narrative economics

Robert J. Shiller

narrative economics

How Stories Go Viral & Drive Major Economic Events

princeton university press

princeton & oxford

Requests for permission to reproduce material from this work
should be sent to permissions@press.princeton.edu

Published by Princeton University Press
41 William Street, Princeton, New Jersey 08540
6 Oxford Street, Woodstock, Oxfordshire OX20 1TR

press.princeton.edu

ISBN 9780691182292
ISBN (e-book) 9780691189970

British Library Cataloging-in-Publication Data is available

Editorial: Peter Dougherty and Alena Chekanov
Production Editorial: Terri O'Prey
Text Design: Leslie Flis
Jacket Design: Faceout Studio
Production: Erin Suydam
Publicity: James Schneider and Caroline Priday

This book has been composed in Arno Pro text with Helvetica Neue display

Printed on acid-free paper. ∞

Printed in the United States of America

10 9 8 7 6 5 4 3 2 1

Contents

List of Figures   vii

Preface: What Is Narrative Economics?   ix

Acknowledgments   xxi

Part I   The Beginnings of Narrative Economics

1 The Bitcoin Narratives   3

2 An Adventure in Consilience   12

3 Contagion, Constellations, and Confluence   18

4 Why Do Some Narratives Go Viral?   31

5 The Laffer Curve and Rubik's Cube Go Viral   41

6 Diverse Evidence on the Virality of Economic Narratives   53

Part II   The Foundations of Narrative Economics

7 Causality and Constellations   71

8 Seven Propositions of Narrative Economics   87

Part III   Perennial Economic Narratives

9 Recurrence and Mutation   107

10 Panic versus Confidence   114

11 Frugality versus Conspicuous Consumption   136

12 The Gold Standard versus Bimetallism   156

13 Labor-Saving Machines Replace Many Jobs   174

14 Automation and Artificial Intelligence Replace
      Almost All Jobs   196

15 Real Estate Booms and Busts   212

16 Stock Market Bubbles   228

17 Boycotts, Profiteers, and Evil Business   239

18 The Wage-Price Spiral and Evil Labor Unions   258

Part IV   Advancing Narrative Economics

19 Future Narratives, Future Research   271

Appendix: Applying Epidemic Models to
   Economic Narratives   289

Notes   301

References   325

Index   351

Figures

2.1 Articles Containing the Word *Narrative* as a Percentage of
All Articles in Academic Disciplines   13

3.1 Epidemic Curve Example, Number of Newly Reported
Ebola Cases in Lofa County, Liberia, by week,
June 8–November 1, 2014   19

3.2 Percentage of All Articles by Year Using the Word
Bimetallism or *Bitcoin* in News and Newspapers, 1850–2019   22

3.3 Frequency of Appearance of Four Economic Theories,
1940–2008   27

5.1 Frequency of Appearance of the Laffer Curve   43

10.1 Frequency of Appearance of *Financial Panic, Business
Confidence,* and *Consumer Confidence* in Books, 1800–2008   116

10.2 Frequency of Appearance of Financial Panic Narratives
within a Constellation of Panic Narratives through Time,
1800–2000   118

10.3 Frequency of Appearance of *Suggestibility, Autosuggestion,*
and *Crowd Psychology* in Books, 1800–2008   120

10.4 Frequency of Appearance of *Great Depression* in Books,
1900–2008, and News, 1900–2019   134

11.1 Frequency of Appearance of *American Dream* in Books,
1800–2008, and News, 1800–2016   152

12.1 Frequency of Appearance of *Gold Standard* in Books,
1850–2008, and News, 1850–2019   159

13.1 Frequency of Appearance of *Labor-Saving Machinery* and
Technological Unemployment in Books, 1800–2008   175

14.1 Percentage of Articles Containing the Words *Automation* and *Artificial Intelligence* in News and Newspapers, 1900–2019   197

15.1 "Housing Bubble" Google Search Queries, 2004–19   226

16.1 Frequency of Appearance of *Stock Market Crash* in Books, 1900–2008, and News, 1900–2019   232

17.1 Frequency of Appearance of *Profiteer* in Books, 1900–2008, and News, 1900–2019   243

18.1 Frequency of Appearance of *Wage-Price Spiral* and *Cost-Push Inflation* in Books, 1900–2008   259

A.1 Theoretical Epidemic Paths   291

Preface: What Is Narrative Economics?

When I was a nineteen-year-old undergraduate at the University of Michigan over a half century ago, my history professor, Shaw Livermore, assigned a short book by Frederick Lewis Allen, *Only Yesterday: An Informal History of the 1920s*, about the run-up to the 1929 stock market crash and the beginnings of the Great Depression of the 1930s. It was a best seller when it was published in 1931. After reading it, I came to believe that the book was extremely important, for it not only described the lively atmosphere and massive speculative booms of the Roaring Twenties but also illuminated the causes of the Great Depression, the biggest economic crisis ever to hit the world economy. It struck me that this period's history of rapid-fire contagious narratives somehow contributed to the changing spirit of the times. For example, Allen wrote an eyewitness account of the spread of narratives throughout 1929, just before the stock market peaked:

> Across the dinner table one heard fantastic stories of sudden fortunes: a young banker had put every dollar of his small capital into Niles-Bement-Pond and now was fixed for life; a widow had been able to buy a large country house with her winnings in Kennecott. Thousands speculated—and won too—without the slightest knowledge of the nature of the company upon whose fortunes they were relying, like the people who bought Seaboard Air Line under the impression that it was an aviation stock. [Seaboard Air Line was a railroad, so named in the nineteenth century, when "air line" meant the shortest conceivable path between two points.][1]

These narratives sound a bit fanciful, but they were repeated so often that they were hard to ignore. It couldn't have been so easy to get rich, and the most intelligent people in the 1920s must have realized that. But the opposing narrative, which would have pointed out the folly of get-rich-quick schemes, was apparently not very contagious.

After I read Allen's book, it seemed to me that the trajectory of the stock market and the economy, as well as the onset of the Great Depression, must have been tied to the stories, misperceptions, and broader narratives of the period. But economists never took Allen's book seriously, and the idea of narrative contagion never entered their mathematical models of the economy. Such contagion is the heart of narrative economics.

In today's parlance, stories of fabulously successful investors who were not experts in finance "went viral." Like an epidemic, they spread from person to person, through word of mouth, at dinner parties and other gatherings, with help from telephone, radio, newspapers, and books. ProQuest News & Newspapers (proquest.com), which allows online search of newspaper articles and advertisements back to the 1700s, shows that the phrase go viral (and variations going viral, went viral, and gone viral) first appeared as an epidemic in newspapers only around 2009, typically in connection with stories about the Internet. The associated term viral marketing goes back only a little further, to 1991, as the name of a small company in Nagpur, India. Today, as a ProQuest search reveals, the phrase going viral itself has gone viral. Google Ngrams (books.google.com /ngrams), which allows users to search for words and phrases in books all the way back to the 1500s, shows a similar trajectory for go viral. Since 2009, trending now, a synonym for going viral, has also gone viral. These epidemics were helped along by the prominent statistics displayed on Internet sites about numbers of views or likes. Both "going viral" and "trending now" characterize the rising part of the infectives curve, when the epidemic is growing. There isn't as much popular attention to the process of forgetting, the later falling part of the infectives curve, though for economic narratives that will likely be as important a cause of changes in economic behavior.

Allen was thinking in terms of stories going viral when he wrote his book, though he did not use the term. He wrote about his "emphasis upon the changing state of the public mind and upon the sometimes trivial happenings with which it was preoccupied,"[2] but he did not formalize his thinking about the contagion of narratives.

We need to incorporate the contagion of narratives into economic theory. Otherwise, we remain blind to a very real, very palpable, very important mechanism for economic change, as well as a crucial element for economic forecasting. If we do not understand the epidemics of popular narratives, we do not fully understand changes in the economy and in economic behavior. There is an extensive medical literature on forecasting disease epidemics. This literature shows that understanding the nature of epidemics and their relation to contagion factors can help us forecast better than those using purely statistical methods can.

Narrative Economics: What's in a Phrase?

The phrase *narrative economics* has been used before, though rarely. R. H. Inglis Palgrave's *Dictionary of Political Economy* (1894) contains a brief mention of narrative economics,[3] but the term appears to refer to a research method that presents one's own narrative of historical events. I am concerned not with presenting a new narrative but rather with studying other people's narratives of major economic events, the popular narratives that went viral. In using the term *narrative economics*, I focus on two elements: (1) the word-of-mouth contagion of ideas in the form of stories and (2) the efforts that people make to generate new contagious stories or to make stories more contagious. First and foremost, I want to examine how narrative contagion affects economic events.

The word *narrative* is often synonymous with story. But my use of the term reflects a particular modern meaning given in the *Oxford English Dictionary*: "a story or representation used to give an explanatory or justificatory account of a society, period, etc." Expanding on this definition, I would add that stories are not limited to simple chronologies of human events. A story may also be a song, joke, theory, explanation, or plan that has emotional resonance and that can easily be conveyed in casual conversation. We can think of history as a succession of rare big events in which a story goes viral, often (but not always) with the help of an attractive celebrity (even a minor celebrity or fictional stock figure) whose attachment to the narrative adds human interest.

For example, narratives from the second half of the twentieth century describe free markets as "efficient" and therefore impervious to improvement by government action. These narratives in turn led to a public reaction against regulation. There are of course legitimate criticisms of regulation as practiced then, but those criticisms were usually not powerfully viral. Viral narratives need some personality and story. One such narrative involved movie star Ronald Reagan, who became a household name as the witty and charming narrator of the highly popular US television show *General Electric Theater* from 1953 to 1962. After 1962, he entered politics in support of free markets. Reagan was elected president of the United States in 1980. In the 1984 reelection, he won every state except his opponent's home state. Reagan used his celebrity to launch a massive free-markets revolution whose effects, some good and some ill, are still with us today.

Contagion is strongest when people feel a personal tie to an individual in or at the root of the story, whether a stock personality type or a real celebrity. For example, the narrative that Donald J. Trump is a tough, brilliant dealmaker and a self-made billionaire is at the core of an economic narrative that led to his unlikely election as US president in 2016. Celebrities sometimes concoct their own narratives, as in the case of Trump, but in many cases the celebrity's name is merely added to an older, weaker narrative to increase its contagion—as in the story of the self-made man told many times over, each time with a different celebrity. (I discuss many celebrity-based narratives throughout this book.)

Narrative economics demonstrates how popular stories change through time to affect economic outcomes, including not only recessions and depressions, but also other important economic phenomena. The idea that house prices can only go up attaches to the stories of rich house flippers seen on television. The idea that gold is the safest investment attaches to stories of war and depression. These narratives have a contagious element, even if their attachment to any given celebrity is tenuous.

Ultimately, narratives are major vectors of rapid change in culture, in zeitgeist, and in economic behavior.[4] Sometimes, narratives merge with fads and crazes. Savvy marketers and promoters then amplify them in an attempt to profit from them.

In addition to popular narratives, there are also professional narratives, shared among communities of intellectuals, that contain complex ideas that subtly affect broader social behavior. One such professional narrative, the *random walk theory of speculative prices*, holds that prices in the stock market incorporate all information, thus implying that attempts to beat the market are futile. This narrative has an element of truth to it, as professional narratives generally do, though there is now a professional literature that finds imperfections not predicted by the theory.

Occasionally these professional narratives translate into popular narratives, but the public often distorts these narratives. For example, one distorted narrative states that a buy-and-hold strategy in the domestic stock market is the best investment decision. That narrative conflicts with the professional canon, despite the popular idea that the buy-and-hold strategy comes from scholarly research. Like the popular interpretation of the random walk, some distorted narratives have an economic impact for generations.

As with any kind of historical reconstruction, we cannot go back in time with a sound recorder to capture the conversations that created and spread the narratives, so we have to rely on indirect sources. However, we can now capture the arc of contemporary narratives through social media and other tools, such as Google Ngrams.

Better Forecasts of Major Future Events

Most contemporary economists tend to think that public narratives are "not our field." If you press them, they might suggest you check with other departments of the university, such as the journalism and sociology departments. But scholars in these other fields often find it difficult to tread in the land of economic theory, thus leaving a gap between the study of narratives and their effects on economic events.

No economist gave a credible forecast of the worldwide nature of the Great Depression of the 1930s before it happened, and only a handful predicted the peak of the US housing boom in 2005 or the "Great Recession" and "world financial crisis" of 2007–9. Some economists in the late 1920s argued that prosperity would reach new heights in the 1930s, while others argued the opposite extreme: unemployment would remain high forever, because labor-saving machinery would permanently replace jobs. But there seems to have been no public economic forecast of the actual events: a decade of very high unemployment and then a return to normal.

Traditionally, economists who study data have excelled in creating abstract theoretical models and in analyzing short-run economic data. They can accurately forecast macroeconomic changes a couple quarters into the future, but for the past half century, their one-year forecasts have been on the whole worthless. When assessing the probability that quarterly US GDP growth will be negative one year in the future, their predictions have had no relation to actual subsequent negative growth rates.[5] There have been, according to a Fathom Consulting study, 469 recessions (defined as a decline in a country's GDP over a year) in 194 countries forecasted since 1988 by the International Monetary Fund in its biannual *World Economic Outlook*. In only 17 of these did they forecast a recession in the preceding year. They predicted recessions that did not occur 47 times.[6]

One might think that this forecasting record is good relative to that of weather forecasting, which is accurate for only a few days. But in economic decisions, people typically think years ahead. They plan to send children to high school or college for four years, and take out thirty-year home mortgages. So it is natural to suppose that we would sometimes know that the next few years will be strong or weak.

Maybe economic forecasters are doing the best they ever could do. But it seems that, with economic events coming again and again for no apparent cause, it would be a time to think whether economic theory could stand some fundamental improvement.

It is rare to see a professional economist, in interpreting the past or forecasting the future, quoting what a businessperson or newspaper writer thinks is going on, let alone what a taxi driver thinks. But to understand a complex economy, we have to take into account many conflicting popular narratives and ideas relevant to economic decisions, whether the ideas are valid or fallacious.

Criticism of traditional approaches to macroeconomic research is not new. In a famous 1947 article, "Measurement without Theory," economist Tjalling Koopmans criticized the then-standard approach of looking exclusively at statistical properties of time-series data like GNP or interest rates to find leading indicators to help in forecasting. He asked for theories based on actual observations of underlying human behavior:

> These economic theories are based on evidence of a different kind than the observations embodied in time series: knowledge of the motives and habits of consumers and of the profit-making objectives of business enterprise, based partly on introspection, partly on interview or on inferences from observed actions of individuals—briefly, a more or less systematized knowledge of man's behavior and its motives.[7]

In short, as Koopmans pointed out, traditional economic approaches fail to examine the role of public *beliefs* in major economic events—that is, narrative. By incorporating an understanding of popular narratives into their explanations of economic events, economists will become more sensitive to such influences when they forecast the future. In doing so, they will give policymakers better tools for anticipating and dealing with these developments. Indeed, my argument in this book is that economists can best advance their *science* by developing and incorporating into it the *art* of narrative economics. The following chapters lay the groundwork for bringing science and art together in a more robust economics.

The Moral Imperative of Anticipating Economic Events

Ultimately, the objective of forecasting is to intervene now to change future outcomes for society's benefit. In his 1969 presidential address to the American Economic Association, Kenneth E. Boulding (another

teacher who influenced me at the University of Michigan) said that economics should be considered a "moral" science, in that it is concerned
with human thought and ideals. He inveighed against:

> a doctrine that might be called the Immaculate Conception of the In-
> difference Curve, that is, that tastes are simply given, and that we
> cannot inquire into the process by which they are formed. This doc-
> trine is literally "for the birds," whose tastes are largely created for them
> by their genetic structures, and can therefore be treated as a constant
> in the dynamics of bird societies.[8]

Economics, Boulding says, "creates the world it is investigating."[9] Often,
we don't want to forecast but to warn. We don't ever want to forecast a
disaster; we want to take actions that will prevent the disaster from
happening.

Newspaper accounts of central bank actions, such as the routine raising or lowering of interest rates, seem to reflect the assumption that the
exact amount and timing of these actions are of central importance, rather
than the words and stories that accompany them. Irving Kristol, writing
in 1977, expresses the typical economist's view succinctly, dismissing public opinion polls purporting to measure business confidence:

> It is all supremely silly. Business confidence—as represented by the
> willingness to invest in new plant and equipment—is not a psychologi-
> cal phenomenon but an economic one. It is what Mr. Carter and what
> Mr. Burns *do* that counts, not what they say. John Maynard Keynes may
> have believed—and some of his disciples obviously still believe—that
> the propensity to invest is governed by the high or low "animal spirits"
> that prevail among businessmen. But then, Keynesian economists have
> always had a poor opinion of the intelligence of businessmen, whom
> they represent as temperamental children, to be paternalistically "man-
> aged." . . . What governs business confidence are the prospects for prof-
> itable investment. That and nothing else—not what the president says,
> not what executives say, not what anyone else says.[10]

Kristol does not identify the economic forces that operate independently
of stories to produce economic crises. He does, however, hint at the

politicization of economics when he argues that economists insult businessmen's intelligence when they try to describe less-than-optimizing business behavior. Many economists have learned that it pays to flatter businesspeople, whose support is useful to economists' careers. Describing the economy as driven only by abstract economic forces suggests that the economy operates in a moral vacuum, that there is no criticism of their leadership.

John Maynard Keynes: Narrative Economist

Kristol's dismissal of opinion polls notwithstanding, some of the most famous economic forecasts in world history appear to be based substantially on observations of narratives and worries about their human consequences. In his 1919 book *Economic Consequences of the Peace*, Cambridge economist John Maynard Keynes predicted that Germany would become deeply embittered by the heavy reparations imposed by the Versailles treaty ending World War I. Keynes was not the only person to make such a prediction at the end of the war; for example, the pacifist Jane Addams led a campaign for compassion for the defeated Germans.[11] But Keynes tied his argument to evidence about economic reality. Germany was indeed unable to pay the reparations, and he was correct about the dangers of forcing Germany to try. Keynes predicted how Germans would likely interpret the reparations and the associated clause in the treaty asserting that Germany was guilty of war crimes. Keynes's insight exemplifies narrative economics because it focuses on how people would interpret the story of the Versailles treaty given their economic conditions. It was also a forecast because he warned, amidst a "cheap melodrama" of foreign policy in 1919, about a war to come:

> If we aim deliberately at the impoverishment of Central Europe, vengeance, I dare predict, will not limp. Nothing can then delay for very long that final civil war between the forces of reaction and the despairing convulsions of revolution, before which the horrors of the late German war will fade into nothing, and which will destroy, whoever is victor, the civilization and the progress of our generation.[12]

Keynes was right: World War II began amidst lingering anger twenty years later and cost sixty-two million lives. His warning was grounded in economics and tied to a sense of economic proportion. But Keynes was not talking about pure economics as we understand it today. His words "vengeance" and "despairing convulsions of revolution" suggest narratives filled with moral underpinnings, reaching to the deeper meaning of our activities.

From Irrational Exuberance to Narrative Economics

This book is the capstone of a train of thought that I have been developing over much of my life. It draws on work that I and my colleagues, notably George Akerlof, have done over decades,[13] culminating in my presidential address, "Narrative Economics," before the American Economic Association in 2017 and my Marshall Lectures at Cambridge University in 2018. This book makes a broad attempt at synthesizing the ideas in all these works, linking these ideas to epidemiology (the branch of science concerned with the spread of diseases) and putting forth the notion that thought viruses are responsible for many of the changes we observe in economic activities. The "story" of our times, and of our personal lives, is constantly changing, thereby changing how we behave.

The insights into narrative economics presented in this book dovetail with recent advances in information technology and social media because these are the conduits through which stories travel the globe and go viral in milliseconds, and which have had profound effects on economic behavior. However, this book also examines a long span of history in which communications were slower, when stories were repeated via telephone and telegraph and via newspapers delivered by truck or train.

This book is divided into four parts. Part I introduces basic concepts, drawing from research in fields as diverse as medicine and history, and offering two examples of narratives that many readers will recognize: (1) the Bitcoin narrative, whose epidemic began in 2009, and (2) the Laffer curve narrative, which went viral mostly in the 1970s and 1980s. Part II provides a list of propositions to help guide our thinking about economic narratives and to help prevent errors in such thinking. For example, many people do not realize that perennial narratives may undergo a process of mutation that renews once-strong stories and makes them strong again. Part III examines nine perennial narratives that have proved their ability to influence important economic decisions, such as narratives about others' confidence or about frugality or job insecurity. Part IV looks to the future, with some thoughts about where narratives are taking us at this point in history and what kind of future research could improve our understanding of them. Following part IV is an appendix that relates the analysis of narratives to the medical theory of disease epidemics.

Acknowledgments

My 2017 American Economic Association (AEA) presidential address, "Narrative Economics," was published in the April 2017 issue of the association's journal, the *American Economic Review*. Many passages from that presidential address have found their way, often with modifications, into this book.

This book is strongly influenced by two books I wrote with George Akerlof, *Animal Spirits* (2009) and *Phishing for Phools* (2015). Another strong influence is the book George Akerlof wrote with Rachel Kranton, *Identity Economics* (2011). Narratives play a role in all these books. Working with George aided my thinking immeasurably.

The research that underlies this book has taken place over decades. I acknowledge research support over the years from the US National Science Foundation, the Cowles Foundation for Research in Economics at Yale University, the Smith Richardson Foundation, the Whitebox Foundation via the Yale School of Management, and the James Tobin research fellowships at Yale.

I thank participants in seminars at which I presented earlier versions of my AEA address, notably as the Marshall Lectures at Cambridge University and as seminars at the Bank of England, at the Toulouse School of Economics/Toulouse Institute for Advanced Study, and at the Yale University Department of Economics. Special thanks go to Bruce Ackerman, Santosh Anagol, Bob Bettendorf, Bruno Biais, Laurence Black, Jean-François Bonnefon, Michael Bordo, Stanley Cohen, Donald Cox, Robert Dimand, William Goetzmann, Emily Gordon, David Hirshleifer, Farouk Jivraj, Dasol Kim, Rachel Kranton, Arunas Krotkus, Naomi Lamoreaux, Terry Loebs, Ramsay MacMullen, Peter Rousseau, Paul Seabright, John Shiller, Thomas Siefert, and Sheridan Titman.

Peter Dougherty, who stepped down in 2017 as director of Princeton University Press and is now editor at large, has been a formative influence on me for twenty years. He has always encouraged me to stay on a true path in my writing, a contribution that has been invaluable to me. He is now, after leaving the helm of the Press, still giving me editorial help.

Research assistance was provided by Logan Bender, Andrew Brod, Laurie Cameron Craighead, Jaeden Graham, Jinshan Han, Lewis Ho, Jakub Madej, Amelie Rueppel, Nicholas Werle, Lihua Xiao, and Michael Zanger-Tishler. I am also indebted to other Yale students who made comments or suggestions: Brendan Costello, Francesco Filippucci, Kelly Goodman, Patrick Greenfield, Krishna Ramesh, Preeti Srinivasan, and Garence Staraci.

My indefatigable administrative assistant at Yale, Bonnie Blake, read and edited the manuscript. Much appreciation, too, needs to be acknowledged for my very thorough and detail-oriented copyeditor, Steven Rigolosi.

Some of the ideas in this book have come from my experience with writing more than two hundred newspaper columns, the equivalent of two books by word count. Since 2003, I have been regularly contributing columns to *Project Syndicate*; these columns are published in newspapers around the world, mostly outside the United States. Writing for *Project Syndicate* has helped me develop a world perspective and avoid an excessively US-centric view. Since 2007, I have also been a contributing columnist for the Sunday Business section of the *New York Times*. I thank my editors at these outlets, Andrzej Rapaczynski (*Project Syndicate*) and Jeff Sommer (*New York Times*), who have given me much attention.

Finally, I thank my wife of forty-three years, Virginia Shiller, for her continuing support and encouragement of my work.

Part I

The Beginnings of Narrative Economics

Chapter 1

The Bitcoin Narratives

This book offers the beginnings of a new theory of economic change that introduces an important new element to the usual list of economic factors driving the economy: contagious popular stories that spread through word of mouth, the news media, and social media. Popular thinking often drives decisions that ultimately affect decisions, such as how and where to invest, how much to spend or save, and whether to go to college or take a certain job. *Narrative economics*, the study of the viral spread of popular narratives that affect economic behavior, can improve our ability to anticipate and prepare for economic events. It can also help us structure economic institutions and policy.

To get a feel for where we are going, let's begin by considering one such popular narrative, recently in full swing. Bitcoin, the first of thousands of privately issued cryptocurrencies—including Litecoin, Ripple, Ethereum, and Libra—has generated enormous levels of talk, enthusiasm, and entrepreneurial activity. These narratives surrounding Bitcoin, the most remarkable cryptocurrency in history as judged by the speculative enthusiasm for it and its market price rather than its actual use in commerce, provide an intuitive basis for discussing the basic epidemiology of narrative economics (which we explore in detail in chapter 3).

An *economic narrative* is a contagious story that has the potential to change how people make economic decisions, such as the decision to hire a worker or to wait for better times, to stick one's neck out or to be cautious in business, to launch a business venture, or to invest in a volatile speculative asset. Economic narratives are usually not the most prominent narratives circulating, and to identify them we have to look at their potential to change economic behavior. The Bitcoin story is an example

3

of a successful economic narrative because it has been highly contagious and has resulted in substantial economic changes over much of the world. Not only has it brought forth real entrepreneurial zeal; it also stimulated business confidence, at least for a time.

Of Bitcoin and Bubbles

The Bitcoin narrative involves stories about inspired cosmopolitan young people, contrasting with uninspired bureaucrats; a story of riches, inequality, advanced information technology, and involving mysterious impenetrable jargon. The Bitcoin epidemic has progressed as a cascading sequence of surprises for most people. Bitcoin surprised when it was first announced, and then it surprised again and again as the world's attention continued to grow by leaps and bounds. At one point, the total value of Bitcoin exceeded US $300 billion. But Bitcoin has no value unless people think it has value, as its proponents readily admit. How did Bitcoin's value go from $0 to $300 billion in just a few years?

The beginnings of Bitcoin date to 2008, when a paper titled "Bitcoin: A Peer-to-Peer Electronic Cash System," signed by Satoshi Nakamoto, was distributed to a mailing list. In 2009, the first cryptocurrency, called Bitcoin, was launched based on ideas in that paper. *Cryptocurrencies* are computer-managed public ledger entries that can function as money, so long as people value these entries as money and use them for purchases and sales. There is an impressive mathematical theory underlying cryptocurrencies, but the theory does not identify what might cause people to value them or to believe that other people will also think they have value.

Often, detractors describe the valuation of Bitcoin as nothing more than a speculative bubble. Legendary investor Warren Buffett said, "It's a gambling device."[1] Critics find its story similar to the famous tulip mania narrative in the Netherlands in the 1630s, when speculators drove up the price of tulip bulbs to such heights that one bulb was worth about as much as a house. That is, Bitcoins have value today because of public excitement. For Bitcoin to achieve its spectacular success, people had to become excited enough by the Bitcoin phenomenon to take action to seek out unusual exchanges to buy them.

For Bitcoin's advocates, labeling Bitcoin as a speculative bubble is the ultimate insult. Bitcoin's supporters often point out that public support for Bitcoin is not fundamentally different from public support for many other things. For example, gold has held tremendous value in the public mind for thousands of years, but the public could just as well have accorded it little value if people had started using something else for money. People value gold primarily because they perceive that other people value gold. In addition, Peter Garber, in his book *Famous First Bubbles* (2000), points out that bubbles can last a long time. Long after the seventeenth-century tulip mania, rare and beautiful tulips continued to be highly valued, though not to such extremes. To some extent, tulip mania continues even today, in a diminished form. The same might happen to Bitcoin.

Nonetheless, the value of Bitcoin is very unstable. At one point, according to a headline in the *Wall Street Journal*, the US dollar price of Bitcoin rose 40% in forty hours[2] on no clear news. Such volatility is evidence of the epidemic quality of economic narratives that may lead to an erratic jostling of prices.

I will make no attempt here to explain the technology of Bitcoin, except to note that it is the result of decades of research. Few people who trade Bitcoins understand this technology. When I encounter Bitcoin enthusiasts, I often ask them to explain some of its underlying concepts and theories, such as the Merkle tree or the Elliptic Curve Digital Signature Algorithm, or to describe Bitcoin as an equilibrium of a congestion-queuing game with limited throughput.[3] Typically the response is a blank stare. So, at the very least, the theory is not central to the narrative, except for the basic understanding that some very smart mathematicians or computer scientists came up with the idea.

Narrative economics often reveals surprising associations. Reaching back into history, we see the beginnings of the emotions behind the Bitcoin epidemic in the origins of the growth of anarchism in the nineteenth century.

Bitcoin and Anarchism

The anarchist movement, which opposes any government at all, began around 1880 and followed a slow growth path, according to a search for *anarchist* or *anarchism* on Google Ngrams. But the term itself dates back decades earlier, to the work of philosopher Pierre-Joseph Proudhon and others. Proudhon described anarchism in 1840 as follows:

> To be GOVERNED is to be watched, inspected, spied upon, directed, law-driven, numbered, regulated, enrolled, indoctrinated, preached at, controlled, checked, estimated, valued, censured, commanded, by creatures who have neither the right nor the wisdom nor the virtue to do so.[4]

Proudhon's words clearly appeal to people who feel frustrated by authority or blame authority for their lack of personal fulfillment. It took about forty years for anarchism to reach epidemic proportions, but it has shown immense staying power, even to this day. Indeed, the Bitcoin.org website carries a passage by anarchist Sterlin Lujan, dated 2016:

> Bitcoin is the catalyst for peaceful anarchy and freedom. It was built as a reaction against corrupt governments and financial institutions. It was not solely created for the sake of improving financial technology. But some people adulterate this truth. In reality, Bitcoin was meant to function as a monetary weapon, as a cryptocurrency poised to undermine authority.[5]

Most Bitcoin enthusiasts might not describe their enthusiasm in such extreme terms, but this passage seems to capture a central element of their narrative. Both cryptocurrencies and *blockchains* (the accounting systems for the cryptocurrencies, which are by design maintained democratically and anonymously by large numbers of individuals and supposedly beyond the regulation of any government) seem to have great emotional appeal for some people, kindling deep feelings about their position and role in society. The Bitcoin story is especially resonant because it provides a counternarrative to the older antianarchist narratives depicting anarchists as bomb-throwing lunatics whose vision for society can lead only to chaos and violence. Bitcoin is a contagious counternarrative because it exemplifies the impressive inventions that a free, anarchist society would eventually develop.

The term *hacker ethic* is another modern embodiment of such anarchism. Before the widespread availability of the World Wide Web, sociologist Andrew Ross wrote, in 1991,

> The hacker ethic, first articulated in the 1950s among the famous MIT students who developed multiple-access user systems, is libertarian and crypto-anarchist in its right-to-know principles and its advocacy of decentralized technology.[6]

In his 2001 book *The Hacker Ethic and the Spirit of the Information Age*, Pekka Himanen wrote about the ethic of the "passionate programmers."[7] In the Internet age, people's willingness and ability to work together with new technology—in new frameworks that do not rely on government, on conventional profit, or on lawyers—have surprised many of us. For example, wikis, notably Wikipedia, encourage cooperation among large numbers of anonymous people to produce amazing information repositories. Another success story is the Linux operating system, which is open-source and distributed for free.

But among the many examples of viral economic narratives, Bitcoin stands supreme. It is a narrative that is well crafted for contagion, effectively capturing the anarchist spirit; and, of course, that is why most of us have heard of it. It is part bubble story, part mystery story. It allows nonexperts and everyday people to participate in the narrative, allowing them to feel involved with and even build their identity around Bitcoin. Equally appealing, the narrative generates stories of untold riches.

Bitcoin as a Human-Interest Narrative

The Bitcoin narrative is a motivating narrative for the cosmopolitan class around the world, for people who aspire to join that class, and for those who identify with advanced technology. And like many economic narratives, Bitcoin has its celebrity hero, Satoshi Nakamoto, who is a central human-interest story for Bitcoin. Adding to the romance of the Bitcoin narrative is a mystery story, for Satoshi Nakamoto has never been seen by anyone who will testify to having seen him. One early Bitcoin code-veloper said that Satoshi communicated only by email and that the two had never met in person.[8] On its website, Bitcoin.org says only, "Satoshi left the project in late 2010 without revealing much about himself."

People love mystery stories and love to unravel the mystery, so much so that there is a rich genre of mystery literature. Bitcoin's mystery story has been repeated many times, especially when intrepid detectives have identified a person who may be Nakamoto. The repeated publicity for an intriguing mystery made the contagion rate of the Bitcoin narrative higher than it would have been otherwise.

Bitcoin and the Fear of Inequality

In addition to tapping into anarchist sentiment and the mystery of Satoshi Nakamoto, the Bitcoin story is a story of the desire for economic empowerment. During the twenty-first century, as economic inequality in advanced countries has increased rapidly, many people feel helpless, and they desire greater control over their economic lives. Bitcoin prices first took off around the time of the 2011 Occupy Wall Street / "We are the 99%" protests. Adbusters, a social activist organization that wanted its message to go viral, launched these protests in the United States, and Occupy protests occurred in many other countries too. It is no coincidence that the Bitcoin narrative is one of individual empowerment, because, according to the narrative, the coins are anonymous and free of government control, management, and reach.

Another part of the underlying narrative that has spurred Bitcoin's and other cryptocurrencies' high contagion rate is the story of computers taking greater and greater control of people's lives. In the twenty-first century, people have access to automated assistants, such as Amazon's Alexa, Apple's Siri, and Alibaba's Tmall Genie, that understand human speech and respond knowledgeably and intelligently to questions with a simulated human voice. In addition, driverless cars, trucks, trains, and ships seem likely in the near future, raising the specter of mass unemployment among truck drivers and other people who drive or navigate for a living. The "technology is taking over our lives" narrative is the most recent incarnation of a labor-saving-machinery narrative that has scared people since the Industrial Revolution.

The insistent fear in this Luddite narrative (to which we will return in chapter 13) is that machines will replace jobs. The fear is not that you will show up for work one day and be told that the company is purchasing a new computer that will do your job. Rather, the changes are more gradual, inevitable, and cosmic. More likely, as computers automate more tasks, you may find that your employer seems increasingly indifferent to your presence, fails to offer pay raises, does not encourage you to stay with the company, and doesn't hire others like you, and eventually no longer even remembers you. Fear about your future is more an existential fear about not being needed.

In such an environment, options are eliminated. Computers can be educated to perform new tasks many orders of magnitude faster than human beings can. Calls for government expenditures on education of people to offset the job loss created by computers seem justified, but it is hard to imagine that people can win in the long run. Millions of students around the world question whether their education is preparing them for success, creating an anxiety that indirectly feeds the contagion of technologically driven cryptocurrencies such as Bitcoin, which seem at least superficially to offer some imaginable hope of mastering the computers.

Bitcoin and the Future

The digital signature algorithm that underlies Bitcoin, that defines a Bitcoin's individual owner, and that makes it prohibitively difficult for thieves to steal Bitcoin has received some attention since the early 1990s, but coverage of that narrative epidemic cannot compare with coverage of Bitcoin itself. ProQuest News & Newspapers finds only one article with the words *elliptic curve digital signature algorithm* in its entire database. It finds only five articles that use the phrase *digital signature algorithm*. The RSA algorithm, the original cryptography algorithm that may have started the Bitcoin revolution, dates back to 1977. ProQuest lists twenty-six articles that mention the RSA algorithm. But that number doesn't begin to compare with the fifteen thousand–plus articles that mention the word *Bitcoin*.

The difference must result from the contagiousness of the larger Bitcoin narrative. The phrase *digital signature algorithm* sounds like something a student would be trying to memorize for an exam: technical, painful, boring. There is so much more to the Bitcoin story. Notably, it is a story about how Bitcoin investors have become rich simply by being aware of new things on the cutting edge. Bitcoin is about the "future." That sound bite is easily remembered, a topic to bring up with enthusiasm in conversation at a social gathering. In short, Bitcoin is a gem of a story.

People often buy Bitcoin because they want to be part of something exciting and new, and they want to learn from the experience. This motivation is particularly strong because of the underlying story, the narrative that computers are poised to replace many of our jobs. But computers can't replace *all* of our jobs. Somebody has to control those computers, and there is a narrative today that the people in charge of the new technology will be the winners. Very few people feel secure that they will be on the winning end of this curve. Even taking a degree in computer science doesn't seem to be a sure path to success today, because it may lead to a humdrum job as a low-level programmer, or even to no job at all. A desire to be on the finance side of the tech business, where Bitcoin sits, is popular because there are so many stories illustrating that financiers take control of things. Bitcoin enthusiasts may think that experimenting with Bitcoin will put them in touch with the people who are going to be winners in the new world, will give them insight about how to stay in (or gain) control. It is easy to jump-start one's connection to this new reality by buying some Bitcoin. Best of all, one doesn't have to understand Bitcoin to buy it. Vending machines at convenience stores now sell Bitcoins and other cryptocurrencies. This "Be a part of the future" narrative, enhanced by regular news of exciting fluctuations in the price of Bitcoins, gives them value. It generates fluctuations in Bitcoin prices in terms of national currencies, and these fluctuations thrive on and produce contagious narratives.

Bitcoin as a Membership Token
in the World Economy

We are living in a peculiar transition period in human history, in which many of the world's most successful people see themselves as part of a broader cosmopolitan culture. Our nation-states sometimes seem increasingly irrelevant to our ambitions. Bitcoin has no nationality, giving it a democratic and international appeal. Inherent in its pan-national narrative is the idea that no government can control it or stop it. In contrast, old-fashioned paper money, typically with historical engravings of famous men in a country's history, suggests an obsolete nationalism, something for losers. Paper currency resembles little national flags in a way; it is a symbol of one's nationality. Having a Bitcoin wallet makes the owner a citizen of the world and in some sense psychologically independent of traditional affiliations.

How, then, do we summarize the popularity of Bitcoin? In the end, people are interested in Bitcoin precisely because so many other people are interested in it. They are interested in new stories about Bitcoin because they believe that other people will be interested in them too.

The surprising success of Bitcoin is not really so surprising when we consider the basic principles of narratives discovered by intellectuals who have thought about the human mind, about history, and about mathematical models of feedback. We discuss these great thinkers and their contributions in the next chapter. Most of these thinkers were not economists by training or profession.

Chapter 2

An Adventure in Consilience

For me, thinking about narrative economics has been an adventure in the discovery of consilience. The word *consilience*, coined by philosopher of science William Whewell in 1840 and popularized by biologist E. O. Wilson in 1994, means the unity of knowledge among the differing academic disciplines, especially between the sciences and the humanities. All these different approaches to knowledge are relevant in understanding the real and human phenomenon of the economy and its sudden and surprising changes. When one reflects that the economy is composed of conscious living people, who view their actions in light of stories with emotions and ideas attached, one sees the need for many different perspectives. Narrative economics therefore requires concepts from most university departments.

Unfortunately, academic disciplines tend to become insular. A researcher cannot know everything, and so the impulse is to think one must specialize, narrowing one's inquiry to the point where one can reasonably judge that one has all relevant knowledge on a narrowly defined subject. To some extent, university researchers must live with this reality. But the impulse can go too far, and it often leads to overspecialization.

When economists want to understand the most significant economic events in history, they rarely focus on the important narratives that accompanied those events. As Figure 2.1 shows, economics has lagged behind most other disciplines in attending to the importance of narratives. And, while all disciplines increasingly pay attention to narratives, economics and finance are still playing catch-up, despite occasional calls for a broader approach to empirical economics.[1]

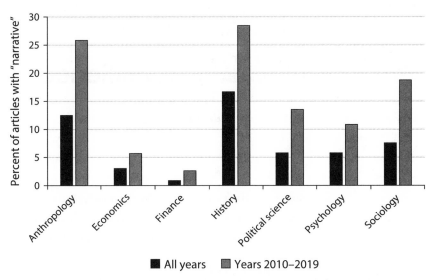

FIGURE 2.1. Articles Containing the Word *Narrative* as a Percentage of
All Articles in Academic Disciplines
All fields show increased attention to narratives in recent years, but economics and
finance are relative laggards. *Source*: Author's calculations using data from JSTOR.

Nor do most economists appear interested in using the enormous databases of written words that they might work with to study narratives.
When they do use the word in published work, they most often do so
casually and tangentially to refer to what they perceive to be a conventional view that they will criticize. In addition, they rarely document the
narrative's popularity, convey its popular human-interest stories, or consider the impact of its popularity on economic behavior. Finally, the
word *narrative* tends to appear in offbeat or popularizing economics journals. However, to the extent that an incipient theory of narrative economics holds promise for helping us better anticipate major economic
events, economists can and should be learning more about narrative,
gathering insights by scholars from the fields discussed in this chapter.
This chapter is an exercise in consilience. It summarizes how thinkers in
a variety of fields have used narrative to advance knowledge within their
disciplines and across disciplines, and it provides a foundation on which
economists might build to think more imaginatively about narrative.

Epidemiology and Narrative

Medical schools have pursued mathematical modeling of the spread of disease epidemics for about a hundred years, making the field well developed and bursting with potential applications to economics. Epidemiology has produced not one model but rather many different models that can be applied to different circumstances, and it is central to this book, as we will see in subsequent chapters. For those who want to examine these mathematical models in detail, the appendix at the end of this book provides a survey of the models and their possible applications to economic narratives.

History and Narrative

Historians have always displayed an appreciation for narratives. However, as historian Ramsay MacMullen noted in *Feelings in History: Ancient and Modern* (2003), a deep understanding of history requires inferring what was on the minds of the very people who made history—that is, what *their* narratives were. He does not literally stress the concept of narratives; he has told me that he would prefer a word conveying "stimulus to some emotional response, and there is no such word." If we want to understand people's actions, he argues, we need to study the "terms and images that energize." For example, he asserts that it is impossible to understand why the American Civil War was fought unless we engage deeply with vividly told stories, such as the 1837 news story reporting an angry mob's shooting of the abolitionist newspaper editor E. P. Lovejoy in Alton, Illinois, in 1837. This evocative story whipped antislavery sentiment in the North to a feverish fury that persisted for years. Academic discussion regarding the extent to which the Civil War was fought over slavery cannot be conclusive unless we take into account the emotional power of relevant narratives.

The late Douglass North, economic historian and Nobel laureate, echoes MacMullen's conviction in his 2005 book, *Understanding the Process of Economic Change*, which emphasizes the importance of human intentionality, essentially in the form of narratives, in the development of economic institutions.

Insights from Sociology, Anthropology, Psychology, Marketing, Psychoanalysis, and Religious Studies

In the social sciences, the last half century saw the blossoming of schools of thought that emphasize the study of popular narratives. Such study has been termed narrative psychology,[2] storytelling sociology,[3] psycho-analysis of narrative,[4] narrative approaches to religious studies,[5] narra-tive criminology,[6] folklore studies,[7] and word-of-mouth marketing,[8] among other terms. The overriding theme is that most people have little or nothing to say if you ask them to explain their objectives or philosophy of life, but they brighten at the opportunity to tell personal stories, which then reveal their values.[9] For example, in interviewing inmates at a prison, we find that the interviewee tends to respond well when asked to tell sto-ries about other inmates, and these stories tend to convey a sense not of amorality but of altered morality.

Another example: anthropologist William M. O'Barr and economist John M. Conley interviewed investment managers about their business and found a widespread tendency for employees at the firm to tell a story about the founding of their firm and about its values.[10] The story has some common features across firms, and it is akin to the creation myths that, as anthropologists have noted, primitive tribes tell about their own origin. The story tends to center on one man (rarely a woman) who showed exceptional foresight or courage in founding the tribe—or, in this case, the firm. The narrative tends to revert to the founding-father story to justify the many stories about the firm as it exists today.

Literary Studies and Narrative

Thinking about economic narratives brings economists to a corner of the university with which they are often unfamiliar: the literature depart-ment. Some literary theorists, inspired in part by psychoanalysis, the *archetypes* of Carl Jung[11] and the *phantasies* of Melanie Klein,[12] have found that certain basic story structures are repeated constantly, though the names and circumstances change from story to story, suggesting that the human brain may have built-in receptors for certain stories. John G. Cawelti (1976) classifies what he calls "formula stories" with names like "the hard-boiled detective story" or the "gothic romance." Vladimir Propp (1984) found thirty-one "functions" present in all folk stories, with abstract names like "violation of interdiction" and "villainy and lack." According to Ronald B. Tobias (1999), in all of fiction there are only twenty master plots: "quest, adventure, pursuit, rescue, escape, revenge, the riddle, rivalry, underdog, temptation, metamorphosis, transformation, maturation, love, forbidden love, sacrifice, discovery, wretched excess, ascension, and descension." Christopher Booker (2004) argues that there are only seven basic plots: "overcoming the monster, rags to riches, the quest, voyage and return, comedy, tragedy, and rebirth."

According to literary theorist Mary Klages (2006), structuralist literary theory considers such efforts to list all basic stories as "overly reductive and dehumanizing."[13] Although she dismisses other scholars' lists of basic plots, she asserts, "Structuralists believe that the mechanisms which organize units and rules into meaningful systems come from the human mind itself."[14] Peter Brooks (1992) says narratology should be concerned with "how narratives work on us, as readers, to create models of understanding, and why we need and want such shaping orders."[15] Well-structured narratives, Brooks argues, "animate the sense-making process" and fulfill a "passion for meaning,"[16] and the study of narratives naturally leads to psychoanalysis.

Russian literature scholar Gary Saul Morson recently collaborated with economist Morton Schapiro in *Cents and Sensibility* (2017), in which they argue that a better appreciation of great novels—which bring us close to the essence of human experience—would help improve the modeling of economic life.

Neuroscience, Neurolinguistics, and Narrative

Narratives take the form of sequences of words, which makes the principles of linguistics relevant. Words have both simple, direct meanings and connotations, in addition to metaphoric use. Modern neurolinguistics probes into the brain structures and organization that support narratives.[17]

Contagious narratives often function as metaphors. That is, they suggest some idea, mechanism, or purpose not even mentioned in the story, and the story becomes in effect a name for it. The human brain tends to organize around metaphors. For example, we freely incorporate war metaphors in our speech. We say an argument was "shot down" or is "indefensible." The human brain notices these words' connection to war narratives, although the connection is not always a conscious one. The connection enriches the speech by suggesting other possibilities. So when we speak of a stock market "crash," most of us are reminded of the rich story of the 1929 stock market crash and its aftermath. Linguist George Lakoff and philosopher Mark Johnson (2003) have argued that such metaphors are not only colorful ways of writing and speaking; they also mold our thoughts and affect our conclusions. Neuroscientist Oshin Vartanian (2012) notes that analogy and metaphor "reliably activate" consistent brain regions in fMRI images of the human brain. That is, the human brain seems wired to respond to stories that lead to thinking in analogies.

Consilience Calls for Collaborative Research

The dazzling array of approaches to understanding the spread of narratives, briefly summarized in this chapter, means that collaborative research between economists and experts in other disciplines holds the promise of revolutionizing economics. Particularly important are the ideas and insights of epidemiologists, whose models successfully forecast the future trajectory of disease epidemics and explain how to counteract these epidemics. As we will see in the next chapter, economists can adapt these epidemiological models to improve their own models and forecasts. The marriage of economics and epidemiology is our first example of consilience in this book.

Chapter 3

Contagion, Constellations, and Confluence

Before we embark on a study of how economic narratives go viral, it is helpful to consider how bacteria and viruses spread by contagion. The science of epidemiology offers valuable lessons and may help explain how the story of Bitcoin (and many other economic narratives) went viral.

Let us consider diseases first, caused by real viruses. Consider as an example the major Ebola epidemic that swept through West Africa—Guinea, Liberia, and Sierra Leone—between 2013 and 2015. Ebola is a viral disease for which there is no approved vaccine or treatment, and it kills most people who contract it. Ebola spreads from person to person via body fluids. Its infectiousness can be lowered through hospitalization and quarantine, and through proper handling and burial of the dead.

In Figure 3.1 we see a typical example of an epidemic curve, for Ebola, in a community, this from Liberia. Note that the number of newly reported Ebola cases has a hump-shaped pattern. The epidemic first rises, then falls. The rising period is a time when the *contagion rate*, the rate of increase of newly infected people, exceeds the recovery rate plus the death rate. During the rising period, the rise in the number of infected people due to contagion outnumbers the fall in the number due to recovery or death. The process is reversed during the falling period. That is, the fall in the number of infected people due to recovery or death outweighs the rise in the number due to contagion, putting the number infected into a steady downward path marking the termination of the epidemic.

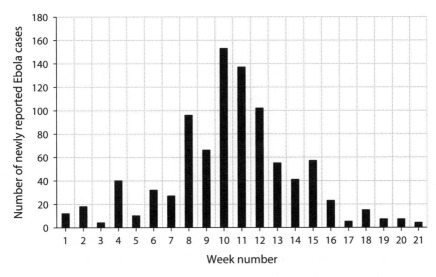

FIGURE 3.1. Epidemic Curve Example, Number of Newly Reported Ebola
Cases in Lofa County, Liberia, by week, June 8–November 1, 2014
We will see many examples of economic narratives whose prevalence in digitized
databases follows a similar hump-shaped pattern. *Source*: US Centers for
Disease Control and Prevention.

After the epidemic started, contagion rates of the Ebola virus eventually fell for various reasons, notably the heroic efforts of Médecins Sans
Frontières (Doctors Without Borders), more than a hundred nongov-
ernmental organizations, and individuals who risked their lives to lower
the contagion in Africa. According to the World Health Organization,
health-care workers were twenty-one to thirty-two times more likely to
catch the disease than the general population there, and there were 815
confirmed and probable cases of health-care worker infection as of 2015.
Most of these workers died.[1]

Contagion, Recovery, and Decline

Efforts to lower contagion rates by avoiding contact with sick people are
hardly new. The history of quarantines extends back at least to 1377 when
the city of Venice imposed during a plague a thirty-day isolation period
on arrivals by sea, and then a forty-day isolation period for travelers by

land (the word *quarantine* derives from the Latin word for *forty*). The world has also seen occasional attempts to increase contagion as an act of war, as with the catapulting of dead bodies of plague victims into a fortified city at the Siege of Caffa, 1346.[2]

Another mechanism for a declining contagion rate is a decrease in the pool of susceptible people. This pool decreases through time because many people who had the disease are now immune to it (or dead). This mechanism, modeled in the appendix (p. 289), occurs even if no health-care workers take action to contain the disease, as in long-ago epidemics before modern medicine. Eventually, those epidemics ended before everyone was infected.

When the contagion rate is lower than the recovery rate plus the death rate, the disease does not disappear immediately. The contagion rate is not reduced to zero. All that is necessary to conquer the epidemic is to lower the contagion rate below the recovery rate. Unless the contagion rate is zero, there will still be new cases of the disease, but the total number of sick people declines, gradually tailing off to zero, at which point the epidemic ends.

We are talking here of the *average* contagion rate and *average* recovery rate, averaging over many people. However, both the contagion rate and the recovery rate can differ greatly from one individual carrier to another. A relatively small percentage of super-spreaders can infect many people. One such super-spreader was Mary Mallon, "Typhoid Mary," who a century ago spread typhoid fever to at least 122 people over an interval of years.[3] In the context of narratives, most of us may not be contagious enough for long enough to cause an epidemic without the presence of these super-spreaders, and because of a small fraction of super-spreaders the average contagion rate can be much higher than the typical contagion rate. Today's narrative super-spreaders may be enabled by marketing using accelerated analytics, such as recently provided by NVIDIA Corporation or Advanced Micro Devices, Inc., which is invisible to most of us. So we can't always accurately judge the contagiousness of a narrative by our own fascination with it.

Both the appearance of the disease epidemic at a given time and place, and the decline in the epidemic after its peak tend to be mysterious. Many factors influence the contagion rate and recovery rate, factors that may be hard to document. For example, the ultimate reason for the recovery could be a change in the weather, which is more readily documented, or it could be a decrease in the number of encounters between people that allow for transmission of the disease, which might be hard to document. Or it might be some combination of the two. The changes need not be big or obvious.

We can apply this same model to epidemics of economic narratives. Contagion occurs from person to person through talk, whether in person or through telephone or social media. There is also contagion from one news outlet and talk show to another, as they watch and read one another's stories. Once again, the ultimate causes of the epidemic might not be obvious. Fortunately, most economic narratives do not result in deaths, but the basic process is the same. The "recovery plus deaths" variable in the medical model is simply recovery, loss of interest in the narrative, or forgetting in the economic model we are developing. Economic narratives follow the same pattern as the spread of disease: a rising number of infected people who spread the narrative for a while, followed by a period of forgetting and falling interest in talking about the narrative.[4]

In both medical and narrative epidemics, we see the same basic principle at work: the contagion rate must exceed the recovery rate for an epidemic to get started. For example, when Ebola is found to have infected hundreds of people in one town and virtually nobody in another, the explanation could be some inconspicuous factor that made Ebola contagion rates higher in Town #1 than in Town #2, putting the Town #1 contagion rate above the recovery rate at the beginning of the epidemic. Meanwhile, in Town #2, there is no epidemic because the contagion rate isn't quite high enough to offset recovery. Similarly, with narrative epidemics there may be two different narratives, one with some minor story details that make it more contagious than the other. The minor story details make the first narrative, and not the second, into an epidemic. Let's apply this insight to the Bitcoin narrative.

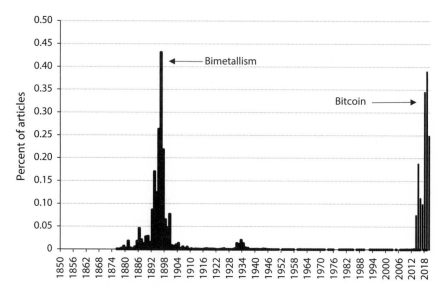

FIGURE 3.2. Percentage of All Articles by Year Using the Word *Bimetallism* or *Bitcoin*
in News and Newspapers, 1850–2019
There is a remarkably similar epidemic pattern to the two popular "bi-" monetary innovation
narratives a century apart and similarity to the disease epidemic curve in Figure 3.1.
Source: Author's calculations using data from ProQuest News & Newspapers.

Contagion of the Bitcoin Narrative

Figure 3.2 plots the frequency of appearance in news articles of the words
bimetallism and *Bitcoin*. This figure is not a plot of a price but rather an
indicator of public attention. Both bimetallism and Bitcoin represent radi-
cal ideas for the transformation of the monetary standard, with alleged
miraculous benefits to the economy. Each word is a marker for a constellation of stories that include not only stories of theory but also human-
interest stories. The plots for both words look quite similar, and each is
similar to a typical infective curve as seen in Figure 3.1. We haven't seen
a definitive end of the Bitcoin narrative yet, as we did with bimetallism;
only time will tell.

We will discuss the remarkable bimetallism epidemic at length in chapter 12, along with other narrative epidemics. For now, it is enough to
know that bimetallism and Bitcoin both invoke monetary theory. In both
cases, an enormous number of people began to regard a particular

innovation as cool, trendy, or cutting-edge. In both cases, the contagion is represented by a hump-shaped curve resembling an epidemic curve. In contrast, in Figure 3.2, the curves look more spiky (that is, compressed left to right) because the figure plots more than a century of data, beyond the virulent periods. In fact, the bimetallism and Bitcoin narratives played out over years, rather than weeks as in the case of Ebola, but the same epidemic theory applies to all three. In the case of bimetallism, we also see a smaller secondary epidemic in the 1930s, during the Great Depression, but it never amounted to much. It was like a secondary epidemic of a disease.

So narrative epidemics really mimic disease epidemics. And it is more than just that. It is interesting also to note that there are co-epidemics of diseases and narratives together. Medical researchers in the Congo during a 2018 outbreak of Ebola linked the high contagion to narratives reaching the population. Over 80% of the interviewees said they had heard misinformation that "Ebola does not exist," "Ebola is fabricated for financial gains," and "Ebola is fabricated to destabilize the region." For each of these statements, over 25% said they believed the narrative. These narratives discouraged prevention measures and amplified the disease.[5] The two epidemics fed on each other to grow large.

The appendix to this book looks at theories and models from epidemiology, including the original 1927 Kermack-McKendrick SIR model, to help explain the spread of economic narratives. These models divide the population into compartments: susceptible to the disease (S), infected and spreading the disease (I), and recovered or dead (R). All of the models feature contagion rates and recovery rates. We can think of Figures 3.1 and 3.2 as evidence on the number of infectives (I). These models tend to predict hump-shaped paths for an epidemic, like that in Figure A.1 in the appendix, page 291, even if there is no medical intervention at all. The epidemic will eventually start weakening because the percentage of the population that has still not been exposed to the disease is declining, bringing down the contagion rate below the recovery rate.

In the appendix we will see also that the time to peak and the duration of an epidemic can vary widely, determined by model parameters. The Ebola epidemic ran for a matter of months in a given locale, but we should not assume that all epidemics must follow that same short time-table. In other words, the Ebola epidemic could have stretched on for years if the initial contagion rate had been lower, so long as contagion did not fall below recovery.

For example, epidemiologists have described the acquired immune deficiency syndrome (AIDS) caused by the human immune deficiency virus (HIV) as not very contagious, and they have recommended that health-care professionals should not shrink from treating HIV patients for fear of catching it.[6] AIDS tends to be transmitted only in certain cir-cumstances involving unsafe practices. AIDS has been a slow epidemic, developing over decades, even slower than the bimetallism and Bitcoin epidemics, and it is able to grow despite low contagion because it has a smaller recovery rate: an HIV-infected person can continue to infect others for many years.

The Contagion of Economic Models

In 2011, Jean-Baptiste Michel and a team of coauthors published an ar-ticle in *Science* providing evidence that mentions of famous people in books tend to follow a hump-shaped pattern through time, rising, then falling, over decades rather than months or years. They amplified their conclusions in a book, *Uncharted: Big Data as a Lens on Human Culture*, by Erez Aiden and Jean-Baptiste Michel (2013).

The same patterns seem to apply to economic theories. In chapter 5 we consider the contagion of one of these narratives, the Laffer curve, a simple model of the relationship between tax rates and the amount of tax revenue collected. But let us first note briefly that these patterns apply even to "highbrow" economic theories that circulate primarily among professional economists. Figure 3.3 shows Google Ngrams results for four economic theories: the IS-LM model (published by Sir John Hicks in 1937), the multiplier-accelerator model (Paul A. Samuelson, 1939),[7] the overlapping generations model (Samuelson, 1958), and the real business cycle model (Finn E. Kydland and Edward C. Prescott, 1982). All show hump-shaped patterns similar to those of disease epidemics.[8] For our purposes here, it doesn't matter what is in these theories. None of them has been proven completely right or wrong. They are all potentially interesting. Each of them is a story whose popularity followed the expected path of an epidemic.

For three of the models, the epidemic first became visible more than a decade after the model was introduced, a phenomenon that we also see in the medical-epidemic framework, where epidemics may go unobserved for a while after very small beginnings. The number of cases may be growing steadily percentage-wise, but the disease fails to be widely noticed until the number of cases hits a certain threshold. In practice, the long lag between the publication of an economic theory and its eventual strong epidemic status represents a time interval over which the model evolves from something regarded as peculiar and thought provoking into something that is clearly correct and recognizably great. Over this gestational interval, other scholars in the discipline increasingly appreciate the model, and the epidemic spreads through academic rituals, such as paper presentations at seminars and major conferences.[9] Eventually the models make their way into textbooks. Still later, the model is talked about enough that the news media begin to feel that it should be mentioned, and people outside of the economics profession who pride themselves on their general knowledge begin to feel they should know something about it. But in this late stage of the epidemic, the model may begin to lose some of its contagion. Some people begin to consider it stale and unoriginal even if it has merit, while others end up forgetting about it completely.

The contagion of these theories did not generally take the form of someone sitting down with a pencil and paper and saying, "Let me explain the IS-LM model to you." In most cases, the communication was probably much more elementary and human. Economic historian Warren Young suspects that the contagion of the IS-LM diagram had something to do with its resemblance to the intersection of supply and demand that is perhaps the most famous image in all of economics.[10]

In addition, the IS-LM model was a formalization of John Maynard Keynes's theory. Keynes was a brilliant writer, but as we have seen, many narratives are associated with celebrities. Keynes himself was a colorful figure and a celebrity in his own right: he hobnobbed with the

Bloomsbury group of artists and intellectuals, among other celebrities (including the writer Virginia Woolf, who was embarking on her own epidemic of fame, which did not peak at least until near the end of the twentieth century, long after her death in 1941). Keynes was reputed to be gay or bisexual, and his male relationships were well known among the tolerant Bloomsbury group, providing a spicy bit of gossip that, at that time, could travel only by word of mouth. Gayness was not generally a good thing for one's career in Keynes's day, but it might have been in the context of a certain narrative. Keynes later married a beautiful ballerina, Lydia Lopokova, who experienced her own epidemic of popularity after she retired from dancing, likely because of her association with Keynes. And, as we have already noted, Keynes was famous for his 1919 best seller, *Economic Consequences of the Peace*, which in effect predicted World War II. In contrast, John Hicks, who first published the IS-LM model, was not quite so colorful a figure. Thus stories about Keynes were possibly "donkeys" that helped carry the IS-LM model to contagion.[11]

Figure 3.3 shows the life history of four economic models. These histories resemble not only the normal course of a disease epidemic but also the life history of other kinds of narratives. Elements of the essential ideas in economic narratives may survive as they are adapted and incorporated in later narratives involving other contagious ideas, but they tend to lose their punch and identity in the process. Their ability to direct thought and action becomes much diminished.

A key proposition of this book is that economic fluctuations are substantially driven by contagion of oversimplified and easily transmitted variants of economic narratives. These ideas color people's loose thinking and actions. As with disease epidemics, not everyone becomes infected. In the case of narrative epidemics, the people who miss the epidemic may tell you that there was no such important popular narrative. But in a historic epidemic, for most people the narrative will be fundamental to their reasons for doing, or not doing, things that affect the economy. Just like the economic theories in Figure 3.3, popular theories among the general public grow on an upward epidemic path, but only for a while. They then recede unless they get renewed.

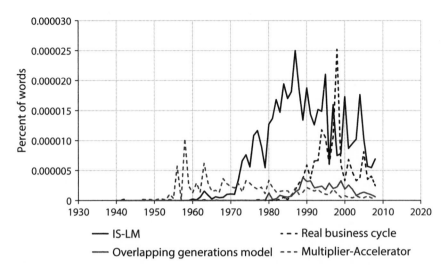

FIGURE 3.3. Frequency of Appearance of Four Economic Theories, 1940–2008
The figure shows four important models: the IS-LM model (Hicks, 1937), the multiplier-accelerator model (Samuelson, 1939), the overlapping generations model (Samuelson, 1958), and the real business cycle model (Kydland and Prescott, 1982). All four show hump-shaped patterns through time. *Source*: Google Ngrams, no smoothing.

It is noteworthy that Keynes's book *The General Theory of Employment, Interest, and Money* (1936) put forth the idea of a perfectly mechanical contagion without using that phrase. According to Keynesian theory, an economic boom starts when some initial stimulus, such as government deficit spending, causes an initial increase in some people's income. These people then spend much of their additional income, which in turn generates income for other people who sell to them or work for companies that sell to them. They in turn spend much of this extra income, thus generating another round of income increases for yet other people, and so on in multiple rounds of expenditure. The Keynesian theory can be tweaked to add some investment dynamics, as Paul Samuelson showed in 1939 with his multiplier-accelerator model, thus creating hump-shaped responses in national income as a result of an economic stimulus. These hump-shaped responses resemble the epidemic curves we have seen. We can view the Keynes-Samuelson model as an epidemic model of sorts, where the contagious element is income. However, it is not enough to think solely in terms of mechanical, multiple rounds of expenditure. We must think of multiple rounds of expansion of economic narratives, and of the ideas and feelings embodied in them.

Constellations and Confluences of Narratives

Just as the world experiences co-epidemics of diseases, where two or more diseases interact positively with each other, we also see co-epidemics of narratives in which the narratives are perceived as sharing a common theme, such as case studies that illuminate a political argument, creating a picture in the mind that is hard to see if one focuses on just one of the narratives. In other words, large-scale economic narratives are often composed of a *constellation* of many smaller narratives. Each smaller narrative may suggest a part of a larger story, but we need to see the full constellation to discern the full theme.

The analogy to constellations should be clarified. Astronomical constellations, such as Cygnus the Swan, are chance alignments of stars, but humans interpret them in a way that seems natural to the human mind— in this case, as a swan. Sometimes humans co-opt constellations for certain purposes. For example, Christians have renamed Cygnus as the Northern Cross to put one of their symbols in the sky. They also paired it with another constellation, the Southern Cross, for people living in the Southern Hemisphere. Other groups and cultures have different narratives with other motivations.

Narratives appear in constellations partly because their credibility relies on a set of other narratives that are currently extant. That is, they sound plausible and interesting in the context of the other narratives. The storyteller does not need to refute the other narratives to set the stage for the current one. Also, the narrative may be based on certain assumed facts that the teller and the listener do not know how to test. Some narratives are contagious because they seem to offer a confirming fact. We can say with some accuracy that most people put on a show of their own knowledgeability and try to conceal their ignorance of millions of facts. Hence narratives that seem contrary to prevailing thought may have lower contagion rates that do not result in epidemics.

Some narrative constellations may at their peak infect only a small fraction of the population, but if that fraction of the population curtails its spending substantially, the narrative may matter a lot. For example, if the narrative has reached only 20% of a country's population, but that fraction decides to postpone purchasing a new car or fixing up their house, the impact of its decreased spending may be big enough to tip the country into a recession.

In addition to a *constellation* of narratives, there is a *confluence* of narratives that may help drive economic events. By a confluence, I mean a group of narratives that are not viewed as particularly associated with one another but that have similar economic effects at a point in time and so may explain an exceptionally large economic event. For example, in my 2000 book *Irrational Exuberance*, I listed a dozen precipitating factors, or narratives, that happened to occur together around 2000 to create the most elevated stock market in the United States ever, soon to be followed by a crash. The list, in brief, comprised the World Wide Web, the triumph of capitalism, business success stories, Republican dominance, baby boomers retiring, business media expansion, optimistic analysts, new retirement plans, mutual funds, decline of inflation, expanding volume of trade, and rising culture of gambling. If we want to know why an unusually large economic event happened, we need to list the seemingly unrelated narratives that all happened to be going viral at around the same time and affecting the economy in the same direction. However, it is important to recognize that big economic events usually can't be described as caused by just a single constellation of narratives. It is far more likely that big economic events are not explainable in such satisfying terms. Instead, explaining those events requires making a list of economic narratives that itself cannot be described as a simple story or a contagious narrative.

In part III of this book, we focus on some of the brighter stars in the narrative constellations, those that are significant enough to contribute substantially to changes in economic motivations. We cannot yet link these constellations precisely to severe economic events. But even with partial views of the constellations and confluences, we are making progress toward understanding the events.

We also have no more than a partial view of the forces that make some narratives into epidemics. The ability of narratives to "go viral" is something of a mystery, which we attempt to unravel in the next chapter.

Chapter 4

Why Do Some Narratives Go Viral?

It is difficult to state accurately or to quantify the reason a few economic narratives go viral while most fail to do so. The answer lies in a human element that interacts with economic circumstances. Beyond some simple and predictable regularities, a network of human minds sometimes acts almost like a random number generator in selecting which narratives go viral. The apparent randomness in outcomes has to do with randomness in the mutation of stories to more contagious forms, and with moments of our individual lives and attentions, that can lead to a sudden climax of public attention to specific narratives. We routinely find ourselves puzzling years later over the reasons for the success of popular narratives in history and for their economic consequences.

The Spontaneity of Narratives in Human Thinking and Actions

At the beginning of the twentieth century, scholars from a wide array of disciplines began to think that narratives, stories that seem to have entertainment value only, are central to human thinking and motivation. For example, in 1938 the existentialist philosopher Jean-Paul Sartre wrote,

> A man is always a teller of tales, he lives surrounded by his stories and the stories of others, he sees everything that happens to him through them; and he tries to live his life as if he were recounting it.[1]

The story of oneself and the stories one tells about others inevitably have diverse connections to what we call "human interest," either directly or indirectly.

When we are asleep at night, narratives appear to us in the form of dreams. We do not dream of equations or geometric figures without some human element. Neuroscientists have described dreaming, which involves characters, settings, and a hierarchical event structure, as based on a storytelling instinct. In fact, the brain's activity during dreaming resembles the activity of certain damaged brains, in which lesions of the anterior limbic system and its subcortical connections lead to spontaneous confabulation.[2]

In their attempts to understand social movements, sociologists have begun to think of the contagion of narratives as central to social change. For example, sociologist Francesca Polletta, who studied the sit-in social movement of the 1960s in which white Americans participated in protests of discrimination against blacks, reported that students described the demonstrations as unplanned, impulsive, "like a fever," and "over and over again, spontaneous."[3] These demonstrations were often driven by a particular popular narrative about blacks demanding service at lunch counters that were labeled as "white only," accompanied by young white supporters who showed moral outrage at the exclusion of blacks. This kind of protest, christened the "sit-in," ultimately became a symbol of a new social movement.

The sit-in story emerged from a single story about a February 1, 1960, protest involving four students from Greensboro Agricultural and Technical College. The story revolved around polite young black people who ignored orders to leave the lunch counter where blacks were not served. The young people sat patiently, waiting to be served, until the restaurant closed, and they returned the next day with more young people. The story went viral, through word of mouth and through news media attention, and within weeks the sit-ins spread throughout much of the United States. The story's spread was not entirely unplanned, Polletta concludes. Activists tried to promulgate the story, but they were not in tight control of the social movement, which was largely viral. The word *sit-in*, coined in 1960, was a true epidemic, with a hump-shaped curve resembling the hump-shaped pattern through time that we see in disease epidemics (see Figure A.1). Use of the term *sit-in*, as revealed by Google Ngrams, grew until 1970, ten years later. In the interim, the movement spawned the word *teach-in*, which had a similar epidemic curve, though less intense and fading earlier.

Several generations earlier, another story had raised white people's sympathy for the plight of black people in the United States. It appeared in Harriet Beecher Stowe's 1852 novel *Uncle Tom's Cabin*. The book was the most successful novel in the nineteenth-century United States, selling over a million copies when the country's population was much smaller and less able to afford books. It tells the story of an older slave, Uncle Tom, who loves children and who tells stories to Little Eva, the white slave owner's innocent little daughter. Eva, still a child, dies of a sudden illness, but not before asking to have locks of her hair cut off and distributed to the slaves, with a wish that she will see them again in heaven. Tom is separated from his wife and children and sold to a vicious slave owner, Simon Legree, who beats him mercilessly for refusing orders to beat another slave.

The book contains some highly evocative scenes, including one of a slave mother, Eliza, fleeing with her four-year-old son after she is told that he will be sold. Pursued by the slave owner's bloodhounds, Eliza clutches her son as she struggles to cross the dangerous ice of the Ohio River. A hit song (in the form of sheet music), "Eliza's Flight," appeared in 1852, and numerous plays, called "Tom shows," typically including the Eliza scene, sprang up all over the northern United States, likely infecting far more people than the printed book did. The Uncle Tom, Simon Legree, and Eliza narratives played an unmistakable role in the North's decision to invade the South after it seceded. The Civil War began in 1861, a historic event with enormous human and economic significance.

On the Universality of Narrative

Anthropologists, who research the behavior of diverse cultures around the world, have observed a class of behaviors that they call "universals," found in every human society if not in every individual. Anthropologist

Donald E. Brown identified a universal that is important to this book: that people "use narrative to explain how things came to be and to tell stories."[4] In fact, the narrative is a uniquely human phenomenon, not shared by any other species. Indeed, some have suggested that stories distinguish humans from animals, and even that our species be called *Homo narrans* (Fisher, 1984), *Homo narrator* (Gould, 1994), or *Homo narrativus* (Ferrand and Weil, 2001). Might this description be more accurate than *Homo sapiens* (i.e., wise man)? It is more flattering to think of ourselves as *Homo sapiens*, but not necessarily more accurate.

In ancient Greece, the philosopher Plato appreciated the importance of narratives; he wrote his philosophy in the form of fictional dialogues featuring the celebrity Socrates. The narrative force helps to explain what makes his work still popular today. In his dialogue *Republic*, written around 380 BCE, Plato has a character argue that the government should censor popular stories. Talking with Adeimantus, Socrates says:

> I do not say that these horrible stories may not have a use of some kind; but there is a danger that the nerves of our guardians may be rendered too excitable and effeminate by them.[5]

In his book *De Oratore* (*On the Orator*, 55 BCE), itself a book about narrative, the Roman senator Cicero says:

> Nature forms and produces men to be facetious mimics or storytellers; their look, and voice, and mode of expression assisting their conceptions.[6]

Other species have culture, but narratives do not transmit that culture. How is it that other animals learn fundamental survival skills, such as fearing specific predators? Experiments have shown that monkeys are genetically predisposed to fear snakes, and birds are genetically predisposed to be afraid of hawks. Moreover, experiments have shown that monkeys and birds acquire fear when they observe others attack their own species. They also acquire fear, even lasting fear, when they observe circumstances that arouse fear among others in their group even if no attack occurs.[7] But that mechanism of cultural transmission is imperfect, and the ability to transfer stories with language is uniquely human.

Human narratives' power in inspiring fear lies in the fact that the information can be transmitted without any observation of the fear-inducing stimulus. If the narrative is strong enough to generate a salient emotional response, it can produce a strong reaction, such as an instinctual fight-or-flight response.

Also universal are norms of polite conversations that facilitate the transmission of narratives. Basic politeness involves simple actions like looking at the person with whom one is speaking, and giving some indication of hello at the beginning of the conversation and good-bye at the end. These norms tend to flatter the other party. They are so engrained that, as experiments have shown, people are somewhat polite when conversing with computers too.[8] Visitors to any human society will observe people facing each other, sitting around the television or the campfire, and talking—and, more recently, tweeting and posting to other social media—to learn others' reactions, to seek feedback that will either confirm or disconfirm their thoughts. It seems that the human mind strives to reach an enduring understanding of events by forming them into a narrative that is embedded in social interactions.

It has also been suggested that our species be called *Homo musicus*, man the musician, because composed music is found in all human cultures, but in no nonhuman species.[9] Linguist Ray Jackendoff sees many parallels between mental processing of narrative and of music.[10] In his book *Music, Language, and the Brain*, Aniruddh Patel concludes there is a "narrative tendency" in music.[11] Purely instrumental music does exist, but when it is successful in the marketplace, it typically merges into program music or symphonic poems whose titles or movements suggested a story that stimulates the listener's imagination. According to musicologist Anthony Newcomb, the classical symphony is in effect a "composed novel" that at least vaguely, emotionally, suggests a story.[12]

Conspiracy Theories in Narrative

Popular narratives often have an underlying "us versus them" theme, a Manichaean tone that reveals the evil or absurdity of certain characters in the story. Jokes are quite often at somebody else's expense—members of some other group. In extreme cases, they may focus on events as evidence of an imagined conspiracy. According to historian Richard Hofstadter, who offers many examples of unfounded conspiracy theories in US history, the narratives tend to show "almost touching concern with factuality,"[13] despite often being almost absurd. Of course, it is rational for people to be alert to conspiracies, because history is filled with real conspiracies. But the human mind seems to have a built-in interest in conspiracies, a tendency to form a personal identity and a loyalty to friends based on the desire to protect oneself from the perceived plots of others. This disposition appears to be related to human patterns of reciprocity and of vengeance against presumed enemies, two tendencies that have been found relevant to economic behavior in terms of willingness to give in bargaining or eagerness to punish unfair behavior, even if doing so means economic loss.[14]

Story and Narrative

The words *narrative* and *story* are often used interchangeably. But according to the Merriam-Webster online dictionary, a narrative is "a way of presenting or understanding a situation or series of events that reflects and promotes a particular point of view or set of values."[15] So a narrative is a particular form of a story, or of stories, suggesting the important elements and their significance to the receiver. Narratives generally take the form of some recounting of events, whether actual or fictional, though often the specific events described are little more than bits of color brightening a concept and making it more contagious.

The human tendency to form simple narratives around even the most complex chains of events infects even the most analytical minds. Garry Kasparov, international chess grandmaster, commented from his own experience:

> The biggest problem was that even the players would fall into the trap of seeing each game of chess as a story, a coherent narrative with a beginning and a middle and a finish, with a few twists and turns along the way. And, of course, a moral at the end of the story.[16]

Historian Hayden White has emphasized the distinction between a historical narrative and a historical chronicle, which merely lists sequences of events:

> The demand for closure in the historical story is a demand, I suggest, for moral meaning, a demand that sequences of real events be assessed as to their significance as elements of a *moral* drama.[17]

Economists have tended to write theories as if a benevolent dictator can implement a specific plan to achieve the greatest social welfare. But we have no such planner. We do have people who can be selfish, altruistic, or both. These people can be influenced by stories.

Of Scripts and Rolling Suitcases

According to psychologists Roger C. Schank and Robert P. Abelson, narratives may be seen as nothing more than *scripts*.[18] These scripts are also called *social norms*, and they partially govern our activities, including our economic actions. For example, the "prudent person rule" in finance is one social norm with economic impact. Fiduciaries and experts do not have the right to act on their own judgment. Instead, they must instead mimic a "prudent person," which in effect means following a script.[19]

When in doubt about how to behave in an ambiguous situation, people may think back to narratives and adopt a role they have heard of, as if they are acting in a play they have seen before. We can debate whether such behavior is rational. In one sense it is rational to copy the behavior of apparently successful people, even if one does not see any logic in the behavior. Those being copied might have mysterious or unobserved reasons for such behavior, and their success suggests they have at least stumbled onto an advantageous behavior. But traditional economic theory does not model this kind of rationality. It sees the following of others' behavior as more reflexive, not as a thoughtful application of the principle "When in doubt, imitate." This reflexivity does not generally follow the typical economic assumption that people attempt to maximize their utility based on all available information. On the contrary, following scripts set by others often looks like quite stupid behavior.

People often fail to notice ideas if those ideas are not part of a script or are not packaged well enough. In my 2003 book *The New Financial Order*, I argued that some obvious financial inventions have not been adopted anywhere, and I asked: Why? As an analogy, I gave the example of wheeled suitcases. These did not become popular until the 1990s, when a Northwest Airlines pilot, Robert Plath, invented his Rollaboard with both wheels and a rigid handle that can collapse into the suitcase. An earlier version of the wheeled suitcase by Bernard Sadow in 1972 had achieved only limited acceptance. The traveler pulled it along by a leather strap, and it worked moderately well, though not perfectly because it tended to flop over sideways. Still, it was a big improvement over non-wheeled suitcases. Sadow had great difficulty getting his wheeled suitcase accepted in the market. Nobody was interested, but why? The idea was good, and today almost every traveler owns Rollaboards or their descendants. Most people wouldn't even think about buying a suitcase without wheels.

Years after *The New Financial Order* was published, I received an email from a former patent examiner who told me of a wheeled trunk patent in 1887, and it looks like much the same idea.[20] But I could not find it advertised in newspapers of that era. I later found a 1951 article by John Allan May, who recounted his efforts to manufacture and sell a wheeled suitcase starting in 1932. May wrote:

> And they laughed. I was very serious about it. But they laughed, the whole lot of them.
>
> When I spoke to any group about the further application of the theory of wheels they would express themselves as vastly entertained in a kind of soporific way.
>
> (Why not make full use of the wheel? Why haven't we fitted people with wheels?) . . .
>
> I calculate I have outlined the wheeled suitcase idea to 125 groups of people and possibly 1,500 individuals. My wife tired of hearing about it back in 1937. The only man who ever took me seriously was an inventor who lived for a time a couple of houses away. The trouble was, nobody took him seriously.[21]

I have never understood why the wheeled-suitcase idea wasn't absolutely contagious. My best guess is that, with Plath's invention, glamour overcame the sense that wheels on a suitcase looked ridiculous. Its 1991 newspaper ads attached the Rollaboard narrative to airlines, which seemed much more glamorous in the 1990s than they do today:

> It's pilot-designed and approved for carry-on aboard most airlines. With its built-in wheels and retractable handle you can roll it through the airport, aboard the plane and down the aisle.[22]

The epidemic was fueled when flight crews adopted the Rollaboards, and passengers saw these glamorous-looking people walking through airports, pulling their Rollaboards effortlessly behind them. By 1993, the ads for Rollaboards took advantage of this publicity, citing them as the "first choice of aircrews worldwide." Maybe that is all it took to make a good idea, over a hundred years old, suddenly contagious.

Experimental Evidence on Virality

Experimental evidence shows that the success of individual creative works depends on how people assess the reactions of others who are observing the work. In one experiment,[23] sociologist Matthew J. Salganik and his colleagues set up an "artificial music market" online. The market included an array of songs that customers could listen to, rate, and, if they chose, download. Unknown bands performed all the songs, and none of the listeners had ever heard any of the songs before taking part in the experiment.

This artificial market simulated real online markets in that subjects never communicated with one another except that they could observe the popularity of songs. This popularity ranking was the only "spark." The subjects were randomly assigned to two conditions: independent and shared. Those in the independent condition had to choose songs entirely independently, never seeing others' choices. Those in the shared condition were divided into eight worlds and saw others' downloads in their own world only. In the extreme shared condition, the computer screen always showed the songs in rank order in terms of popularity measured by downloads. The first subject-customer to buy in each shared-condition world saw no information about others' choices, the second customer saw the first customer's first choice, the third customer saw the first two customers' choices, and so on.

The researchers found that each of the eight worlds developed its own set of hits, only imperfectly correlated across worlds, and that the inequality of success across worlds was uniformly higher than in the independent world where customers never saw information about others' choices. It seems logical to conclude that something about the random initial choices in the shared worlds got amplified as time went on. In the real world, the effect is likely even stronger because real-world marketers attempt to play up the audience size as much as possible. This research may be taken as experimental confirmation that random small beginnings can lead to big epidemics.

The lesson is that history, including economic history, is not the logically ordered sequence of events that is presented by subsequent narratives that try to make sense of it or try to achieve public consensus. Major things happen because of seemingly irrelevant mutations in narratives that have slightly higher contagion rates, slightly lower forgetting rates, or first-mover effects that give one set of competing narratives a head start. These random events can feed back into bigger and more pervasive narrative constellations, as we will see in the next chapter, which examines the narrative constellations associated with the famous (or infamous) Laffer curve.

Chapter 5

The Laffer Curve and Rubik's Cube Go Viral

One of the toughest challenges in the study of narratives is predicting the all-important contagion rates and recovery rates. Despite all the work by epidemiologists and other scholars, we can't precisely observe the mental and social processes that create contagion, and so we have trouble understanding how they play themselves out.[1]

To take an example from popular culture, predicting the success of motion pictures before their release is widely known to be all but impossible.[2] Jack Valenti, former president of the Motion Picture Association of America, said:

> With all the experience, with all the creative instincts of the wisest people in our business, *no one, absolutely no one* can tell you what a movie is going to do in the marketplace. . . . Not until the film opens in a darkened theater and sparks fly up between the screen and the audience can you say this film is right.[3]

Screenwriter William Goldman had a similar thought, in the opening lines of his book:

> Nobody knows anything. Not one person in the entire motion picture field knows for a certainty what's going to work. Every time out it's a guess and, if you're lucky, an educated one.[4]

In fact, many films and songs by one-hit wonders[5] attest to the difficulty of going viral. The same person who's had a hit often can't do it again. Also, hits from past years never seem to become real hits again, at least not without significant modification.

Economics has its own one-hit wonders, including the now-infamous Laffer curve. Examining how this economic narrative went viral provides further insight into how economic narratives lead to real-world results.

The Laffer Curve and the Infamous Napkin

The Laffer curve is a diagram famously used by economist Art Laffer at a dinner in 1974 to justify the government cutting taxes without cutting expenditures, which would please many voters, if the justification were valid. The narrative can be spotted by searching for the words "Laffer curve" (see Figure 5.1). There are two epidemic-like curves (not to be confused with the Laffer curve itself) in succession, the first rising until the early 1980s, the second rising after 2000, when it became involved with another narrative justifying government deficits, associated with the words "modern monetary theory."

The Laffer curve looks like a simple diagram from an introductory economics textbook, with one important difference: it is very famous among the general public. The curve, which takes an inverted U-shape, relates national income tax revenue to the rate at which income is taxed, taking account of the fact that higher tax rates make people work less, thus decreasing national income. The concept sounds like something that most people would find dull and boring. But, somehow, the Laffer curve went viral (Figure 5.1).

The Laffer curve described in the narratives that are tallied in the figure owes much of its contagion to the fact that it was used to justify major tax cuts for people with higher incomes. The Laffer curve's contagion related to fundamental political changes associated with Ronald Reagan, who was elected US president in 1980, and with Margaret Thatcher, who became prime minister in the United Kingdom a year earlier, in 1979. Both were conservatives whose campaigns promised to cut taxes. However, the Laffer curve narrative may not have played a role in France's election of a socialist president, François Mitterrand, around the same time. An analysis of digitized French newspapers shows that

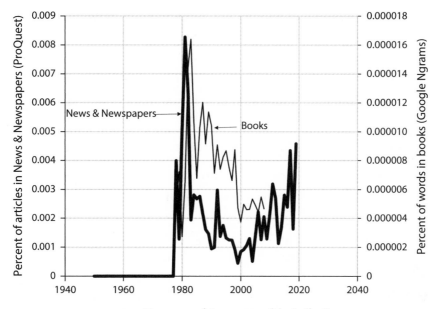

FIGURE 5.1. Frequency of Appearance of the Laffer Curve

The economic narrative of Arthur Laffer's dinner napkin diagram about the effects of taxes on the economy shows a sharp epidemic around 1980 and a secondary epidemic after 2000. *Sources:* Author's calculations using data from ProQuest News & Newspapers 1950–2019, Books (Google Ngrams) 1950–2008, no smoothing.

"la courbe de Laffer" went viral in France too, but not as much it did in the United States and the United Kingdom.

The Laffer curve narrative has a striking punch line that comes as a surprise but usually does not provoke any laughter. The narrative goes like this: What is the relationship between the rate at which income is taxed and the amount of tax revenue collected by the government? Well, it is very clear that if the tax rate is zero, zero tax revenue will be collected. At the other extreme, if the tax rate is 100%, then all income is confiscated by taxes. At a 100% tax rate, no one will work, and again the tax revenue is zero. For tax rates between 0% and 100%, some positive amount of tax revenue will be collected. When you connect the points, you have the Laffer curve. And here is the punch line: because the curve has the shape of an inverted U, there are always *two* tax rates that will collect a given amount of tax revenue. That conclusion is a surprise, for hardly anyone talks of a pair of tax rates for a given revenue. Obviously, to fund the government, it is better to apply the lower of the two tax rates, not the higher.

The notion that taxes might reduce the incentive to earn income and create jobs was hardly new. Adam Smith expressed the idea in the eighteenth century.[6] Andrew Mellon, US treasury secretary from 1921 to 1932, was famous for his "trickle-down" economics, and, along with US president Calvin Coolidge (1923–29), successfully argued for reduction of income taxes that had remained high for a while after World War I. But then the Mellon name began to fade (outside of Carnegie-Mellon University), and the narrative lost its momentum.

The story of the Laffer curve did not go viral in 1974, the reputed year that Laffer first introduced it. Its contagion is explained by an anecdote that was published in Jude Wanniski's 1978 book *The Way the World Works*. An editorial writer for the *Wall Street Journal*, Wanniski wrote a colorful story about Laffer sharing a steak dinner at the Two Continents restaurant in Washington, DC, in 1974 with Wanniski and two top White House powers, Dick Cheney[7] and Donald Rumsfeld.[8] As the story goes, Laffer drew his curve on a napkin at the restaurant table. Years later, after Wanniski's death, his wife found a napkin with the Laffer curve among her late husband's papers. The National Museum of American History now owns the napkin.[9] Museum curator Peter Liebhold writes of this napkin on the museum's website:

> Every museum curator searches for that incredible iconic object, a fabulous artifact that is both physically interesting and represents a great moment in American history. Sadly, such artifacts rarely materialize, and some of the best stories turn out to be apocryphal. However, sometimes you strike gold. It was my luck to beat the odds and collect an incredible story about American business history, a story of political change, economic revolution, and social impact—it was the real deal.[10]

The trouble is, Laffer himself disowned the napkin story. He wrote:

> My only question on Wanniski's version of the story concerns the fact that the restaurant used cloth napkins and my mother had raised me

not to desecrate nice things. Ah well, that's my story and I'm sticking to it.[11]

Laffer was being honest about his recollections, but his honesty could not stop a story that was too good to be stopped.

Visual Aids Go Viral

Why did the napkin story go viral? Good storytelling seems at least partially responsible. After the Wanniski story exploded, Laffer said that he could hardly remember the event, which had taken place four years earlier.[12] But Wanniski was a journalist who sensed that he had the elements of a good story. The key idea, as Wanniski presented it, is indeed punchy.

It may seem absurd to conclude that a story element of a drawing on a napkin helped make the story go viral. But there is ample scientific evidence that unusual visual stimuli aid memory and can help to make a narrative "iconic." It's not that everybody remembers the napkin in the story. Rather, a small detail like a graph drawn on a napkin might have raised the contagion rate at the beginning of the narrative above the forgetting rate.

The Laffer curve embodies a notion of economic efficiency easy enough for anyone to understand. Wanniski suggested, without any data, that we were on the inefficient side of the Laffer curve. The drawing of the Laffer curve seemed to suggest that cutting taxes would produce a huge windfall in national income. To most quantitatively inclined people unfamiliar with economics, this explanation of economic inefficiency was a striking concept, contagious enough to go viral, even though economists protested that the United States was not actually on the inefficient declining side of the Laffer curve.[13] However, there may be some situations in which the Laffer curve offers important policy guidance, notably with taxes on corporate profits. A small country that lowers the corporate profits tax rate below that of other countries may see companies moving their headquarters to that country, enough to raise that country's corporate tax revenue.[14] But an objective analysis of the Laffer curve did not lend itself to a punchy story that could have stifled the Laffer epidemic and the relating of it to personal income taxes. To tell the story really well, one must set the scene at a fancy restaurant, with powerful Washington people and a napkin.

In the end, the Laffer curve napkin story may have gone viral because of the sense of urgency and epiphany conveyed by the story: the idea was so striking, so important, that an economics professor wanted to do something out of place at a fancy restaurant to make government officials see its brilliance.

Ultimately, the story's rich visual imagery helped it evolve from an economic anecdote into a long-term memory. The visual detail of the napkin may have lowered the speed at which people forgot the narrative, which could have helped the epidemic penetrate a large fraction of the population. There is a lesson to be learned here for those who want their stories to go viral: when authors want their audience to remember a story, they should suggest striking visual images. In ancient Rome, the senator Cicero advocated the use of this strategy, quoting the scholar Simonides:

> For Simonides, or whoever else invented the art, wisely saw, that those things are the most strongly fixed in our minds, which are communicated to them, and imprinted upon them, by the senses; that of all the senses that of seeing is the most acute; and that, accordingly, those things are most easily retained in our minds which we have received from the hearing or the understanding, if they are also recommended to the imagination by means of the mental eye.[15]

Indeed, psychology and marketing journals have found that, at least in some circumstances, bizarre mental images do serve as memory aids.[16] For example, Harry Lorayne, a memory-training specialist, has long advocated that people who would like to improve their memory should try to form unusual, highly visual mental images. His suggestion for people who mislay their keys:

> As you drop your keys into the flowerpot, form a mental image of the two vital entities—the keys and the place where you're putting them.

Make it a silly or impossible image. Example: "See" a gigantic key growing in a flowerpot.[17]

As neuroscience has shown us, long-term memory formation involves
many regions of the brain, including visual-image processing regions.[18]

Rubik's Cube, Corporate Raiders,
and Other Parallel Epidemics

Another fad appeared around the same time as the Laffer curve. Rubik's
Cube, invented in 1974 by Ernő Rubik, is a puzzle in the form of a cube-
shaped stack of multicolored smaller cubes. As the narrative went,
Rubik was a creative Hungarian sculptor and architect whose puzzle cap-
tivated the scientific and mathematics community worldwide because
it fostered a narrative that it represented some interesting mathematical
principles. *Scientific American* magazine did a cover story on the cube in
its March 1981 issue, with the lead article by Douglas R. Hofstadter. Author of the best-selling *Gödel, Escher, Bach* (1980), Hofstadter was a science writer with a gift for uniting science with art and the humanities.
His article presented Rubik's Cube as representing deep scientific principles. He described connections to quantum mechanics and the rules for
combining the subatomic particles called quarks. Few people remember
these details today, but they do remember that Rubik's Cube is somehow
impressive. Rubik's Cube was bigger than the Laffer curve on ProQuest
News & Newspapers, but smaller than the Laffer curve on Google
Ngrams. Both show similar hump-shaped paths through time.

Other narratives in the same constellation with the Laffer curve sprang
up around the same time. The terms *leveraged buyouts* and *corporate raiders* also went viral in the 1980s, often in admiring stories about companies that responded well to true incentives and that produced high profits as a result. One marker for such stories is the phrase *maximize
shareholder value*, which, according to ProQuest News & Newspapers and
Google Ngrams, was not used until the 1970s and whose usage grew
steadily until the twenty-first century. The phrase *maximize shareholder
value* puts a nice spin on questionable corporate raider practices, such

as saddling the company with extreme levels of debt and ignoring implicit contracts with employees and stakeholders. *Maximize* suggests intelligence, science, calculus. *Shareholder* reminds the listener that there are people whose money started the whole enterprise, and who may sometimes be forgotten. *Value* sounds better, more idealistic, than *wealth* or *profit*. Use of the three words together as a phrase is an invention of the 1980s, used to tell stories of corporate raiders and their success. The term *maximize shareholder value* is a contagious justification for aggressiveness and the pursuit of wealth, and the narratives that exploited the term are most certainly economically significant.

The Laffer Curve, Supply-Side Economics, and Narrative Constellations

After the Laffer curve epidemic, the Reagan administration (1981–89) reduced the top US federal income tax bracket from 70% to 28%. It also cut the top-bracket US corporate profits tax rate from 46% to 34%, and it reduced the top US capital gains tax rate from 28% to 20% in 1981 (though it returned to 28% again in 1987 during the Reagan presidency). If the Laffer curve epidemic had even a minor effect on these changes, then it must have had a tremendous impact on output and prices.

For these reasons, the Laffer curve is well remembered to this day, but it was only one part of the narrative constellation now known as *supply-side economics*, which holds that governments can increase economic growth by decreasing regulation and lowering taxes. The term *supply-side economics* went viral around the same time the Laffer curve did. The Laffer curve contributed to the impact of the many supply-side narratives because it was a particularly powerful narrative. It had good visual imagery in the form of a scribbled-on napkin, it had authorities behind it just as Rubik's Cube had *Scientific American*, and it suggested that politicians who raised taxes were fools.

One narrative circulating in the supply-side economics constellation was a widely spread story about the consequences of the Swedish Socialist government under Olof Palme, whose government, in a measure of extreme incompetence, inadvertently made the effective income tax rate (on high incomes) go over 100%. People who worked more ended up with *less* after-tax income. The story was reported all over the world, as for example in the United States in 1976 in the *Boston Globe*:

> The typical Swedish dentist works fewer than 30 hours per week because any further earning would actually reduce his retained pay. Film director Ingmar Bergman, probably the country's most famous and admired citizen, left permanently last year after tax inspectors harassed him and seized his records in the middle of a rehearsal—based on a misunderstanding about his corporate rather than personal taxes.[19]

This story of tax rates above 100% in Sweden further mutated in 1976 when Astrid Lindgren, the acclaimed Swedish author of children's books, published an amusing adult fairy tale about it, *Pomperipossa in the World of Money*. The "Pomperipossa Effect" may have contributed to the downfall of the Palme government that year.

Similar narratives of people paying more than 100% of their marginal income in taxes went viral in subsequent years, even in the United States, forming a constellation of narratives.[20] These stories fed on one another. These narratives were about government incompetence, not arguments for lowering tax rates that were already well below 100% overall, but they supported a general impression that tax rates had gone too high. We can find evidence for the existence of this narrative constellation by searching digitized newspapers for the term *highest tax bracket*. In the 1950s, even though the highest US income tax bracket was extremely high, ranging from 84% to 92%, ProQuest News & Newspapers produces only 33 stories with this phrase. In the decade of the 1980s, even though the highest income tax bracket was gradually being reduced from 70% to 28%,[21] there were 520 ProQuest stories featuring the term. Since the 1980s, the epidemic of stories about the highest tax bracket has continued to grow.

Attention to the highest tax brackets naturally drew attention to the lowest tax brackets and to effectively negative tax rates for the poorest, who were now judged in a less sympathetic light. In the United States, the term *welfare mother* refers to an unmarried woman and her children who are supported by unwilling male taxpayers. Use of the term exploded from zero in 1960 to a peak in the early 1970s, after President Lyndon Johnson announced his Great Society plan to eliminate poverty.

Property taxes came in for strong criticism too. In the 1970s, the news media began to notice a public opinion change (strongly in evidence for at least another decade after that) associated not with a celebrity but with a California referendum called Proposition 13. Passage of the proposition led to a 1978 constitutional amendment in California that put a firm limit on property tax increases. The "taxpayer revolt," so named in newspapers of the time, swept the United States:

> The taxpayer revolt that has started in California is about as grass-rootsy as Grape Nuts. But it has California state and local officials shriven with fear and perhaps guilt . . . Proposition 13 is spawning imitators in half the states of the Union.[22]

The stories that were circulating in an epidemic sweeping across the United States in 1978 were of tax rates so high that some homeowners could no longer afford to live in their homes and were forced to sell. Related stories railed against government inefficiency and corruption in the spending of tax revenue. These ideas, and the underlying narrative of a "tax revolt" in the United States, became contagious. But the taxpayer revolt came and went quickly, in the few years around 1978.

In the background was the rise of a free-market, laissez-faire narrative in the second half of the twentieth century in Anglo-Saxon countries. This rise was promoted by stories, such as Ayn Rand's 1943 novel *The Fountainhead*. Its readership was limited in the 1940s, but the novel gradually rose to ever-greater prominence through the rest of the twentieth century. Rand's 1957 novel, *Atlas Shrugged*, went viral. The novel was about a large national strike of productive people against the majority of people, the looters who support government regulation (including taxes) to extract wealth for their own selfish interests. The influence of Rand and her novels has continued to grow since her death in 1982, unlike the taxpayer revolt story, which was contagious only briefly. It seems that the novels were a slower but ultimately larger epidemic. A bit earlier, the phrase *stimulate the economy* had emerged in the late 1950s, and its use grew rapidly from 1978 to 1980, suggesting that tax cuts for higher-income people might serve as an energizer, freeing the supposedly superior people to contribute to society.

Celebrities, Quips, and Politics

Though the Laffer curve epidemic may have played a role in the election of Ronald Reagan and Margaret Thatcher, other narratives were surely influential, such as this quip by Reagan:

> Government's view of the economy could be summed up in a few short phrases: If it moves, tax it. If it keeps moving, regulate it. And if it stops moving, subsidize it.[23]

Reagan used these words in a 1986 speech. But the underlying idea dates back in slightly different form at least to 1967, when Walter Trohan, a conservative commentator for the *Chicago Tribune*, wrote that:

> The federal government operates pretty much in line with the quip, "If it moves, tax it; if you can't tax it, control it; if you can't control it, give it a million dollars."[24]

Thus the quip was already known in 1967. But it needed a celebrity to make it truly contagious, and Ronald Reagan was the celebrity who did just that.

Note the poetic quality of the three elements of the quip, but improved upon between Trohan and Reagan. Each line in Reagan's version has the same basic structure of an "if-then" statement, with the dependent clause starting with "if" and the independent clause a simple two-word statement that is a command in the form of a verb followed by the word "it." The rhetorical form not only added dignity to the quip but also aided its unaltered transmission and contributed to its high rate of contagion, probably because it suggests that everyone is talking about how onerous taxes are and that it isn't just the speaker who is complaining.

In short, it seems likely that narratives like the Laffer curve and other supply-side stories touched off an intense public mandate for tax cutting.

We might argue, too, that the constellation of narratives about tax cutting and smaller government propelled a social movement: entrepreneurship. In 1987, the *New York Times* reported on one of Reagan's pro-entrepreneurship narratives. It is often remembered today for its wit:

> "You know I have a recent hobby," the President remarked in a speech on economic matters earlier this month. "I have been collecting stories that I can tell, or prove are being told by the citizens of the Soviet Union among themselves, which display not only a sense of humor but their feeling about their system."
>
> Mr. Reagan then told his current favorite, about a Russian who wants to buy a car. A Matter of Delivery.
>
> The man goes to the official agency, puts down his money and is told that he can take delivery of his automobile in exactly 10 years.
>
> "'Morning or afternoon?" the purchaser asks. "Ten years from now, what difference does it make?" replies the clerk.
>
> "Well," says the car-buyer, "the plumber's coming in the morning."[25]

Rubik's Cube was just a toy, not support for an economic narrative. But Reagan's lighthearted jokes made for economically powerful entrepreneurial narratives. These new narratives encouraged entrepreneurial spirit and risk taking, and they brought about profound changes in the legal structure of the world's advanced economies.

These examples, the Laffer curve and Rubik's Cube, are just two of a vast universe of narratives. We need to understand their organizing force. The storage points for all these narratives is the human brain, with its prodigious memory capacity. In the next chapter, we use neuroscience to consider the structure of this repository.

Chapter 6

Diverse Evidence on the Virality of Economic Narratives

Further evidence on the impact of narrative contagion on the economy can be found in the story structures in the human brain, in the brain's processing of frightening stories, in the long history of the news media in reinforcing primordial human interactions, in the emotional impact of effective book jackets, logos, and beauty contests.

The Impulse to Convey Stories

In 1958, brain surgeon Wilder Penfield implanted electrodes into the brains of human subjects while performing brain surgery, undertaken for medical reasons on wide-awake patients, under only local anesthesia because the brain itself has no pain receptors. He discovered that electrically stimulating certain narrowly focused parts of the brain caused it to hear a sequence of sounds in chronological order:

> When the electrode was applied in gray matter on the cut face of the temporal lobe at point 23, the patient observed: "I heard some music." Fifteen minutes later, the electrode was applied to the same spot again without her knowledge. "I hear music again," she said. "It is like radio." Again and again, then, the electrode tip was applied to this point. Each time she heard an orchestra playing the same piece of music. It apparently began at the same point and went on from verse to chorus. Seeing the electrical stimulator box, from where she lay under the surgical coverings, she thought it was a gramophone that someone was turning on from time to time.[1]

Stimulating a different part of the brain caused a story to be told, again in chronological sequence:

> A young woman (N. C.) said, when her left temporal lobe was stimulated anteriorly, at point 19 in Figure 5, "I had a dream, I had a book under my arm. I was talking to a man. The man was trying to reassure me not to worry about the book." At a point 1 cm. distant, stimulation at point 20 caused her to say: "Mother is talking to me." Fifteen minutes later the same point was stimulated: The patient laughed aloud while the electrode was in place. After the withdrawal of the electrode, she was asked to explain. "Well, she said, "it is kind of a long story but I will tell you. . . ."[2]

Penfield's work has been highly influential in a number of disciplines. For our purposes, his results indicate the extent to which the human brain structure appears to embody some of the traits that we think of as exclusively human: the propensity to make music and the propensity to tell stories as sequences of events, stories that trigger emotions.

Modern neuroscience is trying to pin down the determinants of the human impulse to tell stories. For example, a team from Emily B. Falk's neuroscience lab at the Annenberg School at the University of Pennsylvania has used functional magnetic resonance imaging to study the brains of people making decisions whether to share health news stories. The team concluded that people tended to share content that enhances self-related thoughts—that is, information that "engages neural activity in regions related to such processes [self-presentation or mental concept], especially in medial prefrontal cortex," and that "involves cognitions or forecasts about the mental states of others."[3] In other words, these people are more willing to share their health information in the form of stories about themselves and others.

Paul J. Zak, a neuroeconomist, has shown experimentally that narratives with a "dramatic arc" increase levels of the hormones oxytocin and cortisol in the listener's bloodstream, as compared with more "flat" narratives.[4] These hormones in turn have well-documented effects on behavior. Oxytocin, sometimes called the "love hormone," plays a role in facilitating relationships. Cortisol, sometimes called the "stress hormone," has been shown to play a role in regulating blood sugar, assisting memory formation, and reducing inflammation.

Neurological Responses to Stories Evoking Fear

News media and popular discussions have long described financial crises as panics created by a spate of sudden economic failures following a period of excessive complacency about economic risks. It may seem like journalistic hype to use charged words such as *panic*, which conjures images of a stampeding mob trying to escape a sudden physical danger, and *complacency*, which suggests a sort of smug stupor. Yet people mostly seem perfectly rational during such financial events, which take place over months and years of largely normal living, and they tend to present themselves as sorting through the facts. Even during a financial "panic," people seem mostly normal and relaxed, joking and laughing.

But are *panic* and *complacency* really so far off the mark? Both words describe mental states that must be supported through neurological structures. We need to study those structures to determine whether there is any common neurology between financial panics and other panics, between financial complacency and other types of complacency.

Consider an example that is current during the writing of this book: the pattern of increasing risk taking by banks as the tenth anniversary of the 2007–9 world financial crisis approached. In 2017, the Federal Deposit Insurance Corporation issued a report expressing concern that US banks, in a reach for yield, were taking excessive risks by extending the maturity of their investments. For nearly ten years after the financial crisis, interest rates had been very low, though higher at longer maturities. Reaching for these higher yields was risky for banks, because if interest rates suddenly increased, they might have to pay more to keep depositors than they earn from the longer-maturity investments, which could cause the banks serious trouble. Ultimately, the banks decided to take the risk, but how did they form their expectations of future interest rates?

No expert has a proven record of forecasting interest rates years into the future. No one can tell a banker how long to wait out a period of low interest rates or guarantee that the low rates will go on forever. All that bankers have are fading memories of narratives of other historical periods when interest rates rose dramatically, leading droves of depositors to run to their banks and withdraw their money. Those stories seem less relevant when interest rates have been low for ten years, but there is no way to quantify how much less relevant.

It may be best to think of bankers' behavior at such times as driven by primitive neurological patterns, the same patterns of brain structure that have survived millions of years of Darwinian evolution. The fact that dogs and rodents today have some of these same fear-management brain structures is evidence for their common Mesozoic origins. Fear is a normal emotion for all mammals and higher animals, and it is supported by brain structures. The extinction of fear is a process that must take place over time to release the fear after the danger has passed.

Scientists first observed the action of these brain structures indirectly. In 1927, Ivan P. Pavlov, a Russian physiologist, reported his research on dogs. If dogs were repeatedly given a dose of acid on their tongue as a metronome clicked in the background, then later the sound of the metronome alone, without the acid, would induce the same involuntary reactions as if acid had been applied. In a subsequent phase of the experiment, Pavlov repeatedly turned on the metronome but withheld the acid, and the dogs' aversive reaction was gradually extinguished. Later, the brain structures involved in such reactions were discovered. In rats, the neurons of the lateral amygdala (an almond-shaped area of the brain) play a fundamental role in both the fear-acquisition stage and the fear-extinction phase, increase their firing during fear acquisition, and reduce their firing during extinction of the fear. Not all of the neurons reduce their firing, keeping a residual fear intact. Neuroscientists have concluded:

> Collectively, there is much evidence suggesting that a distinct neural circuitry involving interactions between the amygdala, vmPFC [ventromedial prefrontal cortex], and hippocampus underlies the ability to extinguish fear, and that this circuitry is preserved across evolution.[5]

Rats show much the same circuitry, and involuntary triggering of fear, that humans do. In humans, thickness of the ventromedial prefrontal cortex is correlated with success in fear extinction.[6] Some human neurological disorders, such as post-traumatic stress disorder (PTSD), represent failures of extinction, and studying these disorders can reveal the underlying structures of fear management.[7] It seems safe to say that the evolutionary process of optimizing the neural circuitry for fear and its extinction has not yet been completed in humans, because civilization is only a few millennia old.

A mental state akin to PTSD may afflict a whole population at times. In his 1951 book *The Captive Mind*, the Polish poet Czesław Miłosz, describing his impressions of the whispered and unofficial narratives that existed late in the Stalinist regime, noted that the atmosphere of fear created by this regime was profoundly important. The fear was of disappearing at the hands of the secret police, of being forcibly transported with one's family to Siberia and, once there, starving or freezing to death:

> Fear is well known as a cement of societies. In a liberal-capitalist economy fear of lack of money, fear of losing one's job, fear of slipping down one rung on the social ladder all spurred the individual to greater effort. But what exists in the Imperium is *naked* fear. In a capitalist city with a population of one hundred thousand people, some ten thousand, let us say, may have been haunted by fear of unemployment. Such fear appeared to them as a personal situation, tragic in view of the indifference and callousness of their environment. But if all one hundred thousand people live in daily fear, they give off a collective aura that hangs over the city like a heavy cloud.[8]

It is reasonable to suggest, as Miłosz does, that the fear of losing one's job is less intense than the fear of being deported to Siberia, and that fear at any level relies on the same brain circuitry. Then, in difficult situations with no logical answer or solution—for example, in the decision whether to make a risky investment—the human mind may delegate the decision to some brain circuitry that is similar to rats'. In such cases, memories of bitter past experience, as well as memories of others' experience transmitted in the form of narratives, may determine the actions taken, and at certain times they may lead to unfortunate economic decisions.

The decline in fear may reflect a gradual process of fear extinction that may be reversed if the narrative experiences a dramatic new development or mutation. Recent narratives about rogue states' possession of nuclear weapons seem possibly intense enough to renew the fear of nuclear annihilation, but apparently they have not done so. Just as it is difficult or impossible to predict which motion picture will be a box office hit, it is difficult to predict which narrative will eventually have economic impact.

Narratives Have Been "Going Viral" for Millennia

People have been spinning narratives since time immemorial. Contagion was increased by communications at bazaars, religious festivals and fairs, as well as casual encounters. In ancient Rome, for example, people who wanted the news would attend the regular *salutatio* at their patron's home, or they went to the *Forum* where they listened to orators or a *praeco,* who wore a special toga to stand out. The *praeco* announced news and stories to the crowd, read advertisements, and handled auctions. *Rumor* is the ancient Latin word for contagious narrative.

The polymath David Hume (1711–76) wrote in 1742:

> When any *causes* beget a particular inclination or passion, at a certain time and among a certain people, though many individuals may escape the contagion, and be ruled by passions peculiar to themselves; yet the multitude will certainly be seized by the common affection, and be governed by it in all their actions.[9]

Hume wrote before the germ theory of disease was established, before bacteria and viruses were identified, but many of his contemporaries understood that both disease and ideas were spread by interpersonal contact.

In 1765, during the economic depression in the American colonies of the United Kingdom following the French and Indian War (Seven Years'

War),[10] a letter to the printer in the *New-London Gazette* (Connecticut) by Alexander Windmill (apparently a pseudonym) identified an epidemic of a narrative that involved the sentence "THERE IS NO MONEY":

> I take it for granted, there is not one of your readers but has heard that most melancholy sentence, repeated times without number, THERE IS NO MONEY: nor scarce one who has not himself frequently joined in this epidemic complaint. Conversation among people of every rank, I have remarked for some months past to run in one invariable channel: and the hackneyed topicks of discourse to be constantly introduced in the same precise order, with admirable uniformity. Benevolent enquiries respecting health, and ingenious observations on the weather, according to the laudable custom of our ancestors, from time immemorial lead the van. As soon as these curious and important articles are discussed; the muscles of the face being previously worked up into a mixt passion of distress and resentment, tempered with a suitable proportion of political sagacity; succeeds the wonderful discovery aforesaid, THERE IS NO MONEY; which is instantly repeated by each party, with every token of astonishment. One would think, by the surprise visible in their countenances, and the vehemence of their expressions, that neither of them had heard of the calamity til that minute, tho', perhaps, it is not two hours since the same persons conversed upon the same subject and, made the same remark.[11]

Windmill goes on to calculate (with some exaggeration perhaps) that the sentence THERE IS NO MONEY was then currently being repeated fifty million times a day by English-speaking inhabitants of the American colonies. He thought it reasonable to assume based on his observations that a million people were saying it every twenty minutes during most of the daylight hours, and some were even sleep-talking it.

Charles Mackay drew attention to the contagious spread of "extraordinary popular delusions" in his 1841 book, *Memoirs of Extraordinary Popular Delusions*. Gustave Le Bon said in his book *Psychologie des foules* (*The Crowd*, 1895), "Ideas, sentiments, emotions, and beliefs possess in crowds a contagious power as intense as that of microbes."[12] Related terms are *collective consciousness* (Durkheim, 1897), *collective memory* (Halbwachs, 1925), and *memes* (Dawkins, 1976).

Of Book Jackets and Company Logos

Those who try to create viral narratives experiment, observe their successes and failures, and try to identify patterns that might suggest further avenues for creation. But the difference between a viral narrative and a nonviral narrative may depend on some aspect of the narrative that is not related to our enthusiasm for the narrative. It may depend, for example, on something hard to observe directly, such as the ability to connect with other topics of conversation, or reminders in other narratives.

The contagion rate is often natural, closely related to an event that launched an epidemic, but it is sometimes engineered by marketers. Their engineering may be almost invisible to us because it happens so frequently that we get used to it, and because we find it difficult to imagine all the thought and research that went into the design of marketing campaigns. For example, consider the modern book jacket, the paper cover that publishers place over their hardcover books and that usually includes endorsements, eye-catching fonts, author photos, and colorful artwork. The modern book jacket was invented during the advertising and marketing revolution around the 1920s, replacing some earlier plain-paper book jackets that were there merely to prevent the book from becoming shopworn.

It is important to note that the jacket looks like the work of the publisher, not the author, so it does not make the author look pandering or boastful. Book jackets permitted an immense step-up in contagion rates for books, despite their sometimes vulgar tone. It may be hard to understand the initial public resistance to book jackets at the time of their introduction. The poet Dorothea Lawrence Mann commented in 1921 on this new phenomenon, noting that it prompted many readers to:

> asseverate with indignation that far from reading or looking at or being influenced by such a blatant advertising scheme as the book-jacket, they throw it away with the greatest celerity and never, never read a book until its jacket has been safely disposed of and forgotten.[13]

Despite such buyer resistance, the modern book jacket flourished because it increased contagion. Most people would never have seen the endorsements that were placed on the book jackets, and soon bookstores learned to place the latest book jackets on display in their shop windows to catch the attention of passersby on the sidewalk. The book jacket was a brilliant marketing innovation precisely because readers made the final decision: they could take the jacket off and throw it away, or they might leave it on and place the book on their coffee table, thus passing along its contagion to people who visited. Once it became established that even dignified authors would allow their publishers to cover their books with a glitzy dust jacket, it became a permanent fixture. In fact, publishers who want to survive in a highly competitive business where others use book jackets have had no choice, for the book jacket is part of what George Akerlof and I called a *phishing equilibrium*. In a competitive market in which competitors manipulate customers, and in which profit margins are competed away to normal levels, no one company can choose not to engage in similar manipulations. If they tried, they might be forced into bankruptcy. A phishing equilibrium with a certain acceptable level of dishonesty in narrative is therefore established.[14] Phishing equilibria may not be all that bad. In the case of the book cover, there has developed an art of book jackets that sometimes have significant value.

Another example of marketing-driven contagion is "the news": the harvest of new information that news publishers hope will grab people's attention on a given day. "Phools," as George Akerlof and I call them, who do not think about the marketing efforts, are apt to think that events exogenously give us the news by jumping out at us. But, in fact, the news media are choosing the news because their financial success depends on their stories' viral impact. A recent example occurred in the United States in 2017 during a total eclipse of the sun that found many people traveling within the country to see the eclipse in its totality. The popular news media were relentless in covering the story, because, no doubt, they recognized its contagion as an experience shared by so many people. Some reporting took on a mystic-patriotic tone, as if God had granted this extremely rare event to the United States. Though the

US media frequently used the phrase "once in a lifetime," they did not mention that another total eclipse of the sun would occur again in the US just seven years later, in 2024. In fact, there was nothing genuinely newsworthy about the 2017 eclipse; eclipses have been studied and understood for centuries.

We also see engineered contagion in company logos on clothing and shoes, especially athletic or work clothing and shoes. The word *logo*, meaning a symbol representing a company or product line, dates back only to the 1930s. An example is the Lacoste clothing line, which displays its crocodile logo on its sportswear, casual clothing, and other products. Jean René Lacoste, the company's founder, was a widely admired tennis star in the 1920s and early 1930s. His nickname was "The Crocodile." Initial contagion for the clothing line, launched in 1933, benefited from his fame. Today, Lacoste the tennis star is mostly forgotten. Still the memory continues, and the logo persists. Those who do not reflect on the imperatives of marketing may imagine that people wear logo-branded clothing because they want to associate themselves with a prestigious clothing designer. But perhaps logo marketing works *because* it increases contagion. Customers may absently reach for the logo product because it is familiar and safe, and because so many others are wearing clothes with the same logo.

The construction of narratives by news media, promoters, and marketers can also help lower the forgetting rate. Narratives can be associated with symbols or rituals that remind people of basic elements of the narrative. A symbol can be incorporated into building architecture, letterheads, email messages, and a million other items, and a narrative can be incorporated into regular rituals, such as traditional parades on national holidays. Experts do not fully understand the role of ritual and symbols in aiding memory, but they do understand that they are associated with success.

All these examples illustrate a fundamental error that people tend to make: phools think that the popularity of a story or of a brand is evidence of its quality and deep importance, when in fact it rarely is. On the contrary, growing evidence in recent years has shown that many consumers detest logos and aggressive marketing.[15] Narrative contagion is often the result of arbitrary details, such as the frequency of meetings among people (many people see a logo on a shirt) and natural links to other contagious narratives (Lacoste's onetime fame as a tennis player).

Beauty Contests and Tail Feathers: How the Theory of Mind Feeds Economic Narratives

Psychologists have noted that the human species is unique in the advanced development of its *theory of mind*—that is, humans' strong tendency to form a model in their own minds of the activities in others' minds. We are thinking about what others are thinking, about their individual thoughts. We observe their actions, their facial expressions, and their vocal intonation, which we then relate to their beliefs and intentions.

The contagion of specific narratives may be related to storytellers' impressions regarding what other people will think. People like to hear stories that they can retell to others who will like the same story, and so storytellers like to tell such stories.

In 1936, Keynes introduced what we now call theory of mind into economic theory with his "beauty contest" metaphor,[16] which he put forth to explain speculative markets, such as the stock market. Keynes thought that people deciding which investments to make were basing their decisions on observations of what other investors were thinking or what they were about to do with their investments (which might cause future price changes). In the case of stock market investments, investors look at what other people whom they randomly encounter are saying and emoting, and they look at patterns in stock prices that offer clues regarding what other people are doing or will soon be doing. They are usually not looking at real evidence based on the firm's technology or management style.

Keynes said he had seen a newspaper contest that displayed a hundred photos, each of a pretty face. But the women in the photos were not the contestants in this unusual form of beauty contest; the readers of the newspaper were. They were asked to mail to the newspaper their list of the six prettiest faces. The person whose list most closely matched the most popular faces as revealed by all the lists together would win the contest prize.[17]

Keynes pointed out that the optimal strategy is not to pick the six prettiest faces based on one's own opinion. Instead, it makes more sense to pick the six that one thinks other people would find prettiest. But this strategy is not optimal either, if we carry the model of mind to the next step in the chain. One should pick the faces that one thinks that others think that others find the prettiest. So, in a rational world, one might suppose that investors, trying to gauge what other investors think other investors are thinking, will try to determine the right thing to think about the speculative investments. However, investors do not necessarily follow this strategy, even if all investors are rational and know that all investors are rational.[18] In addition, we have to account for the investors' less-than-perfect rationality and the investor irrationality expected by other investors.

In our 2009 book *Animal Spirits*, which was in many ways an expansion and elaboration of Keynes's ideas, George Akerlof and I used the beauty contest metaphor to construct a theory of the emotional foundation of business fluctuations in general. The beauty contest metaphor also applies to the contagion of narratives. When we choose to tell a story to others, we base that choice on our perceptions of how people will react to that story in their own minds. We will likely spread a story, whether it is a story about boom-time thinking or about economic despair, if we think that others will like the story enough to want to spread it further. Even if we are spreading an economic narrative for no other reason than trying to amuse ourselves, we are likely to engineer our story to spread based on our model of others' minds.

The stories that go viral are essentially random, just as mutations in evolutionary biology are random. Traditional evolutionary theory suggests that the mutations that survive and spread are those few out of many that are in themselves advantageous for survival. But there is another branch to Darwin's theory, that of sexual selection, and it suggests that the winning mutations may be just as random as the original mutation. Something like this randomness may affect economic narratives going viral as well.

In his 2017 book *The Evolution of Beauty*, ornithologist Richard O. Prum argues that sexual selection gives rise to fluctuations in the animal kingdom that resemble speculative bubbles in economics. Perhaps the most famous example of sexual selection in biology is the male peacock, which has very heavy tail feathers that inhibit his activities. But these feathers are much favored by the female of the species, which facilitates mating and the reproduction of more beautiful tail feathers. Thus the female sexual choice may create an evolutionary advantage for some useless characteristic in a process called a Fisherian runaway, after theorist R. A. Fisher.[19] The mechanism does not even require two distinct sexes, as there is evidence for such sexual selection processes among hermaphrodite species in which each individual has both male and female organs.[20] In both evolutionary biology and narrative economics, some kind of ornament or display can become popular for no more reason than the fact that it randomly began to be popular.

Irrational Impulses Inform Economic Narratives

Psychologist Jerome Bruner, who has stressed the importance of narratives in understanding human culture, wrote that we should not assume that human actions are driven in response to purely objective facts:

> I do not believe that facts ever quite stare anybody in the face. From a psychologist's point of view, that is not how facts behave, as we well know from our studies of perception, memory, and thinking. Our factual worlds are more like cabinetry carefully carpentered than like a virgin forest inadvertently stumbled upon.[21]

That is, narratives are human constructs that are mixtures of fact, emotion, human interest, and other extraneous details that form an impression on the human mind.

Psychiatrists and psychologists recognize that mental illness is often an extreme form of normal behavior or a narrow disruption of normal human mental faculties. So we can learn about the complexities of normal human narrative brain processing by studying *dysnarrativia*, or abnormal narrative phenomena. Neuroscientists Kay Young and Jeffrey

Saver (2001) listed some of its varied forms: arrested narration (the ability to tell only stories learned before a brain injury), undernarration (the telling of vacillating, impulsive stories), denarration (failure to organize a story in terms of an action-generating temporal frame), and confabulation (the fabrication of stories that have little or no relation to reality). Each form of dysnarrativia is related to injury in a specific part of the brain.

Schizophrenia is a serious mental illness that can manifest as a disorder of narrative, as it often involves hearing imaginary voices delivering a fantastic and jumbled narrative.[22] Hearing voices as a symptom of schizophrenia is correlated with volume deficits in specific brain areas.[23] The narrative disruption found in autism spectrum disorder also is related to brain anomalies.[24]

Framing, the Representativeness Heuristic, and the Affect Heuristic

Narrative psychology also relates to the psychological concept of *framing*.[25] If we can create an amusing story that will get retold, it can establish a point of view, a reference point, that will influence decisions. Framing is related to the Daniel Kahneman and Amos Tversky *representativeness heuristic* (1973), whereby people form their expectations based on some idealized story or model, judging these expectations based on the prominence of the idealized story rather than estimated probabilities. For example, we may judge the danger of an emerging economic crisis by its similarity to a remembered story of a previous crisis, rather than by any logic.

George Katona, one of the founders of behavioral economics and author of the 1975 book *Psychological Economics*, noted an odd phenomenon: when he interviewed common people and asked them about their expectations of key economic variables, he had the feeling that they had no clear expectations, and that they made up numbers on the spot to please him. But I would argue that these ordinary people were thinking about narratives that involved people and prices. If asked in an interview about their expectations for inflation, for example, they might not answer the question directly but rather offer a dramatic story with human interest and with clear moralizing, about politicians' or labor unions' activities that might be related to inflation.

Psychologists have also noted an *affect heuristic*, whereby people who are experiencing strong emotions, such as fear, tend to extend those feelings to unrelated events.[26] Sometimes people note strong emotions or fears about possibilities that they know logically are not real, suggesting that the brain has multiple systems for assessing risk. This "risk as feelings" hypothesis holds that some primitive brain system more connected to palpable emotions has its own heuristic for assessing risk.[27]

In joint work with William Goetzmann and Dasol Kim, George Akerlof and I examined data from a questionnaire survey of investors and high-income Americans since 1989. We found that people have exaggerated assessments of the risk of a stock market crash, and that these assessments are influenced by the news stories, especially front-page stories, that they read. One intriguing finding was that a natural event such as an earthquake could influence estimations of the likelihood of a stock market crash. The respondents in our survey assigned statistically significantly higher probabilities to a stock market crash if there had been an earthquake within thirty miles of their zip code within thirty days, triggering the affect heuristic. It seems reasonable to hypothesize that local earthquakes start local narratives with negative emotional valence. Analogous evidence has indicated that seemingly irrelevant events with strong narrative potential can affect economic or political outcomes: the World Cup competition can affect economic confidence,[28] shark attacks at local beaches can affect votes for local incumbents,[29] and background music in advertisements can have a strong effect on consumers.[30] Wine stores find buyers purchasing more expensive wines if the background music is classical versus Top 40.[31]

An affect heuristic also operates in generating activity by Internet trolls (people who send nasty or obscene comments on the Internet).[32] Trolling behavior appears to be contagious: an experimental group randomly selected from the general population was primed with nasty examples of trolling. Members of that group were then much more likely to post similar comments.

Going Forward

The tantalizing evidence about the impact of narratives from neuroscience and related observations suggests some entirely different explanations of the severity of major economic events. In part II of this book we consider some organizing principles for narrative economics. A key issue is assigning the direction of causality from dispersed and ill-defined narrative constellations to actual economic activity, a topic to which we turn in the next chapter. The chapter after that offers key foundations of narrative economics. Part III then presents a list of nine important perennial narrative constellations, one (or a pair) per chapter.

Part II

The Foundations of Narrative Economics

Chapter 7

Causality and Constellations

The goal of this book is to improve people's ability to anticipate and deal with major economic events, such as depressions, recessions, or secular (that is, long-term) stagnation, by encouraging them to identify and incorporate into their thinking the economic narratives that help to define these events. Before we can forecast reliably, we need some understanding of these events' true ultimate causes. The key problem is determining what is a cause versus what is a consequence.

Though modern economists tend to be very attentive to causality, as a general rule they do not attach any causal significance to the invention of new narratives. I want to argue here not only that causality exists, but also that it goes both ways: new contagious narratives cause economic events, and economic events cause changed narratives.

Of course, almost nothing beyond spots on the sun is purely an outside influence on the economy (more on sunspots later in the chapter), but we can think of new narratives as causative innovations, because each narrative originates in the mind of a single individual (or as a collaboration among a few people). Economic historian Joel Mokyr (2016) calls such an individual a "cultural entrepreneur," and he traces the concept back to philosopher and polymath David Hume, who wrote in 1742:

> What depends on a few persons is, in great measure, to be ascribed to chance, or secret and unknown causes; what arises from a great number may often be accounted for by determinate and known causes.[1]

Understanding the effects of the "few persons" who create contagious new narratives is essential to formulating the foundations of a theory of narrative economics.

The effects of a "few persons" sometimes work through the creation of contagious new narratives. Though narratives are commonly connected with celebrities, the "few persons" who *invent* a contagious narrative are usually not famous, and often we will never know who they were. Later on, we can look for celebrities attached to them, but we will usually not find their authors.

In this chapter we will consider the *causal elements* that make economic narratives go viral—especially stories and storytelling—with the aim of developing a better understanding of these narratives' deep structure.

Direction of Causality

It is not easy to prove direction of causality between a narrative and the economy. For example, did the stories of successful speculators and wild enthusiasm for stocks that characterized the 1920s cause increased stock prices and increased corporate earnings? Or did those increased earnings cause the enthusiasm? Was the similar enthusiasm for Bitcoin after 2009 in any way responsible for the increase in Bitcoin's price? Or was Bitcoin's increased value just a logical reaction to news stories and new progress in the mathematical theory of cryptography?

A problem in establishing direction of causality for major economic events is that economists usually cannot run controlled experiments that accurately simulate economic conditions at large. In contrast, laboratory scientists conduct random trials, perhaps by administering a test drug to an experimental group and a placebo to a control group, and then using statistical analysis to determine whether the drug really causes patients to recover. The best economists can often do is to look for events that might be deemed natural experiments. Henry W. Farnam, in his 1912 presidential address before the American Economic Association, addressed economists' inability to conduct controlled experiments, asserting nonetheless that the study of economic history can allow economists to infer causality because random shocks have occurred through history,

as when governments embark on crazy economic policies. In fact, Farnam said, "The economist is really fortunate in having experiments tried
for him without expense."[2]

In their 1963 *Monetary History of the United States*, Milton Friedman
and Anna J. Schwartz gave three examples of what they called "quasi-
controlled experiments" to establish causal impact from monetary
policy to the aggregate economy: the large gold discoveries of 1897 to 1914,
which expanded the money supply, and the periods during and immediately after World War I and World War II. We can debate whether these
events were truly random exogenous shocks (that is, not caused by the
economy), but much more discussion on inferring direction of causality
with economic data has taken place since 1963. The general conclusion
is that it is indeed possible to infer causality even when controlled experiments are impossible. New narratives might be interpreted as exogenous, helping us identify additional quasi-controlled experiments. In fact,
the gold discoveries and wars that Friedman and Schwartz emphasized
likely *were* exogenous because they were made possible by innovations
in popular narratives, such as gold rush stories or fake news about foreign conspiracy.

We must be wary of many (but not all) economists' supposition that
the causality always runs from economic events to narratives, and not the
other way around. There has been a lively debate about the impact of self-
fulfilling prophecies in economics. Sociologist Robert K. Merton
coined the phrase *self-fulfilling prophecy* in 1948, intending to apply the
concept to economic fluctuations. The term often refers to prophecies
stimulated by genuinely extraneous events, with the most popular example being sunspots (spots on the sun, which come and go through
time, and are observable through telescopes).

The economist William Stanley Jevons proposed in 1878 that world
economic fluctuations might be driven by "periodic variation in the sun's
rays, of which the sun-spots are a mere sign."[3] If the heat coming from
the sun is stronger in some years than in others, then crops and other
economic output may be stronger in hotter years, which may lead to
major economic fluctuations. There was by 1878 already astronomical evidence on solar activity, going back centuries, in the form of counts of

sunspots through time. He thought he discerned a correlation between those sunspot counts and economic events. And the cause of this correlation had to be the sun, for there is no conceivable theory that causality could go the other way, from economic events on earth to spots on the sun. His theory sounded plausible, but subsequent economic research did not support it, and variations in solar output are too small to have any substantial such effect. Sunspots should hardly affect the economy, but they may do so if people mystically believe they should, as economists David Cass and Karl Shell explained in 1983. Now, economists use the term *sunspots* to refer to any extraneous noise that affects the economy because people believe it will. Economist Roger E. A. Farmer has been a leader in the field of macroeconomic self-fulfilling prophecies.[4] To his and others' work I add the idea that these self-fulfilling prophecies do not come out of nowhere. Rather, they typically come from millions of mutations in narratives, of which a few are contagious enough in the current environment to become major epidemics. As we have seen, this process can be observed and modeled.

Random Events, Birthdays, and Anniversaries: How Does a Narrative Become an Economic Narrative?

Generally speaking, most people harbor vague fears and concerns stimulated by narratives, but these fears have little or no effect on their actions. The narratives become *economic* narratives when they involve stories in which others take action and describe the actions they take, such as investing in and getting rich in certain financial markets. Economic narratives thus tend to involve scripts, sequences of actions that one might take for no better reason than hearing narratives of other people doing these things.

Trying to understand major economic events by looking only at data on changes in economic aggregates, such as gross domestic product, wage rates, interest rates, and tax rates, runs the risk of missing the underlying motivations for change. Doing so is like trying to understand a religious awakening by looking at the cost of printing religious tracts. But it is easy to see why economists often fall into this trap: abundant data exist for GDP, wage rates, interest rates, and tax rates, but data on narratives are spotty at best. Economists may be falling into what historian Jerry Z. Muller calls the "tyranny of metrics." Muller is not opposed to providing quantitative indexes of important economic phenomena, but he does note that most people overreact to such indexes and fail to see that they are overestimating the importance of arbitrary quantifications that are really of limited value.[5]

The people who make economic decisions against a background of narratives do not usually explain their decisions. If asked to explain, they might be at a loss for words or try to talk like economists. How, for example, can someone explain the ultimate reasons why he or she hesitated to spend during a recession? Hesitation is *not* taking action, and might be caused just by absence of any identifiable thought to take action, amidst a large number of other thoughts.

Contagious stories are largely creative and innovative, not simply a logical reaction to economic events. For example, major stock market corrections take place over many days, during which the public has plenty of time to read the sometimes creative and sensationalistic writing of the various news media, whose job is to attract attention. Over that time period, stock market participants take part in countless conversations that reinterpret the news in efforts not only to inform but also to amuse.

The process is in many ways a random event, like the mutation in a microbe such as a bacterium or virus. A celebrity, for example, may off-handedly voice a colorful phrase. That is what happened on October 15, 1929, two weeks before the 1929 crash, when the famous Professor Irving Fisher of Yale, in a speech before the Purchasing Agents Association of New York, said that the US stock market had reached a "permanently high plateau." The newspapers picked up that new, colorful phrase over the next couple of days.[6] That spectacularly ill-timed and ironic phrase became an epidemic, probably affecting the duration of the market debacle, and it is still widely remembered today. In fact, those three words are more famous today than the title of any of the books that Fisher spent years writing. They are in the same league with other colorful phrases such as *irrational exuberance* and *Laffer curve*. These words and their effects came from outside the economy, and they are therefore exogenous.

Also, anniversaries of past events can resurrect economic narratives. Even though a narrative of years past—such as the 1987 stock market crash—has lost its contagion, it may still exist in the dim recesses of memory, for older people at least. But it has the potential to become contagious again, if it is tweaked (and probably renamed) and reattached to a human-interest story. For example, the news media tend to remind the public about the 1987 crash on major anniversaries, and they will predictably continue to do so until there is a bigger one-day crash. At that point, 1987 will no longer be the record-holder, at which time it won't be of any interest at all.

By 2013, the Bitcoin narrative was beginning to fade. It was an old story, and the price of a Bitcoin dropped from over US $1000 at its 2013 peak to just over $200. But a proliferation of new inventions—or mutations— kept the idea alive. Notable among these inventions was the initial coin offering (ICO), which allowed new cryptocurrencies to be developed with distinctively different stories. These currencies were backed, in effect, as shares of corporations. The ICO brought a flood of new narratives, each tied to a particular coin identified with some line of business. It brought back into public esteem the old sport of picking stocks, which had become somewhat tarnished as a fool's errand. There was something new to talk about. In 2017 alone, there were over nine hundred initial coin offerings for crowdfunded business startups that wanted to raise money for some new venture. Almost half of them failed within a year, but new ICOs kept coming.[7]

Of course, economists are aware of the narratives associated with events, but mostly they work on the assumption that the narratives are nothing more than a bit of silliness that follows the discovery of changing real news about deep economic forces. The presumption is often that these deep economic forces are caused exclusively by scientific advances in production, discovery or unexpected exhaustion of natural resources, demographic changes, or economic research that provides new information on how government policymakers can adopt better rules of action.

But this mode of thinking misses what may be the essential elements that cause change in the economy. As we saw in part I, the economic narratives surrounding these events work in predictable ways: they are contagious, they suggest scripts for people to follow, they repeat their messages, and they thrive on human interest. In doing so, they affect society and the course of economic activity in highly consequential ways.

Controlled Experiments from Outside Economics Show Direction of Causality

While we may sometimes be able to infer direction of causality by studying economic history, we need also to recognize that controlled experiments outside of economics have shown narratives' effects on human behavior.

In the field of marketing, Jennifer Edson Escalas notes, *self-referencing* occurs when the viewer of an advertisement relates a product to his or her personal experiences. But not all self-referencing is equally effective in changing buyer behavior. Using controlled experiments, Escalas has compared analytical self-referencing (an explanation of why *you* need the product) to narrative self-referencing and narrative transportation (which presents a story that causes an individual to imagine himself or herself to be another person, using the word *I* rather than *you*). Escalas found that the narrative transportation is more effective, especially when the analytical case for the product is weak.[8]

In journalism, Marcel Machill and his coauthors, noting evidence that viewers of television news retain little of the news they hear, presented an actual TV news report on the dangers of air pollution to a control group. They also presented a variation of the report to the experimental group in the form of a story with a protagonist, a baker with health problems caused by air pollution, in an unfair struggle against antagonists who benefited from the polluting activities. The experimental presentation of the news was retained better.[9]

In education, Scott W. McQuiggan and his coauthors have found motivational benefits of narrative-centered learning. Each eighth-grade student in the experimental group played a virtual-reality computer game in the role of a young Alyx, whose father, in the fictitious story, is the head of a team of research scientists on Crystal Island. A mysterious grave disease has afflicted some of the scientists, including Alyx's father. Alyx is determined to find out why. Playing involves interacting in dialogues with other simulated people. In the process, the student learns about microbiology, about bacteria, viruses, fungi, and parasites. The study documents an advantage in learning relative to the control group with regard to "self-efficacy, presence, interest, and perception of control."[10]

In health interventions, Michael D. Slater and his coauthors studied how to persuade people to eat more fruits and vegetables. They concluded from experiments that didactic presentations of evidence on nutrition were not effective. Audience response was stronger to narrative messages when the audience identified with persons portrayed in the message. In health interventions, these results underscore the need for carefully pretesting the story and choosing the right persons to convey the message.[11]

In philanthropy, Keith Weber and his coauthors (2006) asked subjects to read a message involving organ donation before asking them to sign an organ donor card. The content of the message (narrative versus statistics) was manipulated. Results indicated that narrative messages were more effective than statistical messages.

In law, Brad E. Bell and Elizabeth F. Loftus (1985) conducted a controlled experiment in which subjects took on the role of jury members. The goal was to determine the jury members' response to vivid prosecutions and nonvivid prosecutions. For example, the vivid prosecution included the irrelevant line that the accused, at the time of the crime, accidentally "knocked over a bowl of guacamole dip onto the white shag carpet." That irrelevant but vivid mental image helped obtain a conviction from the experimental jury.

In sum: economics can learn from other social sciences, including psychology (especially social psychology), sociology, anthropology (especially cultural or historical anthropology), and history (especially cultural and intellectual history or *histoire des mentalités*). Because controlled experiments about whole economies are not readily available to economists, it is all the more important that we specify and understand the building blocks of economic narratives. Stories are one key building block.

The Importance of Stories in Driving Human Activity

Emotion matters in the structure of narratives, economic and otherwise, and it reveals itself in *stories*. The historical novel and historical movie stand outside of mainstream history, but they excel in helping us understand feelings in history and appreciate some of the narratives that drive history. The historical novelist or filmmaker, who constructs dialogue based on imagination and the intuition that research has afforded, looks more like an inventor than a scholar.

In his 2013 presidential address before the American Historical Association, historian William Cronon compared scholarly research in history with the historical novel:

> Historians choose not to represent aspects of the past about which our documents are silent, but some of these—stream-of-consciousness and informal conversation most obviously—are so fundamental to so much of life that it is a little hard to say which depiction of the past is more distorting: a history that says nothing about them, or a fiction that in the absence of authoritative evidence tries to represent them as responsibly as possible.[12]

There is thus a basic question about the primary *metaphor* that we use to understand an economic crisis. Dominating the discussion in popular media is the "economy-as-sick-or-healthy-person" metaphor. The economy is described as healthy at some times, as sick at others, as if it needs a doctor who will administer the right kind of medicine (fiscal or monetary policy). In keeping with the sickness/health metaphor, the popular media often report on a thermometer called "confidence," measured by confidence indexes or the stock market.

The significance of human-interest stories brings to mind the work of psychologist Robert Sternberg. In his book *Love Is a Story* (1998), he describes healthy, loving relationships between two individuals as made possible by a narrative of their relationship. As in loving relationships, the progress of an economy is not one-dimensional. Rather, the story of the economy has dimensions beyond the public's perception of its health. The story has moral dimensions as well, involving attitudes of loyalty versus opportunism, of trust versus distrust, of cutting to the head of the line versus waiting politely. In addition, the story has dimensions of affect, of security versus insecurity, of inner direction versus public direction. The array of stories circulating at any point of time conveys all of these dimensions.

Flashbulb Memory

In addition to having a story-like structure, our memories tend to focus on a few salient, random images. Certain poignant narratives produce such strong emotional reactions that people remember them years later. The narrative may have been transmitted to them only briefly and succinctly, among many other communications that are quickly forgotten. Why can such brief exposures to a narrative cause changes in economic behavior long afterward?

When asked to describe their confidence or current motivations, people can sometimes remember and talk about a sudden change in their mental stance, suggesting a discrete and identifiable causal stimulus. In the extreme form, the establishment of a long-term memory may be so sudden as to be considered a *flashbulb memory*.[13] The experience of a flashbulb memory is similar to the effect of an underexposed movie, filmed in darkness, illuminated for only an instant when a camera flashbulb went off. That flashbulb image may tell quite a story, suggesting an event with a reason, with surroundings and ambience. With many of our memories, we remember points in time, and we have some idea of context, but we cannot move away from the focused, flashbulb memory.

Psychologists have studied how the brain chooses which memories to give flashbulb status, analogous to choosing which photos to put in a family album. It turns out that flashbulb memories are connected not only to the emotions attached to the remembered event but also to social psychological factors. Memories that involve a shared identity with others, or that are rehearsed with others, are more likely to achieve flashbulb status.[14] Thus flashbulb memories are selected in a way that gives them a better chance to be involved in the formation of contagious narratives.

For example, the narrative describing the first shots of the US Civil War near Fort Sumter in 1861 was vividly remembered decades later. Thirty-five years after the event, a former US first sergeant described in great detail just what he was doing when, for the first time in his life, he was told he must lead his men on a mission that might get them killed:

> I was on duty as first sergeant of a company of 100 recruits, well instructed as infantry, on Governor's Island in the New York harbor. We had just about got through with our holiday celebrations, which in antebellum days, were made to last about ten days in the army: and hearty celebrations they used to be. On Saturday, the 5th of January, I was engaged in having the quarters cleaned for the orthodox Sunday-morning inspection, and contemplated having a quiet day, and winding it up with a little more holiday celebration in the evening, when I was summoned to the adjutant's office, where the sergeant-major told me to have my company paraded at 2 p.m. in marching order, for inspection. No use asking questions.[15]

The Japanese attack on the US base in Pearl Harbor in December 1941, which marked the beginning of US involvement in World War II, is similarly described by powerful narratives that explain the commitment to fight the war. Forty years later, people still remembered when they first heard the Pearl Harbor news:

> UniHi classmate John Holmes still remembers precisely where he was and what he was doing:
> "In those days they sold newspapers on street corners. I was a paperboy selling the *Examiner* at the corner of Pico and Prosser. I sold the paper that reported Pearl Harbor had been bombed.

"But I didn't realize what it meant, that it would change my life. I was too immature."

Joe Arnold was working, too, at a gas station at Glendon and Londbrook in Westwood. "It had a big tower. It was foggy that day, and I climbed up to the top of that tower to see if I could see anything. I don't know what I expected to see. . . ."

Barbara Ryan Dunham's memory is typical of that of many Americans.

"We were at the breakfast table," she said. "We had come home from church, and we had the radio on. . . . Nobody could believe it at first."[16]

Flashbulb memory is one aspect of the human tendency to become motivated by seemingly random details of stories, even brief stories that are little more than anecdotes. In the above examples, the stories involved what happened just before or just after the shocking news, in the form of a sequence of mostly meaningless events. In comparison, if we were to ask people to recount such trivial details about another random day decades ago, they would have no memory at all, precisely because the day was not connected with a famous or infamous event.

A famous flashbulb memory event in recent US history is the September 11, 2001, terrorist attack that resulted in the destruction of the World Trade Center in New York City and severe damage to the Pentagon in Washington, DC. Many people in the United States today can remember a story about what they were doing when they heard about the attack. The vividness of these memories is testimony to the attack's causal impact on their economic actions.

At that time, according to the National Bureau of Economic Research (NBER), the US economy had been in a recession since March 2001, following the 2000 peak in the world's stock markets and the subsequent financial crisis and major decline. Right after the September 11, 2001, attacks, in which terrorists crashed commandeered airplanes into symbolically important national targets, there were widespread fears that the recession in the US economy would be prolonged because people would choose to stay at home owing to their fear of another such attack.[17]

Coming a year after the popping of the 2000 stock market bubble, amidst numerous signs of recession, the terrorist attacks were the "perfect storm" for the "economy to hit the wall."[18]

But the attacks appear to have had just the opposite effect. In November 2001, the recession ended and the US economy almost immediately recovered, making that recession one of the shortest in US history. How might we explain the nation's quick recovery? After the attacks, a narrative took hold that involved a plea from national leaders asking the nation's people to do symbolic things to uphold national confidence. Two weeks after the attack, US president George W. Bush gave a talk to airline workers and to the nation as a whole:

> And we must stand against terror by going back to work. Everybody here who showed up for work, at this important industry, is making a clear statement that terrorism will not stand, that the evildoers will not be able to terrorize America and our work force and our people. (Applause.) . . . When they struck, they wanted to create an atmosphere of fear. And one of the great goals of this nation's war is to restore public confidence in the airline industry. It's to tell the traveling public: Get on board. Do your business around the country. Fly and enjoy America's great destination spots. Get down to Disney World in Florida. Take your families and enjoy life, the way we want it to be enjoyed.[19]

President Bush also lavished praise on Americans: "This is a determined nation, and we're a strong nation. We're a nation based upon fabulous values." Like a good sports coach, he was encouraging team spirit, both among the airline workers and among the citizenry as a whole. His narrative suggested a script for strong, courageous, inspired behavior. That narrative was expressly designed to encourage the ideas that we all are watched by others and that we all must set an example of courage. During the economic recovery, however, most economists did not recognize the flashbulb quality of the September 2001 attacks, which encouraged a contagious constellation of narratives and may have profoundly affected US businesses and the US economy.[20]

The Ubiquity of Fake News

In attempting to be vivid, storytellers often resort to fiction or fake news, thereby providing amplified tales. The history of narratives shows that "fake news" is not new. In fact, people have always liked amusing stories, and they spread stories that they suspect are not true, as for example in urban legends. In fact, people often spread titillating stories without making any clear moral decision whether they are spreading falsehoods or not.

Fake news often makes an impression on people because the brain processes that implement reality monitoring are imperfect. According to psychologists and neuroscientists, source monitoring is a difficult process for the brain, which judges sources by their linkages to other memories.[21] Thus, over time, the brain may forget that it once deemed stories unreliable. Also, adeptness in source monitoring differs across individuals, and temporal diencephalic and frontal lobe damage in the brain may contribute to extreme defects in source monitoring.[22]

As an example, let's look at fake wrestling matches, where wrestlers appear to break the rules and almost kill each other. People seem to derive pleasure from watching a match that others would say is obviously fake and trying to pretend that it is real. A word for this strange phenomenon, *kayfabe*, appeared in print starting in the 1970s.

The fake wrestling match does not proceed as a by-the-rules high school or college wrestling match would. Instead, it includes a number of outrageous story elements. One of the combatants may be flamboyantly evil and/or ugly in his near nakedness, while the other is clean-cut, handsome, and honorable. The bad guy acts cowardly, hides behind the ropes, and slips in an illegal strike in plain view of the audience when the referee briefly looks away. He tortures the opponent when he is down, and he climbs up high on the ropes and pretends to jump onto his opponent's abdomen.

The fakery is often so obvious that any observer would see through at least some of it. Spectators sometimes even shout, "Fake!" during a match when the acting is not up to their standards. And yet the match is presented and largely accepted as if it were true. Spectators seem to want it to be possibly true, at least some of the time, and they may pretend it *is* true to stimulate their imaginations. However, as literary theorist Roland Barthes notes, spectators at these matches rarely bet on the outcome as they do in other sports: "That would make no sense . . . wrestling sustains its originality by all the excesses which make it a spectacle and not a sport."[23] In other words, at some level, many people enjoy believing the story and do not care about its factuality.

Fake fighting matches have a long history in many countries, indicating an enduring story. A ProQuest News & Newspapers search for *fake wrestling* shows the phrase dating back to 1890, with a reporter noting that "there have been a lot of fake wrestling matches lately."[24] Even in ancient Rome, in the minutes preceding the real gladiatorial combats that sometimes resulted in death, there was fake combat, *prolusio*, that whetted the audience's appetite for the real thing to follow.[25] *Prolusio* probably resembled modern fake wrestling matches, and in some ways it may even have been more interesting to watch, in that the actors were experienced and skilled in manipulating audiences, and some were celebrities.

Much has improved since ancient Romans released lions to maul and kill criminals, runaway slaves, and Christians in the Colosseum. We have established news media with reputations for honesty. The twenty-first century has seen the birth of fact-checking websites, including AP Fact Check, factcheck.org, politifact.com, snopes.com, USAfacts.org, and wikitribune.com. All of these sites have built their reputation by debunking fake news rather than by reporting all sides of a controversy without taking sides, which was once common in the mainstream news media. Unfortunately, most people do not read these fact-checking websites. In addition, their credibility has recently been compromised by fake news designed to harm their reputations, leading some members of the general public to give up the hope of ever finding the real truth.

What conclusions can we draw? Given its presence over the centuries and millennia, fake news seems to be part of the normal human condition. Fake performances, fake stories, and fake heroes are ubiquitous. The fakery is so creative that we cannot view the performances as caused by fundamental economic forces. Instead, the opposite is true: the fakery, in the form of fake narratives, affects economic outcomes.

Evidence on Causation from
Constellations of Narratives

In studying narratives from archival data, we may miss the constellation of narratives behind any single aspect of cultural change because we may be able to view only some of the superficial narratives. From our vantage point many decades later, it is like standing on the earth on a partly cloudy night and trying to discern the constellations in the sky above. We certainly will not see some of the stars. In addition, narratives typically come and go over a period of years, but economic fluctuations are often sudden, as in a financial panic that unfolds over a matter of days. But the seeds of that panic may well have been planted over months or years.

Ultimately, the mass of people whose consumption and investment decisions cause economic fluctuations are not very well informed. Most of them do not view or read the news carefully, and they rarely get the facts in any discernible order. And yet their decisions drive aggregate economic activity. It must be the case, then, that attention-getting narratives drive those decisions, often with an assist from celebrities or trusted figures.

Once we recognize that newly mutated stories within narrative constellations can cause current economic events, we have made substantial progress. But it is not easy to achieve a secure understanding of how narratives affect the economy. We need to step back first and consider some basic principles, some alluded to in previous chapters, to guide our thinking, which brings us to the next chapter.

Chapter 8

Seven Propositions of Narrative Economics

So far, we've seen that popular narratives gone viral have economic consequences. Ultimately, we want economists to model this relationship to help anticipate economic events. First, though, we want to offer some basic propositions about economic narratives that we can use to understand historically important narratives and to identify new narratives as they develop.

Before we begin, let's review a few key features of economic narratives. As the Bitcoin narrative illustrates, an economic narrative reminds people of facts they might have forgotten, offers an explanation about how things work in the economy, and affects how people think about the justification or purpose of economic actions. The narrative may imply something about the way the world works—in the Bitcoin narrative, the notion that computers are taking over, that we are entering a new cosmopolitan era freed from the perennial problems of local government incompetence and corruption—and how we can use that information to our advantage. Or the narrative may suggest that performing a specific economic action is a useful learning experience that will yield possible benefits in the future. Sometimes, performing the economic action is a way of involving ourselves in the narrative itself. By taking part in the narrative, we can say that we are a part of history. For example, by purchasing Bitcoin, we joined the international capitalist elite.

Proposition 1: Epidemics Can Be Fast or Slow, Big or Small

Economic narrative epidemics come in many different sizes and time frames. There is no standard course for a narrative epidemic, and rapid growth of a fast epidemic does not mean it will have long-run significance. In the appendix to this book we review models from medical epidemiology that show that contagion and recovery parameters can be chosen for the models that imply fast big epidemics, fast small epidemics, slow big epidemics, and slow small epidemics.

Because a narrative can come and go over many decades, it may last longer than any data series on which economists rely to measure the narrative's impact. We must therefore not rush to judgment on the impact of a narrative. For example, if we assume that a viral economic narrative is exactly like a meme that goes viral on Facebook or Twitter over a period of days, then we will miss the possibility that a historic long boom is the result of an epidemic that has occurred over a much longer time frame.

Another example: if we do not appreciate that some epidemics are fast and some are slow, we are likely to overrely on best seller status to judge a work's importance. Best seller lists tend to reflect sales over short intervals of time. The *New York Times* list of best-selling books, for example, reports on the books that sold the most copies in just the current week. (From earlier chapters, we understand why the news media emphasize a short time interval: they have to keep coming up with news stories.) The short time frame explains why the Bible and the Koran are never on the best seller lists. If we look at the *New York Times* best seller lists from decades past, hardly any of the books will be familiar. Most were flash-in-the-pan short-term epidemics.

The contagion rate also varies greatly from one narrative epidemic to another. One example of a narrative epidemic with very high contagion might be that of a national emergency, like the start of a war. With such narratives, people feel that the story is so important that they have license to interrupt any other conversation with the news, or to speak with people with whom they do not normally communicate. An example of a successful narrative with a very low contagion rate might be a patriotic story illustrating a country's national greatness, a story that is brought up only at appropriate times at home, in the classroom, or at events sponsored by civic organizations. Such a narrative can develop (slowly) into a huge epidemic if the forgetting rate is low enough.

Narratives also differ in their recovery rate or forgetting rate. Narratives with high recovery rates often are isolated, not part of a constellation. Narratives with low recovery rates include those with constant reminders. For example, when we see homeless people and beggars on the streets, we remember narratives about massive unemployment during a depression. Longer-term narratives are more likely to have an impact on one's view of the world or one's sense of the meaning of life.

As the mathematical model in the appendix shows, a high contagion parameter and a low recovery rate mean that almost the whole population eventually hears the narrative, sometimes very quickly. But the same narrative can reach most of the population rather slowly if the contagion parameter is low but the recovery rate is even lower. The following example is illustrative.

I conducted a questionnaire survey in the United States right after the October 19, 1987, stock market crash, which was the biggest one-day drop in US history. I asked a random sample of US high-income individuals exactly when they first heard about the crash. Of the respondents, 97% said they heard of it on the day of the drop. The average answer was 1:56 p.m. Eastern Time / 10:56 a.m. Pacific Time.[1] Most of the respondents did not hear about this drop via the morning newspapers or the evening television news. They heard it by direct word of mouth as the event was happening.

Proposition 2: Important Economic Narratives May Comprise a Very Small Percentage of Popular Talk

In trying to judge the importance of economic narrative epidemics, we should not base our conclusions on the assumption that the most economically important narratives are those that are constantly talked about.

Very significant epidemics may generate very little talk. In addition, because people are always talking, some kind of narrative is always spreading. In studying economic narratives, we must not be distracted by the small talk that is not useful in explaining economic changes.

In 1932, near the height of the Great Depression, Franklin Roosevelt challenged incumbent Herbert Hoover in the US presidential election. Writing for the *New York Times*, Pulitzer Prize–winning journalist Arthur Krock tried to summarize what ordinary people were saying about the economic situation. He listened to people talking, "avoiding prompting as much as possible":[2]

> By train, motor car, airplane and on foot I have wandered 10,000 miles. I have talked with, observed and listened to many hundreds of people on trains, in restaurants, on the streets, in speakeasies, in hotel lobbies, in clubs and in their own houses.

He visited twenty US cities over the course of a month and wrote down casual conversations he'd had, or overheard, word for word, that seemed to exemplify what people were saying. He was a little surprised that almost all of the talk was banal:

> Little did I hear of books or plays. Not one new joke was told by a drummer in my hearing. Not a word of personal enthusiasm for any candidate for office did I hear.

Krock's article stands as a warning not to be complacent about narratives that are contagious only in certain venues, and that are not talked about except at certain times. Economic theories are not the topic of casual conversations, even though the news media discuss economic ideas frequently, and people must be thinking about them.

Krock found that people wanted to talk incessantly about the effects and terrors of the Great Depression. For example, he records the words he heard in 1932 from a taxi driver:

> A Taxi Driver in Cleveland—Did you come in from the East? How are things there? If you want to know how they are here, watch the garbage cans behind the all-night restaurants about 3 o'clock mornings.

See the guys who are getting their meals that way. They aren't all bums by a long shot. . . . Do they think East that Roosevelt can make things better? Anyhow they can't be worse. I used to make a good living before Hoover came in. Not on this taxi. I was firing on the Central but they took my job away; no business. This is a good burg, but it is flat now. When do you suppose it will come back?

This quote suggests a contagious narrative about good people made so desperate by the Great Depression that they are reduced to eating garbage. The idea conjures a mental image and an emotion of disgust. The taxi driver also asks a question for which there was no clear answer: When will prosperity return? He wants to know whether the country is stuck in a long-term depression because his economic decisions (for example, how much to spend) depend on the answer. The desperation narrative of people eating garbage may suggest a long haul, which leads the taxi driver to ask the urgent question "When do you suppose it will come back?" The driver wanted some enlightenment about the future from the apparently knowledgeable Krock, but he probably did not expect a quantitative answer. Rather, he probably hoped Krock would provide some kind of narrative offering clues as to the future.[3]

In judging the impact of economic narratives on human economic behavior, we will find it helpful to recall that conversations rarely touch on important economic decisions, such as how much to save for retirement. Should you save 5% of your income? 10%? more? Try to remember any conversation on this topic, and likely you won't dredge up a single one. And yet people have to make decisions about how much to save, and they must base this decision on *something*. Maybe that decision during the Great Depression was influenced by the narratives of depression hardship, like those men eating from garbage cans at 3 a.m. Maybe, too, the decision was based on the impressions of worried experts, whom nobody really knew, suggesting that there might be a reason to fear a long-lived economic downturn with serious human consequences. On their own, any individual, vague narratives might not have determined behavior, but a constellation of such narratives may have.

Proposition 3: Narrative Constellations Have More Impact Than Any One Narrative

Narratives that occur together in a constellation may have different origins, but in our imaginations they seem grouped together in terms of some basic idea, and they reinforce one another's contagion. Alternative terms for *narrative constellations* include *grand narrative, master narrative,* and *metanarrative,* but I prefer not to use them because they suggest more organization or intellectual quality than is warranted when simple story contagion spreads narratives across a broad public.

Sometimes narratives within a constellation are stripped of identifying names or places, and the narrative takes the form of "They say that . . ." without stating who "they" are. In using the pronoun *they,* the teller of the "They say that" narrative conveys that there is a constellation of narratives featuring or told by seemingly authoritative persons. The borders of such narrative constellations may be redrawn from time to time, with a particular narrative borrowing contagion from other currently contagious narratives.

As we've seen, cryptocurrencies are backed by a constellation of related narratives, with a few main stars and thousands or millions of smaller stars. As of 2018, nearly two thousand cryptocurrencies competed with the original Bitcoin. Each of these cryptocurrencies is a story of entrepreneurship, of eager developers with an idea. But the largest constellation of cryptocurrency stories focuses on Bitcoin-related stories. In one narrative, the popular singer Lily Allen turned down an offer in 2009 to do one performance and be paid in Bitcoin. This narrative has a memorable punch line: Allen is kicking herself in regret today, for if she'd accepted the offer and held on to her Bitcoin, she would have been a billionaire by 2017.[4] Stories like this one help sustain the growth of the Bitcoin narrative and Bitcoin prices by invoking people's feelings of regret for not discovering the investment themselves. Like so many other narratives, this story focuses on a celebrity who starts a narrative or keeps it going.

It is difficult to define the exact parameters of narrative constellations. Often we can find only superficial examples of some of their stories.

Most narratives are never written down and are lost forever. Moreover, the narratives sit in the background and are rarely expressed when decisions are made. For example, if you are discussing with your spouse whether to buy a new car this year or wait until times look more secure, you may be unlikely to tell to your spouse one of the stories that makes you feel secure or insecure. Thus it becomes difficult to establish a connection between the narratives and the action. The final link between a verbal narrative and economic action may ultimately be nonverbal.

Proposition 4: The Economic Impact of Narratives May Change Through Time

An economic narrative's impact on behavior depends on details of the narrative's current mutation and other related narratives. When we rely on digitized data on words or phrases that are flags for narratives, we must resist the temptation to assume that all the narratives with these flags have the same meaning through time. We have to read the narratives in terms of their implication for action, in the context in which they were spoken, at least. In the future, some information-processing innovation might make this undertaking less dependent on human judgment.

Let's look again at the October 19, 1987, stock market crash, the biggest one-day crash in percentage terms in history. The topic still comes up regularly, often on major anniversaries of that event. We might believe that memories of that crash make stock markets vulnerable to another crash, because fear of a crash may cause people to react to the apparent beginnings of a drop in stock prices. But the narrative of the 1987 crash need not have any such effect if people do not think current circumstances are similar. In 1987, there was much discussion of a new computerized trading program called *portfolio insurance*. Along with other factors, narratives about portfolio insurance led to a predisposition to consider selling that was peculiar to that time.[5]

Other disturbing stock market events were surrounded by narratives that had nothing to do with portfolio insurance. After Austria-Hungary declared war on Serbia on July 28, 1914, touching off World War I, stock prices began to fall precipitously. Reacting to the panic, the New York

Stock Exchange and all the major European stock exchanges closed their doors. Even though the United States was not involved in the war, the New York Stock Exchange did not reopen until December 12. In his 2014 book about this closing, *When Washington Shut Down Wall Street*, William Silber details a number of stories and rumors that contributed to the market's severe reaction. Notably, panicky European investors scrambled to get their investments out of the United States while they could. During this "European gold rush," massive amounts of gold were shipped from the United States to Europe despite increasing danger to transatlantic shipping. There was much talk about the Panic of 1907 as proof that US markets were unstable, along with fears that another panic might occur. In addition, there was a baseless rumor that the assassination of Archduke Franz Ferdinand, which triggered World War I, was part of a conspiracy involving the Russians, who were hoarding gold in preparation for a great war.

In contrast, the beginning of World War II in 1939 did not close the US stock market. After the United Kingdom declared war on Germany on September 3, 1939, marking the beginning of World War II, the Standard & Poor's Composite Index gained 9.6% in one trading day. Newspapers expressed general surprise at such a positive market reaction and were mostly at a loss to explain why the market did not repeat its 1914 experience. Apparently the very different response had something to do with a narrative that World War I had, ultimately, proven very profitable for some investors who'd held on to their stock market investments and profited from selling armaments or supplies to Europe.[6] The human stories of World War I and World War II might be very similar, but there was a huge difference in the narratives describing successful investors around the start of each war.

We must pay attention to the names that people attach to their narratives. Seemingly minor changes in the name of a narrative can matter a lot, especially if the new name attaches to a different constellation of narratives. In linguistics, synonyms never have exactly the same meaning. If pressed, people can state complex thoughts about the slightly different connotations of synonyms. In neurolinguistics, synonyms have different connections in the neural network. Some of those connections can matter a lot in terms of the economic ideas they support.

Proposition 5: Truth Is Not Enough
to Stop False Narratives

Suddenly prominent economic narratives sometimes appear mysteriously and for no apparent reason. One such narrative occurred after the 2007–9 world financial crisis, when near-zero interest rates were interpreted as a harbinger of a "lost decade," as they had been for Japan in the 1990s. The Japanese "lost decades" story is just one example, just one observation and hence of no statistical significance, but it was contagious enough around the world to rekindle Great Depression narratives, and it launched serious fears about "secular stagnation."

Indeed, such narratives and fears can have serious effects on the economy and our lives. For example, according to political scientist Stephen Van Evera (1984), World War I started at least partly because a false narrative, which he calls "the Cult of the Offensive," went viral. This narrative was a theory that the country that moves first to attack another country will generally have the advantage. The idea was supported by some historical narratives and illustrated by simplistic psychological, mathematical, and bandwagon arguments. Ultimately, Van Evera argues, this theory led to instability: everyone wanted to attack first. Germany thought it had a "window of opportunity" to successfully pursue a "preventive war" against Russia. But the narrative was wrong. It had economic consequences—a huge arms race—and resulted in a war that was disastrous for both the offense and the defense. Norman Angell called the narrative "The Great Illusion" in a 1911 book with that title. Angell's ideas were convincing to many (and he later won the Nobel Peace Prize for his work), but they did not go viral fast enough to prevent the war. The illusion won out even after it had been decisively disproven, because the proof did not spread as fast as the illusion did.

By analogy, we see that economic activities are not always based on up-to-date information. Sometimes they are based on whatever narratives are going viral at a particular time. While general knowledge steadily advances in many respects, we do not necessarily see a steady progression in the knowledge that often importantly affects economic behavior. The narratives that surround and define Bitcoin provide an example. There are brilliant computer scientists who are fascinated by cryptocurrencies but who won't say whether the captivating ideas that generate public excitement are ultimately right or wrong.

Fortunately, in matters of simple fact, unencumbered by any human interest or story quality, modern society stays generally on target, or at least willing to stand corrected if in error. For example, most people can name the various highways around their home correctly and will accept correction if an error is pointed out to them. They also routinely trust medical doctors to tell them the truth about things they know nothing about. Well, sort of, anyway. In a 2003 study, the World Health Organization concluded, "Poor adherence to treatment of chronic diseases is a worldwide problem of striking magnitude."[7] The WHO went on to report that only about 50% of patients in developed countries consistently follow doctor's orders for chronic illnesses, and even fewer do so in emerging countries. Adherence is probably even worse when it comes to following advice from more controversial economic pundits or financial planners. But where does advice end and speculation begin? And how do we distinguish informed speculation from confabulation or fiction? The slope is slippery. Ultimately, a story's contagion rate is unaffected by its underlying truth. A contagious story is one that quickly grabs the attention of and makes an impression on another person, whether that story is true or not.

A study by Soroush Vosoughi and his coauthors published in *Science* in 2018 used social media data to compare the contagion rates of true stories with the contagion rates of false stories.[8] The researchers chose the stories from among those that had been vetted by six fact-checking websites: snopes.com, politifact.com, factcheck.org, truthorfiction .com, hoax-slayer.com, and urbanlegends.about.com. They found 95–98% agreement across these sites as to a story's truth or falsity. They also looked at 126,000 rumors spread by three million people, and they found that false stories had six times the retweeting rate on Twitter as true stories. The researchers did not interpret that finding as specific to

Twitter, and the result may be specific to the time of the study, a time when mistrust of conventional media sources was higher than usual. Rather, these authors interpreted their results as confirming that people are "more likely to share novel information." In other words, contagion reflects the urge to titillate and surprise others. We can add another twist to that conclusion: a new story correcting a false story may not be as contagious as the false story, which means that the false narrative may have a major impact on economic activity long after it is corrected.

Proposition 6: Contagion of Economic Narratives Builds on Opportunities for Repetition

Contagion depends on the frequency of opportunities to slip a narrative into a conversation. It is usually impolite or rude to change the conversation subject, unless justified by some extraordinary circumstance. Novel ideas and concepts may increase opportunities for contagion. For example, the contagion rate of narratives about the stock market probably increased when, in the 1920s and 1930s, the public began paying attention to stock price indexes. The same thing happened with narrative epidemics about housing after the 1970s, when real estate agents and homebuyers began to recognize home price indexes. In both cases, news media writers, looking for new facts to justify writing an attention-grabbing story, found themselves revisiting these indexes frequently.

Consider another example, familiar to almost all of us: the song "Happy Birthday to You." It is probably not an important economic narrative. Some might say it is not even a real narrative because the words of the song do not tell a story. But there is a story attached to the song in practically everyone's consciousness. The story is a sequence of events, repeated with variations on birthdays. The story is this: Based on a long tradition that goes back generations, people have assembled to celebrate the birthday of a loved one. After someone announces that the ceremony is about to begin, a birthday cake is brought in with flaming little candles, one for each year of the person's life (unless he or she is too old, in which case there will be commentary or jokes about the number of candles). The birthday person makes a wish and attempts to blow out all the candles with one breath in order to make the wish come true. Of course, almost no one believes that birthday wishes come true, but they repeat the ritual in deference to long tradition. Sometimes additional words are added to the song, such as "And many more to you," which may make for an awkward moment because the syllables do not match the melody. The ceremony ends with applause.

"Happy Birthday to You" is a good example of a contagious narrative because it has spread around the world in many translations, and it may be the best-known song of all time. It is contagious in part because of the constant reappearance of birthdays, not because it is anybody's favorite song. It is not particularly admired for its beauty or grace. It grew unplanned and uncontrolled. There is no history of a government edict requiring the song to be sung, or a marketing campaign promising lifelong popularity for those who sing it or have it sung to them. Digital counts show that the song grew in English like a disease epidemic in the 1920s and 1930s, faltered around World War II, when people had more important things on their minds, and then took off again.

Warner/Chappell Music had long claimed a 1935 copyright on the song, and it collected millions of dollars per year in royalties, but it lost the copyright in 2016 when it was shown that "Happy Birthday to You" had striking similarities to a published 1893 song, "Good Morning to All."[9] "Good Morning to All" was a virtual nonentity, even though it closely resembles "Happy Birthday to You," with the exact same melody and very similar words:

> Good morning to you
> Good morning to you
> Good morning dear children
> Good morning to all.

The happy birthday version is so similar that it might easily have come into being by accident in some kindergarten classroom when a teacher somewhere, somehow wanted to mark the occasion of a child's birthday. The mutation then went viral from that obscure beginning:

Happy birthday to you
Happy birthday to you
Happy birthday dear [name]
Happy birthday to you.

Let's consider why the seemingly minor mutation has done so much better than the original. The slight change in the lyrics served to make "Happy Birthday to You" part of a new and growing ritual and a symbol of caring, the birthday party, whose popularity began to grow around the 1890s. This association with other infectious narratives enhanced the song's contagion, and, because the ritual recurs from year to year, it reinforced memory and reduced the recovery rate that eventually extinguishes most epidemics. Also, the change in the words allows the singers to insert the birthday person's name, thus personalizing the song and adding more human interest.

Also consider why the authors of "Good Morning to All" did not realize that they could become millionaires if they just changed the song into "Happy Birthday to You" and copyrighted it. At some level, it may seem that they should have realized that the ritual of birthday parties was likely to persist and gain in popularity. They should have known that a song that ties into the birthday ritual—a song that is very short, easy to memorize, and sung frequently—should be a winner. And they should have realized that they could copyright the song and extract millions from commercial outlets.

Easier said than done, as what is obvious now was not so obvious then. There are so many other possible permutations of the song. There are sixteen words in "Good Morning to You." Suppose we decide to change half the words while keeping the total number constant. There are thus $16!/8!$ ($= 518,918,400$) ways to replace the words. Suppose there are one hundred words in the English language that are simple enough to replace eight of the sixteen words. That means there are $100\mathbin{^\wedge}8 =$ ten quadrillion times 518,918,400 possible variants of the song. It would be impossible to think through all of these possibilities in advance and realize how to make a fortune by tweaking the song. So the invention of "Happy Birthday to You" out of "Good Morning to You" was likely just a random event, unlikely ever to happen. But it did happen. It was unappreciated at first, but then a new contagion quietly started without mentioning the author of the change, who is hopelessly forgotten. It led then to a vast constellation of narratives involving the song infused into movies, TV shows, and social media, among other formats.

Proposition 7: Narratives Thrive on Attachment: Human Interest, Identity, and Patriotism

Usually economic narratives rely on human-interest stories for their contagion, because human beings are attracted to such stories. When an identified personality is associated with a narrative, a face we can picture in our minds, then our brains involve our models of people, voices, and faces with the story, lowering the likely rate of forgetting. But the human-interest stories themselves may not be enough to make a narrative contagious. A successful economic narrative is sometimes the invention of creative minds who sense what is contagious and what is not, and who put the elements together well enough to launch a contagious narrative. Those who aspire to create viral narratives must choose their celebrities carefully because the narratives work best when the intended audience personally recognizes and identifies with the celebrity.

For example, there is the George Washington and the cherry tree story, which has been popular for over two hundred years. It first appeared in print soon after Washington's death in 1799, in a new edition of a best-selling book, *The Life of George Washington with Curious Anecdotes, Equally Honourable to Himself and Exemplary to His Young Countrymen* by Mason Locke Weems. Based on the book's title, it is clear that Weems was interested in launching tellable narratives about Washington. Weems said he heard the cherry tree story from "an aged lady, who was a distant relative, and, when a girl spent much of her time in the family":[10]

> "When George," said she, "was about six years old, he was made the wealthy master of a *hatchet!* of which, like most little boys, he was immoderately fond; and was constantly going about chopping every thing that came in his way. One day, in the garden, where he often

amused himself hacking his mother's pea-sticks, he unluckily tried the edge of his hatchet on the body of a beautiful young English cherry-tree, which he barked so terribly, that I don't believe the tree ever got the better of it . . . "George," said his father, "do you know who killed that beautiful little cherry tree yonder in the garden?" This was a *tough question*; and George staggered under it for a moment; but quickly recovered himself: and looking at his father, with the sweet face of youth brightened with the inexpressible charm of all-conquering truth, he bravely cried out, "I can't tell a lie, Pa; you know I can't tell a lie. I did cut it with my hatchet."[11]

This little story is widely remembered in the United States today as a moral lesson. A search on "I can't tell a lie" and "Washington" gets 188,000 Google hits, over a third as many as "I can't tell a lie" by itself. This Washington story is on its way to usurping a basic sentence. Why is it such a contagious story? It must be because it is about the first president of the United States, and it has patriotic appeal. In that context, it is a great narrative; about almost anyone else, it would be nothing. There isn't much to the story, just that as a child Washington didn't lie. "I can't tell a lie" and "Lincoln" gets 102,000 hits on Google, as the equally famous President Lincoln is introduced into the story and sometimes even substituted for Washington. The story, involving two legendary US figures, is part of a constellation of economic narratives about honesty. Those narratives seem to be part of a tradition of honesty, not unique to the United States but maybe stronger than in some other countries, that has likely helped propel the US economy by creating trust in business dealings and by limiting bribery and corruption.

Often, the basic human-interest element of an economic narrative is embodied in somewhat different stories going viral at about the same time. Different versions of the narrative substitute different celebrities who are appropriate for the target audience. For new narratives involving celebrities, there are already familiar narratives about the celebrities in memory, which can enhance contagion.[12] The constellation of narratives built around celebrities is self-reinforcing. In extreme cases, the celebrities attain superhuman status, and associated ideas begin to seem natural and obvious. George Washington's picture is on every one-dollar bill and on every quarter-dollar coin in the United States.

Sometimes, everyday people coin apt or pithy quotes, but those quotes become contagious only after the story is altered to substitute the name of a famous person as the originator of the quote. For example, since the middle of the twentieth century the socialist slogan "From each according to his ability, to each according to his needs" has been attributed to Karl Marx. Actually, those words were emphasized by socialist philosopher Louis Blanc in 1851, when Marx was virtually unknown, and a variation of the phrase appears in the Bible.[13] Louis Blanc was more famous than Marx until after 1900, but today he is largely forgotten. Thus the quote became attributed to Marx in the mid-twentieth century, by unknown persons who started a mutated epidemic by attaching a new celebrity to it.

The website Wikiquotes tracks down the origins of famous quotes, and typically the famous person was quoting someone else, if he or she even said it at all. But, no matter: Wikiquotes notwithstanding, the story of the quote's true source will never go viral because it is not contagious. And contagion is the all-important element: if the narratives are not repeated in human communications, they will be gradually forgotten. Narratives involving celebrities can suddenly lose their contagion if some event discredits the celebrity, whether or not the ideas in the narrative are true or good.

As we've seen, the choice of celebrities has patriotic dimensions, as people have a preference for individuals in their own country or their own ethnic group. This preference helps to explain why the epidemic spread of narratives is often not seen or acknowledged. To acknowledge it typically requires admitting its foreign origin. Practically no one has an incentive to present an idea as coming from abroad, except in unusual circumstances. Thus we have the illusion that important ideas came spontaneously to a compatriot, and we see nothing of the idea's true world epidemic. Beyond celebrities, there are issues of party or regional or religious loyalty.

Patriotism does not mean just flag-waving assertions of loyalty. It is also the feeling that only in our own country does anything important, good or bad, happen. For example, CBS News in the United States has a regular morning feature, "Your World in 90 Seconds," that purports to tell you very succinctly everything you need to know about today's news. But the name is inaccurate because the report doesn't cover the world. Virtually all of the news stories are from the United States (with the exception of tidbits about the British royal family and Vladimir Putin). Maybe the title *is* accurate for many of the Americans who think that the United States is the world, despite having only 5% of the world's population.

———

We have seen seven key propositions with respect to economic narratives:

1. *Epidemics can be fast or slow, big or small.* The timetable and magnitude of epidemics can vary widely.
2. *Important economic narratives may comprise a very small percentage of popular talk.* Narratives may be rarely heard and still economically important.
3. *Narrative constellations have more impact than any one narrative.* Constellations matter.
4. *The economic impact of narratives may change through time.* Changing details matter as narratives evolve over time.
5. *Truth is not enough to stop false narratives.* Truth matters, but only if it is in-your-face obvious.
6. *Contagion of economic narratives builds on opportunities for repetition.* Reinforcement matters.
7. *Economic narratives thrive on human interest, identity, and patriotism.* Human interest, identity, and patriotism matter.

In part III, we use these seven propositions as a framework to look at historically important economic narratives, to identify what we can learn from economic narratives and their consequences in the real world.

Part III

Perennial Economic Narratives

Chapter 9

Recurrence and Mutation

In previous chapters we've focused on the elements of narrative economics, exploring how popular stories go viral, morph into epidemics, and influence economic and political events. We illustrated the discussion with several real-world examples, including Frederick Lewis Allen's insights into the Great Depression, John Maynard Keynes's analysis of the narrative origins of World War II, the Bitcoin narrative, and the Laffer curve narrative.

In this part of the book, we consider nine of the most important narrative constellations. These perennial narratives won't completely go away, and they pop up in many mutated forms. They touch on some of the most important themes in the air today: the idea that machines will replace all workers and cause mass unemployment, that a return to the gold standard would provide greater monetary stability, that real estate and stock markets hold special value, and that businesses or labor unions are evil. These ever-shifting and ever-renewing narratives affect economic behavior by changing the popular understanding of the economy, by altering public perceptions of economic reality, by creating new ideas about what is meaningful and important and moral, or by suggesting new scripts for individual behavior.

The chapters in this part demonstrate these perennial narratives' overarching and ever-shifting influence on society today, explaining how many of the challenges that we tend to attribute to discrete contemporary forces are in fact influenced profoundly by narratives—stories that took root generations and even centuries ago but that reappear in newly configured expressions. Engaging with these examples challenges the way we think about the economy, from large-scale phenomena such as depressions and wars, through major economic forces such as the stock market and real estate, through socially sustaining institutions such as work and technology.

As we've seen, a disease epidemic, such as influenza, measles, or mumps, can recur after a mutation changes its contagiousness. Disease epidemics tend to recur after a mutation overcomes acquired immunity, though sometimes the mutation is a result of a change in environmental conditions that increase the disease's contagion. With influenza, for example, there are regularly recurring epidemics and occasional massive and dangerous epidemics, depending on subtle differences in the viral genome or environmental conditions. Thus the 1918 flu pandemic, often called the Spanish flu, cost more lives than World War I did. The Spanish flu in epidemiology mirrors the trajectory of the Great Depression of the 1930s in economics, except that narratives rather than viruses carried the "disease" of the Great Depression. In both cases, the virulence was especially intense and surprising. So, before we move into the details of perennial economic narratives, it is helpful to detail the ways in which these two essential mechanisms—recurrence and mutation—define and inform economic narratives.

How Economic Narratives Mutate

Just as mutations in influenza may spark a new contagion of a disease with manifestations similar to those of previous outbreaks, so too do economic narratives mutate. But we must be careful in separating the threads of similarity and difference. Typically, when a narrative reappears, say in another country or a few decades later, the mutated narrative tends to have features different from those of the original narrative—a different celebrity, different visual images, a different punch line. For example, in chapter 12 we discuss the gold standard narrative and the bimetallism narrative, which have some deep similarity to the Bitcoin narrative but with William Jennings Bryan substituted for Satoshi Nakamoto. The next new money narrative will have yet another celebrity's name. Just as Bryan is mostly forgotten today, Nakamoto will likely be mostly forgotten in the future. Someone who creates a highly successful new electronic currency in the future will best craft a contagious story about it, as by attaching a popular celebrity's name to it. This variation may be necessary for contagion.

A mutation in a narrative can also occur when some event transpires to change associations of the narrative. For example, some public event may underscore that a narrative is or is not politically correct. People of course hesitate to repeat stories that would now associate them with such a scandalous event.[1]

Mutations in a narrative or in the environment surrounding the narrative may cause it to become an economic narrative by tying it better to economic decisions. A mutation may also occur that increases contagion but twists the story so that it ceases to be the same economic narrative. It may then morph into some different moral or lesson afterward. For example, as we shall see below, a narrative about labor-saving machines replacing jobs (chapter 13) created a sense of fear during the Great Depression of the 1930s, but the same narrative mutated (chapter 14) to create a sense of opportunity during the dot-com boom of the 1990s. These cases can be confusing to those who study a narrative, for some key words in the narrative may come up in searches for a much longer span of time than the period when they had a specific economic interpretation.

Narratives may be relevant to economic events even if the timing of the narrative's appearance does not coincide with the event. When it goes epidemic, a narrative may inspire a latent fear, such as a fear that technology will someday replace one's job, which may result eventually in changes in economic behavior years later when some other narrative or news creates a sense that the feared replacement is imminent.

How Economic Narratives Recur

The mutations that cause the recurrence of narratives can be random accidents, but more likely creative people, including professional marketing experts, politicians, phishers, and just plain social media enthusiasts, have been involved in some element of their design. The creative types know that the older narratives proved their potential by going viral long ago but are no longer contagious. The celebrity attached to the original narrative may be forgotten or discredited. The narrative may have been co-epidemic with another lost narrative. Thus the creative people must try to link it to some extant epidemic.

Recurrent economic narratives tend to have an international scope, partly because people in the news media long ago learned that they should observe the news in foreign countries, for what is viral in one country can often be made contagious in another. But like contagious disease epidemics, at any given time the narrative epidemics tend to be stronger in some countries than in others. In addition, narrative epidemics are more similar in countries that share a language or borders. The examples in this book come mostly from the United States, the country in which I have lived my life and the country about which I have the best intuition and knowledge. Also, the United States has long documented its business cycle history. The National Bureau of Economic Research (NBER) maintains a chronicle of business cycle expansions and contractions back to the year 1854.

Some critics might argue that institutional changes in the United States have been so profound and transformative that there is practically nothing useful to be learned from distant history. However, the events and reactions of 50, 100, and 150 years ago are surprisingly similar to what we see and experience today. In today's narratives, we see the echoes of these historical periods. Remember the story about the huckster who offers a coin toss bet with the words "Heads I win, tails you lose" and the sucker who took the bet? That little gem of a narrative has been in circulation since 1847 (and perhaps earlier). At that time, it was sometimes attached to stories of the Whig Party, Zachary Taylor (twelfth president of the United States), or Richard Cobden, the foremost nineteenth-century advocate of free markets, whom we are unlikely to think about today. In the mid-nineteenth century, people weren't telling exactly the same stories with the same interpretations that we see today, but the themes are surprisingly similar over time.

Big Economic Events, Big Narrative Lessons

The biggest economic events in the United States since 1854 as defined by the NBER include the following. We return to these events frequently in later chapters.

- A depression from 1857 to 1859, followed by the secession of southern states in 1860–61 and the US Civil War (1861–65). The Civil War was the most lethal war in US history, responsible for more US fatalities than all other US wars combined.[2]
- A depression from 1873 to 1879 that led to the publication of the best-selling economics book of all time in the United States, Henry George's *Progress and Poverty* (1879), which accused the unrestrained free-market system of producing worsening inequality.
- A depression in the 1890s comprising two NBER contractions, 1893–94 and 1895–97. The extended depression, during which unemployment always exceeded 8%, ran from 1893 to 1899. This depression coincided with an aggressive phase in US history, with the United States launching the Spanish-American War and the Philippine War.
- A series of three short contractions from 1907 to 1914, starting with the Panic of 1907, which ended only with the heroic advances made by J. P. Morgan and other bankers. These events led to the creation of the Federal Reserve System to prevent such banking crises in the future. These contractions were followed by World War I, which began in 1914.
- A brief but extreme depression from 1920 to 1921 that included the sharpest deflation ever experienced in the United States.
- The Great Depression after the 1929 stock market crash, which morphed into a worldwide depression. In the United States the extended depression ran from 1930 to 1941, with unemployment uniformly exceeding 8%. The Great Depression took its name from the 1934 Lionel Robbins book with that

title. It comprised two NBER contractions, 1929–33 and 1937–38. The worldwide depression immediately preceded World War II.

- A severe recession in 1973–75, associated with a war in the Middle East and an oil embargo. Economist Otto Eckstein called this period the "Great Recession" in his 1978 book with that title, inviting comparison with the Great Depression.
- A severe recession from 1980 to 1982, comprising two NBER contractions, a short contraction within the year 1980 and, soon after, another contraction 1981–82, associated with a war in the Middle East. At the time, this recession was called the "Great Recession," again inviting comparisons with the Great Depression.[3]
- A severe recession from 2007 to 2009, also named the "Great Recession," once again inviting comparisons with the Great Depression, and this time the name really went viral and has stuck to this day.

These recessions and depressions are narratives in themselves, active in producing subsequent events. Thought in any economic downturn tends to emphasize the last large downturn, with attention also paid to the record-holder. In the United States and much of the world the record-holder is, of course, the Great Depression.

Usually, economic historians who attempt to identify the causes of recessions and depressions list events that were contemporary with the downturns: bank failures, strikes, acts of government, gold discoveries, crop failures, stock market events, and so on. Such information is useful, but our goal is to consider these depressions and recessions in terms of the prominent narratives and narrative constellations that likely helped bring them about or increase their severity. Ultimately, however, we can give no final proof of causality because these events are so deeply complicated, and multiple narratives are involved. But the cumulative influence of narratives in the gestation of these very serious economic events is beyond circumstantial.

The first step in our task is organizing and classifying some of the major economic narratives and the mutations that allowed them to recur over long intervals of time. The remaining chapters in this part describe nine perennial economic narratives, along with some of their mutations and recurrences. Most readers will recognize these narratives in their most recent forms but not in their older forms:

1. Panic versus confidence
2. Frugality versus conspicuous consumption
3. Gold standard versus bimetallism
4. Labor-saving machines replace many jobs
5. Automation and artificial intelligence replace almost all jobs
6. Real estate booms and busts
7. Stock market bubbles
8. Boycotts, profiteers, and evil business
9. The wage-price spiral and evil labor unions

Some of these chapters present a pair of opposing narrative constellations (for example, frugality versus conspicuous consumption). These pairs suggest opposite economic actions and opposite moral judgments. At certain times one of the constellations may work toward extinguishing the other, but at other times it may help reinforce the other constellation through the controversy generated.

Note that these chapters are organized thematically, not chronologically, because the themes are relevant beyond the specific historical moment in which they occur. Our main goal is to extract common themes from these narratives that will help us recognize and anticipate the effects of future economic narratives.

Chapter 10

Panic versus Confidence

Since the early nineteenth century, a major class of narratives about confidence has influenced economic fluctuations: people's confidence in banks, in business, in one another, and in the economy. Economically, the most important stories are those about *other people's* confidence and about efforts to promote public confidence.

Among the earliest confidence narratives are those about banking panics—that is, whether we have confidence in the banks to make good on their promises. We mean not only public confidence in the morality of bankers and bank regulators but also confidence in banks' other customers, confidence that they will not all try to withdraw their money at once. Raymond Moley, one of President Franklin Roosevelt's "Brain Trust" experts during the Great Depression, put this idea into a simple narrative:

> A Depression is much like a run on a bank. It's a crisis of confidence. People panic and grab their money. There's a story I like to tell: In my home town, when I was a little boy, an Irishman came up from the quarry where he was working, and went into the bank and said, "If my money's here, I don't want it. If it's not here, I want it."[1]

This and other confidence narratives help us understand major events marking modern history.

Several classes of confidence narratives have characterized the history of the industrialized economies. The first class is a *financial panic narrative* that reflects psychologically based stories about banking crises. The second class is a *business confidence narrative* that attributes slow economic activity not so much to financial crises as to a sort of general pessimism and unwillingness to expand business or to hire. The third is a *consumer confidence narrative* that attributes slow sales to the fears of individual consumers, whose sudden lack of spending can bring about a recession. Figure 10.1 plots the succession of these narratives since 1800. All of these slow-moving narratives have shown growth paths that span lifetimes. Financial panic came first, followed by narratives about crisis in business confidence, followed by narratives of a crisis in consumer confidence.

As narratives spread about the dangers of business losses and decreased consumer confidence, increasing self-censorship of narratives may, and sometimes does, encourage panic. Because people are aware that others self-censor, they increasingly try to read between the lines of public pronouncements to determine the "truth."

Broad public interest in the idea that financial events might be related to psychology began in the early nineteenth century, continued after the panic of 1857 in the run-up to the US Civil War, and then grew over the decades. The phrase *financial panic* peaks on Google Ngrams in 1910, three years after the famous Panic of 1907. The financial panic epidemic was part of a narrative constellation that grew with it. Individual panics ebbed and flowed within the narrative constellation. A particularly strong narrative of the Panic of 1907 involved a celebrity—J. P. Morgan, the most prominent banker in the United States at the time—which made it last for decades. It stands out in Figure 10.1 as the highest point for public attention to financial panics.

Figure 10.2 shows the major US financial panics individually. For example, the panic of 1857 was mostly forgotten within a few years. It later returned as part of a narrative constellation about other panics. During the 1857 financial panic, news reports covered objective events like bankruptcies, bank runs, and suspensions, but they also referred to rumors and emotions. An 1857 newspaper article summarized the panic of that year:

> Brokers and others are highly excited, and circulate monstrous reports. . . . The general disturbance of the public mind makes it impossible to treat the subject coolly, or ascertain the views of the most reliable persons in the business community.[2]

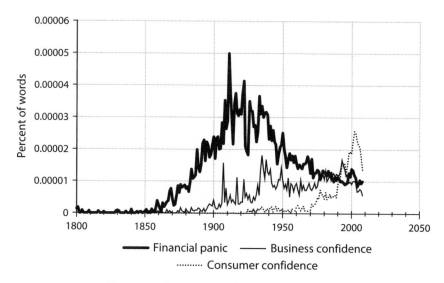

FIGURE 10.1. Frequency of Appearance of *Financial Panic, Business Confidence,*
and *Consumer Confidence* in Books, 1800–2008

The figure shows three separate recurrences of the confidence narrative, but referring to
different sectors, finance, business, and consumer. *Source*: Google Ngrams, no smoothing.

We must reflect on the prevailing nineteenth-century narratives, and
associated views of the world, to understand why people and newspapers spoke of "panics" rather than "depressions" (in the modern sense
of the word) and why they never spoke of consumer confidence. Contemporary narratives about financial panics mostly were viewed as stories about wealthy, pretentious people who had bank accounts and who
perhaps deserved some of the disruption caused by a financial panic and
its associated "depression of trade." In the eighteenth and nineteenth centuries, most people did not save at all, except maybe for some coins
hidden under a mattress or in a crack in a wall. In economic terms, the
Keynesian marginal propensity to consume out of additional income was
close to 100%. That is, most people, except for people with high incomes,
spent their entire income. So, to the spinners of narratives of these past
centuries, there would have been no point in surveying ordinary people
about their consumer confidence.

Most people then had no concept of retirement or sending their
children to college, so they had no motivation to save toward these goals.[3]

If they became bedridden in old age, they expected to be cared for by family or by a local church or charity. Life expectancy was short, and medical care was not expensive. People tended to see poverty as a symptom of moral degradation and drunkenness or dipsomania (now called alcoholism), not as a condition related to the strength of the economy. So there was practically no thought that consumer confidence should be bolstered. The people saw the authorities as responsible for instilling moral virtues rather than building consumer confidence. The idea that the poor should be taught to save grew gradually over the nineteenth century, the result of propaganda from the savings bank movement. But contemporary thought was miles away from the idea that a depression might be caused by ordinary people heeding the propaganda and trying to save too much.

A few years after use of the term *financial panic* peaked, after the Panic of 1907, the United States passed the Aldrich-Vreeland Act (1908), which created national currency associations as precursors to a central bank, and a successor act, the Federal Reserve Act of 1913, which founded the US central bank, whose purpose was to provide a "cure for business panics."[4]

A powerful narrative at that time was the story of a celebrity, J. P. Morgan, widely considered one of the richest people in America. In the absence of any US central bank during the Panic of 1907, he used his own money for, and he prevailed on other bankers to contribute to, a bailout of the banking system. This saving of the United States from a serious depression was a truly powerful story, and Morgan's celebrity only grew. He later built his central office building at 23 Wall Street. Completed in 1913, it is still there today, though he died before he could occupy it. It was directly opposite the New York Stock Exchange (completed in 1903 and still functioning today) and across the street from Federal Hall, which was built in 1842 and replaced the original home of the Congress of the Confederation. George Washington was sworn in as first president of the United States on the steps of Federal Hall in 1789. Morgan chose to make his building strangely small and modest, befitting his public spirit. Thus Morgan emerged in the narrative as a central and model-worthy hero of America. The recovery of confidence after the Panic of 1907 was

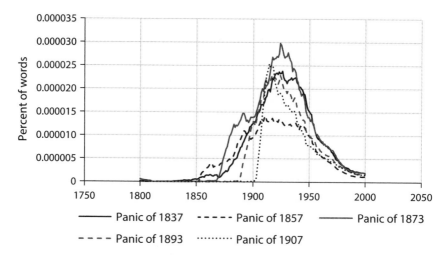

FIGURE 10.2. Frequency of Appearance of Financial Panic Narratives within a Constellation of Panic Narratives through Time, 1800–2000

Each major historical financial panic occurred in a different single year, but the frequency with which each is mentioned follows a multiyear pattern similar to the more general pattern for the phrase "financial panic" in Figure 10.1. *Source*: Google Ngrams (smoothing = 5).

in substantial measure confidence in one man. The Federal Reserve System was modeled after his 1907 consortium of bankers. In accordance with the narrative, the new central bank was technically owned by bankers, though it was created by the federal government. Every Federal Reserve chair since the founding of the Fed fits into the narrative as a J. P. Morgan avatar.

After 1930, the narrative mutated and spread in a different direction. Deficiencies of business confidence, and later consumer confidence, were associated more with despair than with sudden fear. By then, the word *depression* had also taken on another meaning: a psychological state of melancholy or dejection. So the increased use of "depression" to describe an economic contraction reflected a new psychologically based economic narrative of the time.

During the depression of the 1930s, George Gallup, the originator of the Gallup polls and a pioneer in public opinion measurement, became the first social scientist to survey business and consumer confidence using scientific polling methods.[5] Then, in the 1950s, psychologist George Katona at the University of Michigan began constructing an "Index of Consumer Sentiment." The Survey Research Center at the University of Michigan still produces this index, which Katona created in 1952. Later, in 1966, the Conference Board created a Consumer Confidence Index. Both of these indexes are based on questions that consumers answer about their impressions of the strength of the current and near-future economy. None of the questions used to construct these indexes asks respondents about the risk of a banking panic or a sudden stampede of investors, reflecting the changed narrative about business. But the change is not total, and financial panic narratives still have a chance to be rekindled, as we saw, for example, in the United Kingdom with the Northern Rock bank in 2007, the first banking panic there since 1866.

Crowd Psychology Goes Viral

Financial panic narratives have a strong psychological component, and a key concept here is crowd psychology. By the middle of the nineteenth century, Charles Mackay's popular 1841 book *Memoirs of Extraordinary Popular Delusions* began to attract public attention to crowd psychology. Gustave Le Bon popularized the term itself in his best-selling 1895 book, *The Crowd*. Crowd psychology began to become influential around that date and grew in an epidemic-like path, peaking in the early 1930s. The growing number of references to "crowd psychology" appears to have a parallel in the rising level of the booming stock market over the 1920s.

Closely related to the idea of crowd psychology is *suggestibility*, which refers to the idea that individual human behavior is subconsciously imitative of and reactive to others. The word, first seen in the late nineteenth century, appears to be pivotal in narrative constellations and in popular understandings of crowd psychology. *Suggestibility* and its relative *autosuggestion* (which means the practice of suggesting to oneself) follow a fairly standard epidemic curve, peaking around 1920 and mostly declining ever since (Figure 10.3). The concepts likely played a role in the economic exuberance of the 1920s and the depression of the 1930s.

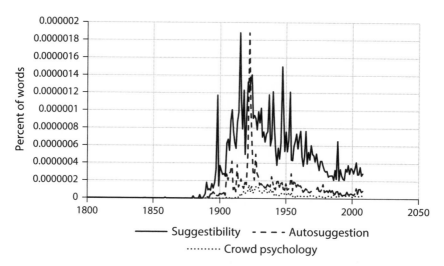

FIGURE 10.3. Frequency of Appearance of *Suggestibility, Autosuggestion,* and *Crowd Psychology* in Books, 1800–2008
This figure shows three recurrences of epidemics of confidence narratives with somewhat different embellishments and contexts. *Source:* Google Ngrams, no smoothing.

The idea that the human mind is suggestible is diametrically opposed to the concept of economic man who is a rational optimizer, who acts as if guided by careful calculations. Suggestibility implies that oftentimes we are acting blind or as in a dream. By 1920, the concept of suggestibility was widely known, indicating that people of that era may have felt that other people are easily influenced by abstract or subtle examples, and are therefore more likely to conduct their economic behavior expecting a highly unstable world. The narrative would lead them to expect herd-like behavior and perhaps to contribute to such behavior. If you think that other people are members of an impressionable herd, you may be more likely to try to anticipate the herd's movements and try to get ahead of them.

We can use the concepts of crowd psychology and suggestibility to understand depressions, such as the Great Depression of the 1930s. In doing so, we should look not only at the direct applications of these concepts but also at the ways in which people *think* that these concepts help explain the depressions. These were their concepts much more than ours.

The Psychology of Suggestion and the Autosuggestion Movement

Close to the beginning of the suggestibility epidemic, in 1898, *The Psychology of Suggestion* was published. The book, written by Boris Sidis, a colleague of psychologist William James, reported on experiments conducted at the Harvard Psychological Laboratory. Sidis defines suggestibility as follows:

> I hold a newspaper in my hands and begin to roll it up; I soon find that my friend sitting opposite me rolled up his in a similar way. This, we say, is a case of suggestion.
>
> My friend Mr. A. is absent-minded; he sits near the table, thinking of some abstruse mathematical problem that baffles all his efforts to solve it. Absorbed in the solution of that intractable problem, he is blind and deaf to what is going on around him. His eyes are directed on the table, but he appears not to see any of the objects there. I put two glasses of water on the table, and at short intervals make passes in the direction of the glasses—passes which he seems not to perceive; then I resolutely stretch out my hand, take one of the glasses and begin to drink. My friend follows suit—dreamily he raises his hand, takes the glass, and begins to sip, awakening fully to consciousness when a good part of the tumbler is emptied.[6]

The term *autosuggestion* came a little later than *suggestibility*, but it led to new expectations that one could manipulate not only oneself but also economic activity. Starting in 1921, the autosuggestion epidemic attracted widespread public interest. Emile Coué, a French psychologist who went on a book tour in the United States in 1922, was the most influential proponent of the autosuggestion movement. The key idea, attractive to so many millions, was that most of us are not successful because we do not believe we can succeed. To achieve success, one must repeatedly suggest to oneself that one will be a success. Coué advised people to recite frequently a key affirmation: "Every day in every way I get better and better." Napoleon Hill, whose varied career included motivational speaking, added to the self-empowerment narrative with his 1925 book, *The Law of*

Success in 16 Lessons and his 1937 best seller, *Think and Grow Rich*. He emphasized channeling the power of the subconscious mind to adopt a positive, wealth-building attitude.

The autosuggestion narrative was a mutation of an earlier hypnosis narrative that went viral over the few decades before the 1920s. That narrative described traveling hypnotists who put people into a trance. Those in a trance then showed immense suggestibility. According to the 1920 book *Success Fundamentals* by Orison Swett Marden:

> One reason why the human race as a whole has not measured up to its possibilities, to its promise; one reason why we see everywhere splendid ability doing the work of mediocrity, is because people do not think half enough of themselves. We do not realize our divinity; that we are part of the great causation principle of the universe. We do not know our strength and not knowing we can not use it. A Sandow could not get out of a chair if a hypnotist could convince him that he could not. He must believe he can rise before he can, for "He can't who thinks he can't," is as true as "He can who thinks he can." [Eugen Sandow, 1867–1925, was a muscleman and bodybuilder who amazed and inspired audiences with his feats.][7]

The autosuggestion movement started to peter out after 1924, but it appears to have had aftereffects. Notably, the highly successful 1935 pro-Nazi film *Triumph of the Will* by Leni Riefenstahl appears to borrow from autosuggestion. Hitler's appeal was based in part on the idea that he would inspire the German nation out of the depression into which it had sunk, despairing and insecure, in the wake of World War I. At the time, it was widely believed that the Depression resulted from a loss of confidence and that Germans needed a leader to restore the nation's confidence. Riefenstahl's movie depicts Hitler, in a speech before the adoring multitudes, saying, "It is our will that this state shall endure for a thousand years. We are happy to know that the future is ours entirely!" Hitler says, "It is our will," as if saying those words will magically turn Germany into the dominant world power.

Behind all this interest in the unseen force of confidence in human affairs was an analogy to the unseen force of air pressure on weather, and the possibility of forecasting both.

Forecasting the Weather, Forecasting Confidence in the Economy

Scientific weather forecasting was a phenomenal new discovery of the mid-nineteenth century. The science advanced shortly after two important inventions of the 1840s: the telegraph, which transmitted information about weather conditions in dispersed locations, and the practical barograph, which created a time-series plot of changes in air pressure. People were impressed by the new weather forecasts, which had (and continue to have) great scientific appeal. For example, in one famous story about the Crimean War, scientists in November 1854 concluded that two apparently separate storms were in fact one storm, enabling them to establish its trajectory and provide a forecast that saved the British and French fleets from destruction.[8]

Weather forecasting stimulated people's imagination as to what modern science could achieve. By the 1890s, newspapers routinely published weather forecasts daily. Such repetition ensures the strong epidemic potential of meteorology narratives. These narratives also suggest an analogy to economic forecasting: changes in public confidence seem analogous to shifting winds or air pressure. Indeed, people will say that recovery, pessimism, or some other inclination "is in the air." It seems natural for people to think that if the meteorologists can forecast the winds, then economists should be able to forecast recessions.

To the extent that the public believes economic forecasts of booms or recessions, there may be an element of self-fulfilling prophecy in the economic forecasts. People hear economists' pronouncements that a recession is imminent and thus postpone activities that might stimulate the economy. Conversely, because these scientists/economists note that past recessions have always ended, people may come to expect any given recession to end. Suppose, by analogy, that weather forecasters everywhere say that they have information to indicate that a certain region is in danger of bad storms, and that the danger from such storms typically lasts six months. People might therefore cancel many activities for six months, and economic activity might fall for six months. With economic forecasts of a recession, people might observe other people decrease their spending after the warning and take that as evidence of a storm of lost confidence.

The idea that economic fluctuations tend to repeat themselves follows an older scientific tradition that has had a prominent place in modern culture. For example, astronomer Edmund Halley noted in the year 1682 that comets sometimes appeared at intervals of 75.3 years. He hypothesized that the same comet was returning again and again, and he predicted it would be visible from Earth again in 1758. Halley was proven right, and to this day Halley's comet returns every 75.3 years, though the comet has faded so much that in its latest arrival in 1985–86 it was almost invisible. The story of Halley's comet is a great one that remains vivid in the popular memory. A constellation of narratives is now built around it, such as the story that Mark Twain, born in a Halley's comet year, predicted his own death 75 years later when Halley's comet returned again.

The earliest ProQuest News & Newspapers mention of the *business cycle* came during the depression of 1858, and it appeared alongside a reference to weather:

> Some, claiming to be learned in meteorology, say the seasons ran in decades: it seems also that there is a sort of business cycle of the same length of time; and it happens very fortunately that the decimal panic comes at the same time with the mildest winter. Whether this is a coincidence or a providence, or whether it is a fact at all, I leave for others to decide.[9]

The idea that business fluctuations are a repetitive cyclical event with a wavelength of a decade, or any other identifiable fixed interval, has become less popular with economists, but the narrative that recessions and drops in confidence are somewhat periodic and forecastable remains entrenched in popular thinking.

Weather forecasting also inspired the idea that there ought to be statistically documented leading indicators of future economic fluctuations. Within a decade after the 1929 stock market crash that preceded the Great Depression, Wesley C. Mitchell and Arthur F. Burns in 1938 pioneered the leading indicators approach to economic forecasting, which encourages people to move into precautionary mode in their economic decision making after a decline in the stock market, thus possibly creating the very recession that was forecast.[10] Leading indicators today include the Department of Commerce's *Business Conditions Developments* (now melded into the *Survey of Current Business*), the Conference Board's *Composite Index of Leading Indicators,* and the OECD's *Composite Leading Indicators.* A ProQuest or Ngrams search for the term *leading indicators* shows that the idea has undergone a long slow epidemic starting around the 1930s and is still going strong.

Confidence as a Barometer for the Economy

Just as we can measure air pressure, we should be able to measure confidence. In addition, unlike air pressure, confidence might be subject to influence, in which case good patriots are morally obligated to support public confidence. Indeed, Calvin Coolidge, the president of the United States from 1923 to 1929, took it upon himself to boost public belief in the economy and in the stock market.

There was great controversy over Coolidge's reassurances, sometimes called the "Coolidge-Mellon bull tips." In a 1928 *Atlantic* article, Ralph Robey identified a pattern: practically every time the stock market declined significantly or the public decried speculators' high level of borrowing to purchase stocks, either President Calvin Coolidge or Treasury Secretary Andrew Mellon made a very optimistic statement about the market or denied any problem with overspeculation.[11] Robey doubted that there was any rational basis for Coolidge's and Mellon's optimism, which he interpreted as an effort to maintain public confidence in the stock market.

The Coolidge-Mellon bull tips may have been part of the administration's attempts to mollify the influentials who feared any disturbance of investor confidence. A 1928 article in the *Wall Street Journal* observed:

> Chief executive of one of our leading industrial corporations was discussing the market with some friends not long ago. "I am bullish on our own stock for the immediate pull," he remarked, "and I would like to take on a line of the stock. I do not speculate, so of course the stock would be put in my name. The trouble is selling it. I have all I want to carry for the future but if I sold any stock the employes would soon hear of it and they are in most instances shareholders and it might not only disturb them but actually give them a hint to get out of their investment holdings. Hence I leave what I know to be a good quick thing alone."[12]

The market crashed in October 1929. Eight months earlier, in February 1929, the Federal Reserve Board had warned that the Federal Reserve would not support banks that loaned into a rising market. It qualified its statement by noting that it "neither assumes the right nor any disposition" to pass judgment on "the merits of a speculation," but the investing public read between the lines and reacted intensely and immediately.[13] The *Washington Post* reported on a "hectic battle between the Federal Reserve and Wall Street," with Wall Street largely of the opinion that the Federal Reserve should mind its own business.[14] On August 9, 1929, just two and a half months before the crash, the Federal Reserve Bank of New York raised its rediscount rate (the rate at which it lends to banks). Never before in the nation's history had there been a government authority with a mission that could be interpreted as stabilizing the stock market. The narrative of the "battle" between Wall Street and the Fed probably added to the contagion of stories that attached great importance to the stock market crash of 1929 in the following months. It also led to a widespread impression that people in the know were sensing overspeculation.

After the crash, disillusionment with prognostications by public officials, businesspeople, and journalists intensified. In 1930, one observer said, "Unfortunately, there appears to be a strong tendency among writers on business subjects to put out nothing but optimistic statements and to avoid all discussion that might be construed as pessimism."[15] In 1931, Alexander Dana Noyes, the financial editor of the *New York Times*, noted, "Men of affairs, when they affix their names to New Year Day prophecies, will seek for a hopeful side and so exclude any disagreeable offsets."[16]

At the same time, no one wanted to be accused of shouting fire in a crowded theater, worsening the public's fears and possibly causing a stampede out of the markets. The original narrative of a fire in a crowded theater goes back to about a half century before the crash, to 1884, as reported in the *New York Times*:

> The curtain rose in a crowded house at the performance of "Storm Beaten" in the Mount Morris Theatre, in Harlem, on Tuesday night. The fire scene was being enacted, when the cry of "Fire!" three times repeated rang through the building. Many blanched faces were visible in the audience but the continuance of the play gave reassurance and a panic, which was imminent, was averted. . . . A youth named Francis McCarron, residing at No. 2,446 Fourth-avenue, was pointed out by Louis Eisler as having caused the alarm, and the Roundsman and Policeman Edmiston took him into custody. . . . Justice Welde sent him to the Island for one month.[17]

The "fire in a crowded theater" narrative did not seem to catch on right away, however. Later, the narrative was mentioned in a 1919 Supreme Court opinion written by then Justice (later Chief Justice) Oliver Wendell Holmes, Jr. It thus became connected with a celebrity. The narrative started to pick up a little in the 1930s, and then went viral after that.

Throughout the 1930s, the idea took root that the Great Depression resulted from an epidemic of "reckless talk" by opinion leaders who were oblivious to its psychological impact.[18] In reality, though, prominent people seem to have been very aware of the possible psychological effects of their talk, which led to the creation of another narrative: thought leaders were now so worried about their talk inciting fear that the public began to assume a general bias toward false optimism. In other words, John Q. Public believed that thought leaders were trying to sound optimistic and that the listener had to correct for that overconfidence. It is easy to see how expectations may have become much more volatile in such an environment.

In keeping with earlier narratives of panic, many people also saw the Great Depression as a stampede or panic. When people saw other people running from the Depression, their fears made them run too. This sense of fear took strong hold on the public imagination. Yale economics professor Irving Fisher wrote in 1930:

> The chief danger, therefore, did not inhere in conditions at all. It was the danger of fear, panicky fear, which might be communicated from the stock market to business. "My only fear is the fear of fear" are the words of a courageous man.[19]

Thomas Mullen, assistant to Mayor James Curley of Boston, made a similar statement in 1931:

> I believe the only thing we need to fear is fear itself.[20]

Later, in 1933, the worst year of the Great Depression, President Franklin Roosevelt said in his inaugural address,

> So, first of all, let me assert my firm belief that the only thing we have to fear is fear itself—nameless, unreasoning, unjustified terror which paralyzes needed efforts to convert retreat into advance.[21]

Thomas Mullen was not a celebrity, but President Roosevelt was. So Roosevelt went viral as the originator of the idea, taking credit for an idea that sounded right because it had already been repeated many times. This articulation of the fear of fear itself may today be Roosevelt's most famous quote,[22] and ProQuest News & Newspapers shows that it was used even more frequently in the first decade of the twenty-first century than it was in the 1930s.

But viral narratives are not easily controlled, and they may have unintended effects. Describing everyone as fearful and emphasizing the need for courage may create some patriotic resolve not to be fearful. At the same time, such exhortations make it doubtful that others will truly cast aside their fear. Thus identifying the problem as one of fear may only worsen the problem.

Other narratives of the 1930s focused on ending up in a poorhouse so overcrowded that one had to open a cot every night to sleep among many others in a common area and to fold up the cot every night to yield the floor space to other activities.[23] There were also narratives of getting sick and having no money to pay a doctor.[24] Even if these narratives were exaggerated, they reduced willingness to spend on anything but the barest necessities. As a result, people neglected routine dental work to conserve money, ultimately leading to painful dental emergencies.

Roosevelt also offered moral reasons to spend. Days after his inauguration in 1933, he took the unusual step of addressing the nation by radio during a massive national bank run that had necessitated shutting down all the banks. In this "fireside chat," he explained the banking crisis and asked people not to continue their demands on banks. He spoke to the nation as a military commander would speak to his troops before a battle, asking for their courage and selflessness. Roosevelt asserted, "You people must have faith. You must not be stampeded by rumors or guesses. Let us unite in banishing fear."[25] The public honored Roosevelt's personal request. The bank run ended, and money flowed into, not out of, the banks when they reopened.

We are still influenced by this narrative constellation. Although the overall narrative has not been powerful enough, or not used well enough, to prevent recessions, it remains in our consciousness and may reassert itself if conditions change. Meanwhile, we are now in the habit of listening to the stock market's closing price at the end of every business day, often interpreting it as an indicator of public confidence. We also follow the various monthly confidence indexes, not because economists urge us to, but because we are still subject to the old narratives suggesting that public confidence can break as suddenly as a shout of fire in a crowded theater.

Narratives Focused on Mass Unemployment

We can look for lists of the causes of the Great Depression created during the Great Depression. These stated or speculated causes tend to correspond to events whose confluence brought on the Depression. For example, Willard Monroe Kiplinger, the founder of today's Kiplinger publications, offered the following list of causes in 1930, early in the Depression:

The causes of unemployment are loosely stated as follows:

1. The development of machines which do the work of many men under the direction of a few men; this is the technological aspect.
2. The overloading of industrial centres with men attracted or driven by circumstances from farms to cities.
3. The entrance of women into jobs formerly held by men.
4. Immigration, which is now less of a factor in unemployment than years ago.
5. Business depression, which is such a broad subject as to include both causes and effects of unemployment.

These are pretty theories, and there is a large element of truth in each of them, particularly the first, relating to the development of labor-saving machinery. The point needing emphasis is, however, that no one of them supplies an answer, nor even all five, for all have ramifications that have never been studied or explored by qualified authorities.[26]

Only one of Kiplinger's five causes would come to mind today in our current popular narrative of the Great Depression: the business depression, which today most would say is related to loss of confidence. But Kiplinger published his list in 1930, and as the Great Depression wore on, more and more people began to think of it as driven by a loss of confidence.

Kiplinger's list refers to facts, not to narratives, but we can suppose that each of the five causes corresponds to a popular narrative of 1930 and thus is connected to other narrative constellations that are difficult to study. It is worth noting that some or many of these narratives probably had a long-term orientation, implying that the Great Depression would go on forever.

As the 1930s wore on, the Great Depression narrative began to be infected with stories of the environmentally catastrophic Dust Bowl in the central United States, the sequence of storms from 1934 to 1940 that hit Oklahoma, Kansas, Colorado, and Texas, blowing off improperly managed dried topsoil and destroying farms. John Steinbeck's 1939 novel *The Grapes of Wrath*, which chronicled the travails of a family of migrant farm workers, helped to cement the association between the Great Depression and the Dust Bowl. *The Grapes of Wrath* was a best seller, later made into a 1940 movie starring Henry Fonda. The book won the Pulitzer Prize, the National Book Award, and the Nobel Prize in Literature, and it has been assigned to US high school and college students ever since. It is part of the constellation that has driven the Great Depression narrative.

In her photographic record of the Great Depression, Dorothea Lange gave us memorable photos of poverty-stricken people in the Dust Bowl. Along with Lange's stark portraits, photos of drab despondent men standing in a breadline; a man selling five-cent apples, stacked neatly on a small wooden box or table on a city street; people lining up outside banks; and life in a Hooverville (shantytown) provide us with a visual memory of the Depression today.

The 1930s represented a turning point in economic measurement. Until then, no statistics reliably measured unemployment. The national census of the United States had provided numbers of people working and not working, but those not working included the elderly, the sick, those pursuing an education, stay-at-home mothers, and vacationers. By the 1930s, the statistics began to focus on the *unemployment rate*, which measures employment based on the size of the labor force, not on the size of the population. Since the end of the Great Depression, the monthly announcement of the unemployment rate may have encouraged thinking that we may be at risk for a repeat of that event. We can see the rise of the term *unemployment rate* sharply in Google Ngrams, though a significant increase did not occur until after 1960.

It may seem odd that the term *unemployment rate* did not receive more coverage in the 1930s, but the lack of coverage may reflect the public's lack of familiarity with its quantitative representation. They did not yet clearly differentiate between involuntary unemployment and laziness and pauperism. In contrast, today's narratives focus on blameless unemployment, the unemployment of those sincerely trying to find a job.

A Different Narrative of the Great
Depression Develops

The narrative of the Great Depression as it stands today would likely mention few of the causes that Kiplinger and others enumerated as it was happening. Instead, people today tend to identify the causes of the Great Depression as fear and a loss of confidence related to bank failures. Bank failures (and shadow-bank failures) were key narratives in the "Great Recession" of 2007–9. In his 1930 list, Kiplinger did not even mention bank failures, most of which happened after 1930.

Some modern theories that seek to explain the extreme length and depth of the Great Depression without relying directly on any of these narratives seem plausible. Harold L. Cole and Lee E. Ohanian (2004) argue that the 1933 National Industrial Recovery Act, which imposed "codes of fair competition" in an effort to combat the Great Depression, actually prolonged the Depression. (The act was in response to another narrative about inadequate purchasing power, described in chapter 13, below.) The act made it easier for businesses to form cartels and more difficult for them to cut wages. Although the Supreme Court declared the act unconstitutional in 1935, Cole and Ohanian argue that the Roosevelt administration managed to keep the codes in effect. In addition, the initial period of high unemployment led to continued high unemployment because the remaining employed labor became "insiders" while those laid off became "outsiders." As Assar Lindbeck and Dennis J. Snower[27] have argued, the insiders tend to band together and ask for higher wages when demand increases, rather than ask for the laid-off "outsiders" to be rehired.

Other theories have merit too. Economic historians Barry Eichengreen and Peter Temin have argued that the length and pain of the Great Depression were related to the unthinking national commitment to the gold standard despite changes in labor markets that made wages more downwardly rigid. They have shown that countries that abandoned the gold standard earlier recovered better.[28]

Milton Friedman and Anna J. Schwartz in their *Monetary History of the United States* had blamed the Great Depression on the Federal

Reserve and its control of the money supply. But Eichengreen and Temin argued that declines in the US money supply were mostly caused by the economy, not the Fed. Declines in the money supply were triggered in part by the bank runs that were caused by the same feedback that created the Great Depression. In effect, Friedman and Schwartz argued that the Fed would have done better if it had offset these declines. Temin also observed that Friedman and Schwartz indicated no substantial correspondence between the bank runs and measures of economic activity.

These economists tell only part of the story of the severity of the Great Depression. The comedian Groucho Marx offered a more entertaining, popular account of the Great Depression. According to his autobiography, published in 1959, Groucho was in his early thirties in the late 1920s, making good money as an actor in popular vaudeville stage shows. He recalls:

> Soon a much hotter business than show business attracted my attention and the attention of the country. It was a little thing called the stock market. I first became acquainted with it around 1926. It was a pleasant surprise to discover that I was a pretty shrewd trader. Or at least so it seemed, for everything I bought went up. . . . My salary in Cocoanuts was around two thousand a week, but this was pin money compared to the dough I was theoretically making in Wall Street. Mind you, I enjoyed doing the show, but I had very little interest in the salary. I took market tips from everybody. It's hard to believe it now, but incidents like the following were commonplace in those days.[29]

Groucho goes on to describe a number of tips that he and his brothers overconfidently bet on: a tip from the elevator man, a Wall Streeter, his theatrical producer, and someone he met on a golf course. He views the whole experience as a great "folly" and struggles to understand his own participation in it. Ideas about the craziness of the Roaring Twenties and the Great Depression became legendary through the persuasive accounts of good storytellers like Groucho Marx, who had much more public influence than economists.

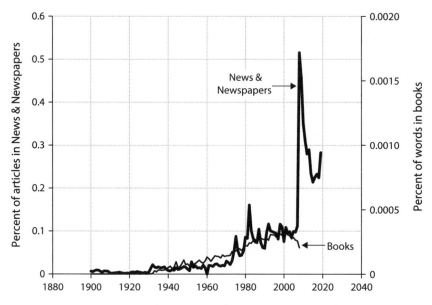

FIGURE 10.4. Frequency of Appearance of *Great Depression* in Books, 1900–2008, and News, 1900–2019

The narrative of the Great Depression has been a long-lasting epidemic that outlasted the Depression itself by many decades. *Sources*: Google Ngrams, no smoothing, and author's calculations from ProQuest News & Newspapers.

In fact, attention to this story has largely kept growing and growing. Figure 10.4 suggests that far more attention was paid to the Great Depression in 2009 than during the Great Depression itself, though we must understand that people hadn't named the economic downturn the "Great Depression" as it was happening. Instead, they called it "hard times." Other Depression-linked narratives of the period were associated with words unusual to that period, such as *breadline*, whose use grew rapidly from 1929 to 1934 and has decayed fairly steadily ever since. The interest in the Great Depression in 2009 is confirmed in Google Trends search counts as well, though not as dramatically as those shown in Figure 10.4.

Ultimately, how do narratives of the Great Depression affect how we think about economic downturns today? Consider a narrative-based chronology of the 2007–9 world financial crisis, which taps into stories about nineteenth-century bank runs that were virtually synonymous with financial crises. After the Great Depression, bank runs were thought to be cured. The Northern Rock bank run in 2007, the first UK bank run since 1866, brought back the old narratives of panicked depositors and angry crowds outside closed banks. The story led to an international skittishness, to the Washington Mutual (WaMu) bank run a year later in the United States, and to the Reserve Prime Fund run a few days after that in 2008. These events then led to the very unconventional US government guarantee of US money market funds for a year. Apparently, governments were aware that they could not allow the old stories of bank runs to feed public anxiety.

In the heart of the 2007–9 recession, the Great Depression narrative may have intertwined with bank run narratives to create this popular perception: "We have passed through a euphoric, speculative, immoral period like the Roaring Twenties. The stock market and banks are collapsing now as they did in 1929, and the entire economy might collapse again, as it did in the 1930s. We might all lose our jobs and crowd around failed banks in a desperate attempt to get our money."

In short, the Great Depression and its causes (after a period of euphoria, loss of confidence) remain a powerful narrative. The Great Depression was a traumatic period in the nation's history that is constantly on people's minds as they listen to other narratives regarding what may happen next. Far less remembered than the confidence and fear constellation of stories is a different constellation that was also prominent in the minds of people who lived during the Great Depression: narratives about modesty, compassion, and simple living. These narratives are mostly in remission and as of this writing have been replaced by success narratives that justify conspicuous consumption, as we discuss in the next chapter.

Chapter 11

Frugality versus Conspicuous Consumption

Frugality and an impulse to maintain a modest lifestyle have roots going back to ancient times. Sumptuary laws in ancient Greece and Rome, as well as China, Japan, and other countries, forbade excess ostentation. Stories about the disgusting flaunting of wealth are one of the longest-running perennial narratives, in many countries and religions. Opposing these frugality narratives are conspicuous consumption narratives: to succeed in life, one must display one's success as an indication of achievement and power. The two narratives are at constant war, with modesty relatively strong during some periods and conspicuous consumption dominant at other times. Both are important economic narratives because they affect how people spend or save, and hence they influence the overall state of the economy. In fact, these narratives can have profound economic consequences that economists and policymakers would not necessarily anticipate.

Frugality and Compassion in the Great Depression

During the Great Depression in the 1930s, frugality narratives were particularly strong amidst the perception of widespread involuntary unemployment. They were also a reaction to the perceived excess of the 1920s, which we can see by the rapid growth then of the phrase *keep up with the Joneses*, generally used to disparage people who think that, to keep up appearances, they have to buy everything that their successful neighbors buy. Indeed, the use of that phrase grew most rapidly during the 1930s. It is difficult to find accounts of depression-induced modesty in the era before the Great Depression.[1] The "new modesty" stayed high during World War II and into the 1950s, and then started to decline.

The new modesty that coincided with the Great Depression and World War II evolved out of the strong narrative that people were suffering through no fault of their own. They lost their jobs because of the Depression, and some lost their lives later because of the war. Maybe your Jones neighbors were doing very well, but your Smith neighbors were having a terribly difficult time, like so many other families during the Depression. A huge constellation of human tragedy narratives prevailed through word of mouth among friends and neighbors, stories of families out on the street after the father lost his job and defaulted on his mortgage and lost the home, through no fault of his own. Under such conditions, the reasonable response even for people who still had a job was to postpone buying a new car, throwing lavish parties, and keeping up with expensive fashions. Such self-imposed austerity helps to explain the severe contraction at the beginning of the Depression as well as the contraction of consumer purchases during World War II.

Depression-Era Narratives in Their Own Words

The talk of the time reflects the dominant narrative. Here is a Depression-era letter to the *Boston Globe*'s "Household Department—Where Women Help Women—Confidential Chat" column, a sort of Twitter, Weibo, or Reddit from another era, where women would write and advise one another under pseudonyms. The following letter appeared in March 1930, six months after the 1929 stock market crash:

> Dear Mikado—In one of your recent letters asking for a budget you said that your savings had been wiped away in the recent financial crash, so I am addressing this letter to you as we surely have something in common, only in my case we not only lost what we had but are deeply in debt as a result.
>
> However, my problem is this: we can pay back this money in about 10 years if we continue to live practically as we are now living, that is, in our present home, by practicing rigid economy. Of course we could

move to a cheaper house, live on only the bare necessities of life and get out of this debt sooner, but what I would like you, Lanceolata, and any of the other sisters who will write to tell me whether you think it wise to do this. . . .

I am afraid to move, for I fear the moral effect on us. Our standard of living will be lowered and I am afraid to think of the readjustment and the effect of such a move on our spirits, our courage and outlook on life. This may not seem very brave, but unless one has been through such a period it is hard to realize the strain and the worry and hard to keep a calm outlook on life . . . Chryold.[2]

When one has neighbors like Chryold, who are desperately hanging on, showing off with extravagant consumption would be seen as deeply unempathetic. It is noteworthy that the writer introspectively refers to "our spirits," which calls to mind Keynes's idea that depressions are caused by declines in "animal spirits." Her decision whether to sell the house is framed in such psychological terms: she has to manage her family's spirits. Managing people's spirits was an important theme of the era's talk, from the common American to the nation's leadership, from individual heads of households to the president of the United States, Herbert Hoover, who spoke optimistically and encouraged optimistic talk in others.

It seems highly likely that Chryold's family and many other families in a similar (or worse) situation would postpone buying a new car. Realistically, the children in each family would receive almost no signal that the family is in financial trouble if their parents postpone the purchase of new car. However, they *would* notice canceled vacations and canceled trips to the movies.

Indeed, concerns about family morale became a new epidemic after 1929, peaking in 1931 but staying high for the rest of the Great Depression. (There had been an earlier rush of stories about family morale during the 1920–21 depression also.) The rising divorce rate was attributed to the loss of morale, especially the shame of a father who was unable to find a job.[3] People considered this loss of morale as a new long-term problem in the making, a problem that might become increasingly significant in the future. A women's group in 1936 asserted:

The family is the unit upon which our whole American system of living is built. . . . Any collapse now of its morale or loss of its solvency will have a disastrous effect on posterity.[4]

This narrative justified postponing unnecessary expenditures while maintaining an attitude of normalcy, but in doing so it contributed to prolonging the economic depression. It also offered a reason for families not affected by the Depression to avoid conspicuous consumption, in deference to the perceived suffering of other families and the outlook for more of the same. Newspapers offered suggestions for maintaining the family morale without spending much:

> Frequently, if resources are at a low ebb, much may be done by rearranging the furniture, changing the positions of heavy pieces (always being careful to maintain a perfect balance in the room) and moving pictures into different spaces. Many a woman by dint of some ingenuity along this line, has secured all the benefits of a trip without leaving her own four walls. Her outlook on life has been cleaned and pressed, in a manner of speaking.[5]

Listening to people's stories of the Great Depression in their own words also offers striking insights. In *Only Yesterday* (1931), Frederick Lewis Allen spoke of a more modest countenance and deeper religiosity, of "striking alterations in the national temper and ways of American life. . . . One could hardly walk a block in any American city or town without noticing some of them."[6] Rita Weiman, an author and actress, described the change too, in the *Washington Post* in 1932, comparing the Great Depression with the 1920s:

> During those years of inflation, when we were right on the edge of a precipice all the time, we lost our sense of perspective. We spent fabulous sums for objects and pleasures out of all proportion to the value received. If it cost a great deal of money, we promptly came to the conclusion that they must be good. . . . Take the matter of home entertainment. Many of us had almost forgotten how much fun it can be to gather friends around one's own table. Any number of us suffered from "restaurant digestion."[7]

The Great Depression became a time of reflection about what is important in life beyond spending money. Writing in the United Kingdom in 1931, columnist Winifred Holtby asked:

> In other words, can we not use this period to get rid of a little snobbery and bunkum and live lives dictated by our own tastes instead of our neighbours' supposed notions of "what is done"? With so much to do, and a world so rich in experience, must we shut ourselves up into little genteel compartments in which we all adopt the same arbitrary standards, wear the same things, eat the same things, and produce the same sad monotony of "appearances"? . . . Can we not remember the wisdom of Marie Lloyd's old song, "It's a little of what you fancy does you good!"?—not a little of what you fancy your neighbours will fancy that you ought to fancy. Can we not dare to be poor?[8]

In 1932, near the lowest ebb of the Great Depression, Catherine Hackett, another writer, explained her view of the new morality in the Great Depression:

> In the old Boom era I could buy a jar of bath salts or an extra pair of evening slippers without an uncomfortable consciousness of the poor who lacked the necessities of life. I could always reflect happily on the much-publicized day laborers who wore silk shirts and rode to their work in Fords. Now it was different. The Joneses were considered to be callous to human misery if they continued to give big parties and wear fine clothes.[9]

Despite such narratives, it appears that some dimensions of the "hard times" of the Great Depression were a desirable improvement over the 1920s. Anne O'Hare McCormick, a Pulitzer Prize–winning journalist for the *New York Times*, wrote in 1932:

> There are times when the complacency, the rugged selfishness and the greed for hokum of one's compatriots are hard to bear. This is not one of those times. At the bottom of the market we are much nicer than we are at the top. Main Street in a depression is the most neighborly street in the world. It is a very patient thoroughfare.[10]

In addition, it was noted during the Great Depression that there was no increase in crime despite the high rate of unemployment.[11] Perhaps this phenomenon was related to the increase in "neighborly" and "patient" sentiments that softened the sense of personal failure created by unemployment that might otherwise have led to crime.

Though the streets may have become more neighborly, the human misery was palpable on the street corners. In the early 1930s there was "a perfect epidemic of pan-handling and street begging."[12] In 1932 the *Washington Post* reported, "Panhandlers have become especially active during the depression. They find that people who do not believe in giving to professional beggars are especially soft-hearted at present."[13]

An epidemic of apple sellers, starting in New York City in the fall of 1930, spread nationwide.[14] The sellers were practically admitting that they were beggars, often displaying signs saying "Unemployed" or "Eat an apple and help me keep the wolf away."[15] In effect, they were begging, but selling the apples made them look more reputable and approachable. Newspapers also carried stories of crimes committed by beggars who hadn't received the requested alms, so their presence created an atmosphere of fear, which surely discouraged conspicuous consumption.[16]

Beyond the visible beggars there were narratives about the internal struggle of others not visibly unemployed. Benjamin Roth, a lawyer, wrote in his personal diary on August 9, 1931:

> Most professional men for the past two years have been living on money borrowed on insurance policies, etc. The only work that comes in now are impossible collections on a contingent fee basis. Everybody is digging up old claims and trying to realize on them. Tempers are short and people are distrustful and suspicious. There is nothing to do but work harder for less money and cut expenses to the bone.[17]

But, mostly, the fundamental change was an atmosphere of collective sympathy, like the feeling in the wake of a shared tragedy. This atmosphere explained people's willingness to work for a contingent fee or to buy apples on a street corner even when they were not in the mood for an apple. However, by stopping any conspicuous consumption, they inadvertently worsened the Depression.

Street begging was not limited to the United States. In Germany, where the unemployment rate was even higher than in the United States, there was a striking rise in panhandlers and in unemployed youths involved in crime in the years just before Adolf Hitler came to power. The higher crime and unemployment rates help explain Hitler's appeal to many voters.[18] After his election in 1933, Hitler dealt with the problem by imprisoning German panhandlers and homeless people in concentration camps.[19]

Meanwhile, much of the world had embraced the frugality narrative. Film critic Grace Kingsley noted in 1932 that motion pictures had become less interested in luxury:

> Due to depression and its effect on the public producers are softpedaling luxury display in their pictures. Whereas heretofore the heroine appeared to live in the public library building, so vast was her domicile, now smaller rooms are shown and display of wealth is not nearly so lavish. . . . And now the elegant Richard Barthelmess and the exotic Marlene Dietrich are scheduled for roles in simple stories of home life.[20]

These movies offered scripts for living. People may find themselves not ever consciously deciding to consume less but consuming less out of pure subconscious suggestibility.

Church sermons also inveighed against the display of wealth, as reported in a newspaper article in 1932:

> In this time of depression, publicly displayed extravagance is an offense, the Rev. Dr. Minot Simons, pastor, asserted yesterday in his Christmas sermon in All Souls Unitarian Church.

The article further quotes his sermon:

> I hope that any one tempted to splurge in costly rejoicings will get that thought that they would be in bad taste. . . . Such things always stir a profound resentment, and this Winter such resentment must not be stirred. [21]

Note that the argument here is basically moral, not an appeal to self-interest.

As Anne O'Hare McCormick had noted when writing about Main Street, USA, people's attitudes toward one another had changed. They became concerned about managing others' perceptions of them. The *Washington Post* observed that the conclusions one might draw about others' status and human worth from observing their frugality had changed entirely:

> And then the mode turned a handspring, as so often happens, and poverty was chic! "I cannot afford it," was said brazenly, even boastingly—because didn't this imply that one had lost lots of money in stocks and things. Whether one had had any or lost any, of course.[22]

Indeed, during the Great Depression, people took (and still sometimes take even today) a strange pleasure in telling Depression hardship and loss stories about themselves, their relatives, and their friends. The narrative has moral dimensions. Because their poverty was not their fault, there was no shame in it; and there was a dignity in sympathizing with those who suffered. In addition, the "sin" of enjoying riches amidst poverty was more immoral when one had long-unemployed neighbors who were barely getting by.

New Modesty Crazes

The "poverty chic" culture spurred new crazes in the 1930s. The bicycle craze was notable: many people began riding bicycles to work or to go shopping in urban environments. Department stores installed bicycle racks for their patrons.[23]

The bicycle craze arose partially from the desire to postpone buying a new car. Those who already owned a car decided to keep the car going rather longer. Those who did not own a car decided to continue taking public transportation as they always had, or to ride a bike. Why did people postpone their car purchases? Being unemployed was one key reason. Another was thinking that they *might* become unemployed.

A 1931 sound movie, *Six Cylinder Love*, based on a play produced during the depression of 1920–21, shows some of the complexities involved in a man's decision to buy an expensive car. As a result of that decision, his wife and daughter are transformed into extravagant spenders, and the family also attracts sponging friends who believe that they are rich because they own a pricey car. The movie plot itself became part of a narrative constellation about the consequences of extravagant purchases. Seeing your neighbor unemployed, and hearing stories of desperation and struggle, made it obvious to many that you should not buy a new car this year. A 1932 article in the *Wall Street Journal* also noted the anti–conspicuous consumption motive for delaying a car purchase:

> One serious but not easily discernible obstacle is now blocking the exercise of their spending power by those who have it and are capable of using it judiciously in the benefit of industry. This is the widespread fear of being considered ostentatiously extravagant. . . . It is no mere guesswork that asserts such a handicap upon efforts to revive trade. The automobile industry, for one, has proved its reality on an extended scale by gathering conclusive evidence that important numbers of people with money and the actual need of a new car are denying themselves through fear of neighborhood criticism. A new species of sales resistance is among the "psychological" products of depression, namely, the haunting doubt whether or not ownership of a new car may be, or may seem to others, an indecent display of affluence.[24]

The *Wall Street Journal* makes an excellent point. A "visibility index" of consumption categories, created by Ori Heffetz, seeks to measure how much other people notice consumption expenditures. The index ranks automobiles as the second most visible consumption category, out of thirty-one categories, second only to cigarettes.[25] If you no longer want to look rich, skipping a new car might be the best thing to do.

The feedback loop soon became apparent: some people postponed buying a car or other major consumer items, which led to loss of jobs in the auto and consumer-products industries, which led to more postponement, which led to a second round of job loss, and so on for several years. The numbers tell the tale: sales of new cars by Ford Motor

Company, which had adopted many labor-saving mass-production machines, fell 86% from 1929 to 1932.

Why was the feedback loop so severe, and why did it happen when it did? To answer these questions, we have to look more closely at the underlying narratives. In the home, there was trouble with the sudden increase in leisure. One anonymous woman wrote to *Confidential Chat* in 1932:

Dear Globe Sisters—May I come to this wonderful column with my problem? I have been married six years and have two children. We were married when quite young and unfortunately my husband had no special trade. I worked, too, but when our first baby was born I had to quit. I got him to take a course to advance himself and I paid for this, also all expenses connected with the baby and our living expenses while he was not working. He worked steadily until a year ago and then like so many others he was laid off. Since then he has had only a few days now and then. I could not work last Summer, as my second baby was only a few months old. This Winter we have spent with relations and I have been helping with the work, occasionally at sewing or nursing, but we don't get by and I am worried.

What bothers me most is the attitude of my husband. It doesn't seem to bother him much of any to live like this. I would hate to have it thrown at my children that they were on the town. I feel the way things are now that we are just living on charity, and this can't go on forever.

Is this attitude on the part of my husband my fault for working in the beginning or is it his fault for being so slow to take the responsibility? Don't think that my husband isn't a good man, for he is a fine fellow in many respects, but he seems to entirely lack any money-making ability. When I earn a few dollars he thinks it is all right for me to take it and pay the bills. I feel so ashamed. I can't accustom myself to a man taking money from a woman, even if she is his wife.

Is there anything I can do to bring him to his senses? I could not let my own people know of this situation. I have the promise of a good job soon myself. If I get it I feel that I shall just pay the children's board and let him shift for himself. Would this do any good, do you think? Please welcome me and advise me.

Lucy Ambler.[26]

Lucy had to be reminded, by one of the "Globe Sisters," that her husband's problems were not her husband's fault:

Dear Lucy Ambler—Your letter regarding an irresponsible husband certainly aroused my interest. I am married to a man who is like your husband in many respects and I think we have a great deal for which to be thankful. You say he is a good man and a fine fellow. Is he to blame if like millions of others he finds himself with no means of support? If he always worked steadily until a year ago and did his best for his family, can anyone look down upon you if you are in need at the present time? Isn't it a fact that your dissatisfaction is really with the present economic conditions and not with your husband? ... Catarina[27]

We can imagine the conversations between husband and wife about the making of large expenditures—if they talk about the topic at all. The feelings of hurt, betrayal, and helplessness would be difficult to talk about, not just for Lucy Ambler and her husband, but also for other couples who feared that they might find themselves in the same situation. We can easily imagine that talk about high-priced expenditures might be verboten, along with the expenditures themselves.

When such stories are rampant, and when unemployment is increasingly long-term, any employer who offers a job to a laid-off worker will be regarded as a sort of hero. But there is an offsetting tendency for the employer to worry about hiring someone with little "money-making ability" and few other options. As a Pennsylvania emergency relief board administrator said in 1936:

Another factor of importance in connection with the unemployment situation, which, of course, is at the basis of relief, is the fact that many men and women who were merely being "carried along" by their employers in the pre-depression days, for sentimental or other reasons, will never get back their old jobs.[28]

Employers need to balance morale and productivity. As Truman Bewley found in his interviews of employers during a recession in the 1990s:

> Managers were concerned about morale mainly because of its impact on productivity. They said that when morale is bad, workers distract one another with complaints and that good morale makes workers more willing to do extras, to stay late until a job is done, to encourage and help one another, to make suggestions for improvements, and to speak well of the company to outsiders.[29]

It seems safe to conclude that employers are particularly concerned about worker morale during hard times. They often try to boost their employees' morale by helping them feel successful in their jobs and by using a nondifferentiation wage policy, paying high performers the same as low performers, despite the negative effects on incentives to work hard.[30] In addition, employers often continue to employ weak employees for sentimental reasons or to maintain workplace morale.

But there is a darker side to the story. The worst days of the Depression gave employers a plausible excuse for laying off weaker employees without generating stories of their inhumanity. When times are a little better, they would rather not rehire the weak employees, which can lead to long-term unemployment for those who have been laid off.

Modesty Fashions: Blue Jeans and Jigsaw Puzzles

Blue denim fabric, formerly considered appropriate only for work clothes, started to become more fashionable during the Great Depression, though earlier celebrities had made denim fashion statements. For example, James D. Williams, governor of Indiana from 1877 to 1880, was nicknamed "Blue Jeans Bill" because of his insistence on wearing them even to formal occasions. According to one observer, for Williams the coarse blue fabric was "a symbol of equality and democracy."[31] But it was not until the

1930s that the material gained popularity. In 1934, the Levi Strauss Company created its first blue jeans for women, naming them "Lady Levi's."[32] Then, in 1936, Levi Strauss put the first fashion logo on the back pocket of its blue jeans. *Vogue* magazine featured its first blue jeans–clad cover model in the 1930s, and women started deliberately damaging their new jeans to make them look worn, putting "an intentional rip here and there."[33]

We can trace blue jeans' associations with different cultures over the decades. In the 1920s and 1930s, blue jeans culture fit in with the poverty-chic culture, the cowboy story culture, and the dude ranch culture. Starting in the 1940s, blue jeans became associated with altogether different cultures, first with Rosie the Riveter during World War II, and then with high school, youthful rebellion, and women's liberation.[34] The blue jeans fashion truly exploded in the 1950s,[35] propelled to new heights by the hit 1955 movie *Rebel Without a Cause* and its handsome star James Dean, who died at age twenty-four, a month before the movie was released, while driving his sports car recklessly. The death was perfect, if ghoulish, publicity for the movie. Some fans of the film went to extremes; for example, Douglas Goodall, a London mail truck driver, not only wore blue jeans but also by 1958 had watched the movie four hundred times and legally changed his name to James Dean.[36] But by this time, the blue jeans narrative was losing its connection with sympathy for poverty, and it may have lost its status as an economic narrative. Nonetheless, the ubiquity of blue jeans (based on their cheapness, practicality, long life, and others' fashion decisions) has allowed the blue jeans epidemic to continue spreading to this day.

Also connected to poverty chic was the jigsaw puzzle craze. To occupy themselves during a quiet, stay-at-home evening, some people bought one of the new cheap cardboard jigsaw puzzles (instead of the more expensive traditional wooden puzzles) at newsstands with the evening newspaper on their way home from work. Jigsaw puzzles were suddenly on sale everywhere, and people wondered, "What psychological quirk lies buried in the human brain to spring to radiant life at the rattle of odd pieces of material in a cardboard box?"[37]

Bicycles, blue jeans, and cardboard jigsaw puzzles might be nothing more than logical, rational responses to the bad economic conditions of the Depression. They were inexpensive. But the enthusiasm for these products, the craze nature of the phenomena, suggests that their narratives help to explain why people stopped buying expensive consumer goods during the Depression—which, by extension, helps to explain the length and severity of the Depression. Perhaps people would never have ridden a bicycle to work in the 1920s not because they were rich but because doing so would have seemed odd. Only after one heard the narrative describing others who rode a bike to work or stayed home assembling jigsaw puzzles in the evening would one be comfortable doing the same things. And then one might continue doing them for many years, weakening the market for more expensive forms of transportation and entertainment, and thus slowing recovery from the Depression. Likewise, if building a beautiful new house is considered to be in bad taste and stirs profound resentment, then those are pretty good reasons not to build the house, thus helping to explain why housing construction virtually stopped during the Depression.

We see here that economic dynamics—the change in demand for goods and services through time—depend on subtle changes in narratives. Over the course of the Great Depression, people started to move beyond poverty chic, perhaps because of changing narratives about what people's apparent poverty implied about them. As the *Washington Post* noted in 1932:

> But now another handspring has been turned. Now it is no longer chic to imply poverty. If one had lost money in unwise speculations or stocks he has had plenty of time to recover from the world-wide upheaval. If he still claims poverty—well, the implication is that perhaps after all he never did have anything![38]

What conclusions can we draw? The modest economic recovery that started at the bottom of the Great Depression in 1933 occurred, at least in part, because people were spending more because poverty was no longer so chic! All of these narratives imply that the causes and effects of the Great Depression extend beyond economists' simple story of multiple rounds of expenditure and the effects of interest rates on rational investing behavior.

The decline in modesty and compassion narratives since the Great Depression may help to explain many economic trends. The modesty decline is likely related to the rise in inequality, in the share of national income earned by the top 1%, documented by Thomas Piketty in his 2014 book *Capital in the Twenty-First Century*.[39] It also is likely related to the long-term decline in managers' feeling of loyalty to their employees, documented by Louis Uchitelle in his 2006 book *The Disposable American*.[40] A narrative downplaying modesty and compassion was supported by Donald Trump in his 2007 book, *Think Big and Kick Ass in Business and Life*, coauthored with Bill Zanker.[41]

The frugality narrative was repeated in Japan after 1990, with different stories and personalities. The high-flying Japanese economy of the 1980s had given way to the "lost decades" of the 1990s and beyond and to stories similar to the modesty and compassion stories in the United States. The *Washington Post* summed these narratives up in 1993:

> Tokyo—The once free-spending Japanese consumers have a new model citizen: Ryokan, an 18th century hermit monk who gave up his worldly goods to seek the pure life.
>
> Ryokan was featured recently in a prime-time television drama and a magazine cover story. A book about him and other ascetics, *The Philosophy of Honest Poverty*, has sold 350,000 copies since September.
>
> These days Japanese consumers seem to be trying to emulate the virtuous Ryokan. Consumers have sobered up and tightened their purse strings after a half-decade spending binge fueled by a roaring economy and soaring financial markets.[42]

Ryōkan (1738–1831) is remembered in many stories for his kindness and generosity to the less fortunate. He let mosquitoes and lice bite him out of sympathy for insects, and he once offered his clothes to a would-be thief who discovered he had nothing to steal.[43] Most Japanese did not go so far, but the new virtue lasted throughout the lost decades in Japan.

"American Dream" and Analogous Narratives
Displace the Frugality Narrative

James Truslow Adams coined the phrase *American Dream* in the first edition of his *New York Times* best-selling book *The Epic of America* (1931). The term is virtually never found on ProQuest News & Newspapers before 1931, except for mentions of a bedspring that promised good sleep, marketed in 1929 and 1930 as "The American Dream." As Figure 11.1 shows, Adams's *American Dream* went viral, vastly outpacing similar terms going back centuries, such as *American character, American principles*, and *American credo*. The "American Dream" was a long slow epidemic that is still growing today, almost a century after Adams coined the term. Adams, who died in 1949, saw only the very beginning of the epidemic.

Adams defined the American Dream as follows:

> The *American dream*, that dream of a land in which life should be better and richer and fuller for every man, with opportunity for each according to his ability or achievement . . . It is not a dream of motor cars and high wages merely, but a dream of a social order in which each man and each woman shall be able to attain to the fullest stature of which they are innately capable, and recognized by others for what they are, regardless of the fortuitous circumstances of birth or position.[44]

Some might say that Adams's account is a somewhat bland description of any country's dream, not a fiery manifesto that we'd expect to go viral. Indeed, it sounds similar to the China Dream, espoused by Chinese premier Xi Jinping; to the French Dream, espoused by former French president François Hollande; and to the Canadian "National Dream," all modeled after Adams. But there must have been something appealing and original about this idea that made it slowly and consistently contagious.

The phrase *American Dream* has a ring of truth to it as a statement of American values. The United States is a proud country that has no aristocracy, allows no titles or royalty, announces in its Declaration of Independence that "all men are created equal," and allows free enterprise to proceed with little government interference. However, it is also a

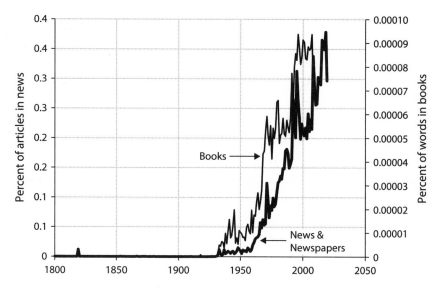

FIGURE 11.1. Frequency of Appearance of *American Dream* in Books, 1800–2008, and News, 1800–2016

The epidemic had hardly begun during the lifetime of its author, James Truslow Adams. *Sources*: Google Ngrams, no smoothing, and author's calculations from ProQuest News & Newspapers.

country that permitted slavery until 1863. Long before Adams defined the American Dream in 1931, slavery was seen as an abomination and an embarrassment inconsistent with the nation's stated commitment to equality. And American blacks have not received equal treatment even long after the abolition of slavery. But by coupling "American" with "Dream," the phrase might have defined a *trend* toward a better social order "in which each man and each woman shall be able to attain to the fullest stature of which they are innately capable." That's what a dream is: the sense of an ideal future, a deep-seated and fervently desired wish that is partly fulfilled today and might become completely fulfilled in the future. When Adams says that the American Dream "is not a dream of motor cars and high wages merely," he seems to assert that the American Dream is *in part* a dream of these material things. Of course people want to provide for their family and they want a good standard of living, but they want everyone to have a chance to achieve the same goals.

The original discussion of the American Dream in the 1930s, before the term went viral, was primarily intellectual. For example, George O'Neil's 1933 intellectual play *American Dream* examined whether American society truly embodied this dream. Later, in 1960, another intellectual play by Edward Albee, similarly titled *The American Dream*, was more critical of consumerism. The phrase *American Dream* cropped up repeatedly in honest discussions about America. Some intellectuals who were critical of the popular notions of economic success in the United States used the term ironically, but other intellectuals thought it measured some real aspect of American character.

For example, civil rights leader Martin Luther King, Jr., used the phrase in his legendary "I Have a Dream" speech, which he delivered during the civil rights march on Washington, DC, to a large crowd stretching between the Washington Monument and the Lincoln Memorial. In that speech on August 28, 1963, he looked confidently forward to a day when "this nation will rise up, live out the true meaning of its creed: We hold these truths to be self-evident, that all men are created equal."

Congress made King's birthday a US national holiday in 1983. When President Ronald Reagan signed the Act of Congress into law, he referred to the "I Have a Dream" speech. Later that year, King's widow, Coretta Scott King, said, "Help us to make Martin's dream—the American Dream—a reality."[45] We see how seemingly small and unpredictable moments in history—the publication of Adams's book and a single speech by King—can develop gradually into the backbone of a powerful narrative that continues to grow by contagion for decades afterward.

The celebrity aspect of narratives, so frequently discussed in these pages, is at work in the American Dream narrative. Martin Luther King, Jr., an inspirational figure who was assassinated as he fought for the American Dream, made for a far better narrative, and he pushed aside James Truslow Adams in the American collective consciousness, giving the American Dream narrative the human interest it needed to achieve enormous contagion. In fact, Adams wasn't enough of a celebrity to have his name attached to the narrative. Less than one-tenth of 1% of ProQuest News & Newspapers hits for *American Dream* since King's "I Have a

Dream" speech mention James Truslow Adams, but 3% mention Martin Luther King, Jr.

Ultimately, the generally accepted narrative of the American Dream includes a wish for prosperity for everyone, framing it in a way that makes it seem not commercial or selfish. It turns upside down Thorstein Veblen's idea of conspicuous consumption undertaken solely to prove one's superiority. As a result, the American Dream became extremely useful in pitches for consumer products that encourage potential purchasers to feel better about their purchases, such as a new home or a second car. In fact, ProQuest News & Newspapers shows that more than half the use of the phrase *American Dream* has occurred in advertisements rather than articles.

The Mutating American Dream: Homeownership

In the 1930s and 1940s, most of the ads using the phrase *American Dream* promoted intellectual products: books, plays, sermons. But as time wore on, and as the epidemic strengthened, the phrase took on a different dimension. The American Dream turned into owning a home, with the underlying sense that owning a home implies patriotism and commitment to the community. While advertisements have used the phrase less in recent decades, they continue the presumption that the American Dream justifies generous expenditures on homeownership. Over two-thirds of ProQuest News & Newspapers hits for *American Dream* since 1931 also include the word *house* or *home*.

The American Dream has been used to justify government actions supporting the housing bubble that eventually collapsed during the world financial crisis of 2007–9. In 2003, near the height of the bubble, Fannie Mae, the government-sponsored mortgage giant, adopted the following slogan for its advertisements: "As the American Dream Goes, So Do We." That same year, the US Congress passed, and President George W. Bush signed, the American Dream Downpayment Assistance Act, which subsidized home down payments. Since 1973, 265 bills and resolutions introduced in the US Congress have included the words "American Dream."

President George W. Bush heavily used the slogan "Ownership Society" during his 2004 reelection campaign. The slogan was a variation on the American Dream theme; Bush was calling attention to a society that respects ownership and in which people "take ownership"—that is, take responsibility for themselves. He said in 2002, "Right here in America if you own your own home, you're realizing the American Dream." He spoke of the good feelings homeownership lent: "All you've got to do is shake their hand and listen to their stories and watch the pride that they exhibit when they show you the kitchen and the stairs."[46]

Controlled experiments have shown that marketing of consumer products may be enhanced by appeals to patriotism.[47] By attaching the term *American Dream* to moral rectitude and to patriotism, this narrative epidemic probably raised the homeownership rate in the United States, as well as stimulating business in general.

The results have been both positive and negative. On the one hand, the American Dream narrative justifies people's desire to purchase expensive cars, extravagant homes, and other lavish consumer products and services. The narrative has probably boosted the real estate sector, both directly through consumer demand and indirectly via government support, or expected future government support, should anything go wrong in that market. On the other hand, the American Dream as embodied in the desire for homeownership played a strong role in the US housing boom before the 2007–9 world financial crisis and thus added to the severity of the crisis.

Today, the American Dream narrative justifies conspicuous consumption and the ownership of a pretentious house, in stark contradiction to the frugality narrative that was popular during the Great Depression. The American Dream narrative offers a justification for feeling proud of one's accomplishments, a sense of moral rectitude. The gold standard narrative, to which we turn in the next chapter, has a similar moral theme.

Chapter 12

The Gold Standard versus Bimetallism

Especially prominent among perennial economic narratives, the gold standard narrative dating back over a century remains somewhat active today. For example, President Donald Trump has repeatedly advocated a return to the gold standard in the United States. In a 2017 interview, he said:

> We used to have a very, very solid country because it was based on a gold standard. . . . Bringing back the gold standard would be very hard to do, but boy, would it be wonderful. We'd have a standard on which to base our money.[1]

Stated simply, bringing back a gold standard means defining the nation's currency in terms of a fixed unchanging amount of gold, and the government promising to redeem currency in gold or to do the reverse, on demand, so that the currency is perfectly interchangeable with gold. The world solidly abandoned the gold standard in 1971. Since then, countries have used fiat money—that is, money not backed by anything.

Central banks (with the notable exception of the Bank of Canada)[2] still own gold, though gold no longer backs their currency. According to the World Gold Council, central banks and finance ministries around the world own a total of 33,000 metric tons of gold, worth approximately $1.4 trillion US dollars.[3] But gold doesn't back the currency, so why do central banks hold it?

US Congressman Ron Paul asked the US chairman of the Federal Reserve, Ben Bernanke, why the Fed holds gold and not diamonds.

Bernanke gave a candid answer: "Well it's tradition—long-term tradition."[4] Bernanke was apparently referring to narratives and to the idea that central banks are apparently worried about stories that upset the public if a central bank rids itself of its gold holdings. Some people even think the United States is still on the gold standard, or at least have no clarity that it is not.

We shall see in this chapter that narratives about gold and money have a peculiar emotional tone, analogous to the emotions we see in cryptocurrency narratives today. There is a mystique about gold and money and innovations, and a mystique about pretentious theories on these topics. This mystique is difficult to explain.

The stories of gold and the gold standard are not simple. In fact, in history the gold standard has long been associated with prolonged deflation and other economic problems. In addition, the narratives about the gold standard have historically been sharply divisive and acrimonious, much like the cryptocurrency narratives in recent years. Let us look first at this long tradition, at the nineteenth-century excitement about gold, and see how it persists today and how it has recurred in mutated form with the cryptocurrencies.

The Crime of 1873 and the Emotional Divide

The United States effectively went onto the gold standard, attaching the US dollar exclusively to gold, with the Coinage Act of 1873 signed by President Ulysses S. Grant. (The Gold Standard Act of 1900 further clarified the standard.) Prior to 1873, the United States had been under a bimetallic standard (in effect, without calling it that), and the Coinage Act of 1834 specified the ratio of silver to gold at sixteen to one. The 1873 move was part of an international standardization of currencies around the gold standard.[5] The 1873 act was followed in the next two decades by persistent deflation (that is, falling consumer prices). Some observers labeled the 1873 Coinage Act "a crime" because the deflation impoverished debtors, especially farmers who bought their farms with a mortgage, by lowering the price at which they could sell their crops and raising the real value of their debts. Also, people who'd made major purchases were dismayed to see that they could have bought them for less if only they'd waited. The talk at that time, notably by farmers, encouraged moral outrage and public support for a return to bimetallism.

The bimetallism proposal, which was discussed internationally in the late nineteenth century and which gained enormous traction in the United States, advocated a return to having two metals backing the currency, enabling people who owed money denominated in dollars in effect to choose which metal to pay in. Under the gold standard as defined in the United States, a contract specifying payment of one dollar was a contract to deliver 1/20.67 of an ounce of gold. Under a bimetallic standard with a 16-to-1 ratio, the contract would have been interpreted as an agreement to deliver either this amount of gold or 16 times as many ounces of silver. Advocates of bimetallism became known as "Silverites," almost as if they were a political party, though in the United States in fact they were allied with the Democratic Party. The Silverites never succeeded in moving the United States to bimetallism, but by the 1890s the Silverites' proposal suddenly gained popularity.

However, by the 1890s the actual market prices of the two metals in world commerce implied a ratio of around 30 to 1. Thus the bimetallism proposal would have allowed debtors to cut their debts roughly in half by choosing to repay them in silver rather than gold. In effect, the result would have been a default on about half the value of all debts denominated in US dollars. Supporters of the gold standard therefore thought of themselves as upholding truth and honesty.

As Figure 12.1 shows, the term *gold standard* has not appeared very often in English-language books, newspapers, or magazines except in two decades: the 1890s and the 1930s. (There is also an uptrend in use of the term after the year 2000, but with "the gold standard" usually meaning just "the best.") Those two decades, the 1890s and the 1930s, were precisely the decades of the two biggest US depressions as measured by the unemployment rate. Because the gold standard was talked about very much during those depressions, we ought to consider how the gold standard narratives relate to the potential for severe depression. In both cases, the 1890s and the 1930s, the talk was of debauching the gold

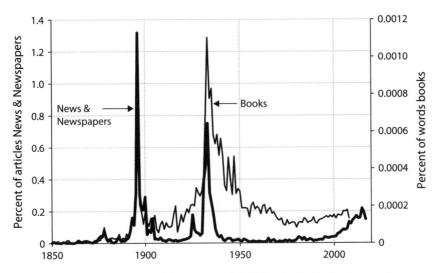

FIGURE 12.1. Frequency of Appearance of *Gold Standard* in Books, 1850–2008,
and News, 1850–2019

The term has had two separate epidemics decades apart, both associated with
major depressions. *Sources*: Google Ngrams, no smoothing, and author's calculations
using data from ProQuest News & Newspapers.

standard, allowing debt to be paid with less gold, and complaining that
ending the gold standard meant ending something traditional and honest. People seem to have a natural respect for ideas that they perceive as
coming from the wisdom of the past and that reflect true or important
values.

The term *devaluation* entered the English language in 1914, referring
to the decline in a currency's value, and it started to become popular in
the 1930s. There was no such word in the 1890s, during the first severe
depression. However, that decade saw a resurgence of Silverite narratives.
Their opponents in the 1890s thought that bimetallism was a dishonest
attempt to avoid national shame for default.

In April 1895, the *Atlanta Constitution* reported on the idea of returning to bimetallism at 16 to 1, an idea that had started going viral:

Representative Hepburn is in town, having spent a month or so traveling in Iowa since the adjournment of congress. He says that he has
visited every county in his district, and various other sections of the

state, and has found that everybody is crazy on the silver question. It is the only topic they will talk about. Whenever two men get together, whether it is at the postoffice or at the street corner, in the railway station, or the corner grocery, or while riding on the cars, they discuss nothing else, and the sentiment is almost unanimous in both parties that the United States government should immediately declare in favor of the free and unlimited coinage of silver regardless of the policy of the European nations.[6]

Belief in bimetallism took on strong geographic and social-class dimensions. Eastern intellectuals favored the gold standard, while westerners, who were more likely to be farmers, favored bimetallism. Supporters of the gold standard tended to appreciate symphony performances, while Silverites liked to watch boxing matches. By some accounts, Silverites tended to be hypermasculine and warmongering. In 1897 the *New York Times* asked, "Is there something in the silver creed that brings out the natural savagery of its sectaries and makes them delight in the barbarous principles and rough ways of early man?"[7]

The debate began to take on strong emotional significance. One observer begged the easterners not to ridicule the Silverites out west:

Some of the Eastern people either misunderstand the character and force of the silver sentiment in the West, or purposely deceive themselves about it. Such epithets as "Western lunatics," "Knaves of the prairies," "lazy shifters," "mining camp robbers," "deadbeats," "repudiationists," and "anarchists," have no other effect than to cause irritation and anger.[8]

This same observer was amazed by the strong differences in ideas, given that most of the westerners had migrated there from the East. He went on to describe the emotionally charged constellation of ideas that the western Silverites seemed to share, particularly their resentment of the monetary experts who believed that any change in the US monetary standard would require delicate international negotiation. Ultimately, he underestimated the power of geographically local idea epidemics.

The contagion of the bimetallism concept was not confined to the United States. The International Bimetallism Conference in London in

1894 noted that a long slow deflation caused by the gold standard had produced depression in agriculture across much of the world.[9] The conference report said that the United States suffered more than other countries, and no other major country saw such a swelling of popular support for bimetallism.

The condescending attitude of eastern intellectuals in the United States was surely noted, and resented, at the height of the bimetallist controversy. We can see how other narratives played on this resentment. *Coin's Financial School*, by lawyer William Hope Harvey, was published in 1894, in the middle of the 1890s depression. It presented an argument in favor of bimetallism. One wonders how a book on such an arcane and technical issue could have become a best seller in the United States. It is widely reputed to have sold a million copies when the US population was only a little over 20% of today's population. But the book is presented in an engaging way, in the form of a fictional dialogue with numerous pictures. The story follows a young man (perhaps in his early teens, based on the pictures) named Coin, a "little financier" lecturing in favor of bimetallism to an audience of argumentative men, including newspaper reporters. They report Coin's first lecture in newspapers, and his insolence angers establishment men, professors, and bankers, who show up for his second lecture in numbers. A "Professor Laughlin, head of the school of political economy in the Chicago University," a real person with fictional lines in the book, tries to embarrass young Coin by questioning him about the facts of the gold standard, but young Coin proves that he knows the facts even better than Professor Laughlin does.[10] In Harvey's book, we see one of the key elements in the contagion of the bimetallism narrative: a good story about an intelligent young man who gets the better of snooty intellectuals and professionals.

Bimetallism and Bitcoin

The enthusiasm for bimetallism in the nineteenth century seems similar to the excitement for Bitcoin we have seen in recent years. Among my students at Yale, some seem passionate about Bitcoin, and others appear extremely intrigued when I bring up Bitcoin. Maybe part of the appeal is that understanding Bitcoin requires some effort and talent. There is an air of mystery around Bitcoin, just as there is with conventional money. Few people understand how paper money gets its value and sustains it either.

As we noted in chapter 1, there is a detective-story-like mystery about Bitcoin, aided by the narrative that it was invented by Satoshi Nakamoto, who might be a multibillionaire as a result of his Bitcoin holdings. However, no one has ever found him or confirmed his existence. Indeed, the Bitcoin narrative is associated with secret codes, like the codes that are still talked about in popular World War II narratives. The idea that savvy young people understand Bitcoin, but that old fogies never will, appeals to many.

It is no coincidence that, a century ago, William Hope Harvey made Coin a young man. In the 1890s, the monetary standard offered some of the same mystery that Bitcoin does today. Young people in the 1890s wondered: What exactly is this money we have, and why does it have value? They might then have asked: How can we be on the gold standard when I almost never see a gold coin, only paper money, copper pennies, and silver dimes? What would happen if I walked into a bank and tried to demand my gold? Most people in the 1890s never tried to do that, and they might have been rebuffed if they did, because banks satisfied their obligations when they gave depositors paper dollars. So, even in the 1890s, the gold standard was a tantalizing mystery.

Silverites and Gold Bugs

In many ways the Silverites of the 1890s anticipated the supporters of Donald J. Trump in the 2016 US presidential election, both in their sympathies and in the contempt that many intellectuals held for them. A *Washington Post* reporter visiting Seattle in July 1896 wrote:

> A spirit of ardent Americanism pervades the entire population. They believe in a nation with a big N, and think America is strong enough to whip the rest of the world, if need be, and surely to put into force any legislation it may undertake without the consent or cooperation

of any other government. They are wide-awake, hospitable, and honorable. "Sunset" Cox, after a trip among them, aptly described the Westerners as "the cream of Eastern young enterprise."

Thousands of them regularly read the Eastern papers from their old homes. For the first time in their lives they now discover in these same papers that they are "idiots" and "anarchists." While editor Dana, of *The New York Sun,* is exhausting the adjectives of abuse for Western people in general, his own nephew and adopted son, John K. Dana, is quietly and industriously earning a living on a wheat and stock farm four miles west of Oakesdale, this State, and is a free silver man of the Populist variety.[11]

The notion that bimetallism is the only route to prosperity became strong among Silverites, who suggested that the 1890s depression would go on forever if the gold standard were allowed to stand. This idea was misguided, for the gold standard had been around for decades and depression had not been permanent. But the idea became ego-involving for Silverites, a core truth that they'd discovered that was nonetheless opposed by pretentious eastern intellectuals. During the presidential election campaign of 1896, William McKinley said that sound money is the route to general prosperity:

> Read the history of the great financial depressions and panics of 1817, 1825, 1837, 1841, 1857, 1873, 1893, and 1896, and see if this is not true. The triumph of sound money and protection at the polls in November will, in my judgment, restore confidence and thereby help every species of business, and when that is done your business will share in the general advancement and profit by the general prosperity.[12]

The implication was that the Silverites, typically rural and ignorant farming people, did not read history. But the idea that the depression would last forever spread among them nonetheless, and the idea itself worked against prosperity, for it discouraged spending and investing.

Meanwhile, those who were fiery in their support of the gold standard became known as *gold bugs.* Rare in 1874, the term took off on what appears to be a hump-shaped infective curve, peaking in 1896 during the depths of the great depression of the 1890s. After McKinley defeated William Jennings Bryan in the 1896 presidential election, a joke went viral. A Silverite would ask a gold bug, "Have you seen the General?" The other would invariably respond, "General who?" The answer was "general prosperity," referring to McKinley's words during the campaign. The joke faded in 1897 around a year after the election; it lost its effect when the economy began showing signs of improvement.[13]

Narratives Trigger the 1893 Bank Runs

The 1893–99 depression in the United States started quite suddenly in the spring of 1893 with a string of bank runs. Depositors rushed to pull their money out of banks, thereby fueling the bank failures that they feared. But what triggered the bank run?

One trigger was a rumor that began on April 17, 1893: the US subtreasury offices would no longer redeem Treasury notes in gold but would provide only silver, in amounts worth about half as much as the notes. There was no basis for this rumor except the news that Treasury reserves were falling. Newspapers had made big news out of the fact that Treasury reserves had fallen below $100 million, just because it was a round number. But the run was on the commercial banks, not on the Treasury. Alexander Dana Noyes, later the financial editor of the *New York Times*, commented in 1898:

> Panic is in its nature unreasoning; therefore, although the financial fright of 1893 arose from fear of depreciation of the legal tenders [federal-government-issued paper money], the first act of frightened bank depositors was to withdraw these very legal tenders from their banks.[14]

Noyes believed that depositors withdrew their money from commercial banks, which had nothing to do with redeeming legal tenders with gold, because the paper money was "the only form of money they were in the habit of using" and because withdrawing from the local bank is what people did in the popular narratives about past times of financial distress. In other words, they were playing by a script that they had seen or heard about many times before. They were used to going to the commercial banks but not to the subtreasury offices where they could demand gold in exchange for notes.[15] So the initial panic of spring 1893 seems to have been the result of the high contagion of stories of bank failures. But this story is not enough to explain the extended depression of 1893 to 1899.

In reading accounts of the gold standard in the 1890s, we see an almost religious attachment to the idea among a large fraction of the US population, largely easterners and the educated. The support for the gold standard was based on the idea that contracts were written with the gold standard as an assumption. Therefore, monkeying with the gold standard could amount to reneging on a contract.

Beyond its business significance, gold has an enormous spiritual significance that economists usually do not consider. Wedding rings are made from it. The word *gold* appears 419 times in the King James version of the Bible. Paintings of saints depict a gold-colored nimbus radiating from their heads. In Christian tradition, these saints were often among the lowly and despised in society, but the nimbus reveals their true worth. In his 1860 poem to his readers "To You, Whoever You Are," Walt Whitman wanted to show that he values every one of his readers:

> But I paint myriads of heads, but paint no head without its
>   nimbus of gold-colored light
> From my hand, from the brain of every man and woman it
> streams, effulgently flowing forever.

The narrative in favor of the gold standard took on strong principle-based symbolic dimensions. In 1874, amidst controversy over the Coinage Act, which demonetized silver and put the United States squarely on a gold standard, US senator John P. Jones of Nevada stated (as recorded in *The Congressional Globe*):

> Gold is the articulation of commerce. It is the most potent agent of civilization. It is gold that has lifted the nation from barbarism. It has done more to organize society, to promote industry and insure its rewards, to inspire progress, to encourage science and the arts than gunpowder, steam or electricity.[16]

In the same debate in 1874, Senator William Morris Stewart, also of Nevada, a gold- and silver-mining state, said:

> You may fix up all the propositions you please, but the real thing is when you come down to it finally, I don't care how much you discuss it or how many resolutions you pass, they don't make any difference; you must come to the same conclusion that other people have, that gold is recognized as the universal standard of value.[17]

These statements, which had political goals, oversimplify history. Indeed, there has not been a gold standard through much of history. The "standard model"—a single gold coin representing legal tender, subsidiary coinage of base metal, and paper money with value based on the government's unqualified willingness to exchange it for legal tender—first came about during the eighteenth century in the United Kingdom. The standard model was not fully adopted in the United States until 1879.[18] Talk about the gold standard began in 1874, but it grew in a nice epidemic curve.

Cross of Gold

The narrative of those opposing the gold standard strongly emphasized unjust inequality. In his 1895 book *The American Plutocracy*, Milford Wriarson Howard wrote of America divided into two classes, the plutocracy and the "toilers of the nation": "The greatest struggle of all the ages is the one now going on between these two classes."[19] He saw the moral value attached to the gold standard as a canard promulgated by a conspiracy of established leaders to justify simple robbery of working people: "This is modern brigandage, upheld by the law and made respectable by society and the plutocratic churches."[20]

That side of the story was contagious in certain quarters, producing a constellation of stories that fed on that contagion, stories of arrogant and grasping business managers who tricked and manipulated innocent people. But it wasn't the only story. On the other side was a story about the stupid masses swept into a dangerous "populist" movement, a movement associated at the time with the Democratic Party but running contrary to that party's traditional values. Henry L. Davis of the California Optical Company said in 1896:

> The riff-raff is a very large proportion of the voters, and there is danger of their gaining control. Our hope lies in educating them to a greater intelligence, to change their views. Their success would destroy confidence, the unrest would be continued and business would continue to suffer.[21]

A constellation of narratives arose to reinforce the idea that Silverites are stupid and that economic disaster was imminent. Charles Merrill of Holbrook, Merrill, and Stetson, a retailer of kitchen appliances and plumbers' supplies, said in 1896:

> I have made this thing a deep study, since it is a matter which interests all citizens—merchants and workingmen alike. I believe that if Bryan is elected and the Democratic platform is carried out it will be the most disastrous thing that could happen to this country. Business is bad enough now, but it would be simply ruined in case of Democratic success, and all classes of people would feel the effect of it equally. If the principles of the Democratic platform were embodied into laws, I might as well go out of business. . . . It would be worse than a civil war. During the late war we managed to maintain our credit but we could not do so if the Democratic platform were put into effect.[22]

Nonetheless, the Democrats understood the power of gold and used it in their narratives. William Jennings Bryan's "Cross of Gold" speech at the July 1896 Democratic National Convention is considered one of the most inspiring American political speeches of all time. It interwove talk of the gold standard with talk of Christian morality. Even today, millions of people remember the concluding lines of the speech:

> Having behind us the commercial interests and the laboring interests and all the toiling masses, we shall answer their demands for a gold standard by saying to them, you shall not press down upon the brow of labor this crown of thorns. You shall not crucify mankind upon a cross of gold.[23]

As Bryan spoke these words, he stretched his arms out as if he were on a cross, to a cheering throng. The reaction was immediate, not only on the convention floor but also nationwide, sometimes to the point of near hysteria, as if a revolution were at hand and the working class would finally prevail.

Why are Bryan's concluding lines so powerful? Likely the working classes connected their economic suffering with the imagery of Jesus's suffering a brutal execution at the hands of the powerful Romans—one of the narratives that helped propel the Christian church through the centuries. Although Bryan spoke the words, he did not write the lines. As many newspapers later reported, a talk by US representative Samuel W. McCall in January 1896, reprinted in the *Congressional Record*, used almost the same words about a crown of thorns and a cross of gold. Bryan had attended McCall's talk, and he'd gauged the audience reaction to those lines. He was doing what great demagogues have always done, observing audiences, experimenting, and searching for something that will take.[24] As the *New York Times* commented:

> Full many a gem of purest ray serene the dark unfathomed files of The Congressional Record may bear. But until the gem has been mined, or rather, until the vein has been worked, by the patient toilers among the back numbers and then issued with an authoritative stamp, it remains useless to man.[25]

The authoritative stamp that Bryan, a celebrity, put on McCall's ruminations was exactly what this story needed to go viral. McCall's words were not a story until a presidential candidate said them in a public forum.

The effect of these conflicting narratives was to leave people unusually uncertain about the value of money and business activity in the near future. Louis Sloss of the Alaska Commercial Company was one of many businessmen who described in 1896 their unwillingness to sign contracts or commit resources at a time when they feared a major devaluation of the money supply and abrogation of contracts:

> Business is very dull, almost at a standstill. Capital is timid and confidence is shaken. Nobody wants to invest in any enterprise, no matter

how alluring the proposition, until this scare of unsound money is over. I know of an instance which illustrates to what extent business suffers from this unrest and agitation and the uncertainty of our financial basis. One of my relatives and a member of this firm contemplated erecting two magnificent houses to cost at least $50,000. The plans were drawn, the bids had been submitted and all was ready, except the signing of the contracts. The prospective builder refused to sign or undertake the building until after the election, when the financial question of the country will be settled. There are undoubtedly many similar instances, and they are the things that stagnate the course of trade.[26]

Among economists and other intellectuals, it was widely thought that moving to a bimetallic standard might double the price level, because the market price of gold meant the ratio should have been 30 to 1. According to classical economics and Gresham's Law ("Bad money drives out good"), silver would drive out gold, putting the United States onto a de facto silver standard.[27] To return to the houses that Sloss wrote about: bimetallism would mean, in effect, that each $50,000 house should sell for $100,000. With that expected sales price, the buyer would be eager to sign at $50,000, while the builder would want $100,000. But expectations were muddy because the politics of bimetallism were uncertain and unprecedented. It is easy to see how the buyer and the builder might find it difficult to come to an agreement.

An 1893 article from the *Chicago Daily Tribune* illustrates how dramatic bimetallism's effects might be:

> If we continue the purchase of silver or make the coinage free at the ratio of 16 to 1 or 20 to 1, we shall practically demonetize gold and drive it out of the country and sink to a silver basis. This would mean to every wage-worker the loss of nearly one-half the purchasing power of his wages—to every bank depositor the loss of nearly one-half the value of his deposit. Free coinage of silver in this country would be the most gigantic fraud and robbery ever perpetrated on a people.[28]

How, then, is it possible that William Jennings Bryan came close to being elected president of the United States and committing that "fraud and robbery"? Bryan's popularity came from a sequence of popular narratives about bimetallism that went viral because they seemed to justify, at least to some voters, that bimetallism was legitimate, or, more precisely, that bimetallism at a 16:1 or 20:1 ratio with gold was legit.

We mustn't assume that the typical American had a deep, or even any, understanding of the monetary system. In the 1890s, most people in the United States were fundamentally confused about bimetallism and the existing monometallic (gold) standard. The confusion came because there were both gold and silver coins in circulation that were freely accepted as of equivalent value even though the gold content of a gold coin was worth in the metals market about twice the market value of a silver dollar. Also, there were paper dollars, the silver certificates, that had inscribed on them, "one silver dollar" and "payable to the bearer on demand." Isn't that a silver standard? In fact, however, if one brought 100 silver dollars or $100 worth of silver certificates to a US subtreasury office, then they would freely give 100 gold dollar coins in exchange. They would do this since failing to do so would disrupt the free convertibility of the gold and silver dollars. The key point that many people did not understand is that the US Treasury would not give gold dollars in exchange for metallic silver. If they did *that*, then the US Treasury would see a vast amount of silver presented for conversion in gold. Anyone could then have done this repeatedly: buy metallic silver on the market, exchange it for gold at the subtreasury, using the gold to buy more silver on the metals market, and repeat the process every day, which would allow one eventually to amass a huge fortune. But the supply of US silver dollars was limited by the US government.

Practically no one paid any attention then to the type of currency they received or spent. In fact, most people didn't even know how to convert their cash into gold if they wanted to.

Why, then, did narratives of unsound money circulate so strongly? Why did the call for a bimetallic standard become so vehement in the last decade of the nineteenth century? One reason is obvious: the idea was promoted that debtors would see their burden cut in half if they could pay in silver at 16 to 1. That idea must have seemed like a form of salvation to them, and any story suggesting the possibility of such a change would certainly be appealing. Recall, too, that the bimetallism narrative often was framed as revenge for the "Crime of 1873" through which an act of Congress ended the bimetallic standard.

Put these together: Bimetallism was a proposal to make a seemingly subtle and clever change in the backing of the currency that most uninformed people wouldn't even grasp, like the cryptography behind Bitcoin that very few understand today. So bimetallism was a cool idea, or a "capital idea" as they would say in the 1890s. On top of that, bimetallism might compensate for perceived injustice, the source of much anger. The two together gave bimetallism intense contagion.

The Yellow Brick Road

The peculiar contagion of gold and silver narratives is exemplified by the appearance of a social epidemic surrounding a children's book by then-obscure author L. Frank Baum. *The Wonderful Wizard of Oz* was published in May 1900, at the start of the second presidential election campaign between McKinley and Bryan, when bimetallism was again an issue. The book is a children's story about a young girl named Dorothy, who, with her little dog Toto, is transported to the mysterious Land of Oz. The story is a sort of odyssey, as Dorothy, wearing magical silver slippers and pursued by a witch, follows a yellow brick road to meet the Wizard of Oz. Accompanying her are Toto and three newfound friends: a scarecrow, a tin man, and a lion. In the end, the Wizard of Oz is shown to be a weak little man who is a phony.

Some people read the book as a parable: the yellow brick road is the gold standard, the silver slippers are the Free Silver movement, the Wizard of Oz is President McKinley, and the Cowardly Lion is William Jennings Bryan. Oz itself is the abbreviation for ounce, the usual unit of measurement for gold or silver.

The book did not garner critical acclaim, but it was a best seller, and became contagious. By 1902 it was a "musical extravaganza" onstage. Its success went meteoric with the release of the movie *The Wizard of Oz*, starring Judy Garland, in 1939. (The film version changed the silver slippers into ruby slippers to take full advantage of the relatively new color film.) Interest was renewed again in 1972 with an animated *Journey Back to Oz* with the voice of Garland's daughter, Liza Minnelli. The best-selling 1995 novel *Wicked: The Life and Times of the Wicked Witch of the West* by Gregory Maguire led to a Broadway musical, *Wicked: The Untold Story of the Witches of Oz*, which has been running continuously on Broadway since 2003, as of 2018 the sixth-longest-running Broadway musical ever.[29] There are other examples too, including a 2013 movie *Oz: The Great and Powerful* and a future Oz TV series under development in 2019 by Legendary Entertainment. The success of the Oz constellation might be a vestige, barely recognizable, of a gold-silver narrative that went viral over a century ago.

The End of the Gold Standard

The Bryan proposal to lower the precious-metal value of the US dollar was an extremely emotional issue in the 1890s. It was so because of a narrative that economic historians Barry Eichengreen and Peter Temin call the "mentality of the gold standard" and the "rhetoric of morality and rectitude" that the gold standard represented.[30]

By the 1930s, with the help of John Maynard Keynes, the narrative had changed owing to the sense that unemployment was at catastrophic levels. An article by Mark Sullivan in the *Hartford Courant* in November 1933, around the time of the devaluation of the US dollar from 1/20.67 ounce of gold to 1/35 ounce of gold and the suspension of convertibility, explained how the new narrative about the gold standard in the 1930s differed from that of earlier years. The difference was partly a matter of new words. Sullivan quotes Talleyrand, Napoleon's chief diplomat, that "the business of statesmanship is to invent new terms for institutions which under their old names have become odious to the public."[31] The supporters of the devaluation apparently understood this. By the 1930s, the new word *devaluation* had massively replaced the negative-sounding *debasement* and *inflation. Devaluation* refers to a constructive action of enlightened governments, while *debasement* and *inflation* connote a moral failing.

Other countries had already suspended convertibility of currency to gold coin before the United States did so in a series of steps in 1933–34. On the advice of eminent economists such as Keynes, the United Kingdom had suspended the gold standard in 1931. The final end of the gold standard occurred in 1971 in the United States under President Richard Nixon, with the switch to a floating dollar. The public accepted the end of the gold standard, and economic dislocations were few.

The gold standard narrative is certainly not prominent today. President Trump tested the waters by advocating for it, but the public reaction was largely neutral. However, the fascination with narratives about money certainly lives on, as our running Bitcoin example illustrates. It seems likely that the future will bring new mutations of the money narratives, which will arouse a segment of the public, and which will affect future economic developments.

In these first three chapters describing perennial narratives, we have seen how narratives can affect confidence in others' confidence, the desire to engage in conspicuous consumption, and beliefs about monetary institutions. In the next two chapters we consider recurring narratives about the advance of dramatic new technologies that had the potential make human skills obsolete and that forced people to think about fundamentally changing standards of living and working.

Chapter 13

Labor-Saving Machines Replace Many Jobs

Concerns that inventions of new machines that are powered by water, wind, horse, or steam, or that use human power more efficiently, might replace workers and cause massive unemployment have an extremely long history. These perennial narratives are reappearing with modification in the twenty-first century and could become important problems damaging confidence, as they did in the past.

In this chapter, we consider a number of technology narratives, often using the terms *labor-saving machinery* or *technological unemployment*, that went epidemic and then faded (Figure 13.1), including the Luddite event in 1811, the Swing Riots in 1830, the depression scare of 1873–79, the depression of 1893–97, and the extended Great Depression of 1930–41.

From Ancient Times to the Swing Riots

Talk of automatic machinery replacing human muscle power goes back to the ancient world. The *Iliad*, Homer's eighth-century BCE epic, describes a driverless vehicle, the tripod of Hephaestus, that navigates on its own. Homer refers to the vehicle as "automatic."[1] Aristotle, around 350 BCE, raised the possibility of machines replacing humans:

> For if every instrument could accomplish its own work, obeying or anticipating the will of others, like the statues of Daedalus, or the tripods of Hephaestus, which, says the poet, "of their own accord

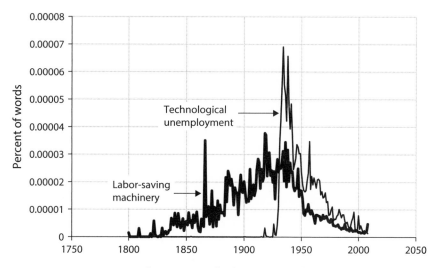

FIGURE 13.1. Frequency of Appearance of *Labor-Saving Machinery* and *Technological Unemployment* in Books, 1800–2008
Narratives of losing one's job to a machine have a long history, with mutations creating different epidemics. *Source*: Google Ngrams, no smoothing.

entered the assembly of the Gods"; if, in like manner, the shuttle would weave and the plectrum touch the lyre without a hand to guide them, chief workmen would not want servants, nor masters slaves.[2]

The statues of Daedalus were said to be able to walk or run, like modern-day robots. Hero of Alexandria in the first century BCE wrote a book, *Automata*, describing how to make a programmable tripod of Hephaestus, as well as a coin-operated vending machine and other remarkable devices. Water-powered mills began grinding grain into flour by the first century BCE. So the idea of machines replacing jobs was in place long before the start of the Common Era, along with fears of unemployment.

Searching eighteenth-century newspapers, we find evidence of great interest in how technological advances are changing the economy, but without much alarm about technology's effects on jobs. The term *industrial revolution* does not come up at all in a search of eighteenth-century newspapers—historians introduced that term later on. But by the nineteenth century, concerns about technology-based unemployment took center stage. The narrative was particularly contagious during economic depressions when many were unemployed.

The defining event was a protest in 1811 in the United Kingdom by a group that claimed a mythical man, Ludd, as their spiritual leader. The mutation that renewed the old narrative and made it so virulent in 1811 was a new kind of power loom that was eliminating weavers' jobs. The word *Luddite* continued to appear regularly in newspapers in following years and today remains a synonym for a person who resists technological progress.

In 1830, the Swing Riots in Britain were a response to the loss of farm jobs that occurred when the new mechanical thresher entered widespread use. The rioters' spiritual leader was the imaginary "Captain Swing," and again rioters destroyed the machinery. Certainly the decline in agricultural employment due to mechanization was widely noted. It was a frightening change for the people in the advanced countries undergoing the fastest mechanization. Living on and working the land was an ancient tradition, and now workers had to do something entirely new to earn their keep, and the new jobs probably required moving to crowded urban areas. In describing their fears, they did not use the words *technological unemployment, computers,* or *artificial intelligence,* but they did have their own terms for the phenomenon, including *labor-saving,* as in labor-saving appliances, labor-saving devices, labor-saving inventions, labor-saving machines, and labor-saving processes.

Depression Narratives of the 1870s

In the depression of 1873–79, a particularly strong depression in the United States and Europe, concern that labor-saving inventions were at least partly to blame for high unemployment took center stage in the popular consciousness, likely worsening the depression. In the United States, this depression is typically attributed to financial speculation leading to the banking panic of 1873, but the fear-inducing narrative about a long-term loss of jobs and job prospects due to labor-saving inventions may help to explain why the depression went global. Certainly the depression of the 1870s was accompanied by farmers' accelerated adoption of labor-saving machinery, along with more workers destroying machines and hired farm laborers threatening violence.[3] Underneath the violence was widespread concern about the outlook for the common laborer.

In the middle of that depression, the famous 1876 Centennial Exhibition in Philadelphia, a celebration of one hundred years of US independence, turned out to be more a testimony to labor-saving machinery than a remembrance of the American Revolution. The exhibition did display some of George Washington's personal items, but not much more about history. Instead, it presented examples of modern industry from twenty countries. The visitor's guide describes one of the most dramatic exhibits in the gigantic Machinery Hall:

> In the centre of this building is located a 1400 horse-power Corliss engine, capable of driving (if required) the entire shafting necessary to run all the machinery exhibits. This engine has a 40-inch cylinder with 120-inch stroke, and was constructed for this especial service. It will be run when required, but it is expected that the engines on exhibition will do a portion of the work of driving the shafting. The main lines of shafting are at a height of 18 feet above the floor, and extend almost the entire length of the building; countershafts extend from the aisles into the avenues at necessary points.[4]

The exhibition also gave reason for alarm regarding jobs in agriculture:

> Among the most extensive and interesting exhibits will be the agricultural machines in active operation, comprising everything used on the farm or plantation, in tillage, harvesting, or preparation for market; manufactured foods of all kinds, and all varieties of fish, with the improved appliances for fish-culture.[5]

Though impressive, the Centennial Exhibition's technological exhibits led to fears about jobs and about the horrible human effects of unemployment. The *Philadelphia Inquirer* in 1876 wrote:

> Want of employment leads to discouragement, hopelessness and despair. It overflows almshouses, charitable institutions, prison houses and penitentiaries. It degrades manhood. It ruins families. Misery,

crime and suicide follow in its wake. It supplies ready victims for the gallows. . . . To-day one man does what would have been the work of a hundred, fifty years ago. The steam-power of seven tons of coal is sufficient to make 33,000 miles of cotton thread in ten hours, while, without machinery, this would equal the hand labor of 70,000 women! Consumption does not keep pace with the production by machinery. Markets become glutted.[6]

As a result of these fears, in 1879 Senator George Frisbie Hoar of Massachusetts set up a committee to "enquire and report as to the extent to which labor-saving processes have entered into production and distribution of products to the displacement of manual labor."[7]

However, by 1879, a counternarrative had already developed: labor-saving processes will increase the number of jobs, not decrease them. One editorial in the *Daily American*, dismissing the worries about replacement of labor by machines, noted,

> The whole tendency of labor-saving processes is towards the elevation of the laboring classes, and if the change is accompanied by some hardship, so is every step in the progress of the human race.[8]

This editorial sounds very much like arguments made today to reassure workers regarding their fear of job loss, but the overall discussion of labor-saving machinery during the depression of the 1870s suggests that such arguments were not persuasive.

Henry George's 1879 best seller, *Progress and Poverty*, faced these issues head on. The book held that the immense technological advances of the time were creating inequality and increasing the number of people who lived in poverty. The book asserted:

> For, if labor-saving inventions went on until perfection was attained, and the necessity of labor in the production of wealth was entirely done away with, then everything that the earth could yield could be obtained without labor, and the margin of cultivation would be extended to zero. Wages would be nothing, and interest would be nothing, while rent would take everything. For the owners of land, being enabled without labor to obtain all the wealth that could be procured

from nature, there would be no use for either labor or capital, and no possible way in which either could compel any share of wealth produced. And no matter how small population might be, if any body [*sic*] but the land owners continued to exist, it would be at the whim or by the mercy of the land owners—they would be maintained either for the amusement of land owners, or, as paupers, by their bounty.[9]

At this time, the phrase *push a button* arose to indicate a mechanical actuation that completes an electrical circuit. For example, in 1879, the news described an invention in France that would allow a horse's rider to push a button to deliver an electrical shock to the horse, a system that could be used to discipline a misbehaving horse.[10]

Labor-Saving Inventions and the Depression of the 1890s

Such inventions only exacerbated fears of unemployment. An 1894 editorial in the *Los Angeles Times* blamed the severity of the 1890s depression on labor-saving inventions:

> There is no doubt that the introduction of labor-saving machinery and the consequent increase of production has had more than a little to do with the present depression in business. . . . It is true that during the past few years the increase in the invention and adoption of labor-saving machinery has been so great that the community has scarcely been able to keep up with it.[11]

The article then went on to list recent examples of labor-saving innovations:

> In the manufacture of hats machinery has multiplied the productive power of labor nearly nine times. Manifestly we can't wear nine times as many hats as formerly.
>
> By the adoption of improved processes the labor involved in the production of flour has been reduced 80 percent, yet we can each eat no more flour.[12]

That same year, the *San Francisco Chronicle* chimed in with an editorial about labor-saving machinery. The editorial was entitled "The Great Problem":

> The rich have grown richer and the poor have grown poorer. Side by side with the growth of enormous fortunes the hovels of the struggling laborers have become more dilapidated. . . . And to further emphasize the seriousness of these considerations it may be said that this problem must soon be solved or there will come a cataclysm which will destroy modern civilization.[13]

In 1895 a new dumbwaiter system was installed in US kitchens in multifloor buildings. The dumbwaiter had an array of buttons, one for each floor of the building. Press the number of the floor, and the elevator would automatically ascend to that floor and stop there, to return if a button was then pressed from that floor.

In "Stores Are Merely Labor-Saving Machines," an 1897 letter to the editor of the *Chicago Daily Tribune*, the letter writer adds to the growing list of labor-saving innovations. He refers to the department store movement, the movement to build gigantic stores that sold everything imaginable under one roof. The movement had started in 1838 with the Bon Marché department store in Paris. By the 1890s, department stores were an accelerating international epidemic, with continued expansions, glamorizing, and advertising over succeeding decades. The letter writer notes that even further expansion of department stores could yet "do away with so many people employed to distribute where one-third of them could do as well."[14]

In Chicago, Marshall Field & Co., established in 1881, built a seven-story department store in downtown Chicago in 1887. It then built an even more glamorous nine-story store in 1893, to coincide with the large crowds expected to attend the international fair, the 1893 Columbian Exposition. In 1897, Chicago's elevated street railway, called "The Loop," was completed, connecting many more people to Marshall Field's, marking an innovation in efficient retailing that may have prompted this letter writer.

Particularly striking during the 1893–99 depression was a spike in public anger about trusts, combinations of companies that fixed prices at a high level. In an 1899 talk in New York, John C. Chase, mayor of Haverhill, Massachusetts, and former trade unionist, said, "The trust is, in my opinion, a labor saving machine," apparently meaning that the modern trust adopts such machines in its inhuman effort to dispense with labor.[15]

Machines, Robots, and Future Technological Unemployment

The notion of a world without labor became more vivid with E. M. Forster, the English novelist famous for such classics as *A Room with a View*, *A Passage to India*, and *Howards End*. Forster's 1909 science fiction story "The Machine Stops" described a future in which machines do everything:

> Then she generated the light, and the sight of her room, flooded with radiance and studded with electric buttons, revived her. There were buttons and switches everywhere—buttons to call for food, for music, for clothing. There was the hot-bath button, by pressure of which a basin of (imitation) marble rose out of the floor, filled to the brim with a warm deodorized liquid. There was the cold-bath button. There was the button that produced literature, and there were of course the buttons by which she communicated with her friends. The room, though it contained nothing, was in touch with all that she cared for in the world.[16]

Forster's story ends when the machine unexpectedly malfunctions, bringing death and destruction to a world that has grown too dependent on it.

A little more than a decade later, during the 1920–21 depression, the labor-saving machine narrative mutated again, leading to the idea of robots. A 1921 Czech play, *R.U.R.: Rossum's Universal Robots*, by Karel Čapek, coined the word *robot*, from the Czech word for *worker*, to replace the earlier terms *labor-saving invention* and *automaton*. The play first appeared in English translation in New York in October 1922, to strong reviews. The play was not a big immediate success, and it was not made into a movie until 1948. But it started a narrative epidemic.

The play and its ideas went viral enough to cause the word *robot* to enter most of the world's languages. The play tells the story of the scientist Rossum, who invents a robot, and the businessman Domin, who starts manufacturing robots and who ultimately faces a revolt of the robots, who have developed minds of their own. The idea of a mechanical man who walks, talks, and fights might seem to be more inherently contagious than stories of push-button devices, but Čapek's initial story reached only a small base of people, and so the robot epidemic was gradual. Perhaps the recovery rate was also low because of the constant reminders of technological innovations in the following decades. Very few newspapers mentioned robots in the 1920s, but use of the term grew over the decades. To become more contagious, the idea of a robot may have needed further development by creative people.

Before 1930: Increasingly Vivid Narratives of Machines Replacing People

The story of an automated future was growing more and more vivid, but the stories still seemed mostly remote. The word *robot* did not become common in newspapers and books until the 1930s, though there were some dramatic exceptions, such as a traffic light, described in the *Los Angeles Times* in July 1929, that replaced policemen who had been directing traffic at an intersection in Medford, Massachusetts:

> The robot, which is made up in the usual form of red, yellow and green-light traffic tower, is operated automatically by the automobiles themselves as they pass over sensitive plates set in the street surface. No car is required to wait when there is no opposing traffic. When the car reaches an intersection and the way is clear the control from the plate in the pavement will give it a green light. If a car is waiting to cross an intersection and the opposing traffic is heavy the light permitting the car to cross will automatically set in its favor whenever there is a

gap and will immediately return in favor of the heavy traffic once the car is clear. The robot handles multiple numbers of machines on the same principle, the streets containing the greatest amount of traffic being emptied or partially emptied first, thus using a smooth even flow of traffic through all parts of the complicated square here.[17]

Reading this paragraph today, almost a century later, we may wonder why we still find ourselves occasionally waiting in our cars at a red light when there is no opposing traffic. There must have been problems with this particular robot, problems that still do not have an inexpensive and practical solution. But this 1929 story was beginning to have an impact.

A decade earlier, a new phrase had appeared in the English language to describe the effects of labor-saving inventions. The phrase was *technological unemployment*. This phrase appeared first in 1917, but it started its epidemic upswing in 1928. The count for *technological unemployment* skyrockets in the 1930s in Google Ngrams into an epidemic curve much like the Ebola epidemic curve in Figure 3.1. The *technological unemployment* curve peaked in 1933, the worst year of the Great Depression. A parallel epidemic occurred with the term *power age*, which is now mostly gone. The power age referred to the perception that activities once done by muscle are now done by powerful machines. During the 1870s depression, about half the US labor force worked in agriculture, and the labor-saving machinery of that decade tended to be agricultural equipment, pulled by horses. By 1880, only a fifth of the US labor force worked in agriculture, and the narratives focused instead on new fuel-powered and electronic machines, threatening the jobs to which agricultural people fled from the farms. (Less than 2% of the US workforce is in agriculture today.) Technological unemployment became a new and persistent worry.

It is curious that the narrative epidemic of technological unemployment began in 1928, a time of prosperity well before the Great Depression. Still, 1928 was a time of heightened concern about unemployment, which was blamed entirely on technological unemployment and not connected in public talk to any weakness in the US economy. Philip Snowden, former and future chancellor of the Exchequer in the United

Kingdom, wrote in the *New York Times* in 1928 that the United States, then the leader in developing labor-saving devices, had a unique problem of technological unemployment:

> But if other countries are compelled to follow America in specialization and in the displacement of human labor, the problem of unemployment in these countries will assume the feature of the existing unemployment problem in America.
>
> This, indeed, is the great problem which every industrial nation must face, namely, to avoid the present hardship which mechanical and scientific advance inflicts upon a mass of the wage-earning class. In other words, the problem is to free the human being from slavery to the iron man.[18]

By the 1920s, there was much talk about "efficiency experts" whose "time and motion studies" treated workers as if they were machines. The experts' goals were to eliminate any unnecessary motions, thereby saving time and labor cost. Like other narratives that took form in the late 1920s and went viral in the Great Depression of the 1930s, efficiency was associated with technological unemployment.

How did the epidemic of technological unemployment fears start? In March 1928, US senator Robert Wagner stated his belief that unemployment was much higher than recognized, and he asked the Department of Labor to do a study of unemployment. Later that month, the department delivered the study that produced the first official unemployment rates published by the US government. The study estimated that there were 1,874,030 unemployed people in the United States and 23,348,602 wage earners, implying an unemployment rate of 7.4%.[19] This high estimated unemployment rate came at a time of great prosperity, and it led people to question what would cause such high unemployment amidst abundance.

In April 1928, a month later, the *Baltimore Sun* ran an article referring to the theories of Sumner H. Slichter, who later became a prominent labor economist in the 1940s and 1950s. In the article, readers are told that Slichter noted several causes of unemployment but pointed out that "at present the most serious is technological unemployment." Specifically,

"The reason we have this unemployment is because we are eliminating jobs through labor-saving methods faster than we are creating them."[20] These words, alongside the new official reporting of unemployment statistics, created a contagion of the idea that a new era of technological unemployment had arrived, and the Luddites' fears were renewed. The earlier agricultural depression, with its associated fears of labor-saving machinery, began to look like a model for an industrial depression to follow.

Stuart Chase, who later coined the term the "New Deal" in the title of a 1932 book, published *Men and Machines* in May 1929, during a period of rapidly rising stock prices. The real, inflation-corrected, US stock market, as measured by the S&P Composite Index, rose a final 20% in the five months after the book's publication, before the infamous October 1929 crash. But concerns about rising unemployment were apparent even during the boom period. According to Chase, we were approaching the "zero hour of accelerating unemployment":[21]

> Machinery saves labour in a given process; one man replaces ten. A certain number of these men are needed to build and service a new machine, but some of them are permanently displaced. . . . If purchasing power has reached its limits of expansion because mechanization is progressing at an unheard of rate, only unemployment can result. In other words, from now on, the better able we are to produce, the worse we shall be off. Even if the accelerating factor has not arrived, the misery of normal unemployment continues unabated.
>   This is the economy of the madhouse.[22]

The book conveyed a sense that the beginnings of the catastrophe were imminent: "Accelerating unemployment . . . if not already here, may conceivably arrive at any moment."[23] This is significant: the narrative of out-of-control unemployment was already starting to go viral before there was any sign of the stock market crash of 1929.

During the days of sharp US stock market drops the week before the October 28–29, 1929, stock market crash, a nationally reported National Business Show was running in New York, October 21–26, in a convention center (since demolished) adjacent to Grand Central Station that many Wall Street people passed through to and from work. The show emphasized immense progress in robot technology in the office workplace. It was described after the show moved to Chicago in November thus:

> Exhibits in the national business show yesterday revealed that the business office of the future will be a factory in which machines will replace the human element, when the robot—the mechanical man—will be the principal office worker. . . .
>
> There were addressers, autographers, billers, calculators, cancelers, binders, coin changers, form printers, duplicators, envelope sealers and openers, folders, labelers, mail meters, pay roll machines, tabulators, transcribers, and other mechanical marvels. . . .
>
> A typewriting machine pounded out letters in forty different languages. A portable computing machine which could be carried by a traveling salesman was on exhibit.[24]

The 1930s: A New Form of Luddism Prevails

Soon after the 1929 stock market crash, by 1930, the crash itself was often attributed to the surplus of goods made possible by new technology:

> When the climax was reached in the last months of 1929 a period of adversity was inevitable because the people did not have enough money to buy the surplus goods which they had produced.[25]

As noted above, fear of robots was not strong in most of the 1920s, when the word *robot* was coined. The big wave of fear had to wait until the 1930s. Historian Amy Sue Bix (2000) offers a theory to explain why the 1920s were fearless: the kinds of innovations that received popular acclaim in the 1920s didn't obviously replace jobs. If asked to describe new technology, people in most of the 1920s would perhaps think first of the Model T Ford, whose sales had burgeoned to 1.5 million cars a year by the early part of the decade. Radio stations, which first appeared around 1920, provided an exciting new form of information and entertainment, but they did not obviously replace many existing jobs. More and more homes were getting wired for electricity, with many possibilities for new gadgets that required electricity. Labor unions in the 1920s tried to sound alarms about machines replacing jobs—and they sounded those alarms with increasing force as the 1920s proceeded—but the public didn't react much. The labor unions' alarms were not contagious because people had not heard many stories about inventions replacing jobs.

By the 1930s, Bix notes, the news had replaced stories of exciting new consumer products with stories of job-replacing innovations. Dial telephones replaced switchboard operators. Mammoth continuous-strip steel mills replaced steel workers. New loading equipment replaced coal workers. Breakfast cereal producers bought machines that automatically filled cereal boxes. Telegraphs became automatic. Armies of linotype machines in multiple cities allowed one central operator to set type for printing newspapers by remote control. New machines dug ditches. Airplanes had robot copilots. Concrete mixers laid and spread new roads. Tractors and reaper-thresher combines created a new agricultural revolution. Sound movies began to replace the orchestras that played at movie theaters. And of course the decade of the 1930s saw massive actual unemployment in the United States, with the unemployment rate reaching an estimated 25% in 1933.

It is difficult to know which came first, the chicken or the egg. Were all these stories of job-threatening innovations spurred by the exceptional pace of such innovations? Or did the stories reflect a change in the news media's interest in such innovations because of public concern about technological unemployment? The likely answer is "a little of both."

Underconsumption, Overproduction, and the Purchasing Power Theory of Wages

Unlike the technological unemployment narrative, the labor-saving machines narrative was strongly connected to an underconsumption or overproduction theory: the idea that people couldn't possibly consume all of the output produced by machines, with chronic unemployment the inevitable result. This theory's origins date back to the mercantilists in the 1600s, but popular use of the terms *underconsumption* and *overproduction* first appears in ProQuest and Google Ngrams around the time of the depression of the 1870s. Henry George described the overproduction theory in his 1879 book *Progress and Poverty*, during the depression of the 1870s, concluding it was an "absurdity."[26]

The theory of overproduction or underconsumption picked up steam in the 1920s. It was mentioned within days of the stock market crash of October 28–29 1929, in interpreting the crash.[27]

The real peak of these narratives was in the 1930s. Underconsumption narratives appeared five times as often in ProQuest News & Newspapers in the 1930s as compared with any other decade. The narrative has virtually disappeared from public discourse, and the topic now appears largely in articles about the history of economic thought. But it is worth considering why it had such a strong hold on the popular imagination during the Great Depression, why the narrative epidemic could recur, and the appropriate mutations or environmental changes that would increase contagion. Today, *underconsumption* sounds like a bland technical phrase, but it had considerable emotional charge during the Great Depression, as it symbolized a deep injustice and collective folly. At the time, it was mostly a popular theory, not an academic theory.

Despite the obvious reality that deflation necessitates wage cuts, an opposing "purchasing power theory of wages" became popular in the 1930s. This theory said that "excessive competition" had forced down wages to such an unfair low level that workers could not afford to consume the output. Thus the Depression could be cured by forcing all employers to raise wages. The economist Gustav Cassel in 1935 called these ideas "charlatan teachings" that "have recently taken a conspicuous place in popular discussion of social economy as well as in political agitation."[28]

But the public did not dismiss such charlatan teachings. In the 1932 presidential campaign, Franklin Roosevelt ran against incumbent Herbert Hoover, who had been unsuccessful with deficit spending to restore the economy. Roosevelt gave a speech in which he articulated the already-popular theory of underconsumption. His masterstroke was putting it in the form of a story inspired by Lewis Carroll's famous children's book

Alice's Adventures in Wonderland. In that book, a bright and inquisitive little girl named Alice meets many strange creatures that talk in nonsense and self-contradictions. Roosevelt's version of this story replaced his opponent Hoover with the Jabberwock, a speaker of nonsense:

> A puzzled, somewhat skeptical Alice asked the Republican leadership some simple questions.
>
> Will not the printing and selling of more stocks and bonds, the building of new plants and the increase of efficiency produce more goods than we can buy? No, shouted the Jabberwock, the more we produce the more we can buy.
>
> What if we produce a surplus? Oh, we can sell it to foreign consumers.
>
> How can the foreigners buy it? Why we will lend them the money.
>
> Of course, these foreigners will pay us back by sending us their goods? Oh, not at all, says Humpty Dumpty. We sit on a high wall of a Hawley-Smoot Tariff.
>
> How will the foreigners pay off these loans? That is easy. Did you ever hear of a moratorium?[29]

Roosevelt used this story to point out the folly of Republican policy, with its attempts at economic stimulus, but his campaign did not suggest any solution to the problem. Instead, in his "Alice" speech, he proposed to install investor protections. He also promised not to make the overly optimistic statements that President Hoover had, and he noted that he would not encourage more stock market speculation. Elected in 1932, Roosevelt signed in 1933 the National Industrial Recovery Act, creating the National Recovery Administration, which attempted to enforce fair wages. We discuss the outcome of this experiment in chapter 17.

On the face of it, underconsumption seemed to explain the high unemployment of the Great Depression, but academic economists never seriously embraced the theory, which had never been soundly explained. Often the theory was presented as an adjunct to technological unemployment: underconsumption suddenly became a problem in the 1930s because of the nation's newfound ability to produce more than it needed. But other accounts of underconsumption make no mention of technology. For example, in 1934, Chester C. Davis, administrator of the Agricultural Adjustment Administration, described how his agency was "redistributing purchasing power to the masses" so as to help them spend more and thereby deal with underconsumption. He explained why he thought technological unemployment had suddenly become so important:

> Why does our nation seem to need this supplement to the market mechanism, after 158 years? You have the answer if you will go back into history and consider the gradual concentration of business into great corporations, of farmers into marketing cooperatives, of labor into collective bargaining associations. These have reduced the area of the free market and have increased the power of individuals controlling these concentrations.[30]

In other words, Davis saw the concentration of business as amplifying the problem of technological unemployment.

The massive unemployment set off serious social problems. For example, in the United States it caused the forced deportation (then called *repatriation*) of a million workers of Mexican origin. The goal was to free up jobs for "real" Americans.[31] The popular narrative supported these deportations, and there was little public protest. Newspaper reports showed photos of happy Mexican Americans waving goodbye at the train station on their way back to their original home to help the Mexican nation.

The dial telephone also played an important part in narratives about unemployment and the associated underconsumption. The older telephone, which had no dial, required a caller to pick up the phone receiver and connect to a telephone operator, who said, "Number please?" The caller had to tell the operator to make the connection. The dial telephone, which required no contact with an operator, was not invented during the Great Depression; in fact, the first patent for a dial telephone dates to 1892. The transition from the non-dial telephone to the dial telephone took many decades. However, during the Great Depression, there rose a narrative focus on the loss of telephone operators' jobs, and the transition to dial telephones was troubled by moral qualms that by adopting the dial phone one was complicit in destroying a job. For example, the US Senate in Washington, DC, replaced its non-dial phones with dial telephones in 1930, the first year of the Great Depression. Three weeks after their installation, Senator Carter Glass introduced a resolution to have them torn out and replaced with the older phones. Noting that operators' jobs would be lost, he expressed true moral indignation against the new phones:

> I ask unanimous consent to take from the table Senate resolution 74 directing the sergeant at arms to have these abominable dial telephones taken out on the Senate side . . . I object to being transformed into one of the employes of the telephone company without compensation.[32]

His resolution passed, and the dial phones were removed. It is hard to imagine that such a resolution would have passed if the nation had not been experiencing high unemployment. This story fed a contagious economic narrative that helped augment the atmosphere of fear associated with the contraction in aggregate demand during the Great Depression.

The loss of jobs to robots (that is, automation) became a major explanation of the Great Depression, and, hence, a perceived major cause of it. An article in the *Los Angeles Times* in 1931 was one of many that explained this idea:

> Whenever a man is replaced by a machine a consumer is lost; for the man is deprived of the means of paying for what he consumes. The greater the number of Robots employed, the less is the demand for what they produce for men cannot consume what they cannot pay for.
>
> This condition is inescapable. No political panaceas can alleviate this purely human distress.[33]

Even if the man hasn't lost his job yet, he will consume less owing to the prospect or possibility of losing his job. The US presidential candidate who lost to Herbert Hoover in 1928, Al Smith, wrote in the *Boston Globe* in 1931:

> We know now that much unemployment can be directly traced to the growing use of machinery intended to replace man power. . . . The

human psychology of it is simple and understandable to everybody. A man who is not sure of his job will not spend his money. He will rather hoard it and it is difficult to blame him for so doing as against the day of want.[34]

Albert Einstein, the world's most celebrated physicist, believed this narrative in 1933, at the very bottom of the Great Depression, saying the Great Depression was the result of technical progress:

> According to my conviction it cannot be doubted that the severe economic depression is to be traced back for the most part to internal economic causes; the improvement in the apparatus of production through technical invention and organization has decreased the need for human labor, and thereby caused the elimination of a part of labor from the economic circuit, and thereby caused a progressive decrease in the purchasing power of the consumers.[35]

By that time, people had begun to label labor-saving inventions as "robots," even if there were no mechanical men to be seen. One article in the *Los Angeles Times* in early 1931, about a year into the Great Depression, said that robots then were already the "equivalent of 80 million hand-workers in the United States alone," while the male labor force was only 40 million.[36]

A Word Is Born: *Technocracy*

By 1932, the bottom of the stock market decline, the US stock market had lost over 80% of its 1929 value in less than three years. We have to ask: Why did people value the market at such a low level? A big part of the answer was a narrative that went viral: modern industry could now produce more goods than people would ever want to buy, leading to an inevitable and persistent surplus.

This new narrative became associated with two new words that left ordinary people out of the economic picture: *technocracy*, a society that is commanded by technicians, and *technocrat*, one of these now-powerful technicians. These words weren't new to the 1930s. They had been used occasionally in the 1920s to refer to a theory that the government should be run by scientists who could assure world peace. Thorstein Veblen had written a book, *The Engineers and the Price System*, during the previous depression, 1920–21, that envisioned a world run by a "soviet of technicians." But the words took on a new meaning with the explosion and duration of unemployment by the early 1930s. A Columbia University group with revolutionary pretensions called itself "Technocracy." Led by engineer Howard Scott, it was composed of scientists from across the United States. By 1933, Scott was as famous as movie stars of that day.

The technocracy movement created its own jargon and proposed a new kind of money, electric dollars. As explained in a 1933 book, *The A B C of Technocracy*, written under the supervision of Howard Scott and published under the pseudonym Frank Arkright, electric dollars represented units of energy. The name Arkright appears to have been inspired by the life of Richard Arkwright, the inventor of the spinning frame, a water-powered spinning machine that displaced jobs and resulted in antimachinery riots in 1779. The Arkright book and its ideas went viral, particularly with the idea that modern science would soon transform the economy, even eliminating money as we know it. The story has many similarities to the Bitcoin story, right down to the use of a pseudonym, Frank Arkright, like Satoshi Nakamoto.

According to *The A B C of Technocracy*, the US economy had an installed capacity of a billion horsepower. It also stated that one horsepower equals ten men's labor and that running the machinery for the ten laborers required only two eight-hour days a week. Thus the book gave credence to the idea that the rising unemployment of the Great Depression was the beginning of an alarming new permanent condition. The conclusions reached by one report were disturbing indeed:

> The situation we are now facing is entirely without precedent in human history, because up to less than 100 years ago the human body was the most efficient machine for energy conversion on earth. The advent of technology makes all findings based on human labor irrelevant because the rate of energy conversion of the modern machine is many thousand times that of man. Up to the year 1890 the movement of the

social body in terms of energy production might be compared to the progress of an ox cart. Since 1890, by comparison, it has attained the speed of an aeroplane and is constantly accelerating.[37]

The idea that the world would now belong to the technicians who designed and ran the machinery was naturally frightening to those who did not deem themselves capable of becoming scientists—that is, most people—and it must have resulted in a hesitation to spend, invest, and hire, which worsened and prolonged the Great Depression.

The *New York Times* in 1933 described some amazement at the strength of the technocracy fad:

> The sensational nature of the technocratic case caused a mass movement that was almost hysterical. Many of those who read Scott's prediction that there would be 20,000,000 unemployed within two years unless something were done along lines set forth by him, vague as these were, looked to the imminent collapse of our industrial and economic system. Business contracts were even held up because of the fear engendered by technocracy.[38]

The technological unemployment narrative appears to have saturated the population by sometime in the 1930s. Afterward, references to it did not need to use the phrase *technological unemployment* because everyone understood the concept. For example, a long 1936 *New York Times* article deploring the tragic effects of long-term unemployment on the human spirit and on family relations did not refer to any theory of unemployment beyond stating that the unemployed people described "have been superannuated less by age than by newly invented machines."[39]

The Narrative Turns to World War II

Though the technological unemployment narrative faded after 1935 (as revealed by Google Ngrams), it did not go away completely. Instead, it continued to exert some influence in the run-up to World War II, until new narrative constellations about the war became contagious.

Many historians point to massive unemployment in Germany to explain the accession to power of the Nazi Party and Adolf Hitler in the election of 1933, the worst year of the Depression. But rarely mentioned today is the fact that a Nazi Party official promised that year to make it illegal in Germany to replace men with machines.[40]

Charlie Chaplin's 1936 movie *Modern Times* marks a narrative that was so powerful that it remains in collective memory today. The movie contained a hilarious scene[41] in which a company adopts a new technology that allows it to streamline the workers' lunch hour by having robotic hands feed the employee his lunch. When Charlie Chaplin is fed his lunch, the machine malfunctions and speeds up to such a rate that it creates a terrible mess. Not coincidentally, the story was contagious at a time of high concern with labor-saving machines.

Searching for mention of robots in the news during World War II, we find some examples. Early in the war a Yale scientist, Clark Hull, was working toward eventually developing armies of robot soldiers.[42] But the account of his efforts sounded far-off and far-fetched. The "robot bombs" and "robot planes" used by the Nazis later in the war were reported to be ineffective.[43] Instead, the news was filled with narratives of great heroism by real human soldiers.

To go viral again, the labor-saving machines narrative needed a new twist after World War II, a twist that could seem to reinforce the newly rediscovered appreciation of human intelligence, and, ultimately, of the human brain. The narrative turned to the new "electronic brains"—that is, computers. The phrase *electronic brain* has a beautiful epidemic curve peaking around 1960, which is indicative of a constellation of machines narratives then that we explore in the next chapter.

Chapter 14

Automation and Artificial Intelligence Replace Almost All Jobs

The narrative of technological unemployment as causing a problem for the indefinite future did not disappear with World War II. In fact, it repeatedly mutated and took on a different sort of virulence, often associated with the terms *automation* or *artificial intelligence*, as Figure 14.1 shows. There were at least four post–World War II narratives about artificial intelligence, peaking, respectively, in the 1960s, 1980s and 1990s, and 2010s. As of this writing, the artificial intelligence narrative of the 2010s looks to be heading even higher.

Each time, the narrative suggested that the world was only just now reaching a frightening major turning point when the machines take over. Because Rossum's Universal Robots (described in the preceding chapter) could talk, they represented a form of artificial intelligence, but there was no story regarding how such intelligence might be achieved. The robots were like the talking animals in children's stories. But the idea of automation and artificial intelligence repeatedly gained new epidemic proportions as the ideas took on new concreteness.

Fears of automation were likely associated with fears of an impending depression. A year-end 1945 *Fortune* public opinion survey conducted by Elmo Roper asked the US public:

Do you expect we probably will have a widespread depression within ten years or so after the war is over or do you think we probably will be able to avoid it?

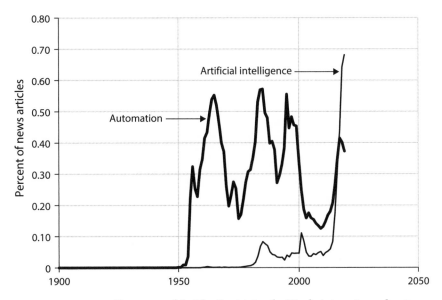

FIGURE 14.1. Percentage of Articles Containing the Words *Automation* and *Artificial Intelligence* in News and Newspapers, 1900–2019
The automation and artificial intelligence narratives have recurred several times, with variations in the story each time. *Source*: Author's calculations from ProQuest News & Newspapers.

The results:

Per cent

Have a depression.. 48.9

Probably avoid it 40.9

Don't know ....10.2[1]

So about half the US population "expected" a depression after World War II. Most likely, their answers reflected their still-strong memories of the Great Depression and post–World War I narratives that we have discussed rather than any clear forecast.

Fortunately, these expectations were wrong; there was no recurrence of depression. Yes, there was a fatalistic fear of a returned depression, but the angry narratives of the recent depressions had faded, including the angry narrative of profiteering that contributed to the post–World War I depression. That narrative just did not restart. In addition, the idea that prices should fall to 1913 levels no longer seemed realistic. The end of World War II was also a distraction that temporarily reduced attention to technological unemployment. Instead, a constellation of economic narratives after World War II began to suggest that it was all right to spend money now that the war was over. (We discuss profiteering and the expectation of lower prices in more detail in chapter 17.)

Among these narratives was the story of the many expensive vacations that Americans were taking right after the war, which offset the frugality narratives of the Great Depression. "The greatest surge in travel in the history of the Americas" was on, and 1946, the year after the end of the war, was dubbed the "Victory Vacation Year."[2] Even a couple years before the war ended, travel agents and vacation resorts in the Western hemisphere had begun promoting the extravagant traveling victory vacation as a way for consumers to spend some of the wealth they'd socked away in government war bonds.

When the vacations actually happened in 1946, the vacationers duly recorded them on new Ready-Mounts (35mm color slides) and stored those slides in a new case that complemented last year's Christmas present, a slide projector.[3] Also, consumers used home movie cameras (which had been mostly unavailable until the years after World War I) to create extensive travelogues. These slides and movies of the vacation, as well as of the new baby (that's me, born in 1946), were shown to friends and relatives back home, spreading the sense of happy times and a patriotic feeling about the shared experience of spending extravagance.

People also began to see their new optimism bolstered by their perceptions of others' optimism. The baby boom, first noted in 1946, marked a big difference from the end of World War I, which was followed by a deadly influenza epidemic instead of a baby boom. The new optimistic stories after 1948 became a self-fulfilling prophecy, a term coined in 1948 by Robert K. Merton. A 1950 newspaper article asserted:

> With such an optimistic consensus as has developed at this year end, the forecasting itself can have the effect of helping to promote high activity.[4]

But the question we must ask is this: Why did so many people in 1945, at the end of World War II, expect a postwar depression? And why did the intermittent recessions in the 1950s and 1960s interrupt the overall optimism? The answer must lie in good part in a Great Depression narrative that still had intermittent power in the postwar period: the same technological unemployment narrative but in mutated form.

The Automation Recession Narrative

The same "zero hour" for the labor-saving machinery economic narrative that appeared in 1929 reappeared late in the second half of the twentieth century, but in mutated forms.

The term *singularity* began to be used after Einstein published his general theory of relativity in 1915. The word denotes a situation in which some terms in the equations became infinite, and it was used to describe the astronomical phenomenon of what came to be called the black hole: a "singularity in space-time." But later the glamorous term *singularity* came to be defined as the time when machines are finally smarter than people in all dimensions.

Such mutations in the economic narrative shifted attention from the muscles being replaced by electrical machines to the brain being replaced by artificial intelligence. The basic technological unemployment narrative is the same, but the examples have a wider scope. First, giant locomotives and electrical power equipment economized on human muscle power. After the mutation, the narrative focused on computers replacing human thinking. This mutation refreshed the narrative.

The term *automation* differs from *labor-saving* in that *automation* suggests no one is near the production process, except perhaps for a technician in a distant control room who presses buttons to start the process. Automation was then described starting in the 1950s not just as machines, but rather as "machines running machines."[5] It suggests a process that runs by itself with no one even paying attention.

Around 1955, the word *automation* suddenly launched into an epidemic. There was considerable public worry that jobs would be replaced.

Notably, electronic data processing began to run whole business operations. The new narrative was of a more wholesale replacement of human involvement in production than in the technological unemployment narrative of the 1920s and 1930s. The year 1956 saw the first "automation strike . . . fomented by fear of the push-button age."[6] Stories were told of an unimaginable leap forward in automation. This from 1956:

> Visitors to an Eastern manufacturing plant stared in amazement recently as they viewed a new type of factory in operation. While they watched, enormous sheets of steel were fed into a conveyor system. Then the steel traveled along 27 miles of conveyors, was worked over by 2,613 machines and tools, and emerged as brand-new refrigerators—packed, crated, and ready for shipment.
>
> What amazed the visitors was the fact that no human hands touched the machines or steel while two gleaming-white refrigerators were being produced each minute.
>
> They were seeing automation in action.[7]

Automation was also seen as foretelling the imminent end of labor unions, which had stood up for workers' rights in the past. It is impossible for labor to organize the machines.[8]

Surveys of workers show a sudden shift around the time of the 1957–58 and 1960–61 twin recessions. Public opinion analyst Samuel Lubell, famous for his success at predicting election outcomes, wrote during the slow economy in 1959 between the two recessions:

> In the Spring of 1958 when I conducted a survey of how the public felt about the recession relatively few persons talked of automation, even as a cause of unemployment.
>
> Currently every third or fourth worker one interviews is likely to cite some case history, drawn from personal experience, of workers displaced by machinery.
>
> Often the tag line to these stories is the rueful comment, "Some men will never get back their jobs." Some say, "It's only the beginning."

The same gloomy prediction, "in two years a machine will be doing my job," was voiced by an elevator operator on Staten Island, an accountant in Cleveland, a switchman in Youngstown and a railway clerk in Detroit.[9]

The twin recessions, the severest since the Great Depression, may have been caused by reduced spending attendant on public fears about the future amidst the automation scare. The 1957–58 recession was then dubbed "the automation recession."[10]

The 1957 motion picture *The Desk Set*,[11] starring legendary actors Katharine Hepburn and Spencer Tracy, is set at a company about to acquire an IBM mainframe computer called Emerac. Hepburn plays the role of Bunny Watson, a super-knowledgeable reference librarian for the company. Tracy plays Richard Sumner, a computer engineer who is working on plans for the new computer. In the course of the movie Richard falls in love with Bunny and proposes to her, amidst tensions that he is working to destroy her livelihood. The movie notes that an earlier computer has already automated payroll and eliminated many jobs in the payroll department. Tension builds in the film when Emerac malfunctions and sends out pink slips firing not only Bunny but also everyone in the whole company. The mistake is later corrected.

The film shows the computer taking over some of the functions of the company's reference library by answering questions typed on a console. For example, Emerac is asked, "What is the total weight of the earth?" Emerac answers, "With or without people?" (I recently asked the voice-activated Google Assistant, OK Google, the same question, and it answered matter-of-factly: 5.972×10^{24} kg.) Bunny then asks Emerac, "Should Bunny Watson marry Richard Sumner?" Emerac answers, "No," perhaps suggesting that the computer was romantically involved with her creator. (I asked OK Google the same question, and it responded by directing me to a 2011 *New Yorker* article, "Is I-Pad the New Emerac?")

Extensive concern about the dangers of automation continued into the 1960s. In 1962, the Center for the Study of Democratic Institutions issued a report on cybernation (a word that started to take off as a synonym for automation but fizzled after the 1960s). The report concluded that:

> Cybernation presages changes in the social system so vast and so different from those with which we have traditionally wrestled that it will challenge to their roots our current perceptions about the viability of our way of life. If our democratic system has a chance to survive at all, we shall need far more understanding of the consequences of cybernation.[12]

In 1963, labor leader George Meany tied a demand for a thirty-five-hour workweek to concerns about automation. In 1964, US president Lyndon Johnson signed into law during the presidential election a bill creating the National Commission on Technology, Automation, and Economic Progress. The commission's report[13] was delayed until 1966, when the scare was mostly over.

The 1957–66 automation scare seemed to dissipate rather quickly, and for a number of years. In 1965, the *Wall Street Journal* ran a story by Alfred L. Malabre, Jr., titled "Automation Alarm Is Proving False." The article noted that people in 1965 seemed just to have forgotten about automation. Malabre found it interesting that automation wasn't even mentioned at a major United Auto Workers labor convention in 1965. The article concluded, "The degree to which this pessimism pervaded the leading councils of labor, the campus, the Government and even management was, to say the least, extensive."[14]

Star Wars Stories

The automation scare came roaring back to life in the 1980s. We've seen that narratives often recur in mutated forms. Sometimes the new narratives make use of new words, but sometimes an old word comes back. Figure 14.1 shows an enormous spike of *automation* in the early 1980s. Use of the word *robot*, coined in the 1920s, also shows an enormous spike in the early 1980s. One possible explanation: the contagiousness of robot stories was encouraged by the phenomenal success of home computer manufacturers Atari and Apple, which led people to believe that technical progress was accelerating. A company called The Robot Store began manufacturing and selling humanoid robots in 1983. These robots looked like people, and the company's president predicted that between 10% and 20% of American households would own robots within two years.[15] In fact, these devices were practically useless, and the product line flopped.

Consistent with this observed spike of the word *robot* around 1980, we observe a sequence of very successful robot movies around the same time, showing how contagion can change over time and bring new viral stories with it. George Lucas's *Star Wars* trilogy, a sequence of three movies that appeared between 1977 and 1983, featured the world's most famous (to date) robots, R2-D2 and C-3PO. The American television cartoon feature *The Transformers*, which focused on the adventures of gigantic robots with the ability to transform themselves into vehicles and weaponry, aired from 1984 to 1987. Both of these series were accompanied by massive sales of children's toy figures. *Blade Runner* (1982) and *The Terminator* (1984) were other successful robot films of that time.

Of course, robots had appeared in movies long before the 1970s, and they continue to do so today. In fact, robots in movies precede even the word *robot* coined by Čapek, the Czech playwright, which started to go viral in 1922. Notably, film robots (or automatons) were called *dummies* (as in *The Dummy*, 1917) or *mechanical men* (as in *L'uomo meccanico*, 1921). Many more robots appeared in movies after 1922, notably Futura in Fritz Lang's 1927 *Metropolis*, which called a robot a Machinen-Mensch, or Machine-Man. However, most films featuring robots were B-grade horror movies with wildly implausible and juvenile themes, analogous to space-aliens-destroy-the-world films that have had relatively little impact on public thinking.[16] These mostly silly movies probably did not have much impact on economic activity except where they may have lent emotional color to fears about the automated future.

Another spike in successful robot movies preceded the automation scare, 1957–64. Film robots of that era included Ro-Man in *The Robot Monster* (1953), Tobor (robot spelled backward) in *Tobor the Great* (1954), Chani in *Devil Girl from Mars* (1954), the Venusian Robots in *Target Earth* (1954), Robby the Robot in *Forbidden Planet* (1956), Kronos in *Kronos: Destroyer of the Universe* (1957), the Colossus in *The Colossus of New York* (1957), and M.O.G.U.E.R.A. in *The Mysterians* (1957).

A significantly mutated form of the automation narrative came back with the twin recessions of 1980 and 1981–82, when the unemployment rate reached into the double digits. The unemployment encouraged the thought that automation might again be responsible for the loss of jobs, an idea that must have fed back into reduced aggregate demand and even higher unemployment. In 1982, Andrew Pollack of the *New York Times* discerned a "new automation," exemplified by the now very visible beginnings of automation of offices:

> Those affected so far by office automation have been mainly secretaries—who are still in short supply—and other clerical workers, whose tasks can be speeded by replacing typewriters with electronic word processors and filing cabinets with computerized storage systems. But new office automation systems are affecting management as well, because they give managers the ability to call up information out of the company computers and analyze it themselves, a function that once required a staff of subordinates and middle-level management.[17]

Once again, a narrative went viral that we had reached a singularity that made all past experience with labor-saving machinery irrelevant, that might just now be producing a huge army of unemployed. "I don't see where we can run to this time,"[18] Pollack says. This viral narrative may well be the real reason that these twin 1980s recessions were so damaging.

As Figure 14.1 shows, there was a third spike in *automation* around 1995. Once again, narratives surged that a singularity was at hand that made all past experience with labor-saving devices obsolete. In 1995 at the very beginning of the Internet boom, there was a narrative about the advent of computer networks:

> Most economists think the ill-effects of automation are transitory, but a growing minority of their colleagues and many technologists think the current surge of technological change differs from anything seen before, for two reasons.
>
> First, tractors put only farmers out of work, and machine-tool automation only factory workers, but smart devices and computer networks can invade almost every job category involving computing, communicating or simple deduction. They can fill out and check mortgage-loan forms and transfer phone calls, and even allow cows to milk themselves without human assistance at microcontrolled milkers. No technology has ever been as protean, so unrestrained by physical limits, so capable of cutting huge swaths through unrelated industries such as banking, power utilities, insurance and telecommunications.
>
> Second, the power of devices and networks run by microprocessors and software is increasing at a rate never seen before, roughly doubling in performance every 18 months or so. Among other things, this trend leads to unprecedented reductions in the cost of microchip-based technology, allowing it to be used much more widely and rapidly.[19]

This new twist in the fear-of-automation narrative around 1995 did not immediately produce a recession. Most people were not moved to curtail spending because of it, and the world economy boomed. The dominant narratives in the 1990s seemed to be focused on the wonderful business opportunities brought by the coming new millennium. The automation narratives trailed off again in the 2000s, with the distractions of the dot-com boom, the real estate boom, and the world financial crisis of 2007–9. But the automation narratives are still with us, described by new catchphrases.

The Dot-Com or Millennium Boom
in the Stock Markets

The Internet, first available to the public around 1994, launched a narrative of the amazing power of computers. Before the turn of the century, the Internet Age appeared to coincide with the coming of the new millennium in 2000, much talked about when it was an imminent future event. Dot-com stocks were the primary beneficiaries in the years leading up to 2000. During the market expansion from 1974 to 2000, stock prices rose more than twentyfold.[20] The period marked the biggest stock market expansion in US history, and descriptions of the expansion suggested exactly that. (This story is beginning to be forgotten now, as it is being replaced by the narratives surrounding the mere threefold expansion following the world financial crisis of 2007–9, which are more contagious at the time of this writing.)

Discussions of the stock market expansion in the last quarter of the twentieth century did not stress fears of being replaced by machines as a motive to buy dot-com stocks. Why? People tend to speak more of the opportunity provided by investments in information-age inventions than of their personal feelings of inadequacy in the face of technological progress. But it appears that such feelings may have driven people's motivation to be part of the dot-com phenomenon as the stockholders of tech companies.

Fears of the Singularity Gain Strength
after the 2007–9 World Financial Crisis

According to Google Trends, the latest wave of automation/technology-based fears began around 2016 and continues unabated at the time of this writing.

How do we explain this recent surge in automation fears? To answer this question, we must consider the advent of Apple's Siri, the iPhone app launched in 2011 that uses automatic speech recognition (ASR) and natural language understanding (NLU) to (attempt to) answer the questions you've asked it.[21] To many, Siri's ability to talk, understand,

and provide information looked like the advent of that long-awaited singularity when machines become as smart as, or smarter than, people. That same year, IBM presented its talking computer Watson as a competitor on the television quiz show *Jeopardy*, and Watson beat the human champions who played against it. Now these are followed by Amazon Echo's Alexa, Google's "OK Google," and other variations and improvements such as Alibaba's Tmall Genie, LingLong's DingDong, and Yandex's Alice. These inventions were amazing; the time prophesied by *Star Wars*, *The Transformers*, and *The Jetsons* seemed finally to have arrived.

Apple bought Siri from its creator, SRI (Stanford Research Institute) International, which had developed it with government funding from the US Defense Advanced Research Projects Agency (DARPA) between 2003 and 2008. These earlier projects did not go viral; 2011 was the year in which, suddenly, people had a device in their pockets to talk with and to show off to almost-unbelieving admirers. Siri, and its soon-to-follow competitors, seemed to start the process of eliminating the need for human conversation. We might imagine preferring Siri as a conversation partner to a human, because Siri's information is much more comprehensive and reliable. The idea that humans were ultimately replaceable was a scary thought, and it is easy to imagine a resulting loss of humanity's collective self-esteem.

Around the same time, other inventions also attracted great public attention, notably driverless cars, which, despite some worries about safety, are predicted to replace many jobs. Though very few of us had actually seen a driverless car, we all knew that prototypes were already on our highways. These autonomous vehicles can already do things that we assumed were not programmable, like slowing down when the car senses children running around near the street. Human common sense can be reduced to a list of signals to a driverless car, which means that human common sense can be replaced.

Recent talk has stressed machine learning, in which computers are designed to learn for themselves rather than be programmed using human intelligence. A Google Trends search for Web searches for *machine learning* reveals a strong uptrend since 2012, with the Google search index more than quadrupling between 2004 and 2019. The narrative is propelled by recent stories. The highly successful chess computer program AlphaZero is described as working purely through machine learning—that is, without use of any human ideas about how to play chess. This narrative describes a tabula rasa program that plays vast numbers of chess games against itself, given no more information than the rules of the game, and learns from its mistakes.[22] In some ways, the machine learning narrative is more troubling than computers running human-generated programs. Historian Yuval Noah Harari describes this narrative as leading toward a "growing fear of irrelevance" of ourselves and worries about falling into a "new useless class."[23] If they grow into a sizable epidemic, such existential fears certainly have the potential to affect economic confidence and thus the economy.

Of Jobs and Steve Jobs

The story of Steve Jobs is a remarkable narrative that ties into the fear of job loss to mechanization. His story was told in many books that appeared around the time of the 2007–9 world financial crisis. Particularly notable was the 2011 book *Steve Jobs* by Walter Isaacson, which sold 379,000 copies in its first week on sale,[24] became a number-one *New York Times* best seller, and has over 6,500 reviews on Amazon with an average ranking of 4.5 stars out of 5. Isaacson specializes in biographies of geniuses (including Albert Einstein, Benjamin Franklin, and Elon Musk), but his book about Jobs was by far his most successful. Why did his book about Jobs go viral? Part of the answer was the timing: the publisher wisely dropped it into the market just weeks after Jobs's death, allowing the news media narrative of his death to interact with the talk about the book.

Interestingly, the Steve Jobs narrative makes it appear that Jobs, a real human being with quirks that no one would program into a robot, was totally indispensable for Apple Computer. Jobs's own story therefore became appealing to people who worry about their own possible obsolescence. He founded the company but was forced out, the story goes, because drab managerial types could not tolerate his eccentricities.

When Apple began to fail, he was called back and breathed new life into the company, which is today one of the most successful in the world. The Steve Jobs narrative is a fantasy for people who don't quite fit into conventional society, as many people with inflated egos but modest success in life may see themselves.

Economic Consequences of the Narratives about Labor-Saving and Intelligent Machines

We have traced much popular attention over two centuries to narratives about machines that will replace jobs. These narratives certainly affected, and continue to affect, people's willingness to spend on consumption and investments, as well as their eagerness to engage in entrepreneurship and speculation. The economic hardships created by a temporary recession or depression are mistaken for the job-destroying effects of the machines, which creates pessimistic economic responses as self-fulfilling prophecies.

Henry George's solution to the labor-saving machines problem—and the defining proposal of his book *Progress and Poverty*, published during the depression of the 1870s—was to impose a single tax on land, to tax away the labor-saving inventions' benefits to landowners. George's proposal assumed that the sole purpose of the new machines was to work the land, which might be the case if the economy is purely agricultural. This proposal is analogous to the much-discussed "robot tax" that appeared in public discussion during the Great Depression and has reappeared in the last few years. Taxing companies that use robots, the argument goes, will provide revenue to help the government deal with the unemployment consequences of robotics.[25]

George proposed to distribute part of the tax proceeds as a "public benefit."[26] His proposal is essentially the same universal basic income proposal that is talked about so often today:

> In this all would share equally—the weak with the strong, young children and decrepit old men, the maimed, the halt, and the blind, as well as the vigorous.[27]

Other incarnations of the universal basic income proposal were offered by Lady Juliet Rhys-Williams in a 1943 book, *Something to Look Forward To; a Suggestion for a New Social Contract*, and by Robert Theobald in a 1963 book, *Free Men and Free Markets*. The Basic Income European Network (BIEN), an advocacy group, was founded in 1986 and later renamed the Basic Income Earth Network. The narrative that the future will be jobless for many or most people has helped sustain support for a progressive income tax and for an earned income tax credit, though in modern times it has not succeeded in producing a universal basic income in any country.

The mutating technology/unemployment narrative tends to attract public attention when a new story creates the impression that the problems generated by technological unemployment are reaching a crisis point. A celebrated 1932 book by Charles Whiting Baker, *Pathways Back to Prosperity*, sought to explain why the public's concerns about labor-saving machines replacing jobs were wrong until *now*, the early 1930s. Baker emphasized the newness: "The widespread use of automatic machinery and economic transportation is only a thing of yesterday." He stressed that unemployment was a new long-term problem, not going away, ever. Thus Baker advocated something like a universal basic income for all:

> We have got to face the fact that there is one way, and only one, whereby we can make a market for our huge surplus of goods. . . . Increase the purchasing power of the 95 percent of the families of the United States who have only tiny incomes, and they will at once buy more.[28]

Recent years have seen a renewal of this great wave of concern as new redistribution proposals are put forth and discussed. Notably, Google Trends shows a huge uptrend in searches for the term *universal basic income* starting in 2012. ProQuest News & Newspapers reveals essentially the same uptrend. Public attention to inequality has burgeoned, with much attention to the increased share of income by the top 1% or the top one-tenth of 1%. Thomas Piketty's *Capital in the Twenty-First Century*, which described this trend, was a best seller that generated intense discussion. The term "digital divide" has gone viral, describing a sort of inequality related to access to digital computers.

No one can predict the effects of labor-saving and intelligent machines on livelihoods and work in the future, but the narratives themselves have the potential to drive amplified economic booms and recessions, as well as public policy. The narratives at the time of this writing about artificial intelligence and machine learning replacing human intelligence and disintermediating skilled workers lend an instability to expenditure and entrepreneurship patterns. These and other economic narratives may show up in the speculative markets, notably the real estate markets and the stock markets, to which we turn in the next two chapters.

Chapter 15

Real Estate Booms and Busts

Real estate narratives—stories about the often tantalizing increase in value of land, housing, locations, and homes—are among the most prominent economic narratives. A strong example of their influence was the talk leading up to the Great Recession of 2007–9, which disrupted economies all over the world. The 2007–9 Great Recession was fueled by stories communicating inflated ideas of the value of housing.

Real estate narratives have a long history. From ancient times through the Industrial Revolution, real estate talk centered on the price of farms. In modern times, attention shifted first to stories about empty city property suitable for building homes, then to actual homes in metropolitan areas. These shifts are just mutations of a perennial narrative about the scarcity of land and its value.

We might think that the real estate boom and bust narratives would be part of the same constellation of panic or confidence narratives that we discussed in chapter 10. But real estate confidence is very different from confidence in the state of the economy, because people tend to view the two as very different things.[1] Real estate is regarded as a personal asset, which one might have useful opinions about, while the economy is seen as the product of myriad forces. As this chapter reveals, however, real estate is also a socially informed asset, with its value depending on how people compare themselves to their neighbors and beyond.

Speculation and Land Bubbles

For much of history before the twentieth century, popular narratives celebrated land speculation (either of farmland or of vacant city lots in burgeoning or promised cities) rather than home speculation or stock speculation. The following land speculator's narrative, full of human interest, was written in 1840, after the collapse of a US land bubble that had started in 1837:

> His father left him a fine farm free of incumbrance [*sic*]; but speculation became rife, fortunes were made in a twinkling, and D. fancied "one thing could be done as well as another." So he sold his farm, and bought wild lands in the prairies, and corner lots in lithographed cities; and began to dream of wealth worthy of "golden Ind." Work he could not: it had suddenly become degrading. Who could think of tilling or being contented with a hundred acres of land, when thousands of acres in the broad west were waiting for occupants or owners. D. was not the man to do it, and he operated to the extent of his means. At last the land bubble broke; lithographed cities were discovered to be mere bogs; and prairie farms, though the basis of exhaustless wealth, worthless unless rendered productive by labor.[2]

Here we see a perennial narrative of a foolish speculator buying unseen land in a bog, a narrative resurrected in the 1920s Florida land bubble, where a swamp replaced the bog.

The Florida Land Boom of the 1920s

There appears to have been little talk of single-family homes as speculative investments until the second half of the twentieth century. A ProQuest News & Newspapers search for *home price* reveals virtually no reference to the term in a speculative context until then. In fact, the phrase *home price* had a different meaning in past centuries, as in the home price of wheat, meaning the price of wheat in the domestic market as opposed to in foreign markets. When the phrase *home price* with its modern meaning was mentioned, it typically appeared in a story about a rich person spending a lot on a home, as a sign of wealth, but with no sense that the home was appreciating in value. For example, an 1889 article in the *St. Louis Post-Dispatch* exclaimed:

> Senator Sawyer, who has for years lived in the house which Jefferson Davis occupied when he was here in Washington, has stopped paying rent and has built a MAGNIFICENT BROWN STONE MANSION within a stone's throw of Dupont Circle. It is worth at least $80,000 and Sawyer's millions will keep it in fine style. There are fine houses all around it.[3]

There is reference to value as if it is unchanging, but no sense that the senator might be making a speculative investment.

A ProQuest News & Newspapers search for *price per acre* shows a very different pattern. The phrase peaked at the beginning of the twentieth century, when it tended to refer to farmland as a speculative investment. The *Florida land boom* of the mid-1920s gets many hits, but the phrase *home price* almost never appears in those articles. During that widely discussed boom, an associated narrative emphasized that the proliferation of motorcars was making Florida land more easily accessible to northerners looking for winter homes. Given the rise of the automobile, it is not surprising that the allegedly beautiful sites that were selling out so fast were empty lots for building new homes. However, by 1926, the Florida land boom had become a widely covered scandal, reported nationally. Newspapers printed stories that promoters were selling undeveloped land divided into home-size parcels, sight unseen, to northerners who would never in their lifetimes see a town built near their isolated homes. These stories rendered such sales of undeveloped land disreputable.

Land has always been only a small part of a home's value. One estimate, by Morris A. Davis and Jonathan Heathcote, suggests that the land's value averaged only 36% of the home's total value from 1976 to 2006.[4] We do not seem to have data on the percentage of land value in home value for earlier years, except in assessments for property tax, but presumably when the US population was more rural, the percentage was even lower.[5]

In contrast to the Florida narrative, with its emphasis on land, investments in homes historically have been viewed as investments in structures that depreciate through weather and use, that require constant maintenance, and that go out of style and get torn down eventually. We can understand why land itself with no structure on it, at least during the Florida boom, seemed a more exciting investment.

Traditionally, prices of new homes were widely thought to be dominated by construction costs.[6] In fact, it used to be conventional wisdom that home prices closely tracked construction costs. A 1956 National Bureau of Economic Research study noted some short-term movements in US home prices not explained by construction costs between 1890 and 1934, but it concluded:

> With regard to long-term movements, however, the construction cost index conforms closely to the price index, corrected for depreciation. . . . For long-term analysis the margin of error involved in using the cost index as an approximation of a price index cannot be great.[7]

Because their construction cost index included only the prices of wages and materials, but not the price of land, the NBER analysts were viewing investments in homes as nothing more than holdings of depreciating structures, wearing out through time and tending to go out of fashion. With such a narrative, housing bubbles have little chance of getting started.

Enter News, Numbers, and Narratives

Newspapers eventually discovered that readers were interested in stories about home prices in congested inner cities, where the price of land is more connected with home prices because land is much more expensive there. These stories may have gained contagion, leading people to think that their properties far from city centers shared some of the same speculative trend to higher prices.

Another factor adding to contagion was the development of home price indexes for existing homes. The first mention of median prices of existing homes in ProQuest News & Newspapers appeared in 1957 in an Associated Press story referring to a US Senate housing subcommittee report, which concluded that low-income families were being priced out of the housing market partly because of the increased price of land.[8] Newspapers began publishing the National Association of Realtors median price of existing homes in 1974. The Case-Shiller home price index (now the S&P/CoreLogic/Case-Shiller home price index), originally created by Karl Case and me, began to appear in 1991. These indexes allowed news media to regularly announce large movements, thereby lending concreteness to stories about movements in home prices.

Before the advent of statistical measures of home prices, it was relatively hard for the news media to come up with regular stories about speculative movements in that market. Before stock price indexes became popular in the 1930s, writers for the news media were able to quote numbers illustrating big movements in the stock market, usually by quoting the one-day change in a few major stocks, which tended to move in the same direction on big move days. They lost no opportunity to write such stories. But it is not so easy to write about regular news in home prices. A house is almost never resold in just one day. Rather, most house sales occur over long intervals of time, years or even decades. Even changes in the median home price month to month were not newsworthy, because one-month changes could be erratic when different kinds of houses sold from one month to the next. The repeat-sales that Karl Case and I first started publishing in 1991 marked the beginning of a new era, one in which month-to-month changes in aggregate home prices could be inferred from highly disparate houses, each of which sells very infrequently. The indexes led to a futures market for single-family homes at the Chicago Mercantile Exchange that has the potential to reveal day-to-day changes in home prices, though activity on that market mostly dried up after the 2007–9 world financial crisis.

A common assumption in accounts of speculative bubbles in stock and housing markets has been that investors are extrapolating recently successful investment performance, expecting the price increases to continue and thereby eagerly forcing prices up even higher. This process repeats again and again in what may be called a vicious circle or feedback loop. However, narratives matter as well. If we listen to the narrative at such times, investors may seem a lot less calculating than they sometimes appear. Instead, the price increase appears to be driven less by future expectations than by the proliferation of stories and talk that draw attention to the asset that is booming, thereby fueling the bubble.

House Lust and Social Comparison

It is vital to listen to what people are saying during a rapid expansion of prices, to understand just what is animating them. In his 2007 book *House Lust: America's Obsession with Our Homes*, Daniel McGinn sees psychological factors at work. The book was published at the beginning of the world financial crisis of 2007–9, right on the heels of the most rapid increase in house prices during the record-setting US national home-price boom of 1997–2006.

McGinn chose the title *House Lust* because he believed that the emotions displayed in conversations during the boom market just before the 2007–9 world financial crisis and recession reflected a true lust: a lust for status, and maybe power, that sometimes drives people to ruinous actions. During this lustful period in US history, people relished stories of higher and higher home prices, and of the people who benefited from them, a bit too much to be rational.

McGinn defines and explains some impulses and motives that are not in most economists' vocabulary. He describes the "high-five effect," which is the "vicarious thrill of cheering on a winner." Most people enjoy seeing their own recent success with their real estate investments, and, so long as they are invested and not envious, they enjoy their friends' and neighbors' successes too. They are happy to share in their neighbors' victories, giving each other "high fives," the celebratory gesture that athletes give to each other after a big win, in a moment of seeming joy.

McGinn also describes an "Our House *Is* Our Retirement Plan" effect: the story that a house is necessary to successful living because it is a recognizable store of value. The narrative in the recent boom fueled house prices by implying the dictum that one should "stretch" or "reach" to buy a house. Buy the biggest house you can afford, because you will be glad that you did so when the house's value goes even higher. McGinn also describes an "It's So Easy to Peek in the Window" effect, caused by the Internet and social media, that allows housing voyeurs to get information about neighbors' and celebrities' home specs and prices as never before. McGinn observed:

> And in many neighborhoods, if you'd judged the nation's interests by its backyard barbecue conversation—settings where subjects like war, death, and politics are risky conversational gambits—a lot of people find homes to be more compelling than any geopolitical struggle.[9]

The Internet adds force to the narrative in today's housing market. People are naturally curious about the amount of money that others make in their jobs, but they can't find such information on the Internet (except in the case of government jobs), and it is considered vulgar to ask. However, McGinn notes, websites such as Zillow and Trulia, both founded in 2006, allow you to find out right away (for free) what anyone's house is worth.

Social psychologist Leon Festinger described a "social comparison process"[10] as a human universal. People everywhere compare themselves with others of similar social rank, paying much less attention to those who are either far above them or far below them on the social ladder. They want a big house so that they can look like a member of the successful crowd that they see regularly. They stretch when they pick the size of their house because they know the narrative that others are stretching. McGinn's "You Are Where You Live" effect confirms the power of the real estate comparison narrative. As of the early 2000s, when the housing boom was at its peak, there was no other comparable success measure that one could just look up on the Internet.

The History of Homeownership Promotion

In another element of the real estate narrative, history shows a succession of advertising promotions for homeownership itself, not just for the sale of individual properties. In the United States, these promotions began with the "Own Your Own Home" campaign, launched by real estate agent Hill Ferguson in 1914 under the auspices of the National Association of Real Estate Boards (precursor to the National Association of Realtors today). The Own Your Own Home campaign, like the savings and loan association movement that preceded it in the United States and the even earlier building society movement in the United Kingdom and Europe, was an attempt to help people build up some savings.

The Own Your Own Home campaign set out to change the widespread presumptions that borrowing is disreputable or dangerous, that people should never go into debt, and that they should accumulate savings to buy a home with an all-cash offer. In a 1919 display ad placed in numerous newspapers, the campaign stated:

> Don't let the idea of a mortgage scare you. Some people think they're a disgrace. But if they're good enough for the biggest corporations and the United States government they needn't frighten you.[11]

Note that the purchase of a home was not cast as part of the more modern concept of "saving for retirement." A ProQuest News & Newspapers search reveals that retirement was virtually never mentioned in advertisements for homes until the 1920s, and the idea did not take off until the 1940s. In the earliest part of the twentieth century, people didn't think of saving for retirement, as they in many cases did not think they would live long enough to spend much time in retirement. Rather, savings were put aside as a safety measure against illness or other misfortune.

The savings bank movement and the Own Your Own Home movement were a moderate success. The homeownership rate rose, and even today low-income people in the United States and other advanced countries tend to have some savings, mostly in the form of home equity.

Next came the Better Homes in America movement launched in 1922 by Marie Meloney, the editor of a woman's magazine, the *Delineator*. Real estate groups continued to pay for advertisements advocating homeownership throughout the rest of the twentieth century. In the years leading up to the 2007–9 world financial crisis, the National Association of Realtors placed numerous ads including the words "Now is a good time to buy or sell a home." After the financial crisis, it launched a new campaign, "Home Ownership Matters." These campaigns emphasized that homeowners tend to be successful and patriotic people. The campaigns not only helped support patriotic ideals but also created a clearer rationale for buying a home, thus enhancing the narrative.

The desire to impress the neighbors is part of the social fabric, but it comes with a psychic cost. Marketing people often find themselves in the position of trying to help people get past their guilt about showing off, which may involve buying land or ostentatious houses. Before the Great Depression, many ads touted purchasing undeveloped land as investments. For example, a large newspaper display ad from 1900 with the headline "A Princely Spot Is Orangewood" offered five-acre plots near Phoenix, Arizona, that could be used either to build a home or to plant an orange grove. The ad featured recent auction prices of oranges from the region as well as text about how fashionable the area was.[12] In response to complaints about such marketing, the individual states of the United States put into place over the period 1911–33 a series of "blue sky laws" prohibiting the selling of "speculative schemes which have no more basis than so many feet of 'blue sky.'"[13]

Mr. Ponzi and His Other Scheme

In 1926, Charles Ponzi, who is said to have invented the Ponzi scheme in 1920, was released from jail. (Also called a *circulation scheme*, a Ponzi scheme is a fraudulent investment fund that pays off early investors with money raised from later investors, creating a false impression of profits to lure yet more victims.) Soon thereafter, Ponzi went back to jail for violating Florida's blue-sky law. During the Florida land boom, he began selling small parcels of Florida land to investors without disclosing that the land was under water, in a swamp.[14] Ponzi's name, and the story of unwitting investors buying land in a swamp, went viral with his circulation scheme, and it remains famous even today, but his name is not so attached to the swamp narrative.

In reaction to such abuses, the United States imposed stronger laws on the subdivision of land for sale to small investors. State laws defined land sales as securities sales, even if the sale was a simple transfer of property, thus making the sales subject to securities regulation. In addition, regulation of the sale of land was reinforced to prevent such abuses.[15] As a result of the scandals and the ensuing legislation, people began to think that investing in undeveloped land based on prospective future use was irresponsible and disreputable, that land needed to generate real income before reputable brokers could sell it. Thus advertising turned to offering investments in going businesses and owner-occupied homes, which continued to feed the real estate narrative.

As people continued to think of home purchases as investments in land rather than reproducible and depreciating structures, the potential for home price bubbles persisted. At the same time, real estate investment remained the simplest of speculative investments. Most people never find the time to get involved in a risky specialized investment, but many people own a home at some point in their lives, and so they typically do not have to work hard to learn about real estate as a speculative investment.

City Land and Stories

Changing narratives do not explain some major swings in home prices afflicting certain cities and sparing others. There is evidence that booms in some cities but not others can be explained merely in terms of supply constraints. For example, undeveloped land available for building is more available in some cities than in others, and there could be a time when a city that once had plenty of land for building finds that its land has been exhausted.

When a city's population is expanding, even if the city is not particularly attractive and has no particularly favorable narratives, there will be *some* people who want to move there. For example, there are always potential immigrants, often from poor or unstable countries, seeking a foothold in advanced countries, and they may choose cities based on arbitrary factors such as proximity to their home country or the existence of a subpopulation speaking their language in the destination city. If land is readily available for purchase there, new houses will be built, and the immigrants' demand for housing may have minimal impact on prices. But if such land has run out, these immigrants will have to outbid others for existing houses, and home prices will rise. In that case, only the wealthier buyers will be able to live in that city. People who are already living in the city but have no special interest in it have an incentive to sell their houses and take the proceeds to another more affordable house in another city. The supply constraint thus results in higher prices and a wealthier population in that city.[16]

Supply constraints also help to explain the differences in home prices across cities and through time. Economist Albert Saiz used satellite data to construct estimates of the amount of available land around major US cities. He found that cities that are boxed in by bodies of water or steep-sloped terrain (which is less suitable for building) tend to have higher home prices.[17] There is also a tendency for people who already own homes in a city to try to block further construction of homes, particularly of affordable housing. They have an economic incentive to do so, for limiting housing supply boosts home prices. The effects of such an incentive may differ across cities. But beyond such conventional economic explanations, there is also evidence that changing narratives play a role in housing booms.

The years leading up to the 2007–9 world financial crisis saw record-breaking increases in home prices in some countries, notably the United States. According to the S&P/CoreLogic/Case-Shiller home price index, home prices in the United States nationwide rose 75% in real (Consumer-Price-Index inflation-corrected) terms between 1997 and 2005, while the Consumer Price Index for Rent of Primary Residence, corrected for Consumer-Price-Index inflation, rose only 8%. This boom in home prices far exceeded anything that could be attributed to increased unmet demand for housing services. This housing boom in the United States and other countries was a major factor in the world financial crisis of 2007–9. Home prices fell dramatically and defaults on mortgage payments surged, plunging mortgage lenders into serious financial difficulty, a crisis that then spread to the rest of the financial sector and the world. By 2012, in the aftermath of the crisis, real US home prices fell to a level that was only 12% above that of 1997, before taking off again in a new boom that continues as of 2019, though the boom shows some signs of weakening and actual price declines in some US cities. US real home prices were up again 35% from 2012 to 2018, while real rents were up only 13%.

The Rise of Flipping

In trying to understand the housing boom leading up to the Great Recession of 2007–9, looking at the usual suspects, such as interest rates, tax rates, or personal income, is not very helpful. Instead we should examine the shift to a more speculative narrative in which people thought of their homes more as speculative investments in land—a narrative that lenders welcomed.

The seeds of the world financial crisis were planted decades earlier. A new meaning for the word *flipper* went viral in the United States in the 1970s and 1980s. At that time, a flipper was a sharp operator who buys a speculative investment and then "flips" it, selling less than a year after purchase, to make a quick profit. The term then became popular during a different kind of housing boom: a condominium conversion boom. Owing to the very high inflation at that time, the tax advantages of homeownership over renting significantly increased, because one could deduct the interest paid on a mortgage (very high because of the inflation) from gross income but could not deduct rent paid. Though high nominal mortgage interest rates deterred some from homeownership, for many others the expected appreciation in home value due to inflation offset the high interest rate.[18]

To meet the demand, developers began buying apartment buildings, evicting the renters of the individual apartments and selling the apartment units as condominiums. Renters, some of whom had lived in their apartment for many years, complained bitterly. To assuage them, the operators offered renters a contract to buy, at the time of conversion, their own apartment at a discounted price. The contract allowed them to resell the contract to people interested in buying it. Many renters chose to "flip" their contract to speculators, who in turn flipped the contract again. Flippers attracted a lot of public attention, and many admired them as entrepreneurs who saw the opportunity quickly enough to cash in on it.

By the 1990s, the term *flipper* was commonly used to describe people who bought shares in initial public offerings (IPOs) and resold them quickly. People often described the flippers in admiring terms, as people who understood that IPOs were typically underpriced on the offering date. When the share price popped up soon after the IPO, the flippers made a quick profit. A famous 1991 article by Jay Ritter showed that the initial IPO price pop tended to be followed by weak performance over subsequent years, so the optimal strategy appeared to be buying IPOs at the offering and then flipping them.

Then, in the early 2000s, during the enormous home price boom, the term *flipper* became attached to people who bought homes, fixed them up a little or a lot, and sold them quickly. Once again admiring stories were told of their successes. While most people were not enthusiastic enough to actually flip houses, they may have imagined that they were engaged in "long-term flipping" simply by purchasing a primary residence as a long-term investment. Thus they engaged the speculation narrative.

Mansions and Modesty

Exuberant real estate narratives did not stop with the 2007–9 world financial crisis. In October 2012, the *Wall Street Journal* launched a new section in the newspaper. Called "Mansion,"[19] it was a response to a section in the *Financial Times* titled "How to Spend It," but "Mansion" focused on housing. Notably, 2012 was the same year that home prices in the United States started rising sharply again after the 2007–9 world financial crisis. It was also the year in which the police finally cleared the Occupy Wall Street movement, which had started a year earlier, from Zuccotti Park in New York City. The movement had been attracting much attention to the slogan "We Are the 99%," referring to the majority of the population who cannot live extravagantly, in a public assertion that these people matter.

The "Mansion" section seemed to scream that the top 1% mattered even more. It featured lush photo spreads of lavish homes and their pretentious occupants in a tone of gushing admiration. But the section also reported on anxieties about ostentation and about fears of public disgust at such extravagance. For example, a 2017 article in "Mansion," "Tech CEOs: Lie Low or Live Large?" discussed in detail the quandary that heads of technology companies face in deciding how big a home to buy. The article made clear that the choice of a home is part of a delicate balancing of forces in a career-optimization strategy. Hence "Bay Area real-estate agents say their clients are becoming reluctant to buy fancy homes, for fear of spooking investors wary of distracted or high-living founders."[20]

The Donald Trump Narrative and Urban Investors

Offsetting the modesty narrative was the Donald Trump narrative, which led to his election as president of the United States in 2016. The Trump narrative proved that many people are not at all "spooked" by those who "live large." On the contrary, as Trump openly states in his various coauthored books, it pays to let people know that one is rich. Here the housing boom narrative is co-epidemic with the conspicuous consumption narrative discussed in chapter 11. Vast numbers of people have taken interest in the Trump narrative, which encourages the idea that the display of wealth is an amazing, affirmative career strategy—and the polar opposite of Occupy Wall Street idealism. The Trump narrative epidemic contributed to the upward turn in home prices in the United States starting after 2012.

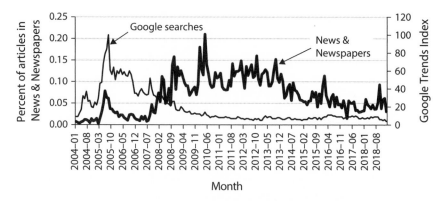

FIGURE 15.1. "Housing Bubble" Google Search Queries, 2004–19
Internet searches shot up just before the world financial crisis of 2007–9; news media
response was partly delayed. *Source*: Google Trends.

In 2005, during the housing boom that preceded the 2007–9 financial
crisis, Web searches for *housing bubble* increased dramatically. The
curve, shown in Figure 15.1, resembles the Ebola epidemic curve (see
Figure 3.1). Something very contagious was clearly happening then.
Some tried to capitalize on the boom, not just by flipping homes but
also by promoting the boom. Enthusiasm for real estate investments
infected a significant portion of the population. In 2005, Trump founded
a business school, Trump University, saying, "I can turn anyone into a
successful real estate investor, including you." Trump's timing was bad—
the *Economist* ran a cover story on June 18, 2005, about the prospect of
a bursting housing bubble.[21] Trump University went out of business
right after the world financial crisis, in 2010, amidst cries of fraud and
deceit.

The Housing Market Today

Since 2003, I have collaborated with my late colleague Karl Case and
now with Anne Kinsella Thompson to conduct an annual survey of recent homebuyers in four US cities. The survey is conducted under the
auspices of the Yale School of Management. One of our questions is "In
deciding to buy your property, did you think of the purchase as an

investment? 1. Not at all; 2. In part; 3. It was a major consideration." The percentage who answered, "It was a major consideration" peaked at 49% in 2004. The percentage choosing that answer fell to 32% in 2010, just after the world financial crisis, and by 2016 it had risen to 42%.

The survey also asks about the general level of conversation about the housing market. Specifically, we ask, "In conversations with friends and associates over the last few months, conditions in the housing market were discussed (circle the one which best applies): 1. Frequently; 2. Sometimes; 3. Seldom; 4. Never." The percentage who answered, "Frequently" reached a high of 43% in 2005, the end of the 1997–2005 boom. By 2012, the percentage choosing "Frequently" reached a bottom of 28%, significantly below the number during the boom periods. The likely interpretation is that the contagion rate for housing market narratives had decreased, and that indeed the decline in home prices could be viewed as the end of an epidemic.

What were the narratives in spring 2005? ProQuest finds 246 stories with the phrase *housing bubble* from March to May 2005, before the cover stories in the *Economist* and other places. One of these stories included a statement from Alan Greenspan, who said that he saw "a little froth" and an "unsustainable underlying pattern" in the housing market. This statement was then compared with his "irrational exuberance" speech about the stock market in December 1996. Between 2005 and 2007, there were 169 news stories with both *Greenspan* and *froth* in them. It was a colorful, quotable story featuring an economic celebrity. It contributed to a colorful, and quotable, constellation of narratives, among them narratives with the power to change economic behavior and to bring on a financial crisis.

We turn in the next chapter from real estate to the stock market, to chart another powerful narrative, putting the stock market at the center of the economy. We shall see some similarities between the narratives, both contagious in the context of perceived grand opportunities for investors, both intertwined with stories of investor greed and foolishness.

Chapter 16

Stock Market Bubbles

Narratives about stock market bubbles are stories about excitement and risk taking, and about relatively wealthy people who buy and sell securities. Like the real estate narratives discussed in chapter 15, narratives about stock market bubbles are driven by social comparison. Because they are fueled by psychology, and because stock prices are related to general confidence, these narratives also relate to the confidence and panic narratives presented in chapter 10.[1] But the stock market is different from the economy as a whole. Therefore, the narratives that create and sustain stock market bubbles constitute another distinct constellation of narratives, with a different path and different sources of contagion.

A Narrative Is Born

The word *crash* quickly became associated with the one-day stock market drop on October 28, 1929, along with a slightly smaller drop on October 29, 1929, and it became inextricably linked to the Great Depression that followed. *Crash* calls to mind reckless or drunk drivers or race cars pushing their limits, and the crash narrative typically implies that a period of exceptional boom, of crazy optimism and maybe even reckless and immoral behavior, preceded the crash. The narrative of human folly expressed in a stock market boom followed by a horrendous stock market crash is still very much with us today.

The atmosphere of speculation in the 1920s was unsurprisingly associated with a technological advancement: the Trans-Lux Movie Ticker (also called the ticker projector). First mentioned in the news in

1925, and proliferating after that in brokerages, clubs, and bars, the ticker projector was invented amidst the public excitement about the stock market. The projector showed the latest trades in the stock market on a screen large enough to be seen by a substantial audience. Watching the information displayed by the projector was like watching a movie, or, as we would say today, like watching a large flat-screen television. A crowd could gather at one of the tickers, thus encouraging the contagion of stock market stories. According to an Associated Press account in 1928, the movie ticker brought in "wild trading":

> This has whetted the speculative appetite of thousands and created many new ones, the thrill of seeing one's stock quoted at advancing prices on a heavy turn-over being akin to that of the race track devotee who sees the horse on which he has placed his bet come thundering down the home stretch in advance of the field.[2]

The persistence of this narrative helps explain the public fascination in subsequent decades, and even today, with domestic stock price indexes, which the news media display constantly. People widely believe that the stock market is a fundamental indicator of the economy's vitality.

The word *crash* was not commonly attached to stock market movements before 1929, and the new use of the word became a name for a different view of the economy, that economic growth depends heavily on the performance of the overall stock market, so that the stock price indexes are taken as oracles. The phrase *boom and crash* had been popular in the nineteenth century, but it was used most often to refer to cannons firing, storm waves beating upon the shore, or even Richard Wagner's music. After 1929, *boom and crash* went viral and usually described the stock market.

Crash: The Breaking Point between Speculative Excess and Hopelessness

Economists still puzzle over the stock market crash of October 28, 1929, a date on which no sudden important news occurred other than the crash itself. Just as baffling, though less discussed, is the exponential growth of stock values over most of the decade of the 1920s that preceded it. The year 1929 saw the most dramatic upswing ever, with more than a fivefold increase between December 1920 and September 1929. By June 1932, the value of the market had fallen back down to below its December 1920 level.

Earnings per share also increased dramatically over the 1920s, but the puzzle is why the stock market responded so heavily to these earnings increases. It is more normal for the stock market to react hesitantly to such upswings in earnings, which are exceptionally volatile from year to year and could even fall to zero in a single year. But surely the stock market should not fall to zero because of one bad year. Nor, normally, should it rise to match earnings in one spectacular year.

The crash of 1929 is not best thought of as a one- or two-day event, though the narrative usually suggests that it was. The combined October 28–29, 1929, crash brought the Standard & Poor's Composite Index down only 21%, a fraction of the decline over the next couple of years, and this drop was half reversed the next day, October 30, 1929. Overall, the closing S&P Composite Index dropped 86% from its peak close on September 7, 1929, to its trough close on June 1, 1932, over a period of less than three years. The October 1929 one-day drops are talked about most often, but much more noteworthy was the stock market's irregular but relentless decline, day after day, month after month, despite the protestations of businessmen and politicians who said the economy was sound.

This narrative was especially powerful in its suddenness and severity, focusing public attention on a crash as never before in America. Certainly, the October 1929 one-day drops set records, and records always make for good news stories. In addition, there was something about the timing of this story that caused an immediate and lasting public reaction. In his 1955 intellectual history of the 1930s, *Part of Our Time: Some Ruins and Monuments of the Thirties*, Murray Kempton wrote:

And it is also hard to re-create that storm which passed over America in 1929, which conditioned the real history of the 1930s. . . . The image of the American dream was flawed and cracked; its critics had never sounded so persuasive.[3]

That storm was not fully unexpected. In October 1928, during the presidential election campaign and a year before the 1929 crash, Alexander Dana Noyes, financial editor of the *New York Times*, wrote:

An observant traveler, returning from a recent tour of the United States, remarked that conversation on the trains and in the hotel sitting-rooms, after directing itself in a perfunctory way to the political campaign, would always turn with real animation to the stock market. Another testifies that even the conversation of women which he happened to overhear, would sooner or later be absorbed in discussion of their favorite stocks. Something like this was observed in 1925, in 1920 and particularly in 1901. . . . In one respect, however, the present situation differs strikingly from all the others. On all these previous occasions sober financiers, perhaps believing that some entirely new economic force had upset accepted precedent, kept silence, hesitating to predict collapse of the speculation. In this present season, on the contrary, conservative opinion has frankly and emphatically expressed the unfavorable view. In a succession of utterances by individual financers [*sic*] and at bankers' conferences, the prediction has been publicly made that the end of the speculative infatuation cannot be far off and that an inflated market is riding for a fall.[4]

Clearly, evidence of speculation was available to the public, which read about it in the news and talked about it on train cars. For example, in the year before its 1929 peak, the US stock market's actual volatility was relatively low. But the implied volatility, reflecting interest rates and initial margin demanded by brokers on stock market margin loans, was exceptionally high, suggesting that the brokers who offered margin loans were worried about a big decline in the stock market.[5]

So the evidence of danger was there in 1929 before the market peak, but it was controversial and inconclusive. A high price-earnings ratio for the stock market can predict a higher risk of stock market declines, but

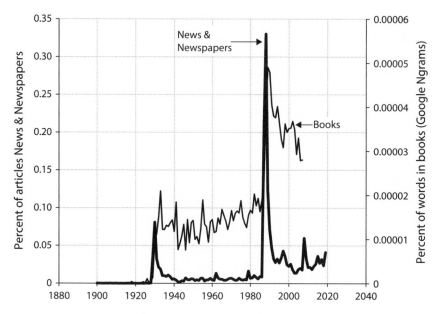

FIGURE 16.1. Frequency of Appearance of *Stock Market Crash* in Books, 1900–2008, and
News, 1900–2019

This graph shows extreme short epidemics in 1929 and 1987 in news, with a long-lagged
response in books. *Sources*: Google Ngrams, no smoothing, and author's calculations
from ProQuest News & Newspapers.

it is not like a professional weather forecast that indicates a dangerous
storm is coming in a matter of hours. Most people will heed that kind
of storm warning. However, in 1929 a great many people did not heed
the warning communicated by the high price-earnings ratio. After the
crash, many of them must have remembered the warnings and wondered why they had not listened.

As Figure 16.1 shows, the stock market crash narrative shot up with
such strength in 1929 that it persists today, though more in books than
in newspapers. The epidemic of *stock market crash*, which even today
generally refers to 1929, seems to have begun weakly in 1926, several
years before the actual crash of 1929, but it was not taken seriously. In
newspapers, there were two fast epidemics, each peaking within a year,
implying very strong short-run contagion. The first assumed massive
proportions in 1929 with the record 12.8% one-day drop in the Dow

Jones Industrial Average on October 28, 1929, and a further drop the next day. The second started on October 19, 1987, when the Dow experienced a 22.6% drop (almost double the percentage of the October 28, 1929, drop, though falling short of the two-day drop in 1929). Apart from the 1987 drop, no other stock price movement since 1929 has been widely called a *crash*. Why? As we've seen, newspapers are very focused on records, presumably because their readers are, and 1987 was the only record one-day drop after 1929. Folklore suggests that the stock market epidemic generated extremely high contagion in 1929. We know there was high contagion in the days before October 19, 1987, too. Stories involving the news media and investors brought to mind and amplified the story of the 1929 crash.[6]

The 1987 crash appears to be a flashbulb memory event (see chapter 7), like a sudden bombing attack, an automobile accident, or a declaration of war, and thus it is not easily forgotten. But after decades its story no longer seems to fit into any lively narrative constellation, and hence it is no longer virulent.

The 1929 Suicide Narrative

The October 28–29, 1929, crash was another flashbulb memory event, one that may have been stronger than the 1987 event. The 1929 flashbulb memory is magnified partly by the stories of death associated with the crash. That is, stories abounded of businesspeople committing suicide.

There is some question whether the crash really led to these suicides or whether writers learned that blaming business conditions for suicides just got a greater reaction from readers. In his best-selling 1955 book *The Great Crash, 1929*, John Kenneth Galbraith argued that there really weren't many more suicides after the crash.[7] But there really were many narratives about such suicides, with twenty-eight such stories in Pro-Quest News & Newspapers in November 1929 alone. The principle of psychology called the affect heuristic, discussed in chapter 6, predicts that such narratives make people temporarily more fearful about everything.[8]

The narrative of death at the time of the 1929 crash was reinforced by many stories of people who were financially "ruined" by the crash and therefore had no reason to continue living. Two months after the crash, a newspaper article in the *Louisville Courier-Journal* implored:

Don't Shoot Yourself!

With amazement I read of men who kill themselves at 50. The stock-market crash has ruined them—but only financially.

Have they not the same brains that made the money for them?[9]

In 1970, Studs Terkel published *Hard Times: An Oral History of the Great Depression*, which was based on Terkel's interviews with people who were of retirement age when Terkel was researching the book. The interviews reveal how the 1929 narrative had evolved in the interviewees' memories after forty years. Suicide and 1929 came up frequently, along with embellishments and obvious exaggerations. One interviewee, Arthur A. Robertson, the chairman of the board of a substantial company when Terkel interviewed him, was thirty-one years old in 1929. Robertson said:

October 29, 1929, yeah. A frenzy. I must have gotten calls from a dozen and a half friends who were desperate. In each case, there was no sense in loaning them the money that they would give the broker. Tomorrow they'd be worse off than yesterday. Suicides, left and right, made a terrific impression on me, of course. People I knew. It was heartbreaking. One day you saw the prices at a hundred, the next day at $20, at $15. On Wall Street, the people walked like zombies.[10]

Knud Andersen, a painter and sculptor, recalled:

When the shock of losing what you had worked for comes, I found refuge in my art. To stew in a deplorable situation . . . where people were affected . . . some to suicide . . . I lost myself in my art. The pain that came with economic loss, I felt would pass. These things, like the eclipse of the sun. . . . People first observed it and committed suicide . . . not realizing that this would pass.[11]

Julia Walther, the wife of a businessman in 1929, said:

> When the Crash came, the banks withdrew their support, stock held on margin was called in. Fred, unable to meet this in the falling market, lost everything he had. He was completely wiped out. Fred always laughingly said, "The only million dollars in my life I ever saw were those I lost."
>
> I felt the fever period was unreal. And the Depression was so real that *it* became unreal. There was a horror about it, with people jumping out of windows.[12]

The 1987 epidemic in Figure 16.1 looks far stronger than the 1929 epidemic. The 1987 epidemic draws much of its strength from memories of 1929. Suicides were attributed to the 1987 crash too, but these stories do not seem to have formed long-term memories, for a strong narrative did not develop and there was no reinforcing story of depression after 1987. A 50% margin requirement in force in 1987, but not in 1929, meant that in the United States many fewer people were "wiped out" or "ruined" by the 1987 crash than by the 1929 crash.

Moral Narratives about 1929

How did the 1929 crash narrative achieve such strength? Ideas about morality may have played a role. The 1920s had been a time not only of economic superabundance but also of chicanery, selfishness, and sexual liberation. Some critics viewed these aspects of the culture negatively, but they were unable to make a case against this putative immorality until the stock market crashed.

Sermons preached on the Sunday after the crash, November 3, 1929, talked about the crash, attributing it to moral and spiritual transgressions. The sermons helped frame day-of-judgment narratives about the Roaring Twenties. Google Ngrams shows that the term *Roaring Twenties* was rarely used in the 1920s. Use of the term, which sounds a bit judgmental, did not become common until the 1930s, when the broad moral story line in the Great Depression gradually morphed into a national revulsion against the excesses and pathological confidence of the

1920s. Purveyors of morality likened the one-day event on October 28, 1929, to a lightning bolt from heaven.

Murray Kempton describes a narrative that began on the day of the 1929 crash, referring to the "myth" of the 1920s and the "myth" of the 1930s:

> The myth of the twenties had involved the search for individual expression, whether in beauty, laughter, or defiance of convention; all this was judged by the myth of the thirties as selfish and footling and egocentric. It did not seem proper at the time to say that the twenties were not quite so simple, and their values were mixed, some good and some bad.[13]

Thus the stock market crash was viewed as a dividing line between the self-centered, self-deceiving 1920s and the intellectually and morally superior, albeit depressed, 1930s. Even today, the narrative notion that a stock market crash is a kind of divine punishment remains with us.

Celebrities and the Shoeshine Boy Narrative

One example of celebrity attachment to the 1929 crash narrative is the shoeshine boy narrative of the late 1920s. In this narrative, a great man, either John D. Rockefeller or Bernard Baruch or Joseph Kennedy (all of them still celebrities today, Kennedy only because he was the father of John F. Kennedy, who later became president of the United States), decided to sell stocks before the peak in 1929 after a shoeshine boy offered him advice on investing in the stock market. Jody Chudley provided a version of this story in *Business Insider* in 2017:

> In 1929, JFK's father Joseph Kennedy Sr. picked up on one of those subtle signs and didn't just get out at the top, he scored a massive windfall on the way down as well.
>
> Like for virtually anyone invested in the stock market, the 1920s were good to Joseph Kennedy Sr. How could they not be, all you had to do was buy all the stock you could and watch it go up.

After having made a bundle owning stocks in the roaring bull market of the 1920's, Joe Kennedy Sr. found himself needing to get his shoes polished up.

While sitting in the shoeshine chair, Kennedy Sr. was alarmed to have the shoeshine boy gift him with several tips on which stocks he should own—yes, a shoeshine boy playing the stock market.

This unsolicited advice resulted in a life-changing moment for Kennedy Sr. who promptly went back to his office and started unloading his stock portfolio.

In fact, he didn't just get out of the market, he aggressively shorted it—and got filthy rich because of it during the epic crash that soon followed.

They don't ring bells at the top, but apparently when shoeshine boys start giving stock advice it is time to head for the exits.[14]

I could not, however, find evidence of this story in the ProQuest News & Newspapers database for the 1920s and 1930s. The earliest mention I found of a shoeshine boy giving stock tips to a rich and important man was in Bernard Baruch's 1957 memoirs,[15] but even there the story is not exactly that of an epiphany at the moment the shoeshine boy spoke.

The shoeshine boy story also has variants that mention bootblacks, barbers, or policemen as the stock tipper. For example, a 1915 article in the *Minneapolis Morning Tribune* argued that the advancing market was not about to turn down because:

We do not hear of the chamber maids and bootblacks who have cleaned up fortunes by lucky plays in the street. These romances usually mark the approach of the culmination of the advance.[16]

This 1915 narrative does not seem to have the moral force of the shoeshine boy narrative, for it is not connected to any catastrophic Armageddon event, it does not moralize as effectively, and it does not effectively tie the story to a celebrity.

Relevance of the Stock Market
Crash Narrative Today

Though much time has passed since the 1929 crash, and much of the zeitgeist of the 1930s is lost to us now, the feeling lingers that the United States *might* experience another stock market crash. This continuing economic narrative is a lasting legacy of 1929, and it probably serves to amplify end-of-boom drops in the stock market and drops in confidence. Moreover, any awareness that some people frame their thinking in terms of such a narrative might lead to expectations that others will also display such amplifying reactions. As of this writing, in 2019, the stock market crash story is not contagious, but it remains a part of public thinking and might return with a mutation or change in the economic environment.

Policymakers might take a lesson from both the real estate bubble narratives and the stock market crash narratives: during economic inflections, there is real analytical value to looking beyond the headlines and statistics. We should also consider that certain stories that recur with mutations play a significant role in our lives. Stories and legends from the past are scripts for the next boom or crash.

The next two chapters describe economic narratives that differ from those we have covered so far in that they engender moral outrage and an impulse to fight back. In both chapters, we examine a dominant emotion of anger—against business in chapter 17, and against labor in chapter 18. This anger takes a form that may cause significant changes in economic behavior.

Chapter 17

Boycotts, Profiteers, and Evil Business

Anger at business varies through time. People may start thinking business is evil when prices of consumer goods increase substantially. Narratives blame business aggressiveness for rising prices, and public anger may continue after the inflation stops, if the public believes that prices are still too high. Anger can also become inflamed when businesses cut wages. Such anger may induce organized boycotts or disorganized decisions to postpone spending until prices are lower. In such cases, people view their buying decisions in moral terms, not just as satisfying their wants. Anger narratives may also interact with self-interested thoughts of postponing expenditures until prices come down. We see the effects of such angry narratives clearly in major economic events, including the depression of the 1890s, the 1920–21 depression, the Great Depression, and the 1974–75 recession. We see glimpses of such anger today, and we may see it strongly again in the future.

The Boycott Narrative

The word *boycott* (with slight modifications reflecting language idiosyncrasies) entered most of the world's major languages starting in 1880. Charles C. Boycott has found eternal fame not because he invented the boycott but because he was its most celebrated victim. Boycott was the land manager for an absentee landlord in Ireland. Responding to a bad crop in 1880, he offered to cut by 10% the rents to be paid by tenant landlords, but the tenants demanded a 25% cut. He resisted. An Irish organization of land tenants then appealed to the broader community for support against Boycott. In October 1880, Boycott described his travails in a letter to the editor of the *Times of London*:

> On the 22d of September a process-server, escorted by a police force of 17 men, retreated on my house for protection, followed by a howling mob of people, who yelled and hooted at the members of my family. On the ensuing day, September 23, the people collected in crowds upon my farm, and some hundred or so came up to my house and ordered off, under threats of ulterior consequences, all my farm labourers, workmen, and stablemen, commanding them never to work for me again. . . . The shopkeepers have been warned to stop all supplies to my house. . . . I can get no workmen to do anything, and my ruin is openly avowed as the object of the Land League unless I throw up everything and leave the country.[1]

This is a vivid story, but why did it go viral worldwide? First, it was controversial. On one side, the action against Boycott seemed to offend human sensibilities, but on the other side, it addressed the prominent questions of rising inequality and the concentration of wealth and power. It was not the first time such actions had been taken. But this time the idea developed that asking for moral support in the form of a boycott from the general community might be a powerful tool. Indeed, the boycott seemed to be a new and superior tactic for labor because it involved the entire community, which did not directly benefit from the boycott. Thus it seemed to be proof that the action was moral, not self-interested. The idea was highly contagious, and it spread far and wide.

Boycott would eventually become the centerpiece of its own economic narrative. Like some other narratives, it centers on an emotional response—in this case, anger against businesspeople. The boycott narrative brings with it a sense of conspiracy also generated by anger. As we will see in this chapter, the boycott narrative and others in its constellation tend to recur when there is a broad-based undercurrent of social opprobrium, and they are economically important because they affect people's willingness to spend and willingness to compromise.

The Boycott Narrative Goes Viral

In *The Boycott in American Trade Unions* (1916), labor historian Leo Wolman wrote:

> Almost without warning the boycott suddenly emerged in 1880 to become for the next ten or fifteen years the most effective weapon of unionism. There was no object so mean and no person so exalted as to escape its power.[2]

By the middle of the depression of the 1890s, the narrative began to change, and the public was becoming fed up with a constant succession of boycotts. The moral authority of boycotts disappears when most people begin to express suspicion and annoyance with them. As Wolman notes:

> The influence of the American Federation of Labor has been exerted in inducing in its members a greater conservatism in the employment of the boycott. Practically the great majority of its legislative acts from 1893 to 1908 have been designed to control the too frequent use of the boycott. At the convention of 1894 the executive council remarked "the impracticability of indorsement of too many applications of this sort. There is too much diffusion of effort which fails to accomplish the best results." Thereafter, every few years saw the adoption of new rules restricting the endorsement of boycotts.[3]

But boycotts did not go away forever, and they have recurred periodically throughout modern economic history. In each case, the boycott lasts only as long as the narrative behind it remains strong. When the underlying narrative weakens, the boycott eventually falls apart.

Profiteer Stories Reinvigorate the Boycott Narrative with World War I

Related to boycotts was the emerging profiteer narrative. Figure 17.1 shows the epidemic contagion of *profiteer*, a new word associated with anger against businesspeople. The term was coined in 1912, according to the *Oxford English Dictionary*. It was mentioned extremely frequently around World War I and just after, with its use peaking during the depression of 1920–21. *Profiteer* is a play on the much older word *privateer*, meaning a pirate ship that has government support to prey on enemy foreign shipping. Such vivid mental images enhanced profiteer contagion. Associated phrases at the time were *excess profits* and, as we have seen, *boycotts*.

In 1918, the last year of World War I, the *New York Tribune* offered an example of these narratives:

> There is a local story, writes "The Cleveland Plain Dealer," to the effect that two men in a streetcar were discoursing upon the great struggle, when one of them said: "The war has been a godsend to my plant," and the other, chuckling, replied: "If it lasts two years longer I'll be on Easy Street." Whereupon, as the story runs, a woman stood up and smote both men grievously with her umbrella, exclaiming as she did so: "If that's what the war means to you, this is what your remarks mean to me!"[4]

This narrative, accompanied here by a powerful visual image of an angry woman using her umbrella as a weapon, was highly contagious. This narrative and similar narratives persisted after the war, strongly affecting attitudes toward business for several more years.

The sharpest depression (meaning fastest decline and recovery) in US history since the advent of modern statistics occurred from 1920 to 1921. At that time, people called the depression the "post-war depression," and the unhyphenated word *postwar* also emerged, unambiguously referring to World War I, which was considered a unique turning point in history. The phrase describing it, *the war to end all wars*, had gone viral during and just after World War I. A few decades later, World War II eclipsed World War I, and the meaning of *postwar* changed to refer to the period after World War II. As a result, the depression of 1920–21 lost a uniquely identifying name. In a 2014 book, James Grant suggested calling it "The Forgotten Depression," which was the title of his book about it.

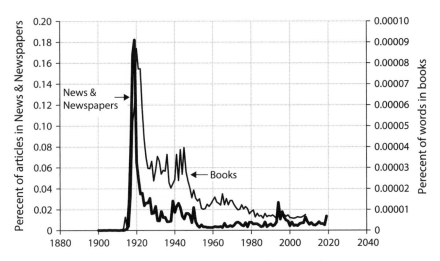

FIGURE 17.1. Frequency of Appearance of *Profiteer* in Books, 1900–2008,
and News, 1900–2019

Profiteer was a strong short epidemic starting during World War I but did not peak until
the 1920–21 depression. *Sources:* Google Ngrams, no smoothing, and author's calculations
from ProQuest News & Newspapers.

Nonetheless, the 1920–21 depression was a powerful narrative at the
time of the Great Depression of the 1930s. It was part of the script for
that depression. Ultimately, every important event from the depression
of the early 1920s through the Great Depression of the 1930s was put in
the emotional context of either "prewar" or "postwar." For example, in
1933, twenty-year-old soldiers who survived World War I, then in their
midthirties, still maintained wartime friendships and in many cases still
nursed wartime wounds. Both depressions also generated an atmosphere of public outrage toward business, as exemplified by the angry
woman attacking the two businessmen with her umbrella.

The Return to "Normalcy"

After World War I, with immediate postwar inflation totaling 100%, a
deflation narrative developed by 1920. The story that consumer prices
would fall dramatically was strongly contagious owing to its association

with the profiteer narrative. Indeed, during the 1920–21 depression, thousands of newspaper articles noted that certain individual prices had fallen to their prewar 1913 or 1914 levels. The newspapers' writers and editors knew that readers would respond well to such stories because, to most people, it seemed natural that once the war was over, prices would return to their old levels: a very important perceived "return to normalcy" that might eventually encourage consumers to buy a new house or a new car, but only after prices came down fully.

The idea that prices would fall to prewar levels was encouraged by the talk during the 1920 presidential campaign. Presidential candidate Warren Harding popularized the word *normalcy* to describe the world's conditions before World War I, promising to bring back those conditions. Use of the word *normalcy* long before 1920 can be documented—it was not Harding's invention—but the word was used so rarely before 1920 that many people believed that Harding had coined it. Harding used *normalcy* much as Donald J. Trump used the words *bigly* and *yuge* in his 2016 election campaign promises to make America great again. In both Harding's campaign and Trump's, words loaned a concreteness to the narrative, were frequently joked about, and seemed almost to provide a name for the narrative. For Harding, the word *normalcy* reflected a tendency to conflate the depression conditions of 1920 with the still-vivid trauma of the war, making for an emotionally intense narrative of the times.

In his March 1921 inaugural address as new president of the United States, Harding summarized what he'd emphasized throughout his 1920 election campaign:

The business world reflects the disturbance of war's reaction. Herein flows the lifeblood of material existence. The economic mechanism is intricate and its parts interdependent, and has suffered the shocks and jars incident to abnormal demands, credit inflations, and price upheavals. The normal balances have been impaired, the channels of distribution have been clogged, the relations of labor and management have been strained. We must seek the readjustment with care and courage. Our people must give and take. Prices must reflect the receding fever of war activities. Perhaps we never shall know the old levels of wages again, because war invariably readjusts compensations, and the necessaries of life will show their inseparable relationship, but we must strive for normalcy to reach stability.[5]

To Buy or Not to Buy

In the still-bruised emotional atmosphere of the 1920s, waiting to buy discretionary items until the prices fell seemed an obvious strategy, both moral and practical, to most consumers. But postponing purchases helped bring on a depression. As one observer wrote in 1920:

> The buying public knows that the war is over and has reached the point where it refuses to pay war prices for articles. Goods do not move, for people simply will not buy.[6]

Populist anger grew, along with protests against profiteering manufacturers and retailers. The protests sought to take advantage of a basic economic principle:

> If people determine to buy foodstuffs or anything else only what they actually cannot do without, the working of the inexorable law of supply and demand will operate automatically to bring conditions to a more normal state.[7]

Thus thrift became a new virtue as people waited for the return of the "normal" prices of 1913.

Why 1913? An authoritative retail price index precursor to the modern Consumer Price Index (CPI) was first published in the United States by the Bureau of Labor Statistics in 1919, just before the 1920–21 depression. The index used past data starting in 1913, the last year of complete peace before the surprise start of World War I in 1914.[8] The index highlighted a very dramatic price increase since 1913. Thus 1913 became the benchmark date for price comparisons, and consumers sought to delay purchases until prices returned to their 1913 levels. In January 1920, the commissioner of labor statistics, Royal Meeker, said, "The prices we kicked about in 1913 have come to be regarded as ideal,"[9] noting that the ideal was mistaken. The Consumer Price Index began with a value of 9.8 in 1913. By 1920, it had more than doubled to 20.9, and by mid-1921 it had fallen to 17.3. It would have to fall a lot further to get back down to 9.8.

In extreme cases of deflation, embellished narratives about deflation might develop enough emotional contagion to go viral, and only in that case would buying behavior be significantly reduced; consumers see some vengeful reward in postponing purchases until prices are at fair levels again. The anger depends on the narrative; thus there is not a strong consistent relationship across countries and through long periods of time between deflation and depression.[10] The economic narrative of the 1920s created an emotionally rich atmosphere of expectations about falling prices. The narrative was not only that it was smart to postpone purchases, but also that it was moral and responsible to do so.

Profiteering and Fair Wage Narratives

The price increase between the end of the war and 1920 was widely blamed on businesspeople who were labeled with the newly popular word *profiteer*. None of the words that were used in previous wars to criticize those who profited from the war (*harpy, racketeer, exploiter, black marketer, bloodsucker, vampire, pilferer*) seem to have the same connotations as *profiteer*, which suggests wartime fortune building at the expense of war heroes. *Profiteer* suggested a big operation, a corporation perhaps, with connections in government, rather than a small-time individual opportunist, and it thus suggested more of a need for collective action in the form of a serious boycott. An added benefit of boycotts, from a US perspective then, was their lack of any connections with communism.

The word *profiteer* during and after World War I appeared in numerous narratives, not just those reported in the business columns. Church sermons began to inveigh against the high price of food during the war, criticizing the selfish behavior of businesspeople who showed little human decency or respect for human suffering.[11] Other narratives described lawyers who discovered the names and addresses of US families who had lost a family member in the war. The lawyers would falsely state

that families of fallen soldiers needed an attorney to demand government benefits, and they asked the families to sign a contract to pay them
20% of any government support in exchange for their help in navigating
the maze of government benefits.[12] Such narratives make it easy to
understand the extremely emotional reactions to such rapacious
profiteering.

The profiteer narratives did not stop with the end of the war in 1918.
During the postwar inflation, in 1920 and 1921, narratives spread of customers angry at high prices chastising their milkman and telling their
butcher they would stop eating meat altogether to spite them. Economists
understood why wartime inflation continued until 1920 (heavily indebted
governments faced troubles from a war-disrupted economy and did not
want to raise taxes or raise interest rates, which would add to their deficit),
but the public at large did not. The public began to view the wartime experience and the immediate postwar experience in terms of a battle between good and evil. The popular author Henry Hazlitt wrote in 1920:

> Hence we have self-righteous individuals on every corner denounc-
> ing the outrages and robberies committed by a sordid world. The
> butcher is amazed at the profiteering of the man who sells him shoes;
> the shoe salesman is astounded at the effrontery of the theatre ticket
> speculator; the theatre ticket speculator is staggered at the high-
> handedness of his landlord; the landlord raises his hands to high
> heaven at the demands of his coal man, and the coal man collapses at
> the prices of the butcher.[13]

We might ask: Did these people deserve to be called profiteers? It
seems that their only crime was selling at higher prices in an inflationary
period. In 1922, Irving Fisher visited Germany, where the post–World
War I inflation continued longer and developed into a hyperinflation.
He recalls the conversation he had with a "very intelligent" woman who
ran a clothing store and who offered him an abnormally low price on a
shirt, given the extremely rapid inflation:

> Fearing to be thought a profiteer, she said: "That shirt I sold you will
> cost me just as much to replace as I am charging you." Before I could

ask her why, then, she sold it at so low a price, she continued: "But I have made a profit on that shirt because I bought it for less."[14]

Fisher then energetically argued that there was nothing moral or special about prewar prices or the "dollar of 1913." German complaints against profiteering were similar to those expressed in the United States in 1920, which saw 28% consumer price inflation over the nineteen months between the World War I armistice and June 1920:

> Syracuse (N. Y.) June 2—The John A. Roberts Corporation of Utica, dealers in wearing apparel, was today fined $55,000 by Federal Judge Harland B. Howe, following its conviction of profiteering on eleven counts. . . . The sales, as explained by the government, were: A dress bought for $16.75, sold for $35 . . . a scarf bought for $6.50 sold for $25.00.[15]

The massive inflation created an illusion of high profits for this seller of apparel. Economists tried to explain some of the mechanisms at work:

> But there is injustice of another kind caused by high prices, and that is the excessive profits which business men of all kinds—manufacturers, jobbers, wholesalers and retailers—are able to reap, indeed almost compelled to take in a period of swiftly rising prices. In these last five years a business man could grow rich by merely keeping his goods on the shelf while the market price continued to rise. This is the real story of "profiteering." It is not a vicious habit which has suddenly come over the business world and which can be stopped by putting men in jail. It is a symptom of the disease, not the disease itself.[16]

This argument probably convinced only a few people who hadn't the faintest idea of inflation's true impact on corporate profits. Instead, most people were likely caught in the profiteer epidemic that business had developed a "vicious habit" of price gouging. The concern with profiteering began to recede only after consumer prices started to fall, but the concern's ebb was not exactly coterminous with that fall, for the epidemic of anger had its own internal dynamics.

In the United States, the inflation ended by June 1920, and although consumer prices never got back to 1913 levels, prices dropped rapidly. Until then, emotions ran very high on the matter. One 1920 letter to the editor stated:

> Excess profit is just what its name indicates—the fruits of profiteering, usury; and if there is anything in the world that should be taxed it is that very thing. In fact, it should be punishable by prison sentence or even more severely still.[17]

The government took these emotions seriously. In 1917, during World War I, the United States imposed a 60% excess profits tax on profits above the prewar 1911–13 level. The excess profits tax was not revoked until October 1921, because anger at corporations lingered long after the war was over. The tax contributed to the 1920–21 depression by encouraging companies to postpone profits until after the tax was revoked. Meanwhile, people held off buying, not only because of their anger at selfish profiteers but also because of the perceived opportunity to profit from postponing their purchases during a time of falling prices.

Perhaps the 1920–21 depression is better thought of as the 1920–21 consumer-boycott-induced depression. In January 1920, US senator Arthur Capper said, "Profiteers are more dangerous than Reds," urging consumers to "boycott the profit hogs by refusing to buy goods offered at extortionate prices."[18] To use another term of that time, perhaps the depression was truly "the 1920–21 buyers' strike," as captured by the word *boycott*.

Also prominent in the depression of 1920–21 was a concern about being paid a "fair wage." Anger against so-called profiteers was sometimes fueled by some companies cutting their employees' wages. These companies defended their actions by noting that they could not continue to pay higher wages when the market prices for their final goods were falling. Any rational person should have seen that wage cuts were sometimes necessary, but an explanation of employers' need to cut wages was not a contagious narrative. Labor union representatives did not have any incentive to explain the employers' predicament to their members. Rather, they found it in their interests to keep alive a story about evil management.

A plot of uses of the term *fair wage* follows a pattern remarkably similar to that of *profiteer*. However, the growth of *fair wage* was steeper and more gradual, starting in the late nineteenth century. In books, the peak usage of *fair wage* was around the time of the 1920–21 depression. In ProQuest News & Newspapers, the peak mention occurred in the Great Depression of the 1930s.

The fair wage-effort hypothesis, as presented by George A. Akerlof and Janet L. Yellen (1990), asserts that workers are inclined to slow down their work in revenge if they feel that they are not being paid a fair wage. Akerlof and Yellen presented their theory as if it applies equally at all times, but it appears that attention to fair wages can be heightened by changing narratives.

Narratives That Suddenly Ended the
Sharp 1920–21 Recession

The abrupt end of the 1920–21 depression and attenuation of public concerns about profiteering do not seem to have any obvious explanation. Presumably there were new popular narratives poorly observable today that induced less expectations of falling prices and less anger about high prices.

There was a good harvest in the summer and fall of 1920, and while that may not be a reliable leading indicator, it was taken by many as such:

> We raised enormous crops this year and there is a definite relation between big crops and good times. The war didn't repeal natural laws.[19]

In late 1920 Sir Edmond Walker, a prominent Canadian banker, offered the theory why prices would not fall to 1913 levels:

> This condition [of consumer prices well above prewar levels] may last for another generation, and must last so long as the weight of war indebtedness causes unusually heavy taxes and high rents.[20]

By April 1921 there were claims that there was "less profiteering going on, as prices settle slowly to peace levels."[21] Many farmers were reportedly already back down to receiving 1913-level prices for much of their produce by 1921.[22]

So by that time there seemed to be less reason to postpone purchases until prices were lower. Also, business—and wealth—were no longer so evil, so there was no more impulse to boycott. People were becoming more comfortable with spending. Women were said to be wearing more conspicuous jewelry by 1921.[23] Children were bringing money to school rather than lunch bags, and they bought expensive lunches for themselves. A "pass it along spirit" was developing by late 1921:

> Everyone is taking more comfort—finding more enjoyment in life— than ever before. For proof of this see the roads filled with automobiles. All that means the expenditure of money.[24]

The sharp recovery in 1921 might be attributed to these new narratives, rather to any active government stimulus to revive the economy.

Contrasting the Depression of 1920–1921 with the Great Depression of the 1930s

Labor historians have found that labor was more acquiescent to wage cuts justified by falling prices in the 1920–21 depression than in the later Great Depression of the 1930s.[25] Labor unions were fewer and weaker in the former episode, and thus union propaganda was less viral. Therefore employers had better success in 1920–21 with arguing that they must cut wages because of deflation; they noted that the lower prices they could charge for their products left them with less revenue to pay wages. In *The Forgotten Depression* (2014), James Grant attributes the relatively rapid end of the 1920–21 depression to such wage flexibility.

In contrast, narratives in the 1930s described employers' justification for cutting wages as purely the result of greed and lies. Clergymen were criticized for becoming politicized against business:

> Some of the clergymen who think they were ordained with a special power to preach economics instead of religion go into wages and

work wholly on emotion. They passionately urge minimum rates and hours on such broad and fine humanitarian grounds that those who oppose regulation on equally fine and broad humanitarian grounds find themselves classed with the sweat-shop employers as enemies of human progress.[26]

Such talk surely made it hard for employers to cut wages to avoid layoffs and to maintain goodwill with the public. In addition, as noted in chapter 13, the National Industrial Recovery Act of June 1933 regulated against wage cuts, and President Franklin Roosevelt's policy, even after the Supreme Court declared the act unconstitutional in May 1935, only made it more difficult for firms to cut wages.[27] These regulations reflected narratives of the Great Depression years that wage cuts were truly evil. Even without such regulations, firms would have found it difficult to cut wages in response to lower prices.

The "return to normalcy" narrative was not so prominent in the Great Depression of the 1930s, and not so easily disposed of with the passage of time. The perception in the depression of 1920–21 that the depression was a transitional phase back to normalcy after a war and an influenza epidemic was a fundamental framing difference when compared to the Great Depression. The unemployment and falling prices in the Great Depression were instead seen through the lens of other narratives that were of epidemic proportions in the 1930s, the confidence narratives (chapter 10 above), the frugality narrative (chapter 11 above), the technological unemployment narrative (chapter 13 above), and the 1929 stock market crash narrative (chapter 16 above).

Boycotts and Profiteers during the Great Depression of the 1930s

References to the 1920–21 depression began during the October 28–29, 1929, stock market crash.[28] The last big crisis always has a special place in people's minds, especially if it was the biggest crisis ever, because such stories rely on people's memories to enhance contagion. Though one narrative at the beginning of the Great Depression held that the current situation was essentially a repeat of the 1920–21 event, the larger Great Depression narrative had to differ in some fundamental ways. The narrative of the 1920s emphasized the recent suffering from World War I, but that narrative was less intense a decade later, in the 1930s. However, the deflation observed was much the same. The consumer price declines in 1920–21 looked like the sharpest ever. Because many people after 1929 expected prices to fall, as they had in 1920–21, they chose to delay their purchases until the price decline was complete.

A month or so after the October 28–29, 1929, stock market crash, the news paid much attention to the signs of weakening retail sales during the annual Christmas shopping season in the United States. News articles described Christmas buying as normal, but weak in luxury items. However, buying was normal only because of price cutting, with the changes attributed to "the psychological effects of the stock market crash."[29]

Economists expected the contraction to be as short-lived as that of 1920–21, which helps explain why President Hoover and others confidently stated in 1930 that the depression that had started in 1929 would soon be over. But the public didn't generally believe President Hoover. Near the bottom of the Great Depression in 1932, the narrative persisted that consumer prices would eventually fall to 1913 or 1914 levels, which would have meant another 20% decline in prices beyond what we know was the bottom level of consumer prices, in 1933.[30] This narrative justified postponing purchases of consumption goods. Catherine Hackett wrote in 1932:

> I have read enough predictions by economists to convince me that my guess is as good as anyone's on the future trend of prices. A housewife plays the falling commodity market just as an investor plays the falling stock market; she sits tight and waits for prices to settle before buying anything but actual necessities. But I do not need to be an economist to realize that if all the twenty million housewives do that, business recovery will be indefinitely delayed.[31]

This quote illustrates some important aspects of consumer behavior. Hackett compares consumer behavior to the behavior of stock market speculators, who do not trust experts and who put emotional energy into forming their own personal forecasts for individual stock prices. She also notes the high contagion of narratives about such speculation. Women must have been talking like speculators, telling stories about some smart decisions and some mistakes with their shopping successes and failures among the unpredictable variability of consumer price changes. Even if the average shopper expected some (nonnegative) inflation, the result could be a significant net decrease in consumer spending if there was a higher contagion rate for emotionally laden narratives about likely price declines.

It is curious that economists haven't looked more at the testimonies of women to understand buying patterns in the depressions of the 1920s and 1930s. Given the sex roles of the era, in which men were likely to play the stock market and women to manage the shopping, women must have been talking extensively about strategizing their shopping based on their hunches. The men who wrote the history attributed everything to important decisions made by male presidents, bankers, and business leaders, but the critical decisions that brought on the depression (that is, the postponement of purchases) may have come more from women. In fact, in 1932, during the depths of the Great Depression, a Mrs. Charles E. Foster reportedly told a women's group:

> One of the most effective weapons in the hands of American women today is their tremendous purchasing power. We are told that they spend eighty-five percent of the incomes of the United States. How could they better create public opinion in favor of spending as usual than by setting the example themselves?[32]

Meanwhile, like the depression of 1920–21, the Great Depression of the 1930s saw many boycotts: against German and Japanese goods, as well as against goods associated with Jewish people. Germans began boycotting Western goods. All of these boycotts must have had economic effects.

The "Buy Now" Campaign

In the early days of the Great Depression there were attempts to create a moral imperative against the bargain craze that led consumers to postpone purchasing.[33] The Washington, DC, Chamber of Commerce launched a campaign in 1930 with the slogan "Buy Now for Prosperity." A "Prosperity Committee" sought the participation of clergymen of all denominations to "preach prosperity through their pulpits" and thereby to "stimulate production, relieving the unemployment situation."[34] When he became president in 1933, Franklin Roosevelt launched his own "Buy Now Campaign," describing patriotic citizens overcoming their impulse to wait for lower prices in order to support a stronger economy.[35] In August 1933, a "Buy in August" campaign described patriotic people as making a special effort to buy retail products in August, the slowest month of the year for retailers. Consumers were reminded that August was "canning time" for many fruits and vegetables and so a good time to buy them. The campaign publicized the seasonality of consumer prices, implying that prices would rise for the rest of the year and that wise consumers should purchase now.[36] Clearly, the "Buy Now" campaign was an attempt to counter the "prices will fall" narrative that had taken hold.

Later Boycott Narratives

After World War II, the United States experienced something akin to a repeat performance of the 1920–21 depression and its boycotts. But this time government authorities remembered the narrative of 1920–21 and used it to guide their response. After the war ended in 1945, the US authorities maintained the wartime price controls for a while to prevent the kind of inflation experienced in 1919 after World War I. From April to October 1945 there was a very brief but sharp recession linked to demobilization, a recession with stable prices as measured. But as the US government lifted the controls, prices began to rise rapidly, and by 1949 they were about 30% higher than they'd been in 1945. Once again there was talk of consumer boycotts and a buyers' strike, and there was a recession in 1949 that resembled that of 1920. Newspapers again reported that buyers were waiting for prices to come down before buying postponable items.

The severe recession of 1973–75 is widely attributed to an embargo, the selling counterpart of the boycott. The Arab oil embargo began in October 1973 during the Arab-Israeli (Yom Kippur) War. The embargo took the form of limiting the supply of oil from the Organization of the Petroleum Exporting Countries (OPEC), which sympathized with the Arab nations that had attacked Israel and were about to be defeated, with US support of Israel. The embargo was a principle- or emotion-driven event, continuing long after the war ended in the same month it started. It was a statement of moral support for the Arab countries, even though only one of the eleven OPEC countries (Iraq) was among the five Arab countries that participated in the war.

Many of the narratives surrounding the recession of 1973–75 had a source in human anger. The most cited cause of this recession—the oil crisis generated by OPEC angrily protesting US support of Israel in the 1973 Yom Kippur War—was only part of the story. The price of oil suddenly quadrupled to unheard-of levels, generating anger among consumers and stories of difficulties dealing with oil rationing in the United States, such as odd-even rationing of gasoline. (Consumers could buy gasoline only on odd-numbered days if their license plate ended with an odd number, and only on even-numbered days if their license plate ended with an even number.) Higher oil prices caused higher electric bills, and anger at the perceived injustice was one of the reasons many people started keeping much of their homes in darkness, as a sort of protest.[37] In the period of runaway US inflation of the 1970s, when many viewed inflation as the nation's most important problem, one observer wrote in July 1974, "Fighting inflation is like fighting a forest fire, it requires courage, team play, and coordinated sacrifice."[38] At the time, US annual inflation was 12%, which was a record high excluding periods surrounding the world wars.

The firefighting metaphor has moral overtones that might have caused people to curtail spending. Indeed, at the very beginning of the severe 1973–75 recession, in April 1973, there had been a "meat boycott" in which consumers protested the high price of meat. That boycott reportedly put twenty thousand US meat industry workers out of their jobs.[39] In August there was a one-day boycott, a "Don't Buy Anything Day."[40] The next year, in January 1974, with the economy well into the recession, angry consumers renewed the meat boycott and extended it to a grain boycott.[41] The boycott sentiment remained in consumer consciousness for some time, generating reduced purchases of a wide array of goods and services, leading to, or at least contributing to, the recession.

During the world financial crisis years 2007–9 thousands of boycotts were reported, including boycotts of mortgage lenders and of gasoline, but boycotts and profiteering did not appear to rise to the level of economic significance seen in earlier episodes. Still, narratives that stimulate angry boycotts will likely appear in the future, just as they have in the past. How emerging businesses and labor unions are perceived—as either good or evil—matters greatly for the future state of the economy, a topic to which we turn in the next chapter.

Chapter 18

The Wage-Price Spiral and Evil Labor Unions

The *wage-price spiral* narrative took hold in the United States and many other countries around the middle of the twentieth century. It described a labor movement, led by strong labor unions, demanding higher wages for themselves, which management accommodates without losing profits by pushing up the prices of final goods sold to consumers. Labor then uses the higher prices to justify even higher wage demands, and the process repeats itself again and again, leading to out-of-control inflation. The blame for inflation thus falls on both labor and management, and some may blame the monetary authority, which tolerates the inflation. This narrative is associated with the term *cost-push inflation*, where *cost* refers to the cost of labor and inputs to production. It contrasts with a different popular narrative, *demand-pull inflation*, a theory that blames inflation on consumers who demand more goods than can be produced.

As Figure 18.1 shows, the two epidemics, *wage-price spiral* and *cost-push inflation*, are roughly parallel. Both epidemics were especially strong sometime between 1950 and 1990. These epidemics reflected changes in moral values, indicating deep concerns about being cheated and a sense of fundamental corruption in society. According to the narratives, labor unions were deceitfully claiming to represent labor as a whole, when in fact they were representing only certain insiders.[1] Meanwhile, politicians and central banks were selfishly perpetuating the upward spiral of inflation, which impoverished real working people not represented by powerful unions. There has been a long downtrend in

FIGURE 18.1. Frequency of Appearance of *Wage-Price Spiral* and *Cost-Push Inflation* in Books, 1900–2008

These two related epidemics helped bring about major changes in labor relations and government regulation of business. *Source*: Google Ngrams, no smoothing.

public support in the United States for labor unions, from 72% in 1936 to 48% in 2009, as documented by the Gallup Poll.[2]

These narratives were enhanced by detailed stories that invited angry responses. For example, around 1950 an outrageous story went viral about labor unions' reframing their wage in terms of miles traveled rather than hours worked. The *New York Times* described it thus in 1950:

> One of the rule changes asked by these two unions is that the pay base for trainmen and conductors on passenger trains be lowered to 100 miles or five hours, from 150 miles or seven and a half hours. The railroads have countered by asking that the basic day's work be increased to 200 miles. . . . Because of recent technological improvements, including the greater use of diesel locomotives, the speed of passenger trains has been increased, where many passenger train service employes now receive a day's pay for two and a half to three hours of work. By reducing the number of miles in the basic day to 100, the mileage rate of pay of the passenger train employes would be increased by 50 per cent.[3]

So, the story went, the conductors would have the opportunity to sit down as passengers after working only two and a half hours, long before the trip was over. Such an outrageous demand made the narrative highly contagious, and it is memorable enough to be remembered today.

Labor unions became associated in the public eye with organized crime. For example, Jimmy Hoffa took over the International Brotherhood of Teamsters union in 1957, despite corruption charges against him then, and led that union as an absolute dictator. There was for years an ongoing story of his investigation for gangster-like activities, in a probe led by Robert F. Kennedy. Hoffa was convicted of bribery and fraud and went to prison from 1967–71. In 1975 he disappeared after being last seen in the parking lot upon leaving the Red Fox Restaurant in Bloomfield Township. Rumors were that he was murdered by rival gangsters. Rumors were that his body "was entombed in concrete at Giants Stadium in New Jersey, ground up and thrown in a Florida swamp, or perished in a mob-owned fat-rendering plant."[4] These colorful theories, which suggest vivid visual mental images of Hoffa's ignominious end, led to the contagion rate of the Hoffa epidemic that further discredited labor unions. The search for his body in a garbage dump, an empty field, and elsewhere created news stories until 2013. This was a viral story, part of a constellation of narratives that described labor unions in negative terms, and which impelled many people to see real evil in them.

The wage-price spiral narrative was reflected in actual inflation rates around the world, which tended to be unusually high when the narrative was strong. The World Bank's Global Inflation Rate peaked in 1980, approximately at the peak of *cost-push inflation* in Figure 18.1, and it has been mostly on the decline ever since. These epidemics also saw high long-term interest rates, reflecting the inflation expectations engendered by the narrative. Today, inflation is down across much of the world, and long-term interest rates have fallen since the epidemic peaked. The dynamics of this worldwide narrative epidemic likely provide the best explanation for these epochal changes in trend of the two major economic variables, inflation and interest rates.

The end of the wage-price spiral narrative was marked by changes in monetary policy and the advent of newly popular ideas: the independent central bank[5] and inflation targeting[6] by central banks. The independent central bank was designed to be free from political pressures, which organized labor tries to exploit. Inflation targeting was designed to place controlling inflation on a higher moral ground than appeasing political forces.

The moral imperative here was strong. On its face, the wage-price spiral may seem purely mechanical. However, many believed it was caused by the greedy (immoral) behavior of both management and labor. President Dwight Eisenhower referred to the spiral in his 1957 State of the Union address:

> The national interest must take precedence over temporary advantages which may be secured by particular groups at the expense of all the people. . . . Business in its pricing policies should avoid unnecessary price increases especially at a time like the present when demand in so many areas presses hard on short supplies. A reasonable profit is essential to the new investments that provide more jobs in an expanding economy. But business leaders must, in the national interest, studiously avoid those price rises that are possible only because of vital or unusual needs of the whole nation. . . . Wage negotiations should also take cognizance of the right of the public generally to share in the benefits of improvements in technology.[7]

Even though 1957 saw only a moderate burst of inflation, from less than zero in 1956 to a peak of 3.7% in 1957 and far smaller than the 23.6% in 1920, it stirred emotions because of the moralizing narrative that attended it. A 1957 editorial in the *Los Angeles Times* exemplifies the reaction:

> What is wrong with our country? A creeping inflation is like a small crack in a dam or dike as it grows menacingly larger by the force of the seeping water. The crack in our national economy is being widened by greed—greed of some leaders of big business and labor as they continue to boost prices and wages, each blaming the other, and neither pausing to realize that the economy of our country is at the

breaking point with a crash being inevitable if we do not level off now and hold prices and wages. It may even be too late.[8]

The moralizing in these narratives, spoken by presidents and prime ministers and published and commented on by journalists, gave the US Federal Reserve and other nations' central banks the moral authority to step hard on the brakes, risking a recession. They did just that, tightening money gradually until the discount rate rose to a peak in October 1957. Allan Sproul, the recently retired president of the Federal Reserve Bank of New York, in 1957 lamented the difficult role of the Fed as the "economic policeman for the entire community." He noted the blame the Fed gets for the expansion before a crackdown:

> As it is, there are times when your Federal Reserve System finds itself in the position of having to validate, however reluctantly, public folly and private greed by supporting increased costs and prices.[9]

Inflation in a Constellation of Injustice and Immorality Narratives

When inflation has been high, many commentators have regarded it as the most important problem facing the nation. Starting in 1935, the Gallup Poll has repeatedly asked its US respondents, "What do you think is the most important problem facing this country [or this section of the country] today?" During the era of highest US inflation, from 1973 to 1981, generally more than 50% of respondents responded by saying either "inflation" or "the high cost of living." This perception appears to have been common across much of the world. Reflecting this view, economist Irving S. Friedman wrote in his 1973 book *Inflation: A World-Wide Disaster* that the increasing inflation was sending "panic signals throughout the world," opining that the inflation crisis was as serious a problem as the Great Depression of the 1930s.[10] Inflation was "eroding the fabric of modern societies" and "threatens all efforts to keep the international monetary system from fragmenting into hostile forces."[11]

The discourse seemed to want to fix blame on some segment of society, either labor or business, for the inflation. Popular syndicated columnist Sydney J. Harris wrote in 1975:

WHAT IS SO frustrating about this kind of thing is the difficulty in pinning down the culprits, if any . . .

Either somebody is lying, or the whole economic process doesn't make sense.

If labor is getting "too much," why are most working families struggling to make ends meet?

If grocers are "profiteering," why do they get glummer as prices go higher?

Where does the buck stop? Nobody knows. And so each segment blames another for the vicious spiral, and each justifies its own increases by pointing to its own rising cost of doing business.

THE MARKET NO longer seems to control prices when they keep escalating despite reduced consumption.

Some strange new twisted law appears to be operating in place of the classical formula of the "free market."

I am not versed enough in economics to understand what is going on; neither are most people.[12]

In contrast to the 1920s and the preceding chapter, there were now multiple possible sources of evil behind inflation, not so focused on evil businesses of various kinds, but now also on evil labor.

In my 1997 study of public views of the inflation crisis in the United States, Germany, and Brazil, conducted after the worst of the inflation had subsided but during a period in which people remained concerned about inflation, I surveyed both the general public and, for comparison, university economists. My research uncovered differences in narratives across countries, across age groups, and, particularly, between economists and the general public.

For the most part, the economists did not think that inflation was such a big deal, unlike Irving Friedman, who was writing for the general public. Meanwhile, although US consumers did not agree on the causes of the inflation, they were nonetheless angry about it. When asked to identify the cause of the inflation, their most common response was "greed," followed by "people borrow or lend too much." In specifying the targets of their anger, the US respondents listed, in order of frequency, "the government," "manufacturers," "store owners," "business in general," "wholesalers," "executives," "U.S. Congress," "greedy people," "institutions," "economists" "retailers" "distributors," "middlemen, "conglomerates, "the President of the United States," "the Democratic party," "big money people," "store employees" (for wage demands that forced price increases), their "employer" (for not raising their salary), and "themselves" (for being ignorant of matters).[13]

In addition, unlike economists, the general public believed in a *wage lag hypothesis*: the idea that wage increases would forever lag behind price increases, and therefore that inflation had a direct and long-term negative impact on living standards. In short, the *wage-price spiral* offered a geometrical mental image of one's economic status spiraling down for as long as strong aggressive demands of labor kept it happening.

In some ways the 1957–58 recession differed substantially from earlier recessions. It did not have the character of a buyers' strike, as the Great Depression did. In fact, sales of luxury items remained very strong. Anger was not so much directed against "profiteers," and there was little shame in living extravagantly. The alarmist talk about the wage-price spiral did not focus anger onto the rich. Rather, sales of postponable everyday purchases suffered more.[14]

At the same time, the public sensed that no feasible government policy could stop the wage price-spiral. The earlier recessions of 1949, 1953, and 1957 had left inflation a little lower, but only temporarily. The lingering narrative of the Great Depression suggested to the general public that it was perhaps too great a risk to try to control inflation by starting a bigger recession. That idea was part of the popular conception of the wage-price spiral model, that the nation should base all of its economic decisions on the assumption that inflation will get worse and worse.

Angry at Inflation

Out-of-control consumer price inflation has occurred many times throughout history, and the phenomenon has always induced anger. The loss of purchasing power is extremely annoying. But the question is this: At whom should the public direct its anger? Anger narratives about inflation reflect the different circumstances of each inflationary period. By studying these narratives, we can see the effects of inflation and how they change through time.

The most extreme cases of inflation tend to happen during wars. When governments are in trouble, they may not be able to collect taxes fast enough to pay for the war, and in desperation they resort to the printing press for more money. But the stories may not resonate, and the public may not see or understand what is happening. That is, narratives that blame the government for the inflation may not be contagious during a war. Instead, it is more likely that people want to blame someone else. Businesspeople, who are staying home safely while others are fighting, are a natural target of narratives.

In chapter 17, we saw the remarkable epidemic of the word *profiteer* during and just after World War I. People were very angry that some businesspeople were made rich by the war, and the result was the imposition of an excess profits tax (not only during World War I but also during World War II). Such anger against the people who get rich during wartime is a perennial narrative, not limited to the twentieth century. For example, there was anger during the US Civil War (1861–65) at those who profited from the war, but it wasn't directed at business tycoons creating inflation to make large profits. The narratives were different. Consider, for example, this sermon by Reverend George Richards of the First Congregational Church of Litchfield, Connecticut, on February 22, 1863:

> How, in contrast with the greedy speculators, in office and out of it, who have prowled, like famished wolves, round our fields of carnage— stealing everything they could lay their hands on—robbing the national treasury—purloining from the camp-chest—pilfering from

the wounded in the hospitals—appropriating to themselves the little comforts meant for the dying, if not stripping the very dead![15]

During the 1917–23 German hyperinflation, the inflation rate was astronomical, and not due to any war. Prices in marks rose on the order of a trillionfold. And yet many people were unable to identify the malefactor who was causing inflation. Irving Fisher, an American economist who visited Germany at the time, found that Germans did not blame their own government, which had been printing money excessively. Fisher wrote:

> The Germans thought of commodities as rising and thought of the American gold dollar as rising. They thought we [the United States] had somehow cornered the gold of the world and were charging an outrageous price for it.[16]

As of this writing, there is some suggestion of resurgence in the strength of labor unions, and of public support for them, in the United States. The wage-price spiral narrative does not seem poised to reappear. Inflation in the United States and other countries seems unusually tame. However, a mutation of the narrative could appear if inflation begins to creep up. The public tends to watch consumer prices closely, because of its constant repetition of purchases. The wage-price spiral narrative, or some variation on that theme, could again create a strong impulse for economic actors to try to get ahead of the inflation game. It could give them newfound zest in this effort by bringing a moral dimension into the mix, a perception of true evil in inflation, personified by certain celebrities or classes of people.

Perennial Narratives: A Summing Up

The list of nine narrative constellations in part III of this book offers a glimpse of the narrative forces that have driven economies into and out of booms and busts. One broad lesson that we may take from this list is the immense complexity of the narrative landscape. No simple index of public opinion, such as the Consumer Confidence Index, summarizes the "strength" of the economy. The various narratives that share the stage at any point have, in a biological analogy, many cellular receptors and signaling molecules. Modern communication means that new and different kinds of epidemics are possible, and economic forecasting requires close attention to many different narratives. Forecasting in the future will require a new attention to data that are becoming available, as we discuss in part IV.

Part IV

Advancing Narrative Economics

Chapter 19

Future Narratives, Future Research

Disease epidemiology has shown us that there will likely be repeats of variants of older epidemics in the future as reservoirs of old epidemics mutate or react to a changed environment to start a new wave of contagion. There will be new forms of influenza and new influenza epidemics. So, too, many of the narratives described in this book will become epidemic again, weaken after years have passed, and then rise more. The timing is unpredictable; unlike the hypothesized business "cycles," narratives don't recur at regular time intervals.

The studies in this book reveal powerful economic narratives of the past that are mostly inactive and sometimes largely forgotten today. However, they are not completely forgotten, and someone seeking a powerful story may rediscover them. The constellations may change, providing new context for, and thereby increasing the contagion rate of, an old narrative and developing the idea into a major epidemic, sometimes after a long time lag.

In this book, I have made unusually heavy use of paragraph-length quotes. I did so to give readers a historical sense of a past narrative that made an impact and might make an impact again if it is repeated in the same words. As with jokes or songs, to be effective a narrative has to be worded and delivered just right.

When it comes to predicting economic events, one becomes painfully aware that there is no exact science to understanding the impact of narratives on the economy. But there can be exact research methods that contribute to such an understanding. There is no exact science about how to evaluate novels or symphonies either, but there are exact methods that may provide information that contributes inspiration to those who involve themselves with such things. We have to avoid the "seductive allure" of superficial arguments about the economy using scientific analogies to lend a sense of precision to a theory that in fact may be of little substance.[1] We need to keep the true scientific method in mind even when trying to use an essentially humanistic approach.

Let us proceed with some suggestions from the analysis in this book about future economic narratives, and how we can in the future direct research that allows a better, if inevitably imperfect, understanding of them.

Altered Forms and Circumstances

The perception from time to time of "economic strength" is driven by narratives, notably an other-people's-confidence narrative (discussed in chapter 10) that is for those times outcompeting other, less optimistic narratives. All narratives have their own internal dynamics, and this "strength" may well be ephemeral. With the Great Recession of 2007–9, we saw a rapid drop in confidence and return of a 1929 stock market crash narrative (chapter 16). The same could happen swiftly again as a result of a small mutation in the narratives or change in circumstances.

The keep-up-with-the-Joneses narrative (discussed in chapter 11) seems especially strong at this writing in the United States. President Donald J. Trump models ostentatious living. In addition, there appears to be less generosity toward hungry families. There had been a distinct downtrend in US charitable giving for basic needs even before Trump's presidency. Research at the Indiana University Lilly Family School of Philanthropy reveals a 29% decline in real, inflation-corrected, basic-needs charity from 2001 to 2014.[2] These declines in the modesty and compassion narratives extend to a lower willingness to help the world's emerging countries.

The intelligent machines narratives (chapters 13 and 14) are still much talked about, though they do not seem to have much economic impact at the moment. Machines do not seem to be very scary at the time of this writing, but should there be some adverse news about income inequality or unemployment, the contagion of scary forms of this narrative could reappear. A sudden increase in concerns about robots has happened before. A search on ProQuest News & Newspapers for articles containing both *robot* and *jobs* reveals that the number of articles almost tripled between the last six months of 2007 and the first six months of 2009. According to the National Bureau of Economic Research, December 2007 was the peak month before the Great Recession, and the recession ended in June 2009.

New Technology Will Change Contagion
Rates and Recovery Rates

Notable changes in information technology, with changes in contagion rates and recovery rates, have occurred over the course of history. The early invention of printed books in China, the invention of Gutenberg's printing press in the fifteenth century, the invention of newspapers in Europe in the seventeenth century, the invention of the telegraph and telephone in the nineteenth century, the invention of radio and television in the twentieth, and the rise of the Internet and social media have all fundamentally altered the nature of contagion, but to date there has been no systematic quantitative study of these inventions' impact on contagion.

Social media and search engines have the potential to alter the fundamentals of contagion. In the past, ideas spread in a random, non-systematic way. Social media platforms make it possible for like-minded people with extremist views to find each other and further reinforce their unusual beliefs. Contagion is not slowed down by fact-checkers. In contrast, the Internet and social media allow ideas to be spread with central control that is nonetheless poorly visible. Designers of social media and search engines have the ability to alter the nature of contagion, and society is increasingly demanding that they do so to prevent devious use of the Internet and the spread of fake news.

But changing communications technology isn't the only factor that can influence contagion rates. It isn't always even the biggest factor.

Cultural factors are also at work. History has shown changes in face-to-face spoken word use that likely affect the nature of contagion. For example, in the 1800s, literature would be read aloud in the *salon* and in the *family circle*, fashions that were especially prominent in the middle of the nineteenth century. Both the salon and the family circle reading began to fade at the turn of the century, as the *Washington Post* noted in 1899:

> Reading aloud to the children and in the family circle—how fast it is becoming one of the lost arts. What multitudes of children of former days were entertained, and instructed, by this practice, and how few there are who are so entertained and instructed nowadays. Children now, after being taught to read, join that great army which takes in the printed word, swiftly and silently. Most parents, doubtless, are too busy to spare time to educate their sons and daughters by reading to them, and as the children grow older they find their hours too crowded to devote any of them simply to listening. "What is the use" they would say, if asked. "Tastes differ, and we can read what we want in a fraction of the time that would be consumed if we had to sit still and hear it.[3]

However, as the salon and family circle faded, magazine clubs and book clubs took off into the twentieth century.

Another cultural factor altering the spread of narratives has been an international movement toward providing mentors for young people, with roots back to the Big Brothers (now Big Brothers and Big Sisters) movement starting in 1904, and later diversifying into an epidemic of sorts since around 1980. Having regular communications with successful or socially committed people helps a young person gain a sense of identity in the mentor's life stories, or in stories that the mentor tells of others in the same circle.[4] Mentoring groups are especially effective for women and minorities who may have felt little ownership of such stories.[5]

Two new phrases, *influencer marketing* (since 2015) and *social media marketing* (since 2009), have been gaining popularity. Marketing firms, notably shareablee.com and hawkemedia.com, offer influencer marketing, systematically finding influential people who allow marketing to them or with them via social media. Such sites should increase contagion rates for promoted stories and ideas.

Even as information technology is affecting the transmission of economic narratives that affect the human mind, it could conceivably go further and replace some of the ultimate decision-making process that individuals use. For example, we already have robo-advisers that offer advice on how much to consume and save and how much to put into the stock market versus other investments. The first robo-adviser was launched in 1996 with William Sharpe's Financial Engines. Since then, automated advisers such as Schwab Intelligent Portfolios, Betterment, and Wealthfront have proliferated. There are other efforts to automate economic decisions too, such as target date funds, first attracting interest around 2007, that automatically rebalance a long-term investor's portfolio based on a target retirement date. There are many other applications of algorithmic trading. Nonetheless, today, people write the programs and make the ultimate foundational decisions. Someday people may defer massively to machines for life decisions, in which case economic processes may be fundamentally altered. But that day appears likely still to be far-off.

Modeling technology's effects on communications will be easier to trace when there is better science behind the spread of economic narratives. Already, our models show that it is not easy to predict these narratives and their effects. For example, the epidemic's ultimate size may not change when an increase in the contagion parameter is matched by a corresponding change in the recovery parameter. Rather, the epidemic will just happen faster. We must integrate formal models of contagion into economic models to begin to understand the impact of such technology.

The Future of Research in Narrative Economics

It is very important, if we are ever to have a substantial understanding of the kinds of big economic events that have surprised us so often in the past, that we have some scientific methods of studying the narrative element of these, even if the science is not complete and still involves some human judgment. Otherwise the field will be left to prognosticators or prophets who give the whole enterprise a bad name.

Economic research has not emphasized the stories that people tell to one another and to themselves about their economic lives. The research misses any discernible meaning that appears in the form of narratives. By missing the popular narratives, it also misses possibly valid explanations of major economic changes.

If one searches newspapers of the twentieth century for contemporary explanations of recessions as they begin, one finds that most talk concerns leading indicators rather than ultimate causes. For example, economists tend to bring up central bank policy, or confidence indexes, or the level of unsold inventories. But if asked what caused the changes in these leading indicators, they are typically silent. It is usually changing narratives that account for these changes, but there is no professional consensus regarding the most impactful narratives through time. Economists are reluctant to bring up popular narratives that they have heard that seem important and relevant to forecasts, since their only source about the narratives is hearsay, friends' or neighbors' talk. They usually have no way of knowing whether similar narratives were extant in past economic events. So, in their analyses, they do not mention changing narratives at all, as if they did not exist.

We can already today learn something about popular economic narratives by counting words and phrases in the digitized texts that are available, but there has not been enough organized research to measure the strength of the competing narratives that combine and recombine over time to cause major economic events. Artificial intelligence can help with this—especially with unstructured data. The perennial narratives described in part III of this book are works in progress, not final and exhaustive quantifications of all truly important narratives.

Research on narrative economics has already begun and surely will continue, but will such research be done on a sufficient scale in the future? How effectively will substantial research on narrative economics use the large and growing amounts of digitized data? Will narrative economics help us create better, more accurate economic models to forecast economic crises before they begin or get out of hand? To move forward, we need to recognize the importance of collecting better data and integrating lessons from data into existing economic models. We need to research issues that today are considered peripheral to economics, and we need to collaborate with non-economists, who have different perspectives. For example, we can incorporate mathematical insights from other fields, such as mathematical epidemiology, to create a link between mathematical economics and the humanities. We must expand the volume of available data and study many economic narratives together. We must account for changing narrative epidemics in our forecasting models.

A Place for Narrative Economics
in Economic Theory

As we saw in chapter 3, narrative economics has been long neglected. That is likely partly because the relationship between narratives and economic outcomes is complex and varies over time. In addition, narratives' impact on the economy is regularly mentioned in journalistic circles, but often without the demands of academic rigor. The public opinion of journalistic accounts of narratives may have been diminished by aggressive economic forecasts that proved wrong.

In addition, economists long assumed that people are consistent optimizers of a sensible utility function using all available information, with rational expectations. As we've noted, this theory omits some clearly important phenomena. Fortunately, the behavioral economics revolution of the last few decades has brought economic research closer to that of other social sciences. No longer do economists routinely assume that people always behave rationally.

One widespread and important innovation is the creation of economic think tanks interested in creating policies based on the insights of behavioral economics. These think tanks have been called "nudge units," following the Behavioral Insights Team in the UK government in 2010. Working with the ideas popularized by Richard Thaler and Cass

Sunstein in their 2008 book *Nudge: Improving Decisions about Health, Wealth, and Happiness,* these units try to redesign government institutions toward "nudging" people away from their irrational behavior without coercing them. According to the Organization for Economic Cooperation and Development, there are now close to two hundred such units around the world.[6]

I advocate formalizing some of the intuitive judgment that national leaders already use to acknowledge and harness changing economic narratives. Leaders must lean against false or misleading narratives and establish a moral authority against them. Their first step is to understand the dynamics of the narratives. Their second step is to design policy actions that take account of narrative epidemics. Policymakers should try to create and disseminate counternarratives that establish more rational and more public-spirited economic behavior. Even if the counternarratives are slower to take effect than a more contagious destructive narrative, they can eventually be corrective.

For example, as noted in chapter 10, US President Franklin Delano Roosevelt in his March 4, 1933 inaugural address[7] at the bottom of the Great Depression asked people to set aside their fears and spend money. In his first fireside chat, March 12, 1933,[8] he appealed to morality, asking people not to withdraw more money than they needed when the banks reopened. He was spinning a narrative of what could happen if unreasoning people with little social consciousness destroyed the economy. We can speculate that President Roosevelt's request worked because it was based on a moral standard; his chats roughly coincided with upturns in the US economy. However, we do not have a way of quantifying exactly how salient the narratives of the time really were. We would know more, perhaps, if economists had collected better data and conducted more analysis on what people were saying in 1933. If they had, we might now have a better understanding about how to frame such moral-appeal narratives in the future.

A problem in using narratives to forecast economic variables is that human judgment and discourse about narratives tend to be politicized and emotion-ridden. It has been difficult for scholars to research popular narratives, focusing on the core elements that make them contagious, without being accused of taking sides in political, or sometimes religious, controversies. Because many professional economists try to remain nonpartisan, they tend to rely on quantitative, rather than qualitative, observations. However, with modern information technology, economists can now collect data on economic narratives themselves, on their essential elements of meaning, without being overly focused just on words, and they can model the transmission of narratives. If we maintain quantitative rigor, we can make narrative epidemics a part of economic science.

Some may doubt that it is possible to have nonpartisan discussion of economic narratives. However, if we are careful and polite, it should be possible to speak in a nonpartisan way about epidemics of economic narratives. Most people have some instinct about how to speak in a nonpartisan way, and they do so when the occasion demands it. We do not have to go so far in our efforts to be nonpartisan that we exclude study of some ideas and emotions that drive economic changes.

Economic research is already on its way to finding better quantitative methods to understand narratives' impact on the economy. Textual search is a small but expanding area. A search of the NBER working paper database finds fewer than one hundred papers with the phrase *textual analysis*. Economists have used textual analysis to document changes in party affiliation (Kuziemko and Washington, 2015), political polarization (Gentzkow et al., 2016), and news and speculative price movements (Roll, 1988; Boudoukh et al., 2013). Much more could be done. For example, economists could carry the historical analysis further into databases of personal diaries, sermons, personal letters, psychiatrists' patient notes, and social media.

Collecting Better Information about Changing Narratives Should Start Now

Economists must make more serious efforts to collect time-series data on narratives, going beyond the passive collection of others' words, toward experiments that reveal meaning and purpose. Such great quantities of digitized data are now available that it boggles the imagination. Even so, this vast dataset is minuscule compared to the even vaster universe of human communications that go on every day, most of which are not adequately sampled, described, or understood.

It is important that such data collection be maintained on a consistent basis through decades, so that we can make intertemporal comparisons of major influencing public narratives in the future. There has been relatively little incentive to undertake such a project, because there is little immediate payoff to doing so. Instead, most narrative data collection focuses on immediate interests, such as marketing specific products or predicting upcoming elections.

It is also important to apply creative energies toward such consistent long-term data collection. Understanding people, their behavior, and their thinking may even require the help of psychoanalysts and philosophers.

It will be difficult to combine these two needs, consistency through time and creativity. But we must do so if we are to make real progress in narrative economics.

The first step requires improving existing search engines so that they can better measure the time-varying incidence of narratives. The search engines do not tell us exactly how they determine the estimated total number of hits. Rather, they are designed primarily to help users find articles or information they are looking for. Thus some anomalies pop up when researchers attempt to count the number of references. For example, Google's search engine instructions say that a search for a phrase should enclose the phrase in quotation marks so that the search is confined to exactly those words in exactly that order. But sometimes including the phrase in quotation marks results in more hits than the phrase without quotation marks. A Google spokesman says that the greater number of hits for the phrase in quotation marks may happen because quotation marks cause Google to "dig deeper" into the database.[9] We need to see evidence that such deeper digging is not compromising the accuracy of counts. Google Ngrams is designed to count phrases, and to compare the counts through time, but Ngrams and other search engines could do much more to ensure that users can accurately compare counts through time.

In addition, we should be collecting time-series data about economic narratives at least once a year, ideally more often than that, and on an uninterrupted basis for decades into the future, and in multiple countries and languages. Such data-collection efforts might include the following:

1. **Regular focused interviews of respondents inviting them to talk expansively and tell stories in response to stimulus questions related to their economic decisions.** The instructions would ask respondents to tell a story that is interesting or suggestive of causes in the current environment. This is the *listening as a research method* advocated by Charlene Callahan and Catherine S. Elliott[10] and the *qualitative research* advocated by Michael Piore.[11] Some researchers have conducted such research, notably Alan Blinder and his coauthors,[12] who interviewed top executives about how they reach decisions about price setting, and Truman Bewley,[13] who asked managers about their wage setting. Still more researchers have studied narratives to try to infer motivations of those who decide on fiscal and monetary policy.[14]

   Focused interviews are interviews of individuals that ask them to focus on their understandings and stories related to current behavior. Focused interviews began to be used as research tools in the 1920s and were given a firm foundation by Robert K. Merton and Patricia L. Kendall in 1946.[15]

   Unfortunately, these researchers usually conducted these interviews as one-time-only events, and they did not try to collect long time-series information that would reveal how answers and stories changed through history. If such data had been collected, the entire stories would have been digitized as sections of long time series and preserved for future textual analysis. The data could then have been added to major economic data collections. These include databases such as the

Panel Study of Income Dynamics at the University of Michigan Institute for Social Research, the Federal Reserve Board's Consumer Expenditure Survey, and the Swedish Household Market and Nonmarket Activities database (HUS) at Gothenburg University. Maintaining a consistent research environment through time would allow intertemporal comparisons, though the list of stimuli would have to be augmented as time goes on and as relevant new words and concepts appear. There would likely be some overlap with other surveys, such as those conducted internationally under the International Social Survey Program.[16] New efforts could go well beyond the work to date of the University of Chicago General Social Survey[17] or the University of Michigan Institute for Social Research,[18] which have been useful for many purposes in the past.

2. **Regular focus groups with members of different socioeconomic groups to elicit actual conversations about economic narratives.** A focus group is a focused interview done on a group of people. The group interview is especially important for narrative economics since it creates an environment that simulates the very interpersonal contagion that underlies the epidemiology of narratives. The focus group is an important and common research method, typically used by marketers to learn how people in various demographic groups talk among themselves about products or political candidates.

In a focus group, the researcher puts together people who likely represent actual groups in human society; participants are typically similar in age, live in the same geographical region, and share other factors that influence social group cohesion. By putting similar people together, the researcher attempts to eliminate barriers of "political correctness" that might inhibit normal conversation in unnatural groups. The focus group leader then facilitates talk about stimulus words related to the subject of the research and records the conversation. Running focus groups requires human judgment on the part of the interviewer. It is an art as well as a science, the art of getting people to think and talk about why they do certain things or hold particular beliefs.

Focus groups are thus experimental situations that could become real observations of the contagion of ideas. Though common, focus groups researchers do not usually seek to provide voluminous data over decades in an attempt to learn about the causes of economic changes. In the case of economic narratives, focus-group participants might be asked to respond to words or phrases such as *stock market, bank, unemployed, the real reason to save,* or *government actions that might impact your future economic welfare or that of your children.* Recorded videos of the focus groups might be digitized, and, in the future, possibly even scanned and analyzed by facial recognition and emotionally categorized algorithms.

Focus groups are now recognized as valid tools for research into popular understandings and motivations. Focus groups have their critics,[19] for they are often poorly managed, but when done well they are extremely useful. Economists, however, have been extremely loath to use them. Economics and finance are the worst fields for references to focus groups. In the decade 2010–2019, only 0.04% of scholarly economics articles and 0.02% of scholarly finance articles mention the term *focus group* despite the fact that focus group methods, developed largely by practitioners of marketing science, are much improved in terms of sampling, directing, and experimenting.[20]

One of the propositions in chapter 8 of this book holds that the economic impact of narratives may change through time, depending on details of the narrative and of the zeitgeist. We saw examples of apparent inconsistencies: The outbreak of World War I caused the US stock market to collapse, while the outbreak of World War II caused the market to soar. The bombing attacks linked with the "big Red scare" in the United States in 1920 were associated with a decline in economic activity, while the 9/11 attacks in 2001 were associated with ample spending and the end of a recession. A timely and appropriately led set of focus groups that homed in on assumptions, emotions, and loyalties might have given us a better understanding of why people behaved as they did.

3. **A historical database of focus groups conducted for other purposes in years past.** The Public Opinion Research Archive provided by the Roper Center for Public Policy Research,[21] now at Cornell University, has since 1947 amassed a database of opinion survey responses, including the Gallup Data Collection. This archive, however, tabulates answers to individual questions about opinions, questions changing in wording through time and as part of changing questionnaires that provide changing context in terms of other questions asked in the same survey. It does not listen to respondents in their own words and their own thought innovations. The archive is useful, but it is hard to appreciate what elements are contagious or to judge changes in thinking from it. There should be a massive database that asks those conducting focus groups around the world to share the results of past focus group results that may be relevant to understanding changing narratives. It would ask them to share the results of past focus group results that may be relevant to economic narratives. The database administrators would ask permission to publish raw data while remaining suitably respectful of past privacy promises made to participants. The administrators would then find some way (a challenge!) to organize these past focus groups into the closest approximations of computer-searchable time series, which would permit researchers to use the data to plot epidemic curves for specific narratives, as I have done in this book for newspapers and books.

4. **Databases of sermons**. Thousands of religious organizations, churches, synagogues, mosques, and the like, must have records of old sermons (derashas, khutbahs, etc.), but databases seem designed for sermon preparation rather than historical research. Sermons are important because they touch on moral values as

they seek the deeper meanings in life. Changes in these moral values and value judgments about what is right and wrong are undoubtedly relevant to changing economic decisions.

5. **Historical databases of personal letters and diaries, digitized and searchable.** There are the beginnings of such databases already, but we could make a more determined effort to encourage families to donate diaries of deceased family members to such databases. Existing databases do not seem to be based on random samples of the world population with associated personal information. They tend to be assemblages selected for research with a specific purpose, such as research on a single war or social issue in a single country. These are still useful, but better sampling would make for better knowledge on how to generalize results to a broader population.

None of the above-listed data collections is likely to reach the desired scope in the academic research mill any time soon. The payoff to such research is far in the future, and the judgment of such resources is too hard to formalize. Academic research conducted by individuals, who are under pressure to "publish or perish," is unlikely to start data-collection efforts that will help us understand the relatively rare, but serious, depressions and financial crises that occur from decade to decade, but perhaps no more than twice in a lifetime.

Many survey organizations have been collecting some of the data outlined in the wish list above. They should be funded to do so systematically and consistently through time. I have collected such data on a small scale, with questionnaire surveys of both individual and institutional investors about the stock market, since 1989. There are parallel surveys in Japan and China. Also, Karl Case, and now Anne Kinsella Thompson, and I have been doing surveys of US homebuyers and their perceptions of the market for single-family homes since 1993. The early surveys received support from the US National Science Foundation, with later surveys supported by the Whitebox Foundation and the Yale School of Management. The questionnaires for these surveys include open-ended questions with space that invites respondents to write a sentence or two. The questions are designed to stimulate respondents to think about what is motivating them, so that their responses can be analyzed in perpetuity. Since I started these survey projects, I have seen other survey organizations pursue sometimes similar objectives, and then stop. New survey tools like SurveyMonkey and Qualtrics are encouraging a proliferation of surveys but not a consistent strategy that is pursued over long periods of time.

As of this writing, there does not appear to be much support for the routine collection of historical data in a form that will allow, decades hence, a truly comprehensive study of the dynamics of economic narratives.

Tracking and Quantifying Narratives

Research today needs improvement in terms of tracking and quantifying narratives. Researchers have trouble dealing with a set of often-conflicting narratives with gradations and overlaps. Even the simplest epidemic model shows that no narrative reaches everyone. In addition, the spread of a particular narrative may be largely random. The meanings of words depend on context and change through time. A story's real meaning, which accounts for its virality, may also change through time and is hard to track in the long run.

There is also the perpetual challenge of distinguishing between causation and correlation. How do we distinguish between narratives that are associated with economic behavior just because they are reporting on the behavior, and narratives that create changes in economic behavior?[22]

Economic researchers have to grapple with the same issues that have troubled literary theorists who try to list the basic stories in all of literature, who attempt to distill what defines these stories and makes them contagious (see chapter 2). At any time in history there are many contagious stories, and it is hard to sort through them. Literary scholars run the risk of focusing on details of the stories that are common just because the events are familiar in everyday life. They also face the difficulty of accounting for changes through time in the list of stories.

Fortunately, research in semantic information and semiotics is advancing. For example, machine translation allows a computer to select the meaning of a word by looking at context, at adjacent words. The user asks, "What is the longest river in South Africa?" and Siri provides a direct verbal answer ("The longest river in South Africa is the Orange River"). Such search is now becoming well established around the world.

However, semantic search may take a long time to reach the human mind's abilities to understand narratives. In the meantime, researchers can still quantify the study of narratives by using multiple research assistants who receive explicit instructions to read narratives and to classify and quantify them according to their essential emotional driving force. Advances in psychology, neuroscience, and artificial intelligence will also improve our sense of structure in narrative economics. Companies like alexability.com (Alexandria), alpha-sense.com, prattle.co, and quid.com are beginning to offer intelligent searches of public documents and the media that could help organize information about shared narratives.

As research methods advance, and as more social media data accumulate, textual analysis will become a stronger force in economics. It may allow us to move beyond 1930s-style models of income-consumption feedback and Keynesian multipliers that are still influential today and get closer to all the kinds of feedback that drive economic events. It will also help us better understand the deliberate manipulations and deceptions we have experienced, and it will help us formulate economic policies that take narratives into account.

We should be looking forward to better understanding the patterns of human thinking about the forces that cause economies to boom at times and to stagnate at others, to go through creative times and backward times, to go through phases of compassion and phases of conspicuous consumption and self-promotion, to experience periods of rapid progress and periods of regression. I hope this book confirms the possibility of real progress in getting closer to the human reality behind major economic events without sacrificing our commitment to sound scholarship and systematic analysis.

Appendix: Applying Epidemic Models to Economic Narratives

Epidemiology, a subfield of medicine, developed most productively in the twentieth century. Its greatest contribution, a mathematical theory of disease epidemics, sheds powerful light on idea epidemics as they influence economic events. We can adapt this theory to model the spread of economic narratives.

A Theory of How Disease Spreads

The mathematical theory of disease epidemics was first proposed in 1927 by William Ogilvy Kermack, a Scottish biochemist, and Anderson Gray McKendrick, a Scottish physician. It marked a revolution in medical thinking by providing a realistic framework for understanding the dynamics of infectious diseases.

Their simplest model divided the population into three compartments: susceptible, infective, and recovered. It is therefore called an *SIR model* or *compartmental model. S* is the percentage of the population who are *susceptible*, people who have not had the disease and are vulnerable to getting it. *I* is the percentage of the population who have caught the disease and are *infective*, who are actively spreading it. *R* is the percentage of the population who are *recovered*, who have had the disease and gotten over it, who have acquired immunity, and who are no longer capable of catching the disease again or spreading it. Nobody dies in this original model. The sum of the percentages is 100%, $100\% = S + I + R$, and the population is assumed constant.

According to the Kermack-McKendrick mathematical theory of disease epidemics, in a thoroughly mixing constant population the rate of increase of infectives in a disease epidemic is equal to a constant contagion parameter c times the *product* of the fraction of the total population who are susceptible S and the fraction infective I, minus a constant recovery rate r times the fraction of infectives I. Each time a susceptible person meets an infective person, there is a chance of infection. In a large population, the chance averages out to a certainty. The number of such meetings per unit of time depends on the number of susceptibleinfective pairs in the population, hence the product SI.[1] The threeequation Kermack-McKendrick SIR model is:

$$\frac{dS}{dt} = -cSI$$

$$\frac{dI}{dt} = cSI - rI$$

$$\frac{dR}{dt} = rI$$

There is no algebraic solution to this model, only approximations.[2] Similar equations also appear in chemistry, where they are called *rate equations* or *consecutive chemical reactions*.[3]

In the model used in this book, the contagion rate is cS, the product of a constant contagion parameter c and the time-varying fraction of susceptible people S. The recovery rate is constant, r. If we divide both sides of the second equation by the fraction of infective people I, we can see that the second equation is nothing more than a statement that the growth rate of the fraction of the population who are infectives is equal to the contagion rate cS minus the recovery (or forgetting) rate r. This conclusion makes sense: if it is to grow, the epidemic has to be spreading faster than people are recovering, and it is common sense that the contagion rate should depend on the fraction of the population susceptible to infection.

The first and third equations are very simple. The first equation says that the number of susceptibles falls by one with every new infection, because a susceptible turns into an infective. The third equation says that the number of recovereds rises by one with every new

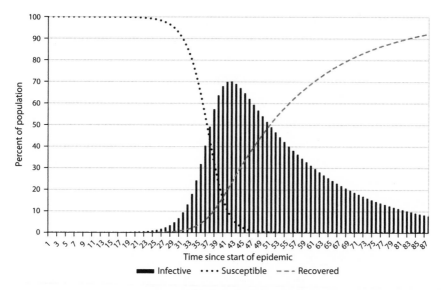

FIGURE A.1. Theoretical Epidemic Paths

Solution to Kermack-McKendrick SIR model for $I_0 = .0001\%$, $c = .5$, $r = .05$. The heavy bars show the percentage of the population who are sick and spreading the disease. The model assumes no medical intervention; the epidemic ends on its own, even though there are still susceptibles in the population, and not everyone was ever infected.

Source: Author's calculations.

recovery, because when a person recovers from the illness (or in our context forgets a narrative) an infective turns into a recovered. We will see below that this elementary model, which carries an essential insight about the path of epidemics, can be modified to include a growing population and many other factors specific to a particular epidemic.

Figure A.1 shows an example, implied by the above three equations, where one person in a million is initially exposed, $I_0 = 0.0001\%$, and parameters $c = .5$, $r = .05$. In this case, almost 100% of the population eventually gets infected. During a disease epidemic, the public tends to focus on the infectives, the bell-shaped curve in the figure. Attention also focuses on the number of newly reported cases, the speed of transition from susceptible to infective, which follows a similarly shaped bell-shaped curve if r is not too far below c. For narratives, we compare plots of counts of words and publications to the infective curve as in the figure.

The SIR model implies that from a small number of initial infectives, the number of infectives follows much the same hump pattern, from epidemic to epidemic, rising at first, then falling. A mutation in an old, much-reduced disease may produce a single individual who is infective with the new strain. Then there will be a lag, possibly a long lag if c is small, before the disease has infected enough people to be noticed in public. The epidemic will then rise to a peak. Before everyone is infected, the epidemic will then fall and come to an end without any change in the infection or recovery parameters c and r.

Not everyone will catch the disease. Some people escape the disease completely because they do not have an effective encounter with an infective. The environment gradually becomes safer and safer for them because the number of infectives decreases as they get over the disease and become immune to it. Thus there are not enough new encounters to generate sufficient new infectives to keep the disease on the growth path. Eventually, the infectives almost disappear, and the population consists almost entirely of susceptible and recovered. Applying this model to narratives: because not everyone is infected, some people will say after an economic narrative epidemic that they never even heard of the narrative, and they will be skeptical of its influence on the economy even if the narrative is indeed very important to economic activity.

Which factors combine to spread a major disease that ultimately reaches a lot of people (the total fraction of the population ever infected and recovered)? The disease's reach is determined by the ratio c/r. As time goes to infinity, the fraction of people who have ever had the disease goes to a limit R_∞ (called the size of the epidemic) strictly less than 1. It follows directly from the first and third equations that $\dfrac{dS}{dR} = -\dfrac{c}{r}S$. Given the initial condition on the fraction of the population initially infected I_0 that $S = (1 - I_0)e^{-\left(\frac{c}{r}\right)R}$, and because $I_\infty = 0$, $1 = S_\infty + R_\infty$, we have:

$$\frac{c}{r} = R_\infty^{-1} \, log \, \frac{1 - I_0}{1 - R_\infty}$$

which provides the relationship between the ultimate number ever infected by the disease and c/r. If we could choose c and r, we could make the size of the epidemic R_∞ anything we want between I_0 and 100%. If we define "going viral" as $R_\infty > \dfrac{1}{2}$, then we see a viral event happening from I_0 close to zero when $\dfrac{c}{r} > 1.386$. If we multiply both parameters, c and r, by any positive constant a, then the same three equations are satisfied by $S(at), I(at), R(at)$.

Higher c/r corresponds to higher size of epidemic R_∞, regardless of the level of c or r, while higher c itself, holding c/r constant, yields a faster epidemic. For an epidemic to get started from very small beginnings, when S is close to 1, c/r must be greater than 1. Depending on the two parameters c and r, there can be both fast and slow epidemics that look identical if the plot is rescaled. If we also vary the ratio c/r, we can have epidemics that play out over days and reach 95% of the population, or epidemics that play out over decades and reach 95% of the population, or epidemics that play out over days and reach only 5% of the population, or epidemics that play out over decades and reach 5% of the population. But in each case, we can have hump-shaped patterns of infected that on rescaling look something like the heavy line in Figure A.1.

Variations on the SIR Model

The Kermack-McKendrick SIR model is the starting point for mathematical models of epidemics that have, over the better part of a century since, produced a huge literature. Among the different versions, the basic compartmental model has been modified to allow for gradual loss of immunity, so that recovereds are gradually transformed into susceptibles again (the SIRS model).[4] The SIR model can also be modified so that an encounter between a susceptible and an infected leads to an increase in exposed E, a fourth compartment who become infected later (the SEIR model). The model has also been modified to incorporate partial immunity after cure, birth of new susceptibles, the presence of superspreaders with very high contagiousness, and geographical patterns of spread.

These models, with modifications appropriate for the disease studied, have been useful for predicting the course of epidemics. For example, the SEIR model has been modified to explain the spread of influenza geographically with the assumption that the exposed but still asymptomatic are capable of long-distance travel. Applying the model to influenza data and data on intercity volume of air transportation, R. F. Grais and her coauthors found that their model helps explain intracity and intercity time patterns of influenza outbreak.[5]

Another compartmental model example is a stochastic extension of an SEIHFR model, where S is susceptible, E is exposed, I is infected, H is hospitalized, F is dead but not buried, and R is recovered or buried. This model has been fitted to data on African Ebola epidemics,[6] and it takes into account public efforts to stem contagion of the disease through hospitalization and proper disposal of bodies.

The SEIHFR compartmental model has six compartments, but future models of economic narratives might well benefit from even more compartments. For example, a model for the spread of the technological unemployment narrative (see chapter 13) might include separate compartments for unemployed and infected and unemployed and uninfected, employed and infected and employed and uninfected, as well as extra equations that come from conventional economic models.

Economic models might also take inspiration from the medical literature on co-epidemics to incorporate contagious economic narratives into economic models. In a medical setting, a co-epidemic occurs when the progress of one disease interacts with the progress of another. For example, HIV and tuberculosis have been identified as coinfective: many more people have both diseases than would be predicted by two independent epidemic models. Elisa F. Long and her coauthors (2008) have proposed a variation of the basic compartmental model along Kermack-McKendrick lines that allows for people infected by one of these diseases to be more likely to catch and spread the other.[7] Models like this one could represent narrative constellations in which multiple narratives support one another by contagion. Such models could also represent the interaction of economic narratives, such as the technological unemployment narrative, with economic status, such as unemployment.

Structural macroeconomic models commonly include simple univariate autoregressive integrated moving average (ARIMA) models to represent error terms or driving variables for which there is no economic theory. George E. P. Box and Gwilym Jenkins first popularized the ARIMA models in a 1970 book. While Box and Jenkins described these models as useful in any realm of science, economists have used them most aggressively.[8] Owing to a well-developed theory of forecasting of times series that can be described in ARIMA terms, the epidemic among economists of ARIMA models led to a slightly delayed epidemic of rational expectations models, which peaked (according to Google Ngrams) around 1990 but still remains prevalent today. The ARIMA models are an alternative to the compartmental models described in this appendix. But there is something essentially arbitrary about the ARIMA models, which, unlike the compartmental epidemic models, lack a theoretical underpinning.[9]

The ARIMA methods can be improved with the theoretical epidemic models, using a combination of simulation, classification, statistical and optimization techniques to forecast the epidemic curve when contagion rates and recovery rates vary through time.[10] We can selectively bring in data other than data on the epidemic itself based on our knowledge of the structure of epidemics, and this takes us well beyond the mindless search for "leading indicators."

Not all data on epidemics fit the compartmental model framework well. Consider the long-slow US epidemic of poliomyelitis enterovirus cases from the late nineteenth century to their peak in 1952, superimposed on seemingly random one-summer epidemics. A gradual trend toward better cleanliness and hygiene should have had the effect of reducing the incidence of the disease, not increasing it. Paradoxically, the lower incidence of the disease, which was in most cases benign, had the effect of making *reported cases* involving paralysis or other consequences more common because nursing infants were less likely to receive antibodies from their mothers, which would have helped them gain immunity to the disease's severe consequences in later reinfections.[11]

When we apply the compartmental model to social epidemics and to epidemics of ideas, certain changes seem natural. One thought is that the contagion rate should decline with time, as the idea becomes gradually less exciting. One way of modeling that notion comes from Daryl J. Daley and David G. Kendall (1964, 1965), who said that the Kermack-McKendrick model could be altered to represent the idea that infectives might tend to become uninfective after they meet another infective person or a recovered person, because they then think that many people now know the story. Because the story is no longer new and exciting, the newly uninfected choose not to spread the epidemic further.

D. J. Bartholomew (1982) argued that when we apply variations of the Kermack-McKendrick model to the spread of ideas, we should not assume that ceasing to infect others and forgetting are the same thing. Human behavior might be influenced by an old idea not talked about much but still remembered, or "behavioral residue" (Berger, 2013).

There is now a substantial economics literature on network models, including the recent *The Oxford Handbook of the Economics of Networks* (Bramoullé et al., 2016). There are only a few behavioral epidemic models. The word *narrative* does not appear even once in the *Handbook*. Some of these modified SIR models involve complex patterns of outcomes and sometimes cycles. Geographic models of spread are increasingly complicated by worldwide social media connections.[12]

Some SIR models dispense with the idea of random mixing and choose instead a network structure.[13] There may be strategic decisions whether to allow oneself to be infected, and the fraction of the population infected may enter into the decision (Jackson and Yariv, 2005). Other models describe individuals as adopting a practice not merely through random infection but rather through rational calculations of the information transmitted through their encounters with others.[14]

The core Kermack-McKendrick model may apply no matter how people connect with one another despite concerns that modern media (especially the Internet) make the original SIR model less accurate in describing social epidemics. For this reason, using the SIR model to explain the spread of ideas or narratives may require modifying it to take account of contagion by broadcast as well as contagion through person-to-person contact.[15] The existing model can accommodate that change with higher contagion rates for narratives owing to social media automatically directing narratives to people with likely interest in them, regardless of their geography.

Sociologists Elihu Katz and Paul F. Lazarsfeld in 1955 showed impressive evidence for a "two-step flow hypothesis" that cultural change begins with the news media but is completed via the "relay function" of word of mouth within primary groups, led by the relatively few group members who pay attention to the news.[16] The marketing profession has responded by promoting word-of-mouth seeding strategies and television ads that feature actors portraying people with whom the common person can identify and simulating direct interpersonal word of mouth. Moreover, marketing literature finds that direct word-of-mouth communications still beat other forms of communication in terms of persuasiveness.[17] In considering whether the Internet and social media affect the SIR model, Laijun Zhao and coauthors (2013) argue for a modified SIR model where the news media increase analogues to the parameters c and r.

Christian Bauckhage gives evidence that the SIRS variant of the Kermack-McKendrick compartmental model fits time-series data reasonably well on Internet memes from Google Insights (now Google Trends.)[18] He looked at silly recent Internet viruses like the "O RLY?" (Oh, really?) meme that displayed nothing more than a picture of a cute owl with what would appear to be a puzzled facial expression. Because the memes are largely nonsensical, we might expect them to follow a course independent of other ideas and thus to fit the SIRS model well, as Bauckhage found. He found roughly the same hump-shaped pattern of infectives among Internet memes again and again.

Further Reasons to Think That Economic Narratives Have Epidemics as Diseases Do

Even though modern communications media have made direct face-to-face communication of ideas less important, the Kermack-McKendrick three-equation model still remains a workable model for idea epidemics. The core model may apply no matter how people connect with one another.

My colleague John Pound and I conducted a survey in 1985 of both institutional and individual investors to try to learn how systematic they are in their investing decisions. We asked all respondents to recall the latest stock market investment they had made. We asked them if they agreed with the following statement about this investment:

> My initial interest was the result of my, or someone else's, systematic search over a large number of stocks [using a computerized or otherwise similar search procedure] for a stock with certain characteristics.[19]

Among institutional investors, 67% agreed with this statement, but only 23% of individual investors did. In a separate survey of investors in rapid-price-increase stocks with high price-earnings ratios, we asked the same question. Here, only 25% of institutional investors agreed, and among individuals only 16% agreed.

How, then, do people start to pay attention to an individual stock? The answer: word of mouth. We asked our respondents in the first survey how many people they talked to about the stock. For institutional investors in the random sample, the average answer was seven. For active individual investors, the average answer was even higher: twenty. The conclusion is that people are not generally systematic: they allow their attention to be swayed by unsystematic responses to hearsay. This lesson from the realm of investing likely extends to other economic decisions beyond investing, because it reflects basic patterns of human decision making. Other suggestions that variants of the SIR model might apply to understanding investments in individual assets include evidence that people tend to invest in companies that are nearby geographically, and that epidemics of interest in individual stocks sometimes proceed very swiftly but do not ever infect a high fraction of the population (which the SIR model can accommodate if both c and r are similarly high or confined to a small geographical area).

Such models could help explain the geographical pattern of the spread of economic narratives, including the Bitcoin narrative, which, though contagious in many countries, does have a geographical distribution. Geoffrey Garrett, dean of the Wharton School at the University of Pennsylvania, remarked on attitudes toward Bitcoin upon his return from a visit to Silicon Valley:

> Whereas most people on Wall Street remain skeptical, playing a wait-and-see game, Silicon Valley is all in. Literally every meeting I participated in, from the biggest tech companies to the smallest startups, was rich with enthusiastic and creative crypto conversations.[20]

Idea Epidemics and Information Cascades

Variations of the SIR model can generate chaos. Chaos theory in mathematics shows that many nonlinear differential equation models can be chaotic in a precise mathematical sense. That is, the system can generate seemingly random variations—variations that never repeat themselves, that appear to be generating random numbers even though the system is deterministic. In fact, random number generators on computers are not really invoking chance but are the product of such chaotic deterministic models. Variations of the SEIR epidemic model can be chaotic, as has been shown and studied mathematically and related to actual disease data.[21]

Chaos theory is associated with the *butterfly effect*, which refers to the idea that a huge, apparently unpredictable storm might have been generated by a seemingly distant and irrelevant event such as a butterfly flapping its wings on the other side of the planet long ago. Another variation of the SIR model can help explain such butterfly effects by adding *information cascades* to the basic model.[22] If people think they are collecting reliable information by observing the numbers of people who make certain choices, then the equilibrium can move off in random directions, much as in the artificial music-market experiment of Salganik and his colleagues discussed in chapter 4. I recall an experience with Professor Ivo Welch of UCLA, one of the authors of the information cascade theory. While driving me to my hotel, he told me he thought we were near the hotel but that he wasn't sure exactly where it was. Then he spotted a taxi with no passenger, and he said that he would just follow the taxi, because there was a good chance that the taxi was on its way to the hotel. His guess that the taxi driver had the information we needed worked perfectly, but it could just as well have led us to a different hotel or to any number of random places. If a lot of people were behaving as Ivo was, then one initial taxi could, in principle, start an epidemic that could set off a deluge of taxis to a random place.

Information cascades can explain how speculative bubbles can be perfectly rational, in accordance with the canon of economic theory. In my view, they are interesting because they describe how bubbles or depressions can start from purely random causes, even if people are fairly sensible. George A. Akerlof and Janet L. Yellen coined the term "near-rational" in 1985, and I wish that term had caught on more, that it had gone viral.[23] However, information cascades may not be so important a problem. In reality, taxi drivers never seem to follow the leader, at least not in terms of driving to destinations in their city. But, like everyone else, taxi drivers may follow others in terms of remembering "facts" of a more ambiguous nature, such as the best restaurant in a city.[24] Ask a taxi driver to take you to the best restaurant: you will likely get laughter in response, and it is unlikely that the destination will be demonstrably the best.[25]

The movements of taxi drivers, just like changes in behavior of consumers, investors, and entrepreneurs and other economic phenomena, can never be properly understood without some input from narrative economics. Making real progress in narrative economics is a big project for serious research in the future.

Notes

Preface: What Is Narrative Economics?

1. Allen, 1964 [1931], p. 261.

2. Allen, 1964 [1931], p. viii.

3. "Descriptive economics again divides into a formal and narrative branch; of which the former analyzes and classifies the conceptions needed for understanding the science in its widest applications, and the latter investigates historically and comparatively the various forms of economic life exhibited by different communities and at different epochs" (within entry "Method of Economics"), Palgrave, 1894, p. 741.

4. Interest in the role of narratives in driving social movements has been expressed by sociologists in the New Social Movement literature; see Davis, 2002.

5. Fair and Shiller (1989) show evidence that forecasting models have some ability to forecast in the short run, but Lahiri and Wang (2013) show with the Philadelphia Federal Reserve Bank Survey of Professional Forecasters that there is no "significant skill" at attaching a probability to a one-quarter GDP decline in the United States one year in the future. The probability of GDP decline that the professionals as a group have been giving at this forecast horizon is worthless.

6. Andrew Brigden, "The Economist Who Cried Wolf." Fathom Consulting, February 1, 2019, https://www.fathom-consulting.com/the-economist-who-cried-wolf/#_ftn2. Other studies that have found little success of professional forecasts of recessions at longer horizons include Zarnowitz and Braun, 1992; Abreu, 2011; and An et al. 2018.

7. Koopmans, 1947, p. 166.

8. Boulding, 1969, p. 2. In January 2018, there was a special posthumous session in Boulding's honor at the annual meeting of the American Economic Association in Philadelphia, "Kenneth Boulding and the Future Direction of Social Science."

9. Boulding, 1969, p. 3.

10. Irving Kristol, "The Myth of Business Confidence," *Wall Street Journal*, November 14, 1977, p. 22.

11. Addams headed an international women's conference in Zurich in 1919 that issued a statement predicting that the Versailles treaty would create animosities that would lead to future wars. She won the Nobel Peace Prize in 1931.

12. Keynes, 1920 [1919], p. 268.

13. My publications started with my 1972 doctoral dissertation at the Massachusetts Institute of Technology entitled "Rational Expectations and the Structure of Interest Rates." That dissertation, written under the supervision of Franco Modigliani, who influenced me in trying to find a realistic grounding for economic theories, was not fully comfortable with the economists'

favorite notion that all people are rational and consistent maximizers. Soon thereafter I wrote "Rational Expectations and the Dynamic Structure of Macroeconomic Models: A Critical Review" (1978). I continued with "Stock Prices and Social Dynamics" (1984); *Irrational Exuberance* (first edition, 2000); and two books coauthored with George Akerlof, *Animal Spirits: How Human Psychology Drives the Economy and Why It Matters for Global Capitalism* (2009), and *Phishing for Phools: The Economics of Manipulation and Deception* (2015).

Chapter 1. The Bitcoin Narratives

1. Quoted by Yun Li, "Warren Buffett says bitcoin is a 'gambling device' with 'a lot of frauds connected with it,'" CNBC May 4, 2019, https://www.cnbc.com/2019/05/04/warren-buffett -says-bitcoin-is-a-gambling-device-with-a-lot-of-frauds-connected-with-it.html.

2. Paul Vigna and Steven Russolillo, "Bitcoin's Wildest Rise Yet: 40% in 40 Hours," *Wall Street Journal*, December 7, 2017, p. 1.

3. The Merkle tree and the digital signature algorithm are essential elements of the Bitcoin protocol described in the original Bitcoin paper signed by Satoshi Nakamoto in 2008. The equilibrium of the congestion queuing game is described in Huberman et al., 2017.

4. Proudhon 1923 [1840], p. 293.

5. Sterlin Lujan, "Bitcoin Was Built to Incite Peaceful Anarchy," https://news.bitcoin.com /bitcoin-built-incite-peaceful-anarchy/. Passage is dated January 9, 2016.

6. Ross, 1991, p. 116.

7. Himanen, 2001.

8. Zoë Bernard, "Satoshi Nakamoto was weird, paranoid, and bossy, says early Bitcoin developer who exchanged hundreds of emails with the mysterious crypto creator," *Business Insider*, May 30, 2018, http://www.businessinsider.com/satoshi-nakamoto-was-weird-and-bossy-says -bitcoin-developer-2018-5.

Chapter 2. An Adventure in Consilience

1. For example, calls for a broader approach to economic research have asked for the study of "social dynamics" and "popular models" (Shiller, 1984), "culturomics" (Michel et al., 2011), or "humanomics" (McCloskey, 2016); or for more "narrativeness" (Morson and Schapiro, 2017) or for "fictional expectations" (Beckert and Bronk, 2018) or "diagnostic expectations" (Gennaioli and Shleifer, 2018), "policy legends and folklists" (Fine and O'Neill, 2010), or "information-processing difficulty" in responding to news that makes "changes in expectations" into "an independent driver of economic fluctuations" (Beaudry and Portier, 2014).

2. Sarbin, 1986.

3. Berger and Quinney, 2004.

4. Rashkin, 1997.

5. Ganzevoort et al., 2013.

6. Presser and Sandberg, 2015.

7. Bettelheim, 1975.

8. Kozinets et al., 2010.

9. O'Connor, 2000.

10. O'Barr and Conley, 1992.

11. Jung, 1919.

12. Klein, 1921.

13. Klages, 2006, p. 33.

14. Klages, 2006, p. 33.

15. Brooks, 1992, location 74.

16. Brooks, 1992, location 749.

17. For a survey of neurolinguistics, see Kemmerer, 2014.

Chapter 3. Contagion, Constellations, and Confluence

1. World Health Organization, 2015.

2. Wheelis, 2002.

3. Marineli et al., 2013.

4. See also Nagel and Xu, 2018.

5. Vinck et al. 2019, especially table 3.

6. Gerbert et al., 1988.

7. Historians of economic thought (including Dimand, 1988) show that the multiplier ac-celerator model has even earlier beginnings, via Keynes (1936); before that, Keynes's student Kahn (1931); before that, a half dozen other multiplier expositors; and before that, even before the 1929 crash, Keynes himself in handwritten notes to himself in preparing for a speech (Kent, 2007). The less pretentious and more metaphoric and visual term "ripple effect" referring to the multiplier (instead of, as formerly, to a pattern or sequence of pleats on clothing) began to go viral around 1970 and by 2000 had surpassed "multiplier effect."

8. The Samuelson overlapping-generations model was anticipated by Allais (1947), but Allais's version received little notice; Samuelson does not reference it.

9. These are examples of the "rational ritual" defined by Michael Suk-Young Chwe (2001), rituals undertaken so that people know that other people recognize the narrative, which makes possible a recognizable "common knowledge."

10. Young, 1987.

11. Writers sometimes describe their craft as looking for stories or vignettes that will serve as "donkeys" for important ideas. See Lawrence Wright, https://www.cjr.org/first_person /longform_podcast_lessons_on_journalism.php.

Chapter 4. Why Do Some Narratives Go Viral?

1. Sartre, 1938, location 952.

2. Pace-Schott, 2013.

3. Polletta, 2002, p. 31.

4. Brown, 1991, location 2852 of 2017 Kindle Edition.

5. Plato, *The Republic*, bk. 3, trans. Benjamin Jowett, https://www.gutenberg.org/files/1497 /1497-h/1497-h.htm.

6. Cicero, 1860 [55 BCE], p. 145.

7. Mineka and Cook, 1988; Curio, 1988.

8. Reeves and Nass, 2003.

9. Brown, 1991; Kirnarskaya, 2009.

10. Jackendoff, 2009.

11. Patel, 2007, p. 324.

12. Newcomb, 1984, p. 234.

13. Hofstadter, 1964.

14. See Fehr and Gächter, 2000.

15. https://www.merriam-webster.com/dictionary/narrative.

16. Kasparov, 2017, p. 138.

17. White, 1981, p. 20.

18. Schank and Abelson, 1977.

19. Shiller, 2002.

20. Thanks to Ryan Larson. It is patent #362,868, 1887, G. I. AP Roberts, https://patents .google.com/patent/US362868A/en.

21. "Come What May: A Wheel of an Idea," *Christian Science Monitor*, October 24, 1951, p. 13.

22. Display ad, *Los Angeles Times*, July 29, 1991, p. A4.

23. Salganik et al., 2016.

Chapter 5: The Laffer Curve and Rubik's Cube Go Viral

1. Shiller, 1995.

2. Litman, 1983.

3. Jack Valenti, in a speech "Motion Pictures and Their Impact on Society in the Year 2001" (April 25, 1978), quoted in Litman, 1983, p. 159.

4. Goldman, 2012, location 695.

5. For lists of exceptional one-hit wonders, see Wikipedia, https://en.wikipedia.org/wiki /One-hit_wonder.

6. "[A tax] may obstruct the industry of the people, and discourage them from applying to certain branches of business which might give maintenance and employment to great multitudes." Smith, 1869, p. 416.

7. Cheney was as of 1978 soon to be White House chief of staff, later secretary of defense and vice president of the United States.

8. Rumsfeld was as of 1978 recently secretary of defense.

9. http://americanhistory.si.edu/blog/great-napkins-laffer.

10. Peter Liebhold, "O Say Can You See," http://americanhistory.si.edu/blog/great-napkins -laffer.

11. Arthur B. Laffer, "The Laffer Curve: Past, Present and Future," January 6, 2004, https:// www.wiwi.uni-wuerzburg.de/fileadmin/12010500/user_upload/skripte/ss09/FiwiI /LafferCurve.pdf.

12. Paul Blustein, "New Economics: Supply-Side Theories Became Federal Policy with Unusual Speed," *Wall Street Journal*, October 8, 1981, p. 1.

13. See Mirowski, 1982.

14. Brill and Hassett, 2007.

15. Cicero, 1860 [55 BCE], pp. 187–88.

16. McDaniel and Einstein, 1986.

17. Lorayne, 2007, p. 18.

18. See Paller and Wagner, 2002.

19. "Second Look in Sweden," *Boston Globe*, September 21, 1976, p. 26.

20. In 1989, it was pointed out that it was possible for an elderly person in the United States to pay more in taxes than 100% of an increase in income because of the combined effect of the tax on Social Security benefits and the Medicare surtax. James Kilpatrick, "Elderly Run Faster, Fall Further Behind," *St. Louis Post Dispatch*, March 19, 1989, p. B3.

21. US Tax Policy Center, https://www.taxpolicycenter.org/statistics/historical-individual-income-tax-parameters.

22. Patrick Owens, "What's behind the Tax Revolt?" *Newsday*, June 2, 1978, p. 75.

23. https://www.gop.gov/9-ronald-reagan-quotes-about-taxes/.

24. Walter Trohan, "Report from Washington," *Chicago Tribune*, February 20, 1967, p. 4.

25. Steven V. Roberts, "Washington Talk; Reagan and the Russians: The Joke's on Them," *New York Times*, August 21, 1987, p. A1.

Chapter 6. Diverse Evidence on the Virality
of Economic Narratives

1. Penfield, 1958, p. 57.

2. Penfield, 1958, p. 57.

3. Scholz et al., 2017, p. 2882.

4. Zak, 2015.

5. Maren and Quirk, 2004.

6. Milad et al., 2005.

7. Milad et al., 2014.

8. Miłosz, 1990 [1951], p. 239.

9. Hume, 1788 [1742], p. 103.

10. An account of this depression, from the viewpoint of the Province of Pennsylvania, is in Berg, 1946.

11. Alexander Windmill, Letter to the Printer, *New-London Gazette*, reprinted in the *Connecticut Courant*, May 20, 1765, p. 1. See also Colin McEnroe, "A Page from History: We Were There," *Hartford Courant*, October 29, 1997, p. F8.

12. Le Bon, 1895.

13. Quoted from the *Boston Transcript* in "Art and Business in Book-Jackets," *Literary Digest* 70 (September 10, 1921): 26–27.

14. Akerlof and Shiller, 2015.

15. Holt, 2002; Klein, 2009.

16. Keynes, 1936.

17. Newspapers used to run many beauty contests. In 1920, the *Evening World* in New York ran a series of photos of beautiful women, some of them famous, not all at once but over weeks, inviting readers to clip out and mail in a nominating coupon with a list of their five favorites. The reader could also suggest a new name and enclose a photo that might be added to the list of contestants for later publication. The list of the readers' favorites was published and updated. There was, however, no prize to the reader, except possibly in the form of pleasure for having picked the winners. Moreover, the newspaper asked readers to select five favorites, not six. I have not been able to find the exact same beauty contest noted by Keynes. https://www .newspapers.com/image/78732551/?terms=Evening%2BWorld's%2BBeauty%2BContest.

18. Allen et al., 2006.

19. R. A. Fisher, 1930.

20. See Leonard, 2006.

21. Bruner, 1998, p. 18.

22. Gaser et al., 2004.

23. Saavedra et al., 2009.

24. Losh and Gordon, 2014; Pierce et al., 2001.

25. Kahneman and Tversky, 2000; Thaler, 2015, 2016.

26. Johnson and Tversky, 1983; Slovic et al., 2007.

27. Loewenstein et al., 2001.

28. Dohmen et al., 2006.

29. Achen and Bartels, 2017.

30. Boltz et al., 1991.

31. Areni and Kim, 1993.

32. Cheng et al., 2017.

Chapter 7. Causality and Constellations

1. Hume, 1788 [1742], essay XIV, p. 101.

2. Farnam, 1912, p. 5.

3. Jevons, 1878, p. 36.

4. Merton, 1948; Azariadis, 1981; Cass and Shell, 1983; Farmer, 1999.

5. In his book *The Tyranny of Metrics* (2018), Jerry Muller details how overreliance on quantitative outcome measures defies sensible decision making in colleges, universities, schools, medicine, policing, the military, business, finance, philanthropy, and foreign aid.

6. "Stock Prices Move Up to Permanently High Plateau," *Toronto Star*, October 16, 1929, p. 14.

7. Kai Sedgwick, "46% of Last Year's ICOs Have Failed Already," February 23, 2018, Bitcoin .com, https://news.bitcoin.com/46-last-years-icos-failed-already/.

8. Escalas, 2007.

9. Machill et al., 2007.

10. McQuiggan et al., 2008, p. 538.

11. Slater et al., 2003.

12. Cronon, 2013, p. 12.

13. Psychologists Roger Brown and James Kulik (1977) coined the term "flashbulb memory" and used the example of the news of the 1963 assassination of US President John F. Kennedy. They hypothesized that flashbulb memory happens when there is both extreme surprise and emotional arousal.

14. Luminet and Curci, 2009.

15. "The First Gun: Its Ominous Report Was Heard Around the World," *Los Angeles Times*, February 1, 1896, p. 11.

16. "University High's Class of '42 Still Remembers Pearl Harbor," *Los Angeles Times*, December 7, 1981, p. F1.

17. The NBER announces US recession dates months after the fact. In this case, the March 2001 beginning of the recession was not announced until November 2001. But economists generally thought the economy was in recession in September 2001.

18. "The Perfect Storm Tears Heart Out of the US Economy," *Guardian*, November 14, 2001, p. 26.

19. "At O'Hare, President Says 'Get on board!'" September 27, 2001, https://georgewbush-whitehouse.archives.gov/news/releases/2001/09/20010927-1.html.

20. Greg Ip mentioned the possibility that "a burst of patriotism" might be a factor in rising confidence then. "After Sept. 11 Attacks, a Rebound, of Sorts," *Wall Street Journal*, October 15, 2001, p. A1.

21. "A central claim of the source-monitoring approach is that people do not typically directly retrieve an abstract tag or label that specifies a memory's source; rather, activated memory records are evaluated and attributed to particular sources through decision processes performed during remembering" (Johnson et al., 1993).

22. Johnson et al., 1993.

23. Barthes, 2013 [1984], http://xroads.virginia.edu/~drbr/wrestlin.html.

24. "Kilrain's Rheumatism," *Cincinnati Inquirer*, February 22, 1890, p. 2.

25. "But a prolusion of that kind [rhetorical] ought not to be like that of gladiators, who brandish spears before the fight, of which they make no use in the encounter." Cicero, 1860 [55 BCE], pp. 178–79.

Chapter 8. Seven Propositions of Narrative Economics

1. Shiller, 1989.

2. Arthur Krock, "What America Is Talking About," *New York Times*, October 30, 1932, p. SM1.

3. Clearly, the original Keynesian idea that current income alone determines current consumption is not accurate, as Milton Friedman (1957) pointed out. He showed that consumption expenditures track current income much more for people in occupations where current income is a better guide to future income—that is, occupations whose incomes are not so volatile year to year. He hypothesized that spending is determined not by an individual's current income, but by permanent income, the expected long-run average future income. But so too, in the Great

Depression, Friedman's permanent-income hypothesis wasn't entirely accurate either. That model has people only reacting to income adjusted for its statistical properties. Christina Romer (1990) pointed out that after the stock market crash of 1929, consumption demand immediately fell, before people's incomes had shown any evidence of decline. She concluded that the reduced demand must have been some reaction to the newfound uncertainty surrounding the crash. Demand depends on both expectations and uncertainty and through these as well on a variety of narratives, which, once experts seem discredited, are all people have to suggest the future. Tobin and Swan (1969) showed further problems with the permanent-income hypothesis.

4. https://www.thesun.co.uk/tech/5067093/lily-allen-bitcoin-billionaire-richer-than-madonna/.

5. See Shiller, 1989.

6. Siegel, 2014 [1994], pp. 250–53. The *New York Herald Tribune*, after expressing puzzlement why the US stock market did not drop after September 3, 1939, offered the possible explanation that "it seems clear that many persons who held on to their securities, or bought securities, were actuated by the belief, or the hope, that the stock market would follow the general pattern of the last world war, when, after eight months of doldrums during part of which there was no formal trading, it leaped upward in 1915 on the stimulus of war orders for Europe." "War and the Markets," *New York Herald Tribune*, September 4, 1939, p. 18.

7. World Health Organization, 2003, p. xiii.

8. Vosoughi et al., 2018.

9. The original song was published in *Song Stories for the Kindergarten* in 1893 by Patty and Mildred J. Hill. https://commons.wikimedia.org/wiki/File:GoodMorningToAll_1893_song.jpg.

10. Weems, 1837, p. 11.

11. Weems, 1837, pp. 13–14.

12. Wang et al., 2012.

13. Blanc, 1851, p. 91: "De chacun selon ses facultés, à chacun selon ses besoins." Matthew 25:15 quotes Jesus: "to each according to his ability."

Chapter 9. Recurrence and Mutation

1. See Kuran and Sunstein, 1999.

2. However, most Civil War deaths were caused by disease, not battle. If considered as a disease epidemic, the Civil War was not the biggest in US history, not even close. See Nicholas Marshall, "The Civil War Death Toll, Reconsidered," *New York Times Opinionator*, March 2014, https://opinionator.blogs.nytimes.com/2014/04/15/the-civil-war-death-toll-reconsidered/.

3. The term "Great Recession" was also attached to the mild 1990–91 recession, associated with another war in the Middle East, and again inviting comparisons to the Great Depression, by US presidential candidate H. Ross Perot during the 1992 presidential campaign. See James Flanagan, "What an Economy in Low Gear Means," *Los Angeles Times*, July 26, 1992.

Chapter 10. Panic versus Confidence

1. Raymond Moley, quoted in Terkel, 1970, location 5151.

2. "The Financial Crisis," *New York Herald Tribune*, September 26, 1857, p. 1.

3. Hannah, 1986.

4. "How the New Banking System Is Expected to Operate as a Cure for Business Panics," *Washington Post*, December 29, 1913, p. 5.

5. George Gallup, "The Gallup Poll: An Increasing Number of Voters Believe Business Will Improve within Six Months," *Washington Post*, February 4, 1938, p. X2.

6. Sidis, 1898, p. 6.

7. Marden, 1920, p. 175.

8. "First Scientific Weather Forecasting," *Chicago Daily Tribune*, December 18, 1898, p. 29.

9. Diogenes, "Correspondence of the Mercury," *Charleston Mercury*, February 15, 1858, p. 1.

10. The term *leading indicators* appears once in 1880 and twice in the 1920s in ProQuest News & Newspapers, but it was not an established public concept until the Great Depression in the 1930s. The significance of the 1938 Mitchell and Burns leading indicators in the history of economic thought is brought out by Moore, 1983. There was also the very influential 1946 book by Burns and Mitchell that expanded on the leading indicators. Arthur Burns later became chairman of the Federal Reserve Board, 1970–78, during a period of exploding inflation that he was blamed for, adding further contagion of talk and celebrity status to his forecasting model.

11. "Lays Bull Market to Coolidge 'Tips,'" *New York Times*, August 24, 1928, referring to an *Atlantic* article of that month.

12. "The Wall Street Journal Straws: Difficult to Take Profits," *Wall Street Journal*, November 5, 1928, p. 2.

13. "'Why Does U.S. Fuss at Us' Traders Ask: Public Eye Battle of Wall Street," *Chicago Daily Tribune*, February 18, 1929, p. 25.

14. "New Threats Made to Cut Speculation," *Washington Post*, April 5, 1929, p. 1.

15. Lewis H. Haney, "Looking 1930 in the Face," *North American Review* 229(3) (March 1930): 365.

16. *New York Times*, January 5, 1931.

17. *New York Times*, September 25, 1884, p. 4.

18. "Reckless Talk in Congress," *New York Times*, May 18, 1932, p. 20.

19. Irving Fisher, 1930, p. 63.

20. Thomas Mullen, quoted in "Money to Move as Fear Leaves, 'Ad' Men Told," *Christian Science Monitor*, June 15, 1931.

21. Franklin Delano Roosevelt, First Inaugural Address, March 4, 1933, http://www .gutenberg.org/files/104/104-h/104-h.htm.

22. Goodreads.com lists "The only thing we have to fear is fear itself" as the most famous out of 139 famous Franklin Roosevelt quotes, in terms of "likes." https://www.goodreads.com /author/quotes/219075.Franklin_D_Roosevelt.

23. Langlois and Durocher, 2011.

24. "In the Wake of Unemployment," *Hartford Courant*, November 8, 1931, p. E5.

25. Roosevelt, first fireside chat, March 12, 1933, https://www.youtube.com/watch?v=r6nYKRLOFWg.

26. W. M. Kiplinger, "Causes of Our Unemployment: An Economic Puzzle," *New York Times*, August 17, 1930, p. 111.

27. Lindbeck and Snower, 2001.

28. Eichengreen,1996; Eichengreen and Temin, 2000.

29. Marx, 2017 [1959], beginning of chap. 15.

Chapter 11. Frugality versus Conspicuous Consumption

1. One might anticipate finding such expectation of moderation in wealthy consumption out of respect for the unemployed in Henry George's book *Progress and Poverty*, published at the end of the depression of the 1870s, but it is not there. Instead, he seems to think just the opposite, for he says, if inequality is someday reduced: "With this abolition of want and the fear of want, the admiration of riches would decay, and men would seek the respect and approbation of their fellows in other modes than by the acquisition and display of wealth" (George, 1886 [1879], chap. 4). One might also expect to see some recognition of moderation, in the extended depression of the 1890s, in Thorstein Veblen's influential 1899 book *The Theory of the Leisure Class*, the book that coined the term "conspicuous consumption." But a new modesty with that depression is not mentioned. Indeed, the panic of 1893 and the ensuing depression are not even mentioned in that book. Veblen, too, seems to think just the opposite, writing, "Freedom from scruple, from sympathy, honesty and regard for life, may, within fairly wide limits, be said to further the success of the individual in the pecuniary culture" (Veblen, 1899, chap. 9).

2. "Financial Crash Left Them Deeply in Debt," *Daily Boston Globe*, March 10, 1930, p. 21.

3. "Family Breakdowns Reported Increasing," *New York Times*, March 21, 1932, p. 2.

4. "Women Make Plea for Family Relief," *New York Times*, May 17, 1936, p. N2.

5. Ruth Ellicott, "Household—Season for Home Refurbishing Arrives: Coziness Is Requisite for Winter, Entire Family Morale May Be Boosted by a Changed Household Environment," *Baltimore Sun*, October 1, 1933, p. TM8.

6. Allen, 1964 [1931], p. 289.

7. Carol Bird, "We're getting 'ANCHORED' Again Says Rita Weiman," *Washington Post*, July 10, 1932, p. SM3.

8. "Keeping Up Appearances: DARE TO BE POOR!" *Manchester Guardian*, October 9, 1931, p. 6.

9. Catherine Hackett, "Why We Women Won't Buy," *Forum and Century*, December 1932, p. 343.

10. Anne O'Hare McCormick, "The Average American Emerges," *New York Times*, January 3, 1932, p. SM1.

11. "Crime Decrease Noted in Depression Years," *New York Herald Tribune*, February 23, 1934, p. 32, and "Crime among Young Shows No Increase," *Globe and Mail*, November 22, 1937, p. 3.

12. "Citizens Advised Not to Give Money to Street Beggars," *Globe* (Toronto), January 14, 1931, p. 14. "Begging in City Increases Daily, Survey Reveals," *New York Tribune*, July 30, 1930, p. 4.

13. "Panhandling," *Washington Post*, November 3, 1932, p. 6.

14. "Bars Apple Sellers from Busy Streets," *New York Times*, April 16, 1931, p. 25.

15. "Apple Sale by Jobless Starts Friday: Unemployed Will Vend Fruit on Hartford Streets as a Way of Providing for Their Families," *Hartford Courant*, November 27, 1930, p. 1. ProQuest Historical Newspapers: *Hartford Courant*.

16. "Holdup in Car Panhandler's Thanksgiving," *Washington Post*, April 28, 1932, p. 18. "Drive Begun on Peddlers," *Los Angeles Times*, December 17, 1932, p. A10.

17. Roth, 2009, p. 12.

18. Stachura, 1986.

19. http://www.pbs.org/auschwitz/40-45/background/auschwitz.html.

20. Grace Kingsley, "Display of Luxury Is Out," *Los Angeles Times*, March 31, 1932, p. A9.

21. "Display of Wealth Viewed as Offense," *New York Times*, December 26, 1932, p. 21.

22. "1932's Bargains Different from Those of 1931: To Claim Poverty No Longer Chic—Furs and Shoes Are Discussed," *Washington Post*, April 7, 1932, p. S6. However, not everyone was enthusiastically involved in modeling poverty: "While poverty has become very *chic*, it is a prevailing negative excuse, the devotees of pleasure find it very hard to refrain." "Baltimoreans Find Europe Alluring," *Baltimore Sun*, June 14, 1931, p. SA13.

23. "Bicycle Riding Fad Strikes Washington," *New York Times*, July 31, 1933, p. 15.

24. "Is a New Car a Sin?" *Wall Street Journal*, February 18, 1932, p. 8.

25. Heffetz, 2011, p. 1106.

26. "Confidential Chat: Husband Lacks All Sense of Responsibility," *Boston Daily Globe*, May 12, 1932, p. 18.

27. "Confidential Chat: Don't Blame the Men; They Can't Help It," *Boston Daily Globe*, May 28, 1932, p. 18.

28. "Relief to Stay, Says State Director," *Pittsburgh Post-Gazette*, January 30, 1936, p. 26.

29. Bewley, 1999, pp. 49–50.

30. Fang and Moscarini, 2005.

31. "Blue Jeans and Calico," *New York Tribune*, April 13, 1920, p. 14.

32. Nerissa Pacio Itchon, "S.F.'s First Fashion Icon: Levi's 501s," *San Francisco Chronicle*, May 19, 2017, https://www.sfchronicle.com/style/article/SF-s-first-fashion-icon-Levi-s-501s -11153403.php. Lady Levi's were first marketed as cowgirl or riding clothes, as in the Levi Strauss display ad "An Old Timer Advises the Dude Ranch Guest," *New York Herald Tribune*, April 28, 1935, p. I13.

33. Judy Horton, "Dude Dressing," *Vogue*, June 1, 1935 p. 121.

34. Sullivan, 2006.

35. https://www.liveabout.com/the-history-of-jeans-2040397.

36. "Briton Changes Name; 'Becomes James Dean,'" *Minneapolis Sunday Tribune Picture Magazine*, January 5, 1958.

37. "The Country Is Off on a Jig-Saw Jag," *New York Times*, February 12, 1933, p. 100.

38. "1932's Bargains Different from Those of 1931: To Claim Poverty No Longer Chic—Furs and Shoes Are Discussed," *Washington Post*, April 7, 1932, p. S6.

39. Piketty, 2014. See also http://piketty.pse.ens.fr/files/capital21c/en/Piketty2014Fig-uresTablesLinks.pdf. Table I.1 on that site shows the fraction of income accruing to the top

decile in income in the United States 1910–2010, reflecting the dramatic rise in inequality since 1970.

40. Uchitelle, 2006.

41. Trump and Zanker, 2007. The title of the book was later changed to *Think Big: Make It Happen in Business and Life*.

42. Paul Blustein, "In Japan, Consumption's No Longer Conspicuous; Consumers' Newly Frugal Mood May Prolong Nation's Recession," *Washington Post*, February 28, 1993, p. H01.

43. Charles Fisher, *Meditation in the Wild: Buddhism's Origin in the Heart of Nature* (Alresford, UK: John Hunt Publishing, 2013).

44. Adams, 1931, p. 404.

45. "A Martin Luther King Center to Open in Phila.," *Philadelphia Inquirer*, November 23, 1983, p. 4-B.

46. "President Calls for Expanding Opportunities to Home Ownership, Remarks by the President on Homeownership," St. Paul AME Church, Atlanta, Georgia, June 17, 2002, https://georgewbush-whitehouse.archives.gov/news/releases/2002/06/20020617-2.html.

47. Pecotich and Ward, 2007.

Chapter 12. The Gold Standard versus Bimetallism

1. Quoted by Ralph Benko, "President Trump: Replace the Dollar with Gold as the Global Currency to Make America Great Again," *Forbes*, February 25, 2017.

2. https://www.bankofcanada.ca/rates/related/international-reserves/.

3. World Gold Council, https://www.gold.org/what-we-do/official-institutions/accounting-monetary-gold. There are 32,150 troy ounces in a metric ton, and the price of a troy ounce of gold at this writing is US $1294.

4. Daniel Indiviglio, "Bernanke to Ron Paul: Gold Isn't Money," *Atlantic*, July 13, 2011.

5. See Flandreau, 1996.

6. *Atlanta Constitution*, April 19, 1895, p. 4.

7. "The Treaty," *New York Times*, February 10, 1897, p. 6.

8. "Silver in the West: Some Easterners Misjudge the Sentiment for It," *Washington Post*, July 28, 1896, p. 4.

9. International Bimetallic Conference, *Report of Proceedings* (London, 1894).

10. Today's University of Chicago opened in 1890. It had as one of its first professors J. Laurence Laughlin, who, before his Chicago years, wrote a book, *The History of Bimetallism* (1886), which strongly opposed bimetallism. The real Professor Laughlin then challenged Harvey to a real debate in which Laughlin did much better than in the fictional exchange, and so became a leading public intellectual with influence on the Gold Standard Act of 1900 and on the creation of the Fed. See André-Aigret and Dimand, 2018.

11. "Silver in the West: Some Easterners Misjudge the Sentiment for It," *Washington Post*, July 28, 1896, p. 4.

12. "M'Kinley on Hard Times," *New York Times*, October 7, 1896, p. 3.

13. "NO MORE: Do Silverites Ask about General Prosperity," *Courier-Journal*, September 11, 1897, p. 6.

14. Noyes, 1898, p. 190.

15. In New York, there was a subtreasury office on Wall Street near the New York Stock Exchange. You can still see the open vault today, with an explanatory plaque, but the office no longer redeems in gold. The building is now a museum.

16. "The Pedigree of the Gold-Bug: The First Pair Imported from Nevada," *Louisville Courier-Journal*, July 28, 1896, p. 2.

17. "The Pedigree of the Gold-Bug," p. 2.

18. See Sargent and Velde, 2002.

19. Howard, 1895, p. 7.

20. Howard, 1895, p. 76.

21. Henry L. Davis, of the California Optical Company, quoted in "San Francisco Business Men Tell Why Times Are Hard and Name the Remedy," *San Francisco Chronicle*, August 21, 1896, p. 8.

22. Charles Merrill, quoted in "San Francisco Business Men," *San Francisco Chronicle*.

23. *Official Proceedings of the Democratic National Convention Held in Chicago, Ill., July 7th, 8th 9th, 10th and 11th, 1896* (Logansport, IN: Wilson, Humphries & Co., 1896).

24. "Where Bryan Got Them," *Louisville Courier Journal*, July 29, 1896, p. 4.

25. "Fiat Oratory," *New York Times*, July 24, 1896, p. 4.

26. Louis Sloss, quoted in "San Francisco Business Men Tell Why Times Are Hard and Name the Remedy," *San Francisco Chronicle*, August 21, 1896, p. 8.

27. The law was enunciated by Scottish economist Henry Dunning Macleod in 1857, at the very beginnings of the bimetallism controversy, and he generously attributed his law to British financier Thomas Gresham (1519–79). The law is very simple: if a bimetallic standard's ratio is contrary to the ratio established in world markets, people will generally choose to pay in the less valuable currency, which will drive the other metal out of circulation.

28. "Voice of the People: A Correspondent's Sensible Letter on the Money Question," *Chicago Daily Tribune*, August 26, 1893, p. 14.

29. On top of the puzzle of the amazing success of this story, there is another puzzle. Baum's book appears to be a parable on the gold standard and the Free Silver movement, but this was not generally recognized until 1964, when an article by Henry M. Littlefield pointed out the allegory. How odd that the parable was not noted in print for the better part of a century afterward. Littlefield is convincing, though, that Baum did intend to refer to the gold standard and the Free Silver movement, especially since Baum, as Littlefield points out, was himself active in the Free Silver movement, went to some of its parades, and lived in a free-silver-leaning rural area. Also despite defeat in the 1896 presidential election, Bryan was gearing up to run for the second time, in 1900, again advocating free silver, against McKinley again, and so the issues were still under public scrutiny in the book's publication year.

30. Eichengreen and Temin, 2000, pp. 206–7.

31. Mark Sullivan, "Inflation's Danger Begins When People Scramble to Get Rid of Their Dollars," *Hartford Courant*, November 26, 1933, p. D5.

Chapter 13. Labor-Saving Machines Replace Many Jobs

1. Our word *automatic* goes back to the seventh century BCE, Homer's *Iliad*, bk. 18, line 376: "Him [Hephaestus] she found sweating with toil as he moved to and fro about his bellows in eager haste; for he was fashioning tripods, twenty in all, to stand around the wall of his well-built hall, [375] and golden wheels had he set beneath the base of each that of themselves (αὐτόματοι) they might enter the gathering of the gods at his wish and again return to his house, a wonder to behold." http://www.perseus.tufts.edu/hopper/text?doc=Perseus %3Atext%3A1999.01.0133%3Abook%3D18%3Acard%3D360.

2. Aristotle, *Politics*, trans. Benjamin Jowett, bk. 1, pt. 4.

3. Argersinger and Argersinger, 1984. However, Walter Smith, in his 1879 book on the causes of the depression of the 1870s, makes no mention of labor-saving machines. The narrative did not reach everyone.

4. *Visitors' Guide to the Centennial Exhibition and Philadelphia* (Philadelphia: Lippincott, 1876), https://archive.org/details/visitorsguidetocoophil.

5. *Visitors' Guide to the Centennial Exhibition and Philadelphia.*

6. Charles M. Depuy, "The Question of the Hour," *Philadelphia Inquirer*, February 3, 1876, p. 1.

7. "Labor-Saving Machinery," *Daily American*, December 11, 1879, p. 2.

8. "Labor-Saving Machinery."

9. George, 1886 [1879], pp. 227–28.

10. "The General Omnibus Company of Paris," *Times of India*, June 4, 1879, p. 3.

11. "Labor-Saving Machinery and Overproduction," *Los Angeles Times*, June 28, 1894, p. 4.

12. "Labor-Saving Machinery and Overproduction."

13. "The Great Problem," *San Francisco Chronicle*, April 22, 1894, p. 6.

14. "Stores Are Merely Labor-Saving Machines," *Chicago Daily Tribune*, March 14, 1897, p. 26.

15. "Trade Unionists' Remedy," *Boston Daily Globe*, April 24, 1899, p. 5.

16. https://www.ele.uri.edu/faculty/vetter/Other-stuff/The-Machine-Stops.pdf.

17. "Robot Cop Dictator: Rules Five-Way Intersection," *Los Angeles Times*, July 29, 1929, p. 1.

18. Phillip Snowden, M.P., "Snowden Fears Trade War," *New York Times*, June 10, 1928, p. 133.

19. "Unemployment Called Serious," *Atlanta Constitution*, March 27, 1928, p. 4.

20. "Mayor Scored for Failure to Help Jobless," *Baltimore Sun*, April 16, 1928, p. 22.

21. Chase, 1929, p. 209

22. Chase, 1929, pp. 215–16.

23. Chase, 1929, p. 323. Chase used the phrase "technological unemployment" (p. 212), but only rarely.

24. "Steno in the Future May Be a Robot, Show Indicates," *Chicago Daily Tribune*, November 12, 1929, p. 45.

25. "Cause of the Crash," *Washington Post*, November 9, 1930, p. S1.

26. George, 1886 [1879], p. 259.

27. "Topics of the Markets: Another Gloomy Day on the Stock Market," *Globe and Mail*, October 29, 1929, p. 8. "Ford Would Raise Wages, Cut Prices Down to Actual Values," *St. Louis Post-Dispatch*, November 21, 1929, p. 2a.

28. Cassel, 1935, p. 66.

29. "Text of Governor Roosevelt's Address Opening His Campaign," *New York Herald Tribune*, August 21, 1932, p. 17.

30. Chester C. Davis, "Underconsumption of Goods: A Challenge to the Nation," *New York Times*, December 9, 1934, p. XX5.

31. See Balderrama and Rodríguez, 2006.

32. "Senators Invoke Ancient Rights Declare War on Dial Phone," *Baltimore Sun*, May 23, 1930, p. 2.

33. Fred Hogue, "Robots Menace World's Wage-Earners," *Los Angeles Times*, February 1, 1931, p. 23.

34. "Fear of Losing Job Makes Worker Curtail Spending," *Boston Globe*, November 1, 1931, p. A60.

35. "Einstein Sees U.S. Troubles Internal," *Boston Globe*, January 24, 1933, p. 17.

36. Fred Hogue, "Robots Menace World's Wage-Earners," *Los Angeles Times*, February 1, 1931, p. 23.

37. Wayne Parrish, "Ten-Year Survey Points to End of Price System," *New York Herald Tribune*, August 21, 1932, p. 1. The "Technocracy" group fell apart in discord by January 1933.

38. "Technology Cult Is Now on the Wane," *New York Times*, January 29, 1933, p. N1.

39. Aubrey Williams, "A Crisis for Our Youth," *New York Times*, January 19, 1936, p. SM4.

40. "Nazis to Bar Replacing of Men with Machines," *Hartford Courant*, August 6, 1933, p. B5.

41. https://www.youtube.com/watch?v=n_1apYo6-Ow.

42. "Yale Scientist Proposes Building Robot Army," *Nashville Tennessean*, January 25, 1941, p. 1.

43. "Robots Not War-Winners," *Globe and Mail*, July 7, 1944, p. 6.

Chapter 14. Automation and Artificial Intelligence Replace Almost All Jobs

1. Elmo Roper, "What People Are Thinking," *New York Herald Tribune*, December 28, 1945, p. 15A.

2. Ralph Reed, "1946 Sees First Traveling Vacations since the War," *Daily Boston Globe*, April 14, 1946, p. B9. The term "victory vacation" had also been used earlier, since 1942, to refer to an economical stay-at-home vacation motivated by a desire to save money and resources for the war.

3. Slide projectors have a long history (https://www.ithaca.edu/hs/vrc/historyofprojectors/), but Ready-Mounts, the convenient slides mounted in cardboard by the photo lab, were first advertised in 1946.

4. Harry T. Montgomery, "Confidence Marks Business Outlook," *Los Angeles Times*, January 3, 1950, p. 35.

5. Alfred L Malabre, Jr., "Automation Alarm Is Proving False," *Wall Street Journal*, December 23, 1965, p. 6.

6. "Automation Strike Deadlock in U.K.," *South China Morning Post*, May 3, 1956, p. 17.

7. John Hoggatt, "What Automation Means to You," *Austin American*, December 16, 1956, p. SM1.

8. Roscoe Born, "Men & Machines: Industrial Unions Fear Automation Will Cut Membership and Power," *Wall Street Journal*, April 7, 1959, p. 1.

9. Samuel Lubell, "Disturbing Paradox: Insecurity Blot on Recovery," *Boston Globe*, May 5, 1959, p. 19.

10. "Automation Blamed for Recession," *Washington Post*, April 23, 1958, p. A2.

11. https://www.youtube.com/watch?v=244SeRiP__M.

12. Michaels, 1962, pp. 13–14.

13. US Department of Health, Education and Welfare, National Commission on Technology, Automation, and Economic Progress, *Technology and the American Economy* (Washington, DC: US Government Printing Office, 1966).

14. Alfred L. Malabre, Jr., "Automation Alarm Is Proving False," *Wall Street Journal*, December 23, 1965, p. 6.

15. Mark Potts, "Personal Robots: The Future Is Now," *Washington Post*, December 12, 1983, p. WB33.

16. https://www.pastemagazine.com/articles/2015/11/the-100-greatest-movie-robots-of-all -time.html?p=5.

17. Andrew Pollack, "A New Automation to Bring Vast Changes," *New York Times*, March 28, 1982, p. HT1.

18. Pollack, "A New Automation."

19. G. Pascal Zachary, "Worried Workers," *Wall Street Journal*, June 8, 1995, p. A1.

20. Stock prices measured by the nominal price per share of the S&P 500 index, not corrected for inflation or share repurchase.

21. A year earlier, in 2010, Google Voice Action allowed verbal commands to be executed.

22. Silver et al., 2017. There are also AlphaZero skeptics, who doubt the program works as claimed, https://medium.com/@josecamachocollados/is-alphazero-really-a-scientific -breakthrough-in-ai-bf66ae1c84f2.

23. Harari, 2018.

24. http://www.cnn.com/2011/11/03/tech/innovation/steve-jobs-book-sales/.

25. "Proposing to Tax Labor-Saving Machines," *Sun*, January 18, 1933, p. 8, and Mady Delvaux, *Draft Report*, European Parliament, May 2016, http://www.europarl.europa.eu/sides/getDoc.do ?pubRef=-//EP//NONSGML%2BCOMPARL%2BPE-582.443%2B01%2BDOC%2 BPDF%2BV0//EN.

26. George, 1886 [1879], p. 395.

27. George, 1886 [1879], pp. 395–96.

28. Quoted in "An Engineer Turns Diagnostician," *St Louis Post-Dispatch*, June 5, 1932, p. 1.

Chapter 15. Real Estate Booms and Busts

1. For example, the correlation between the monthly Michigan Consumer Sentiment Index and the S&P/CoreLogic/Case-Shiller home price index corrected for inflation January 1978 to September 2018 is only 0.035.

2. Observer, "Making Auger Holes with a Gimlet," *Cultivator*, September 1840, p. 146.

3. "Where They Live," *St. Louis Post-Dispatch*, December 29, 1889, p. 18.

4. Davis and Heathcote, 2007.

5. A "traditional" ratio of land value to home value was 10%. Paul F. Kneeland, "This Land Boom Is a Land Boom with a Difference," *Boston Globe*, June 15, 1958, p. A31.

6. For example, during the baby boom in post–World War II US home prices, one article described rising construction costs as the cause: "U.S. Construction Costs Grind Upward: Prices on New Homes Follow Suit: Experts Differ on Why Prices Should Zoom," *Christian Science Monitor*, August 18, 1950, p. 13.

7. Grebler et al., 1956, p. 358.

8. "Housing Prices Nip Low Income Groups," *Arizona Republic*, January 25, 1957, p. 43.

9. McGinn, 2007, p. 6.

10. Festinger, 1954.

11. "Own Your Own Home," *Washington Post*, May 19, 1919, p. 9.

12. *Arizona Republican*, January 1, 1900, p. 3.

13. US Supreme Court Justice Joseph McKenna in *Hall v. Geiger-Jones Co.*, 242 U.S. 539 (1917).

14. "Ponzi's Florida Wizarding Pays Big—for Ponzi," *Chicago Daily Tribune*, January 16, 1926, p. 9.

15. Notably, the US federal government now regulates interstate land sales with the Interstate Land Sales Full Disclosure Act of 1968 (ILSFDA), and the law clearly discourages the kind of advertising and sales tactics that caused land booms in the past. See Loyd, 1975, and Pursley, 2017. ILSFDA now falls under the jurisdiction of the Consumer Financial Protection Bureau, which was created by the Dodd-Frank Act of 2010, and it has been actively prosecuting land promoters who fail to comply.

16. See Gyourko et al., 2013 for such a model.

17. Saiz, 2010.

18. "In fact, from the point of view of the median husband-wife household considering the consumption of a marginal unit of housing services, the after-tax cost is estimated to have declined by 30 percent from 1970 to 1979. This was due primarily to a decline in the before-tax real cost of capital and a large inflation-induced increase in the tax subsidy to owner-occupied housing." See Diamond, 1980, p. 295.

19. "WSJ 'Mansion' Section Makes Its Debut," *Wall Street Journal*, October 4, 2012, http://www.wsj.com/video/wsj-mansion-section-makes-its-debut/5BAD7D1C-77FA-4057-9E3A-19446C5F2F52.html.

20. Katherine Clarke, "Tech CEOs: Lie Low or Live Large?" *Wall Street Journal*, November 17, 2017, p. M1.

21. "House Prices: After the Fall" cover story, *Economist*, June 18–24, 2005.

Chapter 16. Stock Market Bubbles

1. For example, the correlation between the Michigan Consumer Sentiment Index and the Cyclically Adjusted Price Earnings (CAPE) Ratio for the Standard & Poor's 500 Stock Price

Index from January 1978 to November 2018 is 0.57. The correlation between the CAPE ratio and real home prices over the same interval is 0.42.

2. "Movie Ticker Blamed for Wild Trading in Stocks," *Austin Statesman*, May 24, 1928, p. 3.

3. Kempton, 1998 [1955], prelude, location 153.

4. Alexander Dana Noyes, *Globe* (Toronto), October 22, p. 8, 1928, quoting "Financial Markets," *New York Times*, October 22, 1928, p. 36.

5. Rappoport and White, 1994.

6. Robert Shiller, "Lessons from the October 1987 Market Plunge," *New York Times*, October 22, 2017, p. BU3, https://www.nytimes.com/2017/10/19/business/stock-market-crash-1987 .html.

7. Galbraith, 1955. He contradicted others' claims: "Rise in Suicide Rate Laid to Depression: National Survey Shows 20.5 of 100,000 People Took Their Lives in 1931—Highest Figure since 1915," *New York Times*, June 23, 1939, p. 24. Webb et al. (2002) show a modest positive correlation between unemployment for the past year and suicide, especially for white men.

8. Johnson and Tversky, 1983.

9. "When Youth and Beauty Go—What Then?" *Louisville Courier-Journal*, January 19, 1930, p. 87.

10. Terkel, 1970, p. 67.

11. Terkel, 1970, p. 376.

12. Terkel 1970, p. 164.

13. Kempton, 1998 [1955], prelude, location 118.

14. Jody Chudley, "JFK's Father Used a Simple Trick to Spot Market Bubbles—and You Can Too," *Business Insider*, October 12, 2017, http://www.businessinsider.com/how-to-spot-stock -market-bubbles-2017-10.

15. Baruch, 1957.

16. "Conservatives Begin to Realize Value of War Specialty Stocks," *Minneapolis Morning Tribune*, July 26, 1915, p. 15.

Chapter 17. Boycotts, Profiteers, and Evil Business

1. Charles C. Boycott, "The State of Ireland," *Times* (London), October 18, 1880, 6.

2. Wolman, 1916, p. 24.

3. Wolman, 1916, p. 34.

4. "Who Is a Profiteer, and What Shall Be Done with Him?" *New York Tribune*, June 16, 1918, p. D3.

5. http://avalon.law.yale.edu/20th_century/harding.asp.

6. "General Drop in Prices Forecast: Bankers and Traders Expect a Material Reduction in Practically All Lines—Say Era of Extravagance Has Passed," *Christian Science Monitor*, September 25, 1920, p. 4.

7. "Women Fight High Prices," *Globe*, September 4, 1920, p. 6.

8. US Bureau of Labor Statistics, *Monthly Labor Review*, September 2014, https://www.bls .gov/opub/mlr/2014/article/the-first-hundred-years-of-the-consumer-price-index.htm.

9. "Sees High Prices for Several Years," *Boston Daily Globe*, January 5, 1920, p. 13.

10. Atkeson and Kehoe (2004) argue with one hundred years' data from seventeen countries on five-year inflation rates and five-year economic growth rates. They believe that there is no significant association between the two if one excludes the Great Depression, 1929–34.

11. "Attacks Profiteers in Immorality," *Boston Daily Globe*, May 5, 1919, p. 2.

12. Mortimer Fishel, "Lawyers Who Feed on Soldiers' Kin," *New York Times*, August 11, 1918, p. 41.

13. Henry Hazlitt, "Profiteers as Public Benefactors," *New York Times*, March 21, 1920, p. xxx10.

14. Fisher, 1928, p. 7.

15. "Federal Judge Whacks Profiteers Hard Blow," *Los Angeles Times*, June 3, 1920, p. 11.

16. Jacob H. Hollander, Ph.D., "How Inflation Touches Every Man's Pocketbook," *New York Times*, May 2, 1920, p. XX1.

17. "Letters from the People: Excess Profits Tax, M. Hartley a Veteran of the Uncivil War," *St. Louis Post-Dispatch*, December 29, 1920, p. 28.

18. "Profiteers Are Incubators for 'Reds'—Capper," *Chicago Daily Tribune*, January 25, 1920, p. A9.

19. "No Time for Pessimism," *Baltimore Sun*, December 17, 1920, p. 8.

20. "Prices Will Never Reach 1914 Level," *Globe and Mail*, August 27, 1920, p. 7.

21. "Trade Revival Coming, Hoover Tells Business," *New York Tribune*, April 29, 1921, p. 9.

22. "Disjointed Prices," *Nashville Tennessean*, September 26, 1921, p. 4.

23. "Summer Jewelry Is Conspicuous," *St. Louis Post-Dispatch*, July 23, 1921, p. 13.

24. "Children Nowadays Are Spending Money as If It Grew on Bushes," *Boston Daily Globe*, October 23, 1921, p. E6.

25. Mitchell, 1985.

26. Samuel Crowther, "Fixing Wages," *Philadelphia Inquirer*, June 8, 1936, p. 7.

27. Cole and Ohanian, 2004.

28. "Favorable Conditions in Industry Cited," *Detroit Free Press*, October 29, 1929, p. 25.

29. Claude A. Jagger, "Large Holiday Retail Sales Add Impetus to Business," *Atlanta Constitution*, December 23, 1929, p. 15.

30. "If Deflation 'Runs Its Course,'" *Christian Science Monitor*, April 22, 1932, p. 16.

31. Catherine Hackett, "Why We Women Won't Buy," *Forum and Century*, December 1932.

32. "Jersey Clubwomen Urged to Arouse Public Opinion in Favor of Spending," *New York Herald Tribune*, February 7, 1932, p. E11.

33. "What Is a Bargain?" *Jewish Advocate*, October 4, 1932. p. 3.

34. "Buy-Now Campaign Started in Capital," *Washington Post*, October 25, 1930, p. 7.

35. "The Buy Now Campaign," *Hartford Courant*, October 16, 1933, p. 8.

36. Arthur Brisbane, "Buy in August Campaign Will Help City Merchants," *Austin Statesman*, August 2, 1933, p. 4.

37. "Angry Americans Lead Charge on Big Energy Bills," *Boston Globe*, March 9, 1975, p. 2.

38. Richard L. Strout, "Fighting Back at Inflation: Will Nixon Be Able to Put Out Flames?" *Christian Science Monitor*, July 11, 1974, p. 1.

39. Lawrence Van Gelder, "Some Prices Cut by Meat Boycott," *New York Times*, April 6, 1973, p. 1.

40. "A Boycott Fizzle—Little There to Boycott," *Atlanta Constitution*, August 8, 1973, p. 26E.

41. "High Meat Prices: Housewives to Mobilize Again," *Los Angeles Times*, January 20, 1974, sf_a1; "Nationwide Meat, Grain Boycott Launched by Consumer Group," *Los Angeles Times*, January 24, 1974, p. A1.

Chapter 18. The Wage-Price Spiral and Evil Labor Unions

1. Lindbeck and Snower, 2001.

2. https://news.gallup.com/poll/12751/labor-unions.aspx. Gallup-documented public support in the United States for labor unions has been gaining strength since 2009, reaching 62% support in 2018.

3. J. H. Carmical, "Railroads Facing New Labor Crisis," *New York Times*, March 12, 1950, p. F1.

4. Joe Edwards, "Transcripts Cite Hoffa Allies' Plot against FBI," *Boston Globe*, July 25, 2009, p. A10.

5. Blinder, 2004.

6. Bernanke et al., 1998.

7. Eisenhower, State of the Union Address, January 10, 1957, https://www.eisenhower.archives.gov/all_about_ike/speeches/1957_state_of_the_union.pdf.

8. Virgil P. Pownall, "Greed Blamed for Inflation," *Los Angeles Times*, August 26, 1957, p. B4.

9. "Our Price Policeman," *New York Times*, June 18, 1957, p. 32.

10. Friedman, 1973, p. ix.

11. Friedman, 1973, p. xi.

12. Sydney J. Harris, "Nothing about our Current Wage-Price Spiral Makes Sense," *Arizona Republic*, October 8, 1975, p. 7.

13. Shiller, 1997, p. 16.

14. Donald I. Rogers, "Cause of Recession? No One Really Knows: It Came Like a Sudden Shower and Is the Oddest in History," *New York Herald Tribune*, March 31, 1958, p. 1.

15. Richards, 1863, p. 12.

16. Fisher, 1928, p. 7.

Chapter 19. Future Narratives, Future Research

1. Hopkins et al., 2016.

2. Indiana University Lilly Family School of Philanthropy, GenerosityForLife.org, *Charitable Profile*, http://generosityforlife.org/generosity-data/data-tools/generosity-reports/.

3. "Reading Aloud," *Washington Post*, October 25, 1899, p. 6.

4. See Colley, 2003.

5. Regarding women, see Driscoll et al., 2009.

6. OECD, "Behavioral Insights," 2017, http://www.oecd.org/gov/regulatory-policy /behavioural-insights.htm. See also Zeina Afif, "'Nudge Units'—Where They Came From and What They Can Do," World Bank "Let's Talk Development" blog, October 25, 2017, http://blogs .worldbank.org/developmenttalk/nudge-units-where-they-came-and-what-they-can-do.

7. https://millercenter.org/the-presidency/presidential-speeches/march-4-1933-first -inaugural-address.

8. https://millercenter.org/the-presidency/presidential-speeches/march-12-1933-fireside -chat-1-banking-crisis.

9. See https://www.sistrix.com/ask-sistrix/google-index-google-bot-crawler/why-does-a -google-search-with-the-parenthesis-operator-sometimes-deliver-more-results-than-the-same -search-without-it/.

10. Callahan and Elliott, 1996.

11. Piore, 2010.

12. Blinder, 1990; Blinder et al., 1998.

13. Bewley, 1999.

14. David Romer and Christina Romer (1989), using what they called a "narrative approach," studied the Record of Policy Actions and Minutes of the Federal Open Markets Committee of the US Federal Reserve to discern the real impact of monetary policy. Valerie Ramey (2011) and Alberto Alesina, Carlo Favero, and Francesco Giavazzi (2019) have used narrative approaches to study the effects of fiscal policy. All these studies were focused on finding the real exogenous component of government policy, rather than, as in this book, on understanding the thinking of the broader public.

15. Merton and Kendall, 1946.

16. http://www.issp.org/menu-top/home/.

17. http://gss.norc.org/.

18. https://isr.umich.edu/. See also the book from the director of the ISR's consumer sur-veys, Richard Thomas Curtin (2019).

19. https://medium.com/ideo-stories/the-focus-group-is-dead-24e1ec2dda82.

20. See, for example, Edmunds, 2000.

21. https://ropercenter.cornell.edu/.

22. For example, Chen et al. (2016) compute a "propagation score" of narrative contagion based on citations and citations within citations. Such measures relate to the contagion impor-tance of narratives beyond the mere count of numbers of mention.

Appendix: Applying Epidemic Models
to Economic Narratives

1. Miller (2012) derives this equation from a stochastic model based on Poisson processes and generalizing to variants of the Kermack-McKendrick model.

2. See Carvalho and Gonçalves, 2016, https://arxiv.org/pdf/1609.09313.pdf.

3. The common rate equations in chemistry resemble closely the three-equation system shown here, but with SI in the first two equations replaced with just S. https://bio.libretexts

.org/TextMaps/Map%3A_Biochemistry_Online_(Jakubowski)/06%3A_TRANSPORT
_AND_KINETICS/B._Kinetics_of_Simple_and_Enzyme-Catalyzed_Reactions/B2._Multi
-Step_Reactions.

Here S, I, and R are three chemicals together, and the model is, for example, applied to ra-
dioactive decay of three elements together, where S, I, and R are the quantities of the elements,
where I refers to the intermediate element, and R the last element, which is stable. There are the
same two parameters c and r, and plots of S, I, and R may look similar to those here, with a
hump-shaped pattern for I, and there are both fast and slow reactions depending on c and r. But
in that consecutive chemical reactions model, the size of the epidemic is always 100%. More
similar models in chemistry involve reactions that require the pairing of chemicals in a solution.
https://www.chemguide.co.uk/physical/basicrates/arrhenius.html.

4. The SIRS model is the same as the SIR model above except that a term $+sR$ is added to
the right-hand side of the first equation and $-sR$ to the right-hand side of the third equation,
where $s > 0$ is a re-susceptibility rate. In this model the infectives' path may, depending on parameters, look similar to that in Figure A.1 but approaching a nonzero horizontal asymptote as
time increases: the infectives never effectively disappear, and the disease becomes endemic. See
Breda et al., 2012.

5. Grais et al., 2004.

6. Legrand et al., 2007.

7. Long et al., 2008.

8. JSTOR catalogs over nine million scholarly articles and books in all fields, and 7% of these
are in business or economics, but 25% of the articles with "ARIMA," "ARMA," or "autoregressive" are in business or economics.

9. Moving average models are sometimes justified by reference to the Wold decomposition
theorem (1954), which shows that any covariance stationary stochastic process can be modeled
as a moving average of noise terms plus a deterministic component. But there is no justification
for assuming that simple variants of ARIMA models are so general. We may be better able to
do economic forecasting in some cases if we represent these error terms or driving variables as
the result of co-epidemics of narratives about which we have some information.

10. See Nsoesie et al., 2013.

11. Nathanson and Martin, 1979.

12. Bailey et al., 2016.

13. Surveyed in Lamberson, 2016.

14. See Banerjee, 1992; Bikhchandani et al., 1992.

15. Goel et al., 2016.

16. Katz and Lazarsfeld, 1955, pp. 44–45.

17. Herr et al., 1991.

18. Bauckhage, 2011.

19. Shiller and Pound, 1989, p. 54. The words in square brackets were omitted from the version of this question given to individual investors.

20. http://knowledge.wharton.upenn.edu/article/is-this-the-end-of-money/.

21. Rand and Wilson (1991), Zeng et al. (2005), Zheng et al. (2015), and Olsen et al. (1988) claim that a chaotic form of the SEIR model fits data on epidemics of measles, mumps, and rubella.

22. The basic idea of an information cascade was developed by Banerjee (1992) and Bikhchandani et al. (1992), carried further by Vives (1996) and Banerjee and Fudenberg (2004).

23. Akerlof and Yellen, 1985.

24. Restaurant choice is the featured example in Banerjee, 1992.

25. Banerjee and Fudenberg (2004) address the question, from game theory, when thoroughly rational actors may form a consensus on false information.

References

Abreu, Ildeberta. 2011. "International Organizations' vs. Private Analysts' Forecasts: An Evaluation." Bank of Portugal, https://www.bportugal.pt/sites/default/files/anexos/papers/ab201105_e.pdf.

Achen, Christopher H., and Larry M. Bartels. 2017. *Democracy for Realists: Why Elections Do Not Produce Responsive Government*. Princeton, NJ: Princeton University Press.

Adams, James Truslow. 1931. *The Epic of America*. Boston: Little Brown & Co.

Aiden, Erez, and Jean-Baptiste Michel. 2013. *Uncharted: Big Data as a Lens on Human Culture*. New York: Riverhead Books, Penguin Group.

Akerlof, George A. 2007. "The Missing Motivation in Macroeconomics" (AEA Presidential Address). *American Economic Review* 97(1):3–36.

Akerlof, George A., and Rachel Kranton. 2011. *Identity Economics: How Our Identities Shape Our Work, Wages, and Well-Being*. Princeton, NJ: Princeton University Press.

Akerlof, George A., and Robert J. Shiller. 2009. *Animal Spirits: How Human Psychology Drives the Economy and Why It Matters for Global Capitalism*. Princeton, NJ: Princeton University Press.

———. 2015. *Phishing for Phools: The Economics of Manipulation and Deception*. Princeton, NJ: Princeton University Press.

Akerlof, George A., and Janet L. Yellen. 1985. "A Near-Rational Model of the Business Cycle, with Wage and Price Inertia." *Quarterly Journal of Economics* 100(1):823–88.

———. 1990. "The Fair Wage-Effort Hypothesis and Unemployment." *Quarterly Journal of Economics* 105(2):255–83.

Alexander, Kristin J., Peggy J. Miller, and Julie A. Hengst. 2001. "Young Children's Emotional Attachments to Stories." *Social Development* 10(3):374–98.

Allais, Maurice. 1947. *Économie et intérêt*. Paris: Librairie des publications officielles.

Allen, Franklin, Stephen Morris, and Hyung-Song Shin. 2006. "Beauty Contests and Iterated Expectations in Asset Markets." *Review of Financial Studies* 19(3):719–52.

Allen, Frederick Lewis. 1964 [1931]. *Only Yesterday: An Informal History of the Nineteen-Twenties*. New York: Harper & Brothers.

Alesina, Alberto, Carlo Favero, and Francesco Giavazzi. 2019. *Austerity: When It Works and When It Doesn't*. Princeton, NJ: Princeton University Press.

Aly, Samuel. 2017. "The Gracchi and the Era of Grain Reform in Ancient Rome." *Tenor of Our Times* 6(6):10–21, https://scholarworks.harding.edu/tenor/vol6/iss1/6.

American Psychiatric Association. 2013. *Diagnostic and Statistical Manual of Mental Disorders*. 5th ed. Arlington, VA: American Psychiatric Association.

An, Zidong, João Tovar Jalles, and Prakash Loungani. 2018. "How Well Do Economists Forecast Recessions?" Washington, DC: International Monetary Fund, March 5.

Anderson, Benedict. 1991. *Imagined Communities: Reflections on the Origin and Spread of Nationalism*. London: Verso.

André-Aigret, Constance, and Robert Dimand. 2018. "Populism versus Economic Expertise: J. Laurence Laughlin Debates William (Coin) Harvey." *Forum for Social Economics* 47(2):164–72.

Angell, Norman. 1911. *The Great Illusion: A Study of the Relation of Military Power in Nations to Their Economic and Social Advantage*. New York: G. P. Putnam's Sons.

Areni, C. S., and D. Kim. 1993. "The Influence of Background Music on Shopping Behavior: Classical versus Top-Forty Music in a Wine Store." *Advances in Consumer Research* 20:336–40.

Argersinger, Peter H., and Jo Ann E. Argersinger. 1984. "The Machine Breakers: Farmworkers and Social Change in the Rural Midwest of the 1870s." *Agricultural History* 58(3):393–410.

Arkright, Frank. 1933. *The A B C of Technocracy: Based on Authorized Material*. New York: Harper & Brothers.

Ashenfelter, Orley. 2012. "Comparing Real Wage Rates: Presidential Address." *American Economic Review* 102(2):617–42.

Atkeson, Andrew, and Patrick J. Kehoe. 2004. "Deflation and Depression: Is There an Empirical Link?" National Bureau of Economic Research Working Paper 10268.

Azariadis, Costas. 1981. "Self-Fulfilling Prophecies." *Journal of Economic Theory* 25:380–96.

Bailey, Michael, Ruiqing Cao, Theresa Kuchler, and Johannes Stroebel. 2016. "Social Networks and Housing Markets." Presented at NBER behavioral finance workshop.

Baker, Charles Whiting. 1932. *Pathways Back to Prosperity: A Study of Defects in Our Social Machine and How to Mend Them*. New York: Funk & Wagnalls Company.

Balderrama, Francisco E., and Raymond Rodríguez. 2006. *Decade of Betrayal: Mexican Repatriation in the 1930s*. Albuquerque: University of New Mexico Press.

Banerjee, Abhijit. 1992. "A Simple Model of Herd Behavior." *Quarterly Journal of Economics* 107(3):797–817.

Banerjee, Abhijit, and Drew Fudenberg. 2004. "Word-of-Mouth Learning." *Games and Economic Behavior* 46(1):1–22.

Banks, Elizabeth L. 1898. "American Yellow Journalism." *Nineteenth Century*, August, 328–40.

Bardhan, Nilanjana. 2001. "Transnational AIDS-HIV News Narratives: A Critical Exploration of Overarching Frames." *Mass Communication and Society* 4(3):283–309.

Barthes, Roland. 2013 [1984]. *Mythologies*. New York: Hill and Wang.

Bartholomew, D. J. 1982. *Stochastic Models for Social Processes*. Chichester, UK: Wiley.

Baruch, Bernard. 1957. *Baruch: My Own Story*. New York: Henry Holt.

Bauckhage, Christian. 2011. "Insights into Internet Memes." Proceedings of the Fifth AAAI Conference on Weblogs and Social Media, http://www.aaai.org/ocs/index.php/%20ICWSM/ICWSM11/paper/viewFile/2757/3304.

Beaudry, Paul, and Franck Portier. 2014. "News-Driven Business Cycles: Insights and Challenges." *Journal of Economic Literature* 52(4):993–1074.

Beck, Andrew T., Andrew C. Butler, Gregory K. Brown, Katherine K. Dahlsgaard, Cory F. Newman, and Judith S. Beck. 2001. "Dysfunctional Beliefs Discriminate Personality Disorders." *Behavioral Research and Therapy* 39(10):1213–25.

Beckert, Jens, and Richard Bronk. 2018. *Uncertain Futures: Imaginaries, Narratives and Calculation in the Economy*. Oxford: Oxford University Press.

Bell, Brad E., and Elizabeth F. Loftus. 1985. "Vivid Persuasion in the Courtroom." *Journal of Personality Assessment* 49(6):659–64.

Bell, Brian, Anna Bindler, and Stephen Machin. 2017. "Crime Scars: Recessions and the Making of Career Criminals." *Review of Economics and Statistics* 100(3):392–404.

Benabou, Roland. 2013. "Groupthink: Collective Delusions in Organizations and Markets." *Review of Economic Studies* 80:429–62.

Bennett, W. Lance, and Amoshuan Toft. 2009. "Identity, Technology and Narratives: Transnational Activism and Social Networks." In Andrew Chadwick, ed., *Routledge Handbook of Internet Politics*, 246–60. London: Routledge.

Berg, Harry D. 1946. "The Economic Consequences of the French and Indian War for the Philadelphia Merchants." *Pennsylvania History* 13:185–92.

Berger, Jonah. 2013. *Contagious: Why Things Catch On*. New York: Simon and Schuster.

Berger, Ronald J., and Richard Quinney. 2004. *Storytelling Sociology: Narrative as Social Inquiry*. Boulder, CO: Lynne Rienner Publishers.

Bernanke, Ben S. 1983. "Non-Monetary Effects of the Financial Crisis in the Propagation of the Great Depression." *American Economic Review* 73(3):257–76.

———. 2015. *The Courage to Act: A Memoir of a Crisis and Its Aftermath*. New York: W. W. Norton.

Bernanke, Ben, Thomas Laubach, Frederic Mishkin, and Adam Posen. 1998. *Inflation Targeting: Lessons from the International Experience*. Princeton, NJ: Princeton University Press.

Bernstein, Michael J., Steven G. Young, Christina M. Brown, Donald M. Sacco, and Heather M. Claypool. 2008. "Adaptive Responses to Social Exclusion: Social Rejection Improves Detection of Real and Fake Smiles." *Psychological Science* 19(10):981–83.

Bettelheim, Bruno. 1975. *The Uses of Enchantment: The Meaning and Importance of Fairy Tales*. New York: Doubleday.

Bewley, Truman. 1999. *Why Wages Don't Fall in a Recession*. Cambridge, MA: Harvard University Press.

Bikhchandani, Sushil, David Hirshleifer, and Ivo Welch. 1992. "A Theory of Fads, Fashion, Custom, and Cultural Change as Informational Cascades." *Journal of Political Economy* 100(5):992–1026.

Bix, Amy Sue. 2000. *Inventing Ourselves Out of Jobs? America's Debate over Technological Unemployment*. Baltimore: Johns Hopkins University Press.

Blanc, Louis. 1851. *Plus de Girondins*. Paris: Charles Joubert.

Blei, David M., Andrew Y. Ng, and Michael I. Jordan. 2003. "Latent Dirichlet Allocation." *Journal of Machine Learning Research* 3:993–1022.

Blinder, Alan. 1990. "Learning by Asking Those Who Are Doing." *Eastern Economic Journal* 16:297–306.

———. 2004. *The Quiet Revolution: Central Banking Goes Modern*. New Haven, CT: Yale University Press.

Blinder, Alan, Elie R. D. Canetti, David E. Lebow, and Jeremy B. Rudd. 1998. *Asking About Prices: A New Approach to Understanding Price Stickiness*. New York: Russell Sage Foundation.

Blyth, Mark. 2013. *Austerity: The History of a Dangerous Idea*. New York: Oxford University Press.

Bodkin, Maud. 1934. *Archetypal Patterns of Poetry: Psychological Studies of Imagination*. London: Oxford University Press.

Boltz, Marilyn, Matthew Schulkind, and Suzanne Kantra. 1991. "Effects of Background Music on the Remembering of Filmed Events." *Memory & Cognition* 19(6):593–606.

Booker, Christopher. 2004. *The Seven Basic Plots: Why We Tell Stories*. New York: Bloomsbury.

Boudoukh, Jacob, Ronen Feldman, Shimon Kogan, and Matthew Richardson. 2013. "Which News Moves Stock Prices? A Textual Analysis." National Bureau of Economic Research Working Paper 18725.

Boulding, Kenneth E. 1969. "Economics as a Moral Science." *American Economic Review* 59(1):1–12.

Box, George E. P., and Gwilym Jenkins. 1970. *Time Series Analysis: Forecasting and Control*. San Francisco: Holden-Day.

Bramoullé, Yann, Andrea Galeotti, and Brian Rogers, eds. 2016. *The Oxford Handbook of the Economics of Networks*. Oxford: Oxford University Press.

Breda, D., O. Dieckmann, W. F. de Graaf, A. Pugliese, and R. Vermiglio. 2012. "On the Formulation of Epidemic Models (an Appraisal of Kermack and McKendrick)." *Journal of Biological Dynamics* 6(2):103–17.

Briggs, Robin. 1998. *Witches and Neighbors: The Social and Cultural Context of European Witchcraft*. New York: Penguin.

Brill, Alex, and Kevin A. Hassett. 2007. "Revenue-Maximizing Corporate Income Taxes: The Laffer Curve in OECD Countries." Washington, DC: American Enterprise Institute.

Brooks, Peter. 1992. *Reading for the Plot: Design and Intention in Narrative*. Cambridge, MA: Harvard University Press.

Brown, Donald E. 1991. *Human Universals*. Boston: McGraw-Hill.

Brown, Roger, and James Kulik. 1977. "Flashbulb Memories." *Cognition* 5(1):73–99.

Bruner, Jerome. 1991. "The Narrative Construction of Reality." *Critical Inquiry* 18(1):1–21.

———. 1998. "What Is a Narrative Fact?" *Annals of the American Academy of Political and Social Science* 560:17–27.

Burns, Arthur, and Wesley C. Mitchell. 1946. *Measuring Business Cycles*. New York: National Bureau of Economic Research, https://www.nber.org/books/burn46-1.

Callahan, Charlene, and Catherine S. Elliott. 1996. "Listening: A Narrative Approach to Everyday Understandings and Behavior." *Journal of Economic Psychology* 17:79–114.

Calomiris, Charles W., and Larry Schweikart. 1991. "The Panic of 1857: Origins, Transmission, and Containment." *Journal of Economic History* 51(4):807–34.

Campbell, Joseph. 1949. *The Hero with a Thousand Faces*. New York: Pantheon Books.

Carey, Henry Charles. 1861. *The French and American Tariffs Compared*. Detroit, MI: J. Wareen.

Carvalho, Alexsandro M., and Sebastián Gonçalves. 2016. "An Algebraic Solution for the Kermack-McKendrick Model," https://arxiv.org/pdf/1609.09313.pdf.

Cass, David, and Karl Shell. 1983. "Do Sunspots Matter?" *Journal of Political Economy* 91:193–227.

Cassel, Gustav. 1935. *On Quantitative Thinking in Economics*. Oxford: Clarendon Press.

Cawelti, John G. 1976. *Adventure, Mystery, Romance: Formula Stories as Art and Popular Culture.* Chicago: University of Chicago Press.

Chandani, Sushil, David Hirshleifer, and Ivo Welch. 1992. "A Theory of Fashions, Fads, Customs and Cultural Change as Informational Cascades." *Journal of Political Economy* 100(5):992–1026.

Chase, Stuart. 1929. *Men and Machines.* New York: Macmillan.

Chen, Daniel Li, Adithya Parthasarathy, and Shivam Verma. 2016. "The Genealogy of Ideology: Predicting Agreement and Persuasive Memes in the U.S. Courts of Appeals." Unpublished paper, Toulouse School of Economics.

Cheng, Justin, Michael Bernstein, Cristian Danescu-Niculescu-Mizil, and Jure Leskovec. 2017. "Anyone Can Become a Troll: Causes of Trolling Behavior in Online Discussions." Unpublished paper, Stanford University, https://arxiv.org/abs/1702.01119.

Chetty, Raj. 2015. "Behavioral Economics and Public Policy: A Pragmatic Perspective." *American Economic Review* 105(5):1–33.

Chwe, Michael Suk-Young. 2001. *Rational Ritual: Culture, Coordination and Common Knowledge.* Princeton, NJ: Princeton University Press.

Cicero, Marcus Tullius. 1860 [55 BCE]. *On Oratory and Orators.* New York: Harper and Brothers.

Clark, John Bates. 1895. "The Gold Standard of Currency in the Light of Recent Theory." *Political Science Quarterly* 10(3):383–97.

Clayton, Blake C. 2015. *Market Madness: A Century of Oil Panics, Crises, and Crashes.* New York: Oxford University Press.

Clayton, N. S., D. P. Griffiths, N. J. Emery, and A. Dickinson. 2001. "Elements of Episodic-Like Memory in Animals." *Philosophical Transactions of the Royal Society B* 356(1413): 1483–91.

Cochrane, John. 1994. "Shocks." *Carnegie-Rochester Conference Series on Public Policy* 41:295–364.

Cohen, Gillian, and Dorothy Faulkner. 1989. "Age Differences in Source Forgetting: Effects on Reality Monitoring and on Eyewitness Testimony." *Psychology and Aging* 4(1):10–17, http://dx.doi.org/10.1037/0882-7974.4.1.10.

Cole, Harold L., and Lee E. Ohanian. 2004. "New Deal Policies and the Persistence of the Great Depression: A General Equilibrium Analysis." *Journal of Political Economy* 112(4):779–816.

Colley, Helen. 2003. *Mentoring for Social Inclusion: A Critical Approach to Nurturing Mentor Relationships.* London: Routledge Falmer.

Collier, Paul, and Anke Hoeffler. 1998. "On Economic Causes of Civil War." *Oxford Economic Papers* 50(4):563–73.

———. 2002. "On the Incidence of Civil War in Africa." *Journal of Conflict Resolution* 46(1):13–28.

Crane, Stephen. 1895. *The Red Badge of Courage.* New York: D. Appleton & Co.

Cronon, William. 2013. "Storytelling." *American Historical Review* 118(1):1–19.

Curio, E. 1988. "Cultural Transmission of Enemy Recognition in Birds." In Thomas R. Zentall and Bennett G. Galef Jr., eds., *Social Learning: Psychological and Biological Perspectives*, 75. Mahwah, NJ: Lawrence Erlbaum Associates.

Curtin, Richard Thomas. 2019. *Consumer Expectations: Micro Foundations and Macro Impact.* Cambridge: Cambridge University Press.

Cutler, David, James M. Poterba, and Lawrence H. Summers. 1989. "What Moves Stock Prices?" *Journal of Portfolio Management* 15(3):4–12.

Daley, Daryl J., and David. G. Kendall. 1964. "Epidemics and Rumors." *Nature* 204:1118.

———. 1965. "Stochastic Rumors." *IMA Journal of Applied Mathematics* 1(1):42–55.

Davis, Forrest. 1932. *What Price Wall Street?* New York: William Godwin.

Davis, Joseph E. 2002. *Stories of Change: Narratives and Social Movements.* Albany: State University of New York Press.

Davis, Morris A., and Jonathan Heathcote. 2007. "The Price and Quantity of Residential Land in the United States." *Journal of Monetary Economics* 54(8):2595–620.

Davis, Shelby Cullom. 1940. *America Faces the Forties.* Philadelphia: Dorrance and Company.

Dawkins, Richard. 1976. *The Selfish Gene.* Oxford: Oxford University Press.

De Long, J. Bradford, Andrei Shleifer, Lawrence H. Summers, and Robert J. Waldmann. 1990. "Noise Trader Risk in Financial Markets." *Journal of Political Economy* 98(4):703–38.

Desmond, Matthew. 2017. *Evicted: Poverty and Profit in the American City.* New York: Broadway Books.

Diamond, Douglas B., Jr. 1980. "Taxes, Inflation, Speculation and the Cost of Homeownership." *Real Estate Economics* 8:281–97, https://doi.org/10.1111/1540-6229.00218.

Dickstein, Morris. 2009. *Dancing in the Dark: A Cultural History of the Great Depression.* New York: W. W. Norton.

Dimand, Robert W. 1988. *The Origins of the Keynesian Revolution: The Development of Keynes's Theory of Employment and Output.* Stanford, CA: Stanford University Press.

Dohmen, Thomas J., Armin Falk, David Huffman, and Uwe Sunde. 2006. "Seemingly Irrelevant Events Affect Perceptions and Expectations—The FIFA World Cup 2006 as a Natural Experiment." CEPR Discussion Paper No. 5851, https://ssrn.com/abstract=951789.

Driscoll, Lisa G., Kelly A. Parkes, Gresilda A. Tilley-Lubbs, Jennifer M. Brill, and Vanessa R. Pitts. 2009. "Navigating the Lonely Sea: Peer Mentoring and Collaboration among Aspiring Women Scholars." *Mentoring and Tutoring: Partnership in Learning* 17(1):5–25.

Duesenberry, James S. 1949. *Income, Saving, and the Theory of Consumer Behavior.* Cambridge, MA: Harvard University Press.

Durkheim, Emile. 1897. *Le Suicide.* Saint-Germain: Ancienne Librairie Germer Baillière et Cie.

Dynan, Karen E., Jonathan Skinner, and Stephen P. Zeldes. 2004. "Do the Rich Save More?" *Journal of Political Economy* 112(2):397–444.

Eckstein, Otto. 1978. *The Great Recession with a Postscript on Stagflation.* New York: Elsevier Scientific.

Edmunds, Holly. 2000. *The Focus Group Handbook.* New York: McGraw-Hill.

Ehrlich, Paul. 1968. *The Population Bomb.* New York: Ballantine Books.

Eichengreen, Barry. 1996. *Golden Fetters, The Gold Standard and the Great Depression, 1919–1939.* New York: Oxford University Press.

Eichengreen, Barry, and Peter Temin. 2000. "The Gold Standard and the Great Depression." *Contemporary European History* 9(2):183–207.

Eichholtz, Piet M. A. 1997. "A Long Run House Price Index: The Herengracht Index, 1628–1973." *Real Estate Economics* 25(2):175–92.

Escalas, Jennifer Edson. 2007. "Self-Referencing and Persuasion: Narrative Transportation versus Analytical Elaboration." *Journal of Consumer Research* 16:421–29.

Fair, Ray C. 1987. "Sources of Output and Price Variability in a Macroeconomic Model." Yale University: Cowles Foundation Discussion Paper 815.

Fair, Ray C., and Robert J. Shiller. 1989. "The Informational Content of Ex Ante Forecasts." *Review of Economics and Statistics* 71(2):325–31.

Falk, Armin, and Jean Tirole. 2016. "Narratives, Imperatives, and Moral Reasoning." Unpublished paper, University of Bonn.

Falter, Jürgen W. 1986. "Unemployment and the Radicalisation of the German Electorate 1928–1933: An Aggregate Data Analysis with Special Emphasis on the Rise of National Socialism." In Peter Stachura, ed., *Unemployment and the Great Depression in Weimar Germany*, 187–208. London: Palgrave Macmillan.

Fama, Eugene F., and Kenneth R. French. 1993. "Common Risk Factors in the Returns on Stocks and Bonds." *Journal of Financial Economics* 33(1):3–56.

Fang, Hanming, and Giuseppe Moscarini. 2005. "Morale Hazard." *Journal of Monetary Economics* 52(4):749–77.

Farmer, Roger E. A. 1999. *Macroeconomics of Self-Fulfilling Prophecies*. Cambridge, MA: MIT Press.

Farnam, Henry W. 1912. "The Economic Utilization of History: Annual Address of the President." *American Economic Review* 2(1):5–16.

Fearon, James, and David Laitin. 2003. "Ethnicity, Insurgency and Civil War." *American Political Science Review* 97(1):75–90.

Fehr, Ernst, and Simon Gächter. 2000. "Fairness and Retaliation: The Economics of Reciprocity." *Journal of Economic Perspectives* 14(3):159–81.

Ferrand, Nathalie, and Michèle Weil, eds. 2001. *Homo narrativus: dix ans de recherche sur la topique romanesque*. Montpellier: Université Paul-Valéry de Montpellier.

Festinger, Leon. 1954. "A Theory of Social Comparison Processes." *Human Relations* 7:117–40.

Field, Alexander J. 2011. *A Great Leap Forward: 1930s Depression and U.S. Economic Growth*. New Haven, CT: Yale University Press.

Fine, Gary Alan, and Barry O'Neill. 2010. "Policy Legends and Folklists: Traditional Beliefs in the Public Sphere." *Journal of American Folklore* 123(488):150–78.

Fischer, Conan J. 1986. "Unemployment and Left-Wing Radicalism in Weimar Germany." In Peter Stachura, ed., *Unemployment and the Great Depression in Weimar Germany*, 209–25. London: Palgrave Macmillan.

Fisher, Irving. 1928. *The Money Illusion*. New York: Adelphi.

———. 1930. *The Stock Market Crash—and After*. New York: Macmillan.

———. 1933. "The Debt-Deflation Theory of Great Depressions." *Econometrica* 1(4):337–57.

Fisher, R. A. 1930. *The Genetical Theory of Natural Selection*. Oxford: The Clarendon Press.

Fisher, Walter R. 1984. "Narration as a Human Communication Paradigm: The Case of Public Moral Argument." *Communication Monographs* 51(1):1–22.

Flandreau, Marc. 1996. "The French Crime of 1873: An Essay on the Emergence of the International Gold Standard 1870–1880." *Journal of Economic History* 56(4):862–97.

Fogel, Robert W. 2000. *The Fourth Great Awakening and the Future of Egalitarianism*. Chicago: University of Chicago Press.

Foner, Eric. 1974. "The Causes of the American Civil War: Recent Interpretations and New Directions." *Civil War History* 20(3):197–214.

Fougère, Denis, Francis Kramarz, and Julien Pouget. 2009. "Youth Unemployment and Crime in France." *Journal of the European Economic Association* 7(5):909–38.

Francis, Peter. 1997. "The Beads That Did 'Not' Buy Manhattan Island." *New York History* 78(4):411–28.

Freeman, Richard B. 1976. "A Cobweb Model of the Supply and Starting Salary of New Engineers." *Industrial and Labor Relations Review* 29(2):236–48.

———. 1999. "The Economics of Crime." In Orley Ashenfelter and David Card, eds., *Handbook of Labor Economics*, chap. 52. New York: Elsevier Science.

Frey, Bruno, and Hannelore Weck. 1981. "Hat Arbeitlosigkeit den Aufstieg des Nationalsozialismus Bewirkt? / Did Unemployment Lead to the Rise of National Socialism?" *Jahrbücher für Nationalökonomie und Statistik* 196(1):1–31.

Friedman, Benjamin M. 2005. *The Moral Consequences of Economic Growth*. New York: Knopf.

Friedman, Irving S. 1973. *Inflation: A World-Wide Disaster*. Boston: Houghton Mifflin.

Friedman, Milton. 1957. *A Theory of the Consumption Function*. A study by the National Bureau of Economic Research, New York. Princeton, NJ: Princeton University Press, http://www.nber.org/books/frie57-1.

Friedman, Milton, and Anna J. Schwartz. 1963. *A Monetary History of the United States 1867–1960*. Princeton, NJ: Princeton University Press.

———. 1982. *Monetary Trends in the United States and the United Kingdom: Their Relation to Income, Prices, and Interest Rates, 1867–1975*. Chicago: University of Chicago Press.

Friedman, Monroe. 1996. "A Positive Approach to Organized Consumer Action: The 'Buycott' as an Alternative to the Boycott." *Journal of Consumer Policy* 19(4):439–51.

Gabaix, Xavier. 2016. "A Behavioral New-Keynesian Model." National Bureau of Economic Research Working Paper 22954.

Galbraith, John Kenneth. 1955. *The Great Crash, 1929*. Boston: Houghton-Mifflin.

Ganzevoort, R. Ruard, Maaike Hardt, and Michael Scherer-Rath. 2013. *Religious Stories We Live By: Narrative Approaches in Theology and Religious Studies*. Leiden: Brill Academic Publishers.

Garber, Peter. 2000. *Famous First Bubbles*. Cambridge, MA: MIT Press.

Garon, Sheldon. 2012. *Beyond Our Means: Why America Spends While the World Saves*. Princeton, NJ: Princeton University Press.

Gaser, Christian, Igor Nenadic, Hans-Peter Volz, Christian Büchel, and Heinrich Sauer. 2004. "Neuroanatomy of 'Hearing Voices': A Frontotemporal Brain Structural Abnormality Associated with Auditory Hallucinations in Schizophrenia." *Cerebral Cortex* 14(1):91–96.

Geanakoplos, John. 2010. "The Leverage Cycle." In Daron Acemoglu et al., eds., *NBER Macroeconomics Annual 2009*, vol. 24. Chicago: University of Chicago Press.

Gennaioli, Nicola, and Andrei Shleifer. 2018. *A Crisis of Beliefs: Investor Psychology and Financial Fragility*. Princeton, NJ: Princeton University Press.

Gentzkow, Matthew, Jesse M. Shapiro, and Matt Taddy. 2016. "Measuring Polarization in High-Dimensional Data: Method and Application to Congressional Speech." Unpublished paper, Stanford University.

George, Henry. 1886 [1879]. *Progress and Poverty: An Inquiry into the Causes of Industrial Depressions and of Increase of Want with Increase of Wealth. The Remedy.* New York: D. Appleton and Company.

Gerbert, Barbara, Bryan Maguire, Victor Badner, David Altman, and George Stone. 1988. "Why Fear Persists: Health Care Professionals and AIDS." *Journal of the American Medical Association* 260(23):3481–83, doi: 10.1001/jama.1988.03410230099037.

Gervais, Matthew, and David Sloan Wilson. 2005. "The Evolution and Functions of Laughter and Humor: A Synthetic Approach." *Quarterly Review of Biology* 80(4):395–430.

Gillers, Stephen. 1989. "Taking L.A. Law More Seriously." *Yale Law Journal* 98(8): 1607–23.

Gino, Francesca, Michael I. Norton, and Roberto A. Weber. 2016. "Motivated Bayesians: Feeling Moral While Acting Egoistically." *Journal of Economic Perspectives* 30(3):189–212.

Glaeser, Edward L. 2005. "The Political Economy of Hatred." *Quarterly Journal of Economics* 120(1):45–86.

Goel, Sharad, Ashton Anderson, Jake Hofman, and Duncan J. Watts. 2016. "The Structural Virality of Online Diffusion." *Management Science* 62(1):1–17.

Goetzmann, William N., Dasol Kim, and Robert J. Shiller. 2016. "Crash Beliefs from Investor Surveys." National Bureau of Economic Research Working Paper 22143.

Goldberg, Stanley. 1970. "In Defense of Ether: The British Response to Einstein's Special Theory of Relativity, 1905–1911." *Historical Studies in the Physical Sciences* 2:89–125.

Goldin, Claudia. 2014. "A Pollution Theory of Discrimination: Male and Female Differences in Occupations and Earnings." In Leah Platt Boustan, Carola Frydman, and Robert A. Margo, eds., *Human Capital in History: The American Record*, 313–48. Chicago: University of Chicago Press.

Goldman, William. 2012. *Adventures in the Screen Trade.* New York: Grand Central Publishing.

Gordon, Robert J. 1983. "A Century of Evidence on Wage and Price Stickiness in the United States, the United Kingdom, and Japan." In James Tobin, ed., *Macroeconomics, Prices and Quantities*, 85–121. Washington, DC: Brookings.

———. 2016. *The Rise and Fall of American Growth.* Princeton, NJ: Princeton University Press.

Gould, Eric D., Bruce A. Weinberg, and David B. Mustard. 2002. "Crime Rates and Local Labor Market Opportunities in the United States 1979–1997." *Review of Economics and Statistics* 84(1):45–61.

Gould, Stephen Jay. 1994. "So Near and Yet So Far." *New York Review of Books*, October 20.

Grais, R. F., J. H. Ellis, A. Kress, and G. E. Glass. 2004. "Modeling the Spread of Annual Influenza Epidemics in the U.S.: The Potential Role of Air Travel." *Health Care Management Science* 7(2):137–34.

Grant, James. 2014. *The Forgotten Depression: 1921; The Crash That Cured Itself.* New York: Simon & Schuster.

Graves, Lloyd Milner. 1932. *The Great Depression and Beyond.* New York: Press of J. D McGuire.

Grebler, Leo, David M. Blank, and Louis Winnick. 1956. *Capital Formation in Residential Real Estate: Trends and Prospects.* A study by the National Bureau of Economic Research, New York. Princeton, NJ: Princeton University Press.

Grönqvist, Hans. 2011. "Youth Unemployment and Crime: New Lessons Exploring Longitudinal Register Data," https://www.sole-jole.org/12129.pdf.

Grossman, Sanford J., and Robert J. Shiller. 1981. "Determinants of the Variability of Stock Market Prices." *American Economic Review* 71(2):221–27.

Gyourko, Joseph, Christopher Mayer, and Todd Sinai. 2013. "Superstar Cities." *American Economic Journal: Economic Policy* 5(4):167–99.

Hacker, Jacob S., and Paul Pierson. 2016. *American Amnesia: How the War on Government Led Us to Forget What Made America Prosper.* New York: Simon and Schuster.

Halbwachs, Maurice. 1925. "Les cadres sociaux de la mémoire." In *Les travaux de l'année Sociologique.* Paris: Alcan.

Haldrup, Michael, and Jonas Larsen. 2003. "The Family Gaze." *Tourist Studies* 3(1):23–46.

Hall, Todd W. 2007. "Psychoanalysis, Attachment, and Spirituality II: The Spiritual Stories We Live By." *Journal of Psychology and Theology* 35(1):29–42.

Hamilton, James. 1983. "Oil and the Macroeconomy since World War II." *Journal of Political Economy* 91(2):228–48.

Hane, Christopher, and John A. James. 2012. "Wage Rigidity in the Great Depression." Unpublished working paper, State University of New York at Binghamton.

Hanke, Steven H., and Nicholas Krus. 2013. "World Hyperinflations." In Randall Parker and Robert Whaples, eds., *The Handbook of Major Events in Economic History*, 367–77. London: Routledge.

Hannah, Leslie. 1986. *Inventing Retirement.* Cambridge: Cambridge University Press.

Hansen, Alvin H. 1938. *Full Recovery or Stagnation?* New York: W. W. Norton.

———. 1939. "Economic Progress and Declining Population Growth" (1938 presidential address before the American Economic Association). *American Economic Review* 29(1):1–15.

———. 1942. *After the War—Full Employment.* Natural Resources Planning Board. Washington, DC: US Government Printing Office.

Hansen, Lars Peter, and Thomas J. Sargent. 2005. *Recursive Models of Dynamic Linear Economies.* Princeton, NJ: Princeton University Press, http://home.uchicago.edu/~lhansen/mbook2 .pdf.

Harari, Yuval Noah. 2018. "Why Technology Favors Tyranny." *Atlantic*, October.

Harvey, William Hope. 1894. *Coin's Financial School.* Chicago: Coin Publishing Company.

Hassler, John. 2001. "Uncertainty and the Timing of Automobile Purchases." *Scandinavian Journal of Economics* 103(2):351–66.

Haugen, Steven E. 2009. "Measures of Labor Underutilization from the Current Population Survey." US Department of Labor, https://www.bls.gov/ore/pdf/ec090020.pdf.

Heathcote, Jonathan, Gianluca Violante, and Fabrizio Perri. 2010. "Inequality in Times of Crisis: Lessons from the Past and a First Look at the Current Recession." Vox EU, voxeu.org/article /economic-inequality-during-recessions.

Heffetz, Ori. 2011. "A Test of Conspicuous Consumption: Visibility and Income Elasticities." *Review of Economics and Statistics* 93(4):1101–17.

Hegel, Georg Wilhelm Friedrich. 1841 [1807]. *Phänomenologie des Geistes*. Edited by D. Johann Schulze. Berlin: Duncker und Humblot.

Henderson, Willie. 1982. "Metaphor in Economics." *Economics* 18(4):147–53.

Hennig-Thurau, Thorsten, Mark B. Houston, and Torsten Heitjans. 2009. "Conceptualizing and Measuring the Monetary Value of Brand Extensions: The Case of Motion Pictures." *Journal of Marketing* 73(6):167–83, http://dx.doi.org/10.1509/jmkg.73.6.167.

Herr, Paul M., Frank R. Kardes, and John Kim. 1991. "Effects of Word-of-Mouth and Product-Attribute Information in Persuasion: An Accessibility-Diagnosticity Perspective." *Journal of Consumer Research* 17(4):454–62.

Herrera-Soler, Honesto, and Michael White. 2012. *Metaphor and Mills: Figurative Language in Business and Economics*. Berlin: De Gruyter.

Hicks, John. 1937. "Mr. Keynes and the 'Classics'; A Suggested Interpretation." *Econometrica* 5(2):147–59.

Higgs, Robert. 1997. "Regime Uncertainty: Why the Great Depression Lasted So Long and Why Prosperity Resumed after the War." *Independent Review* 1(4):561–90, http://www.jstor.org/stable/pdf/24560785.pdf.

Hill, Napoleon. 1925. *The Law of Success in 16 Lessons*. New York: Tribeca Books.

———. 1937. *Think and Grow Rich*. Meriden, CT: The Ralston Society.

Himanen, Pekka. 2001. *The Hacker Ethic and the Spirit of the Information Age*. New York: Random House.

Hofstadter, Douglas R. 1980. *Gödel, Escher, Bach: An Eternal Golden Braid*. New York: Vintage Books.

———. 1981. "Metamagical Themas: The Magic Cube's Cubies Are Twiddled by Cubists and Solved by Cubemeisters." *Scientific American* 244(3):20–39.

Hofstadter, Richard. 1964. "The Paranoid Style in American Politics." *Atlantic*, November.

———. 1967. *Cuba, the Philippines, and Manifest Destiny*. New York: Vintage Books.

Hoganson, Kristin L. 2000. *Fighting for American Manhood: How Gender Politics Provoked the Spanish-American War*. New Haven, CT: Yale University Press.

Holt, Douglas B. 2002. "Why Do Brands Cause Trouble? A Dialectical Theory of Consumer Culture and Branding." *Journal of Consumer Research* 29(1):70–90.

Hopkins, Emily J., Deena Skolnick Weisberg, and Jordan C. V. Taylor. 2016. "The Seductive Allure Is a Reductive Allure: People Prefer Scientific Explanations That Contain Logically Irrelevant Reductive Information." *Cognition* 155:67–76, https://doi.org/10.1016/j.cognition.2016.06.011.

Howard, Milford Wriarson. 1895. *The American Plutocracy*. New York: Holland Publishing Co.

Howell, David R., and Anna Okatenko. 2010. "By What Measure? A Comparison of French and US Labor Market Performance with New Measures of Employment Adequacy." *International Review of Applied Economics* 24(3):333–57.

Huberman, Gur, Jacob D. Leshno, and Ciamac C. Moallemi. 2017. "Monopoly without a Monopolist: An Economic Analysis of the Bitcoin Payment System." Unpublished paper, Columbia Business School, October 17.

Hume, David. 1788 [1742]. "On the Rise and Progress of the Arts and Sciences." In *Essays and Treatises on Several Subjects*, vol. 1. London: T. D. Cadell.

Huston, James L. 1987. *The Panic of 1857 and the Coming of the Civil War*. Baton Rouge: Louisiana State University Press.

Ibn Khallikan, Ahmad Ibn Muhammad. 1868 [1274]. *Biographical Dictionary*. Translated from the Arabic by Baron William Mac Guckin De Slane. Paris: Édouard Blot, Oriental Translation Fund of Great Britain and Ireland.

Irwin, Douglas A. 2011. "Anticipating the Great Depression? Gustav Cassel's Analysis of the Interwar Gold Standard." Unpublished paper, Dartmouth College.

———. 2012. *Trade Policy Disaster*. Cambridge MA: MIT Press.

Isenhour, Cindy. 2012. "On the Challenge of Signalling Ethics without the Stuff: Tales of Conspicuous Green Anti-Consumption." In James B. Carrier and Peter Luetchford, eds., *Ethical Consumption: Social Value and Economic Practice*. New York: Berghahn Books.

Jackendoff, Ray. 2009. "Parallels and Nonparallels between Language and Music." *Music Perception: An Interdisciplinary Journal* 26(3):195–204.

Jackson, Matthew O., and Leeat Yariv. 2005. "Diffusion in Social Networks." *Économie Publique* 16(1):2–16.

Jacobs, Alan, 2016. "The Watchman: What Became of the Christian Intellectuals?" *Harper's Magazine*, September, 54–60.

Jevons, William Stanley. 1878. "Commercial Crises and Sun-Spots." *Nature* 19:33–37.

Johnson, Edgar H. 1910. "The Economics of Henry George's 'Progress and Poverty.'" *Journal of Political Economy* 18(9):714–35.

Johnson, Eric J., and Amos Tversky. 1983. "Affect, Generalization, and the Perception of Risk." *Journal of Personality and Social Psychology* 45(1):20–31.

Johnson, Marcia K., and Mary Ann Foley. 1984. "Differentiating Fact from Fantasy: The Reliability of Children's Memory." *Journal of Social Issues* 40(2):33–50.

Johnson, Marcia K., Shahin Hashtroudi, and D. Stephen Lindsay. 1993. "Source Monitoring." *Psychological Bulletin* 114(1):3–28.

Jones, Charles M., and Owen A. Lamont. 2002. "Short-Sale Constraints and Stock Returns." *Journal of Financial Economics* 66(2–3):207–39.

Jung, Carl. 1919. "Instinct and the Unconscious III." *British Journal of Psychology* 10(1):15–23.

Kahn, Richard F. 1931. "The Relation between Home Investment and Unemployment." *Economic Journal* 41(162):173–98.

Kahneman, Daniel, and Amos Tversky. 1973. "On the Psychology of Prediction." *Psychological Review* 80(4):237–51.

———. 2000. *Choices, Values and Frames*. Cambridge: Cambridge University Press.

Kasparov, Garry. 2017. *Deep Thinking: Where Machine Intelligence Ends and Human Creativity Begins*. New York: PublicAffairs.

Katona, George. 1975. *Psychological Economics*. New York: Elsevier Scientific Publishing Co.

Katz, Elihu, and Paul F. Lazarsfeld. 1955. *Personal Influence: The Part Played by People in the Flow of Mass Communication*. New York: The Free Press of Glencoe.

Kemmerer, David. 2014. *Cognitive Neuroscience of Language*. Hove, East Sussex: Psychology Press.

Kemmerer, Edwin Walter. 1920. *High Prices and Deflation*. Princeton, NJ: Princeton University Press.

Kempton, Murray. 1998 [1955]. *Part of Our Time: Some Ruins and Monuments of the Thirties*. New York: New York Review of Books Classics.

Kent, Richard J. 2007. "A 1929 Application of Multiplier Analysis by Keynes." *History of Political Economy* 39(3):529–43.

Kermack, William Ogilvy, and Anderson Gray McKendrick. 1927. "A Contribution to the Mathematical Theory of Epidemics." *Proceedings of the Royal Society* 115(772):701–21.

Keynes, John Maynard. 1920 [1919]. *Economic Consequences of the Peace.* London: Macmillan.

———. 1932. "Economic Possibilities for Our Grandchildren (1930)." In *Essays in Persuasion,* 358–373. New York: Harcourt Brace.

———. 1936. *The General Theory of Employment, Interest, and Money.* London: Palgrave Macmillan.

Kirnarskaya, Dina. 2009. *The Natural Musician: On Abilities, Giftedness, and Talent.* Oxford: Oxford University Press.

Klages, Mary. 2006. *Literary Theory: A Guide for the Perplexed.* London: Bloomsbury Academic.

Klein, Melanie. 2002 [1921]. "The Development of a Child." In *Love, Guilt and Reparation: And Other Works 1921–1945.* New York: Free Press, 2002.

Klein, Naomi. 2009. *No Logo.* Tenth Anniversary Edition. New York: Picador.

Koopmans, Tjalling. 1947. "Measurement without Theory." *Review of Economics and Statistics* 29(3):161–72.

Kozinets, Robert V., Kristine de Valck, Andrea Wojnicki, and Sarah J. S. Wilner. 2010. "Networked Narratives: Understanding Word-of-Mouth Marketing in Online Communities." *Journal of Marketing* 74:71–89.

Kuran, Timur. 2012. *The Great Divergence: How Islamic Law Held Back the Middle East.* Princeton, NJ: Princeton University Press.

Kuran, Timur, and Cass Sunstein. 1999. "Availability Cascades and Risk Regulation." *Stanford Law Review* 51(4):683–768.

Kuziemko, Ilyana, and Ebonya Washington. 2015. "Why Did the Democrats Lose the South? Bringing New Data to an Old Debate." National Bureau of Economic Research Working Paper 21703.

Kydland, Finn E., and Edward C. Prescott. 1982. "Time to Build and Aggregate Fluctuations." *Econometrica* 50(6):1345–70.

Laffer, Arthur. 2004. "The Laffer Curve, Past, Present and Future." Executive Summary Backgrounder No. 1765. The Heritage Foundation.

Lahiri, Kajal, and J. George Wang. 2013. "Evaluating Probability Forecasts for GDP Declines Using Alternative Methodologies." *International Journal of Forecasting* 29(1): 175–90.

Lakoff, George, and Mark Johnson. 2003. *Metaphors We Live By.* Chicago: University of Chicago Press.

Lamberson, P. J. 2016. "Diffusion in Networks." In Yann Bramoullé, Andrea Galeotti, and Brian Rogers, eds., *The Oxford Handbook of the Economics of Networks.* Oxford: Oxford University Press.

Lanchester, John. 2018. "Can Economists and Humanists Ever Be Friends?" ["Doesn't Add Up" in print edition]. *New Yorker,* July 23, https://www.newyorker.com/magazine/2018/07/23/can-economists-and-humanists-ever-be-friends.

Langlois, Janet L., and Mary E. Durocher. 2011. "The Haunting Fear: Narrative Burdens in the Great Depression." In *Nobody's Burden: Lessons from the Great Depression on the Struggle for Old-Age Security*, 245–67. Lanham, MD: Lexington Books.

League of Nations, Economic and Finance Section. 1922. *Brussels Financial Conference, 1920. The Recommendations and Their Application; A Review after Two Years.*

Le Bon, Gustave. 1895. *Psychologie des foules (The Crowd)*. Paris: Alcan.

Legrand, J., R. F. Grais, P. Y. Boelle, A. J. Valleron, and A. Flahault. 2007. "Understanding the Dynamics of Ebola Epidemics." *Epidemiology and Infection* 135:610–21.

Leonard, Janet L. 2006. "Sexual Selection: Lessons from Hermaphrodite Mating Systems." *Integrative and Comparative Biology* 46(4):349–67.

Leonard, Mark. 1997. *Britain^{TM}: Renewing Our Identity*, https://www.demos.co.uk/files/britaintm.pdf?1240939425.

LeRoy, Stephen F., and Richard D. Porter. 1981. "Stock Price Volatility: Tests Based on Implied Variance Bounds." *Econometrica* 49:97–113.

Leskovec, Jure, Lars Backstrom, and Jon Kleinberg. 2009. "Meme-Tracking and the Dynamics of the News Cycle." KDD '09 Proceedings of the 15th ACM SIGKDD International Conference on Knowledge Discovery and Data Mining, 497–506.

Lin, Yuri, Jean-Baptiste Michel, Erez Lieberman Aiden, Jon Orwant, Will Brockman, and Slav Petrov. 2012. "Syntactic Annotations for the Google Books Ngram Corpus." Proceedings of the 50th Annual Meeting of the Association for Computational Linguistics, July 8–14, 169–74. Jeju Island, Korea, http://aclweb.org/anthology/P12-3029.

Lindbeck, Assar, and Dennis J. Snower. 2001. "Insiders versus Outsiders." *Journal of Economic Perspectives* 15(1):165–88.

Litman, Barry R. 1983. "Predicting Success of Theatrical Movies: An Empirical Study." *Journal of Popular Culture* 16(4):159–75.

Littlefield, Henry M. 1964. "*The Wizard of Oz*: Parable on Populism." *American Quarterly* 16: 47–58. Reprinted in *The American Culture: Approaches to the Study of the United States*, edited by Hennig Cohen. Boston: Houghton Mifflin, 1968.

Loewenstein, George F., Elke U. Weber, Christopher K. Hsee, and Ned Welch. 2001. "Risk as Feelings." *Psychological Bulletin* 127(2): 267–86.

Long, Elisa F., Naveen K. Vaidya, and Margaret L. Brandeau. 2008. "Controlling Co-Epidemics: Analysis of HIV and Tuberculosis Infection Dynamics." *Operations Research* 56(6):1366–81.

Loomes, Graham, and Robert Sugden. 1982. "Regret Theory: An Alternative Theory of Rational Choice under Uncertainty." *Economic Journal* 92(368):805–24.

Lorayne, Harry. 2007. *Ageless Memory: The Memory Expert's Prescription for a Razor-Sharp Mind.* New York: Black Dog and Leventhal Publishers.

Losh, Molly, and Peter C. Gordon. 2014. "Quantifying Narrative Ability in Autism Spectrum Disorder: A Computational Linguistic Analysis of Narrative Coherence." *Journal of Autism and Developmental Disorders* 44 (12): 3016–25.

Lowen, Anice C., Samira Mubareka, John Steel, and Peter Palese. 2007. "Influenza Virus Transmission Is Dependent on Relative Humidity and Temperature." *PLOS Pathogens*, https://doi.org/10.1371/journal.ppat.0030151.

Loyd, Jere L. 1975. "Consumer Affairs—State Securities Regulation of Interstate Land Sales." *Urban Law Annual* 10:271–82, http://openscholarship.wustl.edu/law_ubranlaw/vol10/iss1/9.

Lucas, Robert E. 1978. "Asset Prices in an Exchange Economy." *Econometrica* 46:1429–45.

Luminet, Olivier, and Antoinietta Curci. 2009. "The 9/11 Attacks inside and outside the US: Testing Four Models of Flashbulb Memory Formation across Groups and the Specific Effects of Social Identity." *Memory* 17(7):742–59.

Machill, Marcel, Sebastian Köhler, and Markus Waldhauser. 2007. "The Use of Narrative Structures in Television News." *European Journal of Communication* 22(2):185–205.

Mackay, Charles. 1841. *Memoirs of Extraordinary Popular Delusions.* London: Richard Bentley.

Macmillan, R. H. 1956. *Automation: Friend or Foe?* Cambridge: Cambridge University Press.

MacMullen, Ramsay. 2003. *Feelings in History: Ancient and Modern.* Claremont, CA: Regina Books.

Malthus, Thomas Robert. 1798. *An Essay on the Principle of Population.* Anonymously published, 1798.

Marcus, George E., and Peter Dobkin Hall. 1992. *Lives in Trust: The Fortunes of Dynastic Families in Late Twentieth Century America (Institutional Structures of Feeling).* Boulder, CO: Westview Press.

Marden, Orison Swett. 1920. *Success Fundamentals.* New York: Thomas Y. Crowell.

Maren, Stephen, and Gregory J. Quirk. 2004. "Neuronal Signalling of Fear Memory." *Nature Reviews: Neuroscience* 5(11):844–52.

Marineli, Filio, Gregory Tsoucalas, Marianna Karamanou, and George Androutsos. 2013. "Mary Mallon (1869–1938) and the History of Typhoid Fever." *Annals of Gastroenterology* 26(2):132–34.

Marx, Groucho. 2017 [1959]. *Groucho and Me.* Muriwai Books.

McCabe, Brian J. 2016. *No Place Like Home: Wealth, Community, and the Politics of Homeownership.* New York: Oxford University Press.

McCaffery, Edward. 2000. "Cognitive Theory and Tax." In Cass Sunstein, ed., *Behavioral Law and Economics.* Cambridge: Cambridge University Press.

McCloskey, Deirdre. 2016. "Adam Smith Did Humanomics: So Should We." *Eastern Economic Journal* 42(4):503–13.

McCullough, David. 1993. *Truman.* New York: Simon & Schuster.

McDaniel, M. A., and G. O. Einstein. 1986. "Bizarre Imagery as an Effective Memory Aid: The Importance of Distinctiveness." *Journal of Experimental Psychology: Learning, Memory, and Cognition* 12(1):54–65.

McGinn, Daniel. 2007. *House Lust: America's Obsession with Our Homes.* New York: Currency Doubleday.

McHugh, Richard. 1991. "Productivity Effects of Strikes in Struck and Nonstruck Industries." *ILR Review* 44(4):722–32.

McQuiggan, Scott W., Jonathan P. Rowe, Sunyoung Lee, and James C. Lester. 2008. "Story-Based Learning: The Impact of Narrative on Learning Experiences and Outcomes." In Beverley P. Woolf, Esma Aïmeur, Roger Nkambou, and Susanne Lajoie, eds., *Intelligent Tutoring Systems,* 530–39. Berlin: Springer Verlag.

Meadows, Donnella, et al. 1972. *Limits to Growth: A Report for the Club of Rome's Project on the Predicament of Mankind.* New York: Universe Books.

Merton, Robert K. 1948. "The Self-Fulfilling Prophecy." *Antioch Review* 8(2):193–210.

Merton, Robert K., and Patricia L. Kendall. 1946. "The Focused Interview." *American Sociological Review* 51(6): 541–57.

Michaels, Donald N. 1962. *Cybernation: The Silent Conquest.* Santa Barbara, CA: Center for the Study of Democratic Institutions, 1962, http://ucf.digital.flvc.org/islandora/object /ucf%3A5123.

Michel, Jean-Baptiste, Yuan Kui Shen, Aviva Presser Aiden, Adrian Veres, Matthew K. Gray, The Google Books Team, Joseph P. Pickett, Dale Hoiberg, Dan Clancy, Peter Norvig, Jon Orwant, Steven Pinker, Martin A. Nowak, and Erez Lieberman Aiden. 2011. "Quantitative Analysis of Culture Using Millions of Digitized Books." *Science* 331(6014):176–82.

Miguel, Edward, Shanker Satyanath, and Ernest Sergenti. 2004. "Economic Shocks and Civil Conflict: An Instrumental Variables Approach." *Journal of Political Economy* 112(4):725–53.

Milad, Mohammed R., Brian T. Quinn, Roger K. Pitman, Scott P. Orr, Bruce Fischl, Scott L. Rauch, and Marcus E. Raichle. 2005. "Thickness of Ventromedial Prefrontal Cortex in Humans Is Correlated with Extinction Memory." *Proceedings of the National Academy of Sciences of the United States of America* 102(30):10706–11.

Milad, Mohammed R., Blake L. Rosenbaum, and Naomi M. Simon. 2014. "Neuroscience of Fear Extinction: Implications for Assessment and Treatment of Fear-Based and Anxiety Related Disorders." *Behaviour Research and Therapy* 62:17–23.

Miller, Joel C. 2012. "A Note on the Derivation of Epidemic Final Sizes." *Bulletin of Mathematical Biology* 74(9):2125–41.

Miłosz, Czesław. 1990 [1951]. *The Captive Mind.* Translated from the Polish by Jane Zielonko. New York: Vintage International.

Mineka, Susan, and Michael Cook. 1988. "Social Learning and the Acquisition of Snake Fear in Monkeys." In Thomas R. Zentall and Bennett G. Galef Jr., eds., *Social Learning: Psychological and Biological Perspectives,* 51–74. Mahwah, NJ: Lawrence Erlbaum Associates.

Mirowski, Philip. 1982. "What's Wrong with the Laffer Curve?" *Journal of Economic Issues* 16(3):1815–28.

Mitchell, Daniel J. B. 1985. "Wage Flexibility: Then and Now." *Industrial Relations* 24(20):266–79.

Mitchell, Wesley C., and Arthur F. Burns. 1938. *Statistical Indicators of Cyclical Revivals, Bulletin 69.* New York: National Bureau of Economic Research, 1938, https://www.nber.org /chapters/c4251.pdf. Reprinted in Geoffrey Moore, *Business Cycle Indicators.* Princeton, NJ: Princeton University Press, 1961.

Mokyr, Joel. 2013. "Culture, Institutions, and Modern Growth." In Sebastian Galiani and Itai Sened, eds., *Institutions, Property Rights, and Economic Growth: The Legacy of Douglass North.* Cambridge: Cambridge University Press.

———. 2016. *Culture and Growth: The Origins of the Modern Economy.* Princeton, NJ: Princeton University Press.

Moore, Geoffrey H. 1983. "The Forty-Second Anniversary of the Leading Indicators." In Geoffrey Moore, ed., *Business Cycles, Inflation and Forecasting.* 2nd ed. Cambridge, MA: Published for the National Bureau of Economic Research by Ballinger Publishing Co., https://www .nber.org/chapters/c0710.pdf.

Morson, Gary Saul, and Morton Schapiro. 2017. *Cents and Sensibility: What Economics Can Learn from the Humanities*. Princeton, NJ: Princeton University Press.

Mullainathan, Sendhil, and Eldar Shafir. 2013. *Scarcity: Why Having Too Little Means So Much*. New York: Times Books.

Muller, Jerry Z. 2018. *The Tyranny of Metrics*. Princeton, NJ: Princeton University Press.

Myrdal, Gunnar. 1974. "The Case against Romantic Ethnicity." *Center Magazine* 7(4):26–30.

Nagel, Stefan, and Zhengyang Xu. 2018. "Asset Pricing with Fading Memory." Unpublished paper, University of Michigan.

Nakamoto, Satoshi. 2008. "Bitcoin: A Peer-to-Peer Electronic Cash System," https://Bitcoin .org/Bitcoin.pdf.

Narayanan, Arvind, Joseph Bonneau, Edward Felten, Andrew Miller, and Steven Goldfeder. 2016. *Bitcoin and Cryptocurrency Technologies*. Princeton, NJ: Princeton University Press.

Nathan, Robert R. 1944. *Mobilizing for Abundance*. New York: McGraw-Hill.

Nathanson, N., and J. R. Martin. 1979. "The Epidemiology of Poliomyelitis: Enigmas Surrounding Its Appearance, Epidemicity, and Disappearance." *American Journal of Epidemiology* 110(6):672–92.

Neftçi, Salih N. 1984. "Are Economic Time Series Asymmetric over the Business Cycle?" *Journal of Political Economy* 92(2):307–28.

Newcomb, Anthony. 1984. "Once More 'Between Absolute and Program Music': Schumann's Second Symphony." *19th-Century Music* 7(3):233–50.

Nørgård, Jørgen Stig, John Peet, and Kristín Vala Ragnarsdóttir. 2010. "The History of the Limits to Growth." *Solutions Journal* 1(2):59–63.

North, Douglass. 2005. *Understanding the Process of Economic Change*. Princeton, NJ: Princeton University Press.

Noyes, Alexander Dana. 1898. *Thirty Years of American Finance*. New York: G. P. Putnam's Sons.

Nsoesie, Elaine O., Richard J. Beckman, Sara Shashaani, Kalyani S. Nagaraj, Madhav V. Marathe. 2013. "A Simulation Optimization Approach to Epidemic Forecasting." *PLoS ONE* 8(6):e67164 doi:10 1371/journal.pone.0067164.

O'Barr, William M., and John M. Conley. 1992. *Fortune and Folly: The Wealth and Power of Institutional Investing*. Homewood, IL: Business-One Irwin.

O Broin, Turlach. 2016. "Mail-Order Demagogues: The NSDAP School for Speakers, 1928–34." *Journal of Contemporary History* 51(4):715.

O'Connor, Patricia E. 2000. *Speaking of Crime: Narratives of Prisoners*. Lincoln: University of Nebraska Press.

Okun, Arthur. 1980. "The Invisible Handshake and the Inflationary Process." *Challenge* 22(6):5–12.

Olsen, L. F., G. L. Truty, and W. M. Schaffer. 1988. "Oscillations and Chaos in Epidemics: A Nonlinear Dynamic Study of Six Childhood Diseases in Copenhagen, Denmark." *Theoretical Population Biology* 33:344–70.

Olson, Mancur. 1971. *The Logic of Collective Action: Public Goods and the Theory of Groups*. Cambridge, MA: Harvard University Press.

Ong, Walter J. 1982. "Oral Remembering and Narrative." In Deborah Tannen, ed., *Analyzing Discourse: Text and Talk*. Washington, DC: Georgetown University Press.

Pace-Schott, Edward F. 2013. "Dreaming as a Story-Telling Instinct." *Frontiers in Psychology* 4:159.

Palgrave, R. H. Inglis. 1894. *Dictionary of Political Economy.* London: Stockton Press.

Paller, Ken A., and Anthony D. Wagner. 2002. "Observing the Transformation of Experience into Memory." *Trends in Cognitive Sciences.* 6(2):93–102.

Palmer, Jay. 1987. "What Do You Think? A Nationwide Poll of Reaction to the Crash." *Barrons,* November 9, 16ff.

Patel, Aniruddh D. 2007. *Music, Language, and the Brain.* New York: Oxford University Press.

Pavlov, Ivan P. 1927. *Conditioned Reflexes: An Investigation of the Physiological Activity of the Cerebral Cortex.* London: Oxford University Press.

Payne, Robert. 1968. *Marx.* New York: Simon and Schuster.

Pecotich, Anthony, and Steven Ward. 2007. "Global Branding, Country of Origin, and Expertise: An Experimental Evaluation." *International Marketing Review* 24(3):271–96, https://doi.org/10.1108/02651330710755294.

Penfield, Wilder. 1958. "Some Mechanisms of Consciousness Discovered during Electrical Stimulation of the Brain." *Proceedings of the National Academy of Sciences* 44(2):51–66.

Pierce, Karen, R. A. Müller, J. Ambrose, G. Allen, and E. Courchesne. 2001. "Face Processing Occurs Outside the Fusiform 'Face Area' in Autism: Evidence from Functional MRI." *Brain* 124(10):2059–73.

Piketty, Thomas. 2014. *Capital in the Twenty-First Century.* Cambridge, MA: Harvard University Press.

Piore, Michael. 2010. "Qualitative Research: Does It Fit in Economics?" *European Management Review* 3(1):17–23.

Polletta, Francesca. 2002. "Plotting Protest Mobilizing Stories in the 1960 Student Sit-Ins." In Joseph E. Davis, ed., *Stories of Change.* Albany: State University of New York Press.

Poole, Debra A., and Lawrence T. White. 1991. "Effects of Question Repetition on the Eyewitness Testimony of Children and Adults." *Developmental Psychology* 27(6):975–79.

Posner, Michael I. 2012. *Cognitive Neuroscience of Attention.* 2nd ed. New York: The Guilford Press.

Presidential Task Force on Market Mechanisms. 1988. *Report* (Brady Commission Report). US Department of Treasury, Washington DC, https://archive.org/details/reportofpresiden01unit.

Presser, Lois, and Sveinung Sandberg. 2015. *Narrative Criminology: Understanding Stories of Crime.* New York: New York University Press.

Propp, Vladimir. 1984. *Theory and History of Folklore.* Minneapolis: University of Minnesota Press.

Proudhon, Pierre-Joseph. 1923 [1840]. *The General Idea of the Revolution in the Nineteenth Century.* Translated by John Beverly Robinson. London: Freedom Press.

Prowaznik, Bruno E. 2006. *Homo artifex: Von der Magie der Kunst.* Infothek.

Prum, Richard O. 2010. "The Lande-Kirkpatrick Mechanism Is the Null Model of Evolution by Intersexual Selection: Implications for Meaning, Honesty, and Design in Intersexual Signals." *Evolution* 64(11):3085–100.

———. 2017. *The Evolution of Beauty: How Darwin's Forgotten Model of Mate Choice Shapes the Animal World—And Us.* New York: Doubleday.

Pursley, Denise. 2017. "Understanding the Full Effects of the Interstate Land Sales Full Disclosure Act." *New England Real Estate Journal*, http://nyrej.com/understanding-the-full-effects-of-the-interstate-land-sales-full-disclosure-act.

Ramey, Valerie A. 2011. "Can Government Purchases Stimulate the Economy?" *Journal of Economic Literature* 49(3):673–85.

Rand, Ayn. 1957. *Atlas Shrugged*. New York: Random House.

Rand, D. A., and H. B. Wilson. 1991. "Chaotic Stochasticity: A Ubiquitous Source of Unpredictability in Epidemics." *Proceedings of the Royal Society B*, https://doi.org/10.1098/rspb.1991.0142.

Rappoport, Peter, and Eugene White. 1994. "Was the Crash of 1929 Expected?" *American Economic Review* 84(1):271–81.

Rashkin, Esther. 1997. *Family Secrets and the Psychoanalysis of Narrative*. Princeton, NJ: Princeton University Press.

Redish, Angela. 2000. *Bimetallism: An Economic and Historical Analysis*. Cambridge: Cambridge University Press.

Reeves, Byron, and Clifford Nass. 2003. *The Media Equation: How People Treat Computers, Television, and New Media Like Real People and Places*. Cambridge: Cambridge University Press.

Rhys-Williams, Juliet. 1943. *Something to Look Forward To*. London: MacDonald.

Richards, George. 1863. *The Memory of Washington: A Sermon Preached in the First Congregational Church, Litchfield CT, February 22, 1863*. Philadelphia: Henry B. Ashmead.

Ritter, Jay. 1991. "The Long-Run Performance of Initial Public Offerings." *Journal of Finance* 46(1):3–27.

Robbins, Lionel. 1932. *An Essay on the Nature and Significance of Economic Science*. London: Macmillan.

———. 1934. *The Great Depression*. New York: Macmillan.

Rockoff, Hugh. 1990. "*The Wizard of Oz* as a Monetary Allegory." *Journal of Political Economy* 98(4):739–60.

Roden, Donald. 1980. "Baseball and the Quest for National Dignity in Meiji Japan." *American Historical Review* 85(3):511–34.

Roll, Richard. 1988. "Orange Juice and Weather." *American Economic Review* 74(5):861–80.

Romer, Christina. 1990. "The Great Crash and the Onset of the Great Depression." *Quarterly Journal of Economics* 105(3):597–624.

Romer, Christina, and David Romer. 1989. "Does Monetary Policy Matter: A New Test in the Spirit of Friedman and Schwartz." Edited by Olivier J. Blanchard and Stanley Fischer. *NBER Macroeconomics Annual*, 63–129.

———. 1994. "What Ends Recessions?" National Bureau of Economic Research Working Paper 4765.

———. 2004. "A New Measure of Monetary Shocks." *American Economic Review* 94(4):1055–84.

Ross, Andrew. 1991. "Hacking Away at the Counterculture." In Andrew Ross and Constance Penley, eds., *Technoculture*. Minneapolis: University of Minnesota Press, 1991.

Roth, Benjamin. 2009. *The Great Depression: A Diary*. Edited by James Ledbetter and Daniel B. Roth. New York: Public Affairs.

Rubin, David C. 1997. *Memory in Oral Traditions: The Cognitive Psychology of Epic, Ballads, and Counting-Out Rhymes*. Oxford: Oxford University Press.

Rubinstein Mark, and Hayne Leland H. 1981. "Replicating Options with Positions in Stock and Cash." *Financial Analysts Journal* 37(4):63–72.

Rudebusch, Glenn D., and John C. Williams. 2009. "Forecasting Recessions: The Puzzle of the Enduring Power of the Yield Curve." *Journal of Business and Economic Statistics* 27(4):492–503.

Saavedra, Javier, Mercedes Cubero, and Paul Crawford. 2009. "Incomprehensibility in the Narratives of Individuals with a Diagnosis of Schizophrenia." *Qualitative Health Research* 19(11):1548.

Saiz, Albert. 2010. "The Geographic Determinants of Housing Supply." *Quarterly Journal of Economics* 125(3):1253–96.

Sala-i-Martin, Xavier. 2006. "The World Distribution of Income: Falling Poverty and . . . Convergence, Period." *Quarterly Journal of Economics* 121(2):351–97.

Salganik, Matthew J., Peter Sheridan Dodds, and Duncan J. Watts. 2016. "Experimental Study of Inequality and Unpredictability in an Artificial Cultural Market." *Science* 311(5762):854–56, doi: 10.1126/science.1121066.

Samuelson, Paul A. 1939. "Interactions between the Multiplier Analysis and the Principle of Acceleration." *Review of Economics and Statistics* 21(2):75–78.

———. 1948a. *Economics: An Introductory Analysis*. New York: McGraw-Hill.

———. 1948b. "International Trade and the Equalization of Factor Prices." *Economic Journal* 58(230):163–84.

———. 1958. "An Exact Consumption-Loan Model with or without the Social Contrivance of Money." *Journal of Political Economy* 66(6):467–82.

Sarbin, Theodore R. 1986. *Narrative Psychology: The Storied Nature of Human Conduct*. Santa Barbara, CA: Praeger.

Sargent, Thomas J., and François Velde. 2002. *The Big Problem of Small Change*. Princeton, NJ: Princeton University Press.

Sartre, Jean-Paul. 1938. *Nausea*. Translated by Robert Baldick. Harmondsworth, UK: Penguin.

Sayles, John. 2011. *A Moment in the Sun*. San Francisco: McSweeney's Publishers.

Schank, Roger C., and Robert P. Abelson. 1977. *Scripts, Plans, Goals, and Understanding: An Inquiry into Human Knowledge*. Hillsdale, NJ: Lawrence Erlbaum Associates.

Scheidel, Walter. 2017. *The Great Leveler: Violence and the History of Inequality from the Stone Age to the Twenty-First Century*. Princeton, NJ: Princeton University Press.

Scheve, Kenneth, and David Stasavage. 2017. *Taxing the Rich: A History of Fiscal Fairness in the United States and Europe*. Princeton, NJ: Princeton University Press.

Scholz, Christin, Elisa C. Baek, Matthew Brook O'Donnell, Hyun Suk Kim, Joseph N. Cappella, and Emily B. Falk. 2017. "A Neural Model of Valuation and Information Virality." *Proceedings of the National Academy of Science of the United States of America* 114(11):2881–86, doi: 10.1073/pnas.161259114, 2017, http://www.pnas.org/content/114/11/2881.abstract#aff-1.

Shapiro, Matthew D. 2016. "How Economic Shocks Affect Spending." *NBER Reporter* 2016(2):11–13.

Shiller, Robert J. 1981. "Do Stock Prices Move Too Much to Be Justified by Subsequent Changes in Dividends?" *American Economic Review* 71(3):421–36.

———. 1984. "Stock Prices and Social Dynamics." *Brookings Papers on Economic Activity* 15(2):457–98.

———. 1987. "Ultimate Sources of Aggregate Variability." *American Economic Review Papers and Proceedings* 77(2):87–92.

———. 1989. *Market Volatility*. Cambridge, MA: MIT Press.

———. 1995. "Conversation, Information, and Herd Behavior." *American Economic Review* 85:181–85.

———. 1997. "Why Do People Dislike Inflation?" In Christina Romer and David Romer, eds., *Reducing Inflation: Motivation and Strategy*. Chicago: University of Chicago Press.

———. 2000. *Irrational Exuberance*. Princeton, NJ: Princeton University Press.

———. 2002. "Bubbles, Human Judgment, and Expert Opinion." *Financial Analysts Journal* 58(3):18–26.

Shiller, Robert J., and John Pound. 1989. "Survey Evidence on the Diffusion of Interest and Information among Investors." *Journal of Economic Behavior and Organization* 12: 47–66.

Shiller, Virginia M. 2017. *The Attachment Bond: Affectional Ties across the Lifespan*. New York: Lexington Books.

Shleifer, Andrei, and Robert W. Vishny. 1997. "The Limits of Arbitrage." *Journal of Finance* 52(1):35–55.

Sidis, Boris. 1898. *The Psychology of Suggestion: A Research into the Subconscious Nature of Man and Society*. New York: Appleton & Co.

Siegel, Jeremy J. 2014 [1994]. *Stocks for the Long Run*. New York: Irwin.

Silber, William. 2014. *When Washington Shut Down Wall Street: The Great Financial Crisis of 1914 and the Origins of America's Monetary Supremacy*. Princeton, NJ: Princeton University Press.

Silver, David, et al. 2017. "Mastering Chess and Shogi by Self-Play with a General Reinforcement Learning Algorithm." Cornell University, arXiv:1712.01815 [cs.AI], https://arxiv.org/abs /1712.01815.

Skousen, Mark. 2001. *The Making of Modern Economics*. Armonk, NY: M. E. Sharpe.

Slater, Michael D., David B. Buller, Emily Waters, Margarita Archibeque, & Michelle LeBlanc. 2003. "A Test of Conversational and Testimonial Messages versus Didactic Presentations of Nutrition Information." *Journal of Nutrition Education Behavior* 35:255–59.

Slovic, Paul, Melissa L. Finucane, Ellen Peters, and Donald G. MacGregor. 2007. "The Affect Heuristic." *European Journal of Operational Research* 177(3):1333–52.

Smith, Adam. 1869 [1776]. *An Inquiry into the Origin and Causes of the Wealth of Nations*. Oxford: Clarendon Press. [London: W. Strahan].

Smith, Walter E. 1879. *The Recent Depression of Trade: Its Nature, Its Causes, and the Remedies Which Have Been Suggested for It*. London: Trübner & Co.

Smith, William, William Wayte, and G. E. Marindin. 1890. *A Dictionary of Greek and Roman Antiquities*. London: John Murray.

Snyder, Timothy. 2010. *Bloodlands: Europe between Hitler and Stalin*. New York: Basic Books.

Stachura, Peter D. 1986. "The Social and Welfare Implications of Youth Unemployment in Weimar Germany 1929–1933." In Peter Stachura, ed., *Unemployment and the Great Depression in Weimar Germany*, 121–47. London: Palgrave Macmillan.

Stern, Barbara B., Craig J. Thompson, and Eric J. Arnould. 1998. "Narrative Analysis of a Marketing Relationship: The Consumer's Perspective." *Psychology & Marketing* 15(3):195–214.

Sternberg, Robert. 1998. *Love Is a Story: A New Theory of Relationships*. Oxford: Oxford University Press.

Stowe, Harriet Beecher. 1852. *Uncle Tom's Cabin; Or Life Among the Lowly*. Boston: John P. Jewett and Company.

Sullivan, James. 2006. *Jeans: A Cultural History of an American Icon*. New York: Gotham Books.

Summers, Lawrence H. 1986. "Does the Stock Market Rationally Reflect Fundamental Values?" *Journal of Finance* 41(3):591–601.

Temin, Peter. 1975. "The Panic of 1857." *Intermountain Review* 6:1–12.

———. 1976. *Did Monetary Forces Cause the Great Depression?* New York: W. W. Norton.

———. 1989. *Lessons from the Great Depression*. Cambridge, MA: MIT Press.

Terkel, Studs. 1970. *Hard Times: An Oral History of the Great Depression*. New York: Random House.

Thaler, Richard. 2015. *Misbehaving: The Making of Behavioral Economics*. New York: W. W. Norton.

———. 2016. "Behavioral Economics: Past, Present, and Future" (AEA Presidential Address). *American Economic Review* 106(7):1577–1600.

Thaler, Richard, and Cass Sunstein. 2008. *Nudge: Improving Decisions about Health, Wealth, and Happiness*. New Haven, CT: Yale University Press.

Theobald, Robert. 1963. *Free Men and Free Markets*. New York: C. N. Potter.

Thibault, Pascal, Manon Levesque, Pierre Gosselin, and Ursula Hess. 2012. "The Duchenne Marker Is Not a Universal Signal of Smile Authenticity—But It Can Be Learned!" *Social Psychology* 43(4):215–21.

Tobias, Ronald B. 1999. *Twenty Master Plots and How to Build Them*. London: Piatkus.

Tobin, James, and Craig Swan. 1969. "Money and Permanent Income: Some Empirical Tests." *American Economic Review* 59(2):285–95.

Trump, Donald J., and Meredith McIver. 2004. *How to Get Rich*. New York: Random House.

Trump, Donald J., and Bill Zanker. 2007. *Think Big and Kick Ass in Business and Life*. New York: HarperBusiness.

Uchitelle, Louis. 2006. *The Disposable American: Layoffs and Their Consequences*. New York: Alfred A. Knopf, 2006.

US Bureau of Labor Statistics. 2014. *Monthly Labor Review*. April, https://www.bls.gov/opub/mlr/2014/article/the-first-hundred-years-of-the-consumer-price-index.htm.

US Centers for Disease Control and Prevention. 2014. "Morbidity and Mortality Weekly Report: Evidence for a Decrease in Transmission of Ebola Virus—Lofa County, Liberia." November 14, https://www.cdc.gov/mmwr/preview/mmwrhtml/mm63e1114a1.htm.

US Department of Health, Education and Welfare. 1966. Report of the National Commission on Technology, Automation, and Economic Progress, *Technology and the American Economy*, vol. 1, https://files.eric.ed.gov/fulltext/ED023803.pdf.

US Department of Labor. 1948. *Construction in the War Years 1942–45: Employment, Expenditures, and Building Volume*. Washington, DC: US Government Printing Office, https://fraser.stlouisfed.org/title/4358.

US Securities and Exchange Commission, Trading and Exchange Division. 1947. *A Report on Stock Trading on the New York Stock Exchange on September 3, 1946*. Washington, DC: Securities and Exchange Commission.

Uscinski, Joseph E. 2018. *Conspiracy Theories and the People Who Believe Them*. Oxford: Oxford University Press.

Van Evera, Stephen. 1984. "The Cult of the Offensive and the Origins of the First World War." *International Security* 9(1):58–107.

Vannucci, Manila, Claudia Pelagatti, Carlo Chiorri, and Giuliana Mazzoni. 2015. "Visual Object Imagery and Autobiographical Memory: Object Imagers Are Better at Remembering Their Personal Past." *Memory* 24(4):455–70.

Vartanian, Oshin. 2012. "Dissociable Neural Systems for Analogy and Metaphor: Implications for the Neuroscience of Creativity." *British Journal of Psychiatry* 103(3):302–16.

Veblen, Thorstein. 1899. *The Theory of the Leisure Class: An Economic Study of Institutions*. New York: Macmillan.

———. 1921. *The Engineers and the Price System*. New York: B. W. Huebsch.

Vernon, J. R. 1991. "The 1920–21 Deflation: The Role of Aggregate Supply." *Economic Inquiry* 29(3):572–80.

Vinck, Patrick, Phuong N. Pham, Kenedy K. Bindu, Juliet Bedford, and Eric J. Nilles. 2019. "Institutional Trust and Misinformation in the Response to the 2018–19 Ebola Outbreak in North Kivu, DR Congo: A Population-Based Survey." *Lancet Infectious Diseases* March 27, https://www.thelancet.com/journals/laninf/article/PIIS1473-3099(19)30063-5/fulltext.

Vives, Xavier. 1996. "Social Learning and Rational Expectations." *European Economic Review* 40:589–601.

Vosoughi, Soroush, Deb Roy, and Sinan Aral. 2018. "The Spread of True and False News Online." *Science* 359(6380):1146–51, doi: 10.1126/science.aap9559.

Wang, Hongbin, Xun Liu, and Jin Fan. 2012. "Symbolic and Connectionist Models of Attention." In Michael Posner, ed., *Cognitive Neuroscience of Attention*, 2nd ed., 47–56. New York: Guilford Press.

Wanniski, Jude. 1978a. "Taxes, Revenues and the 'Laffer Curve.'" *Public Interest* 38:3–16, https://www.nationalaffairs.com/storage/app/uploads/public/58e/1a4/c54/58e1a4c549207669125935.pdf.

———. 1978b. *The Way the World Works: How Economies Fail and Succeed*. New York: Basic Books.

Watson, William, and Jason Clemons. 2017. *The History and Development of Canada's Personal Income Tax*. Fraser Institute, https://www.fraserinstitute.org/studies/history-and-development-of-canadas-personal-income-tax-zero-to-50-in-100-years.

Webb, L. Dean, Gene Glass, Arlene Metha, and Casey Cobb. 2002. "Economic Correlates of Suicide in the United States (1929–1992): A Time Series Analysis." *Archives of Suicide Research* 6:93–101.

Weber, Keith, Matthew M. Martin, Members of COMM 401, and Michael Corrigan. 2006. "Creating Persuasive Messages Advocating Organ Donation." *Communication Quarterly* 54:67–87.

Weber, Max. 1950 [1904]. *The Protestant Ethic and the Spirit of Capitalism (Die protestantische Ethik und der Geist des Kapitalismus)*. New York: Scribner's.

Weems, Mason Locke. 1837. *The Life of George Washington with Curious Anecdotes, Equally Honourable to Himself and Exemplary to His Young Countrymen*. Philadelphia: Joseph Allen.

Wertsch, James V. 2008. "Collective Memory and Narrative Templates." *Social Research* 75:133–56.

Wheelis, Mark. 2002. "Biological Warfare at the 1346 Siege of Caffa." *Emerging Infectious Disease Journal* 8(9):971–75.

Wheen, Francis. 1999. *Karl Marx: A Life*. New York: W. W. Norton.

Whewell, William. 1840. *The Philosophy of the Inductive Sciences, Founded upon Their History*. London: John W. Parker.

White, Hayden. 1981. "The Value of Narrativity in the Representation of Reality." In W.J.T. Mitchell, ed., *On Narrative*, 1–25. Chicago: University of Chicago Press.

Wilson, Edward O. 1998. *Consilience: The Unity of Knowledge*. New York: Alfred A. Knopf.

Wold, H. 1954. *A Study in the Analysis of Stationary Time Series*. 2nd ed. Uppsala: Almqvist and Wiksell Book Co.

Wolfe, Tom. 1975. *The Painted Word*. New York: Farrar, Straus and Giroux.

Wolman, Leo. 1916. *The Boycott in American Trade Unions*. Baltimore: Johns Hopkins University Press.

World Health Organization. 2003. *Adherence to Long-Term Therapies: Evidence for Action*. Geneva: WHO, http://www.who.int/chp/knowledge/publications/adherence_full_report.pdf.

———. 2015. *Health Worker Ebola Infections in Guinea, Liberia and Sierra Leone, Preliminary Report*, http://www.who.int/csr/resources/publications/ebola/health-worker-infections /en/.

Wyatt, H. V. 2011. "The 1916 New York City Epidemic of Poliomyelitis: Where Did the Virus Come From?" *Open Vaccine Journal* 4:13–17.

Young, Kay, and Jeffrey Saver. 2001. *The Neurology of Narrative*. Madison: University of Wisconsin Press.

Young, Warren. 1987. *Interpreting Mr. Keynes: The IS-LM Enigma*. Boulder, CO: Westview Press.

Zak, Paul J. 2015. "Why Inspiring Stories Make Us React: The Neuroscience of Narrative." *Cerebrum*, January–February, 2, https://www.ncbi.nlm.nih.gov/pmc/articles/PMC4445577/.

Zarnowitz, Victor, and Philip Braun. 1992. "Twenty-Two Years of the NBER-ASA Quarterly Economic Outlook Surveys: Aspects and Comparisons of Forecasting Performance." Cambridge MA: National Bureau of Economic Research Working Paper 3965.

Zeng, Guang Zhao, Lan Sun Chen, and Li Hua Sun. 2005. "Complexity of an SIR Epidemic Dynamics Model with Impulsive Vaccination Control." *Chaos, Solitons & Fractals* 26(2):495–505.

Zhang, Sarah. 2015. "The Pitfalls of Using Google NGRAM to Study Language." *Wired*, https:// www.wired.com/2015/10/pitfalls-of-studying-language-with-google-ngram/.

Zhao, Laijun, Hongxin Cui, Xiaoyan Qiu, Xiaoli Wang, and Jiajia Wang. 2013. "SIR Rumor Spreading Model in the New Media Age." *Physica A: Statistical Mechanics and Its Applications* 392(4):995–1013.

Zheng, Muhua, Chaoqing Wang, Jie Zhou, Ming Zhao, Shuguang Guan, Yong Zou, and Zonghua Liu. 2015. "Non-periodic Outbreaks of Recurrent Epidemics and Its Network Modelling." *Scientific Reports* 5, Article number: 16010 (2015).

Index

A page number followed by f refers to a figure or its caption.

The A B C of Technocracy (Arkright), 193

Abelson, Robert P., 37

Adams, James Truslow, 151, 153–54

Adbusters, 8

Addams, Jane, xvii

Advanced Micro Devices, Inc., 20

advertisements: for homeownership, 219–20; online searching of, x; phrase *American Dream* in, 154

affect heuristic, 67, 233

Aiden, Erez, 24

AIDS (acquired immune deficiency syndrome), 24

Akerlof, George, xviii, 61, 64, 67, 250, 300, 301n13

Aldrich-Vreeland Act, 117

Alexa, of Amazon Echo, 8, 207

Alibaba's Tmall Genie, 207

Alice, Yandex, 207

Alice's Adventures in Wonderland (Carroll), 189

Allen, Frederick Lewis, ix–xi, 139

Allen, Lily, 92

AlphaZero chess computer program, 208, 316n22

Amazon's Echo, 207

American Dream (O'Neil), 153

The American Dream (Albee), 153

American Dream Downpayment Assistance Act, 154

American Dream narrative, 151–55, 152f; stock market crash of 1929 and, 231

American Federation of Labor, 241

The American Plutocracy (Howard), 166

analogies, brain response to, 17

anarchism: Bitcoin narrative and, 5–7; history of, 6

Angell, Norman, 95

anger about inflation, 239, 263–64, 265–66; during wars, 265; after World War I, 245, 247

anger at businesspeople: boycott narrative and, 240; cuts in wages and, 239; depressions of 1920–21 and 1930s and, 243; inflation and, 239, 245, 247, 263–64, 265; profiteer narrative and, 241–43, 245, 247, 248–49, 250. *See also* boycott narrative

anger at oil crisis of 1970s, 256

animal spirits: business confidence and, xvi; Keynes's idea of, 138

Animal Spirits (Akerlof and Shiller), 64

Anthropology: creation myths in, 15; economists learning from, 78

Apple Computer: Siri and, 8, 206–7, 287; Steve Jobs and, 208–9

Arab oil embargo of 1973, 256

archetypes, Jungian, 15

ARIMA (autoregressive integrated moving average) models, 295, 322n9

Aristotle, 174–75

Arkright, Frank, 193

Arkwright, Richard, 193

artificial intelligence, in narrative economics research, 276, 287

artificial intelligence narrative, 196, 197f, 199, 211. *See also* robots

Atari, 203

Atlas Shrugged (Rand), 50

autism spectrum disorder, narrative
  disruption in, 66
Automata (Hero of Alexandria), 175
automated assistants, 8. *See also* Siri (Apple)
automation narrative: difference from
  labor-saving machinery narrative, 199;
  as epidemic around 1955–66, 199–202;
  mutated in recessions of early 1980s, 204;
  with new catchphrases in 2000s, 205;
  offices and, 204; percentage of articles
  containing *automation*, 197f; post–World
  War II, 196; robots and, 191; second scare
  during 1980s, 202–4; surge in fears
  beginning around 2016, 206–8; third
  spike in concern around 1995, 204–5;
  unemployment and, 199–200, 204. *See
  also* robots
"automation recession" of 1957–58, 201, 264
autosuggestion narrative, 119, 120f, 121–23

baby boom, optimism associated with, 198
baby boomers retiring, elevated stock
  market and, 29
Baker, Charles Whiting, 210
bank failures: Great Recession of 2007–9
  and, 132; loss of confidence during Great
  Depression and, 132
Bank of Canada, 156\
bank runs: during 1857 financial panic, 115;
  in 1873, during depression, 176; in 1893,
  164–65; in 2007 and 2008, 119, 134–35; as
  crisis of confidence, 114; Great Depression and, 133, 134–35; Roosevelt's "fireside
  chat" during, 129, 278
banks taking risk, ten years after 2007–9
  financial crisis, 55–56
Barthes, Roland, 85
Bartholomew, D. J., 296
Baruch, Bernard, 236, 237
Basic Income Earth Network, 210
basic story structures, 15–16
Bauckhage, Christian, 297–98
Baum, L. Frank, 171, 313n29

"beauty contest" metaphor, 63–64
behavioral economics, 277–78. *See also*
  economic behavior affected by narratives
beliefs of public, and major economic
  events, xv
Bell, Brad E., 78
Bergman, Ingmar, 49
Bernanke, Ben, 156–57
best seller lists, 88
Bewley, Truman, 147, 281
bicycle craze in the Depression, 143, 149
Big Brothers movement, 274
bimetallism: appearance in news articles by
  year, 22, 22f; arguments in opposition to,
  169; Bitcoin and, 108, 161–62, 171; epidemic
  theory applied to, 22–23; geographic
  and social-class dimensions of, 160, 161,
  162–63; international contagion of,
  160–61; popular in late nineteenth century,
  158, 159–61; prior to being ended in 1873,
  157; reasons for popular narratives about,
  170–71; secondary epidemic in 1930s, 23.
  See also gold standard
Bitcoin narrative, xviii, 3–11; anarchism and,
  5–7; bimetallism and, 108, 161–62, 171;
  cause of increased value and, 72;
  contagion of, 21–23; cosmopolitan
  culture and, 4, 11, 87; cryptocurrencies
  competing with, 92; epidemic theory
  applied to, 21–23; fading by 2013, 76;
  fascination with narratives about money
  and, 173; fear of inequality and, 8–9; the
  future and, 9–10, 87; geographic pattern
  of spread, 299; history of, 4; as human-
  interest story, 7–8; key features of, 87;
  mathematical concepts underlying, 5,
  302n3; membership in world economy
  and, 11; as mystery story, 7, 8, 162; in news
  articles by year, 22, 22f; in news articles
  compared to relevant algorithms, 9–10;
  sale of Bitcoin in convenience stores
  and, 10; similarity to gold standard
  and bimetallism narratives, 108–9; as

successful economic narrative, 3–4; technocracy movement and, 193; uncertain truth of, 96; volatility of value in, 5, 10. *See also* Nakamoto, Satoshi

Bix, Amy Sue, 186–87

Blade Runner (film), 203

Blanc, Louis, 102

Blinder, Alan, 281

blockchains, 6

blue jeans, 147–48, 149

blue sky laws, 220, 221

Booker, Christopher, 16

book jackets, 60–61

Boulding, Kenneth E., xv–xvi

Box, George E. P., 295

Boycott, Charles C., 239–40

The Boycott in American Trade Unions (Wolman), 241

boycott narrative, 239–43; in 1973–75 recession, 256–57; contributing to 1920–21 depression, 249; going viral, 241; during Great Depression, 254; origins of, 239–40; profiteer stories in World War I and, 241–42, 246; recurring periodically, 241; during world financial crisis of 2007–9, 257; after World War II, 255. *See also* anger at businesspeople

brain: activated by analogy and metaphor, 17; basic story structures and, 15–16; being replaced by artificial intelligence, 199, 211; in dreaming, 32; fear-related structures in, 56–58; flashbulb memory and, 80–81; long-term memory formation and, 47; narrative processing disrupted by injury to, 65–66; narrative tendency in music and, 35; neurolinguistics of narrative and, 16–17; risk assessment by, 67; sharing content in form of stories and, 54; source monitoring by, 84, 307n21. *See also* neurolinguistics and narrative; neuroscience and narrative

breadline, 134

Brooks, Peter, 16

Brown, Donald E., 33

Brown, Roger, 307n13

Bruner, Jerome, 65

Bryan, William Jennings, 108, 164, 167–68, 170, 171, 172, 313n29

Buffett, Warren, 4

Burns, Arthur F., 125, 309n10

Bush, George W., 83, 154–55

business confidence narrative, 114–15, 116f, 118–19; conventional economists' view and, xvi–xvii; gold standard and, 167, 168–69; stimulated by Bitcoin narrative, 4

business cycle, 124–25, 271. *See also* economic fluctuations

butterfly effect, 299–300

buy-and-hold strategy, xiii

"Buy Now Campaign" during Great Depression, 255

Callahan, Charlene, 281

Canada, National Dream, 151; Bank of Canada, 156

Čapek, Karel, 181–82, 203

Capital in the Twenty-First Century (Piketty), 150, 210–11

capitalism: Bitcoin narrative and, 87; triumphant narrative of, 29

Capper, Arthur, 249

The Captive Mind (Milosz), 57

Carroll, Lewis, 188

Case, Karl, 216, 226, 285

Case-Shiller home price index, 216, 222

Cass, David, 74

Cassel, Gustav, 188

causality between narratives and events, 71–74; controlled experiments and, 72–73, 77–79; vs. correlation, 286; direction of, 71, 72–74; economists' presumption about, 73, 76–77; flashbulb memory and, 80; for recessions and depressions in US, 112. *See also* self-fulfilling prophecies in economics

Cawelti, John G., 16
celebrities: adding human interest to narratives, xii, 100–102, 153; Alan Greenspan as, 227; American Dream narrative and, 153; in Bitcoin-related stories, 7–8, 92; of Bloomsbury group, 26; changed in mutated narrative, 108–9; economic events affected by colorful phrases of, 75–76; forgotten or discredited, 110; Franklin Roosevelt as, 128; J. P. Morgan as, 115, 117–18; Keynes as, 25–26; not usually the inventors of narratives, 72; Oliver Wendell Holmes, Jr., as, 127; preference for one's country or ethnic group, 102; quotes associated with, 102; Reagan's free-market revolution and, xii; Reagan's supply-side rhetoric and, 51; shoeshine boy narrative and, 236–37; substituted as originator of a quote, 102; substituted for different target audience, 101; substituted to increase contagion, xii; Trump as, xii; Virginia Woolf as, 26; William Jennings Bryan as, 168
Centennial Exhibition of 1876, 177
central bank: end of wage-price spiral narrative and, 261; inflation targeting by, 261, 262; words and stories that accompany actions of, xvi. See also Federal Reserve
Cents and Sensibility (Morson and Schapiro), 16
chaos theory, 299–300
Chaplin, Charlie, 195
charitable giving in US, declining from 2001 to 2014, 272
Chase, John C., 181
Chase, Stuart, 185
chemical reactions, rate equations for, 290, 321n3
Cheney, Dick, 44
Chudley, Jody, 236
Chwe, Michael Suk-Young, 303n9
Cicero, 34, 46

Civil War, US: anger at those profiting during, 265–66; depression prior to, 111; emotional power of narratives and, 14; narrative describing first shots of, 81; panic of 1857 in run-up to, 115; Uncle Tom narrative and, 33
Cobden, Richard, 110
co-epidemics: of diseases, 294–95; of diseases with narratives, 23; of narratives, 28, 110, 225, 322n9 (see also constellations of narratives)
Coinage Act of 1834, 157
Coinage Act of 1873, 157, 165
Coin's Financial School (Harvey), 161, 162
Cole, Harold L., 132
collective consciousness, 60
collective memory, 60
communications technology. See information technology
compartmental models of epidemics, 23, 289–93, 291f; applications that don't fit such models well by, 295–96; ARIMA models and, 295; changed for social epidemics and epidemics of ideas, 296, 297; geographic, 296, 299; network models, 296. See also Kermack-McKendrick SIR model
compassion narrative, 137, 140, 141–42; decline in, 150, 272; in Japanese "lost decades," 150
complacency, before financial crisis, 55–56
computer networks, singularity associated with, 204–5
computers: automation narrative mutated by, 204–5; "electronic brain" narrative and, 195; fear that jobs will be replaced by, 9, 10, 201; inequality in access to, 211; replacing human thinking, 199; successful in the home beginning in 1980s, 203; taking control of people's lives, 8–9, 87
condominium conversion boom, 223–24
confabulation, 32, 66, 96

confidence indexes, 79, 119, 129, 266–67

confidence narratives: of 1930s still affecting public confidence, 129, 252; business cycle and, 124–25; causes of Great Depression and, 130, 132; classes of, 114–15, 116f; Hitler's appeal and, 122; labor-saving machinery narrative and, 174; opinion leaders' optimistic assurances and, 125–26, 127–28; other people's confidence and, 114, 272; rapid changes in, 272; real estate and, 212; seemingly irrelevant events affecting, 67; stock market crash narrative and, 238; stock prices and, 228; weather forecasting and, 123. *See also* business confidence narrative; consumer confidence narrative; financial panic narrative

confluence of narratives, 29–30

Conley, John M., 15

consilience, 12–17

conspicuous consumption narratives, 136; American Dream narrative and, 154, 155; delaying car purchase during Depression and, 144; depression prolonged by avoidance of, 139, 142, 144–46; housing boom narrative and, 225; Veblen and, 154, 310n1

conspiracy theories in narrative, 35–36

constellations of narratives, 28–30; built around celebrities, 101–2; class struggle over gold standard and, 166–67; co-epidemic models applied to, 295; economic decision-making and, 91; of financial panic narratives, 115, 118f; Great Depression and, 129, 131, 135, 144; about Halley's comet, 124; "Happy Birthday to You" and, 100; about housing market, 227; impact of, 29, 92–93; Laffer curve in, 47–48; names attached to, 94–95; as new context for old narratives, 271; not obvious from archival data, 86; opposing pairs of, 113; overview of, 28–30; on people paying more than 100% in taxes,

49; random events feeding into, 40, 99–100; recovery rates and, 89; after September 2001 terrorist attacks, 83, 307n20; about stock market bubbles, 228; suggestibility and, 119; supply-side economics as, 47–48; on tax cutting and smaller government, 52; on Wizard of Oz, 172

Consumer Confidence Index, 119, 266–67

consumer confidence narrative, 115, 116f, 118–19; nineteenth-century worldviews and, 116–17

Consumer Expenditure Survey of Federal Reserve, 282

Consumer Financial Protection Bureau, and interstate land sales, 317n15

consumerism, Albee's criticism of, 153

Consumer Price Index (CPI), 245

consumers, theories based on motives and habits of, xv

consumption: depression prolonged by avoidance of, 139, 142, 144–46, 149; excesses of 1920s, 139; feedback loop between job loss and, 144–45; frugality narratives in Great Depression and, 136–37; labor-saving machinery narrative and, 209; underconsumption theory and, 187–92; visibility index of categories of, 144. *See also* conspicuous consumption narratives; spending

contagion of economic models, 24–28

contagion of economic narratives: affecting economic activity, 77; attached to celebrities, xii, 51; based on citations, 321n22; bimetallism and, 171; Bitcoin and, 21–23; consumer behavior and, 254; enhanced by memories, 252; focus group research and, 283; Frederick Lewis Allen and, x, xi; as heart of narrative economics, x; home prices and, 215, 226, 227; marketing-driven, 60–63, 297; medical model of epidemics and, 21, 23; by modern media, 297; mutation of

contagion of economic narratives (continued)
narrative and, 109; new theory of
economic change based on, 3; opportunities for repetition and, 97; perceptions
of other people's reactions and, 64;
profiteer narrative and, 241–42; stock
market crash of 1987 and, 233; wage-price
spiral narrative and, 260
contagion of ideas or social epidemics, 296,
297
contagion of narratives: caused by
unknown processes, 41; celebrity as
source of, 102; functioning as metaphors,
17; historical recognition of, 58–60; by
modern media, 297; often resulting from
arbitrary details, 62–63; opportunities for
repetition and, 97–100; theory of mind
and, 63. See also contagion of economic
narratives
contagion rates: book jackets and, 60–61;
credibility of narrative and, 28–29;
cultural factors affecting, 274; declining
with time, 296; difficulty of predicting,
41; in disease epidemics, 18–21, 289, 290;
effect of slight changes in, 40; engineered
by marketers, 60; great variability of,
88–89; increased by new context, 271;
increased by social media, 297; models
from epidemiology and, 23–24, 295, 296;
new technology leading to changes
in, 273–75; novel ideas and concepts
affecting, 97; raised by small detail, 45; of
true vs. false stories, 96–97; varying
through time, 295
controlled experiments on causality, 72–73;
from outside economics, 77–79
Coolidge, Calvin, 44, 125
Coolidge-Mellon bull tips, 125–26
corporate profits: taxes on, 45, 48; viral
narratives associated with, 47–48
corporate raiders, as viral term in 1980s, 47–48
cortisol, 54–55
cosmopolitan culture, and Bitcoin, 4, 11, 87

cost-push inflation, 258–59, 259f, 260
Coué, Emile, 121
CPI (Consumer Price Index), 245
crash narrative, 228, 229–33. See also stock
market crash narrative
creative people: of news media, 75;
recurrent narratives due to, 109–10; viral
narratives due to, 60
credibility of narratives in a constellation,
28–29
Crimean War, effect of weather forecasting
on, 123
Crime of 1873, 157–58, 171
criminology, narrative, 15
crocodile logo, 62
Cronon, William, 79
"Cross of Gold" speech, 167–68
cryptocurrencies: concept of, 3, 4;
constellation of related narratives about,
92; gold standard and, 157; initial coin
offerings (ICOs) and, 76; lack of definite
knowledge about, 96; sold by vending
machines, 10. See also Bitcoin narrative
"Cult of the Offensive," 95
cultural change: constellations of narratives
behind, 86; narratives as vectors of, xiii;
two-step flow hypothesis of, 297
cultural entrepreneur, 71–72
cultural factors affecting contagion rates,
274
Curley, James, 128
cybernation, 202

Daley, Daryl J., 296
databases for studying narratives, 279,
281–82, 284–85. See also search engines;
searching digitized data; textual analysis
Davis, Chester C., 190
Davis, Henry L., 167
Davis, Morris A., 214
Dean, James, 148
debt, and promotion of homeownership,
219

decision-making: automated by technology, 275; changed by economic narratives, 3; constellations of narratives in determination of, 91; fear-related brain circuitry and, 57–58; focused interviews for research on, 281; framing and, 66; of investors in stock market, 298–99; leading indicators approach and, 125; by mass of people not well-informed, 86

deficit spending: of Hoover administration, 188; Laffer curve and, 42

deflation: in depression of 1920–21, 111, 243–45, 246, 251, 253; gold standard and, 157, 161; in Great Depression, 253; wage cuts necessitated by, 188, 251

demand, depending on changes in narratives, 149–50

demand-pull inflation, 258

De Oratore (Cicero), 34

department store movement, 180

depression of 1873–79, 174, 176–79, 183, 188, 209

depression of 1893–99, 158, 159, 161, 163–65, 174, 179–81, 239, 241

depression of 1920–21, 111, 242–43; angry narratives in, 239, 241, 242; boycotts during, 254; deflation in, 111, 243–45, 246, 251, 253; excess profits tax contributing to, 249; fair wage narrative in, 250; family morale in, 138; fear of ostentation in, 144; Great Depression of 1930s and, 243, 251–53; labor-saving machine narrative and, 181–82; narratives causing abrupt end of, 250–51; postponement of purchases contributing to, 245, 246, 249; technocracy and, 193

depression of 1930s. See Great Depression of 1930s

depressions: in American colonies following French and Indian War, 58–59; biggest in US since 1854, 111–12; causes listed by economic historians, 112; crowd psychology and suggestibility in

understanding of, 120; expected after World War II, 196–97, 199; gold standard narrative during, 158–59; information cascades and, 300; as narratives in themselves, 112; nineteenth-century worldviews and, 116–17; psychologically based economic narrative of, 118; technological unemployment narrative during, 176

The Desk Set (film), 201

devaluation: entering English language in 1914, 159; as positive terminology, 172–73; of US dollar in 1933, 172

dial telephone, and unemployment, 187, 190–91

digital divide, 211

digital signature algorithm, 5, 9–10

The Disposable American (Uchitelle), 150

donkeys for important ideas, 26, 303n11

dot-com boom, 109, 205, 206

dreaming: narrative form of, 32; suggestibility and, 120, 121

driverless vehicles, 8–9, 174–75, 207, 314n1

Dust Bowl, 130–31

dysnarrativia, 65–66

Ebola epidemics, 18–19, 19f, 21, 23–24; co-epidemics with narratives, 23; SEIHFR model of, 294

Eckstein, Otto, 112

eclipse of the sun in 2017, 61–62

economic behavior affected by narratives, xi, xiii, xviii, 3; brief exposure to narrative and, 80; difficulty in establishing connection, 93, 286; false narratives and, 97; forgetting and, x; with impact changing through time, 93–95, 283–84; scripts involved in, 74; in small fraction of population, 29; uncertain knowledge and, 96; years after the relevant narrative, 109. See also consumption; economic events affected by narratives; investment; saving; spending

Economic Consequences of the Peace (Keynes), xvii, 26
economic events affected by narratives, xii; biggest such events in US since 1854, 111–12; celebrities' phrases with impact on, 75–76; difficulty of predicting, 58; economists' presumption about economic forces and, 76–77; by fake narratives, 85; by false narratives, 95; by frugality vs. conspicuous consumption narratives, 136; by latent narratives of earlier years, 109; limited value of quantitative indexes and, 74–75; seemingly irrelevant factors and, 67. *See also* causality between narratives and events; depressions; economic behavior affected by narratives; recessions
economic fluctuations: driven by attention-getting narratives, 86; leading indicators approach to, 125; seen as repetitive and forecastable, 124–25; self-fulfilling prophecies and, 73–74
economic forecasting: analogy to weather forecasting, 123–25; ARIMA models in, 295; business cycle and, 124–25; causes of events and, 71; economists' poor record of, xiii–xv, 301nn5–6; epidemic models and, xi, 295; leading indicators approach to, 125, 309n10; many different narratives required for, 267; moral imperative of, xv–xvii; promise of narrative economics for, xi, xiv–xv, 13, 277; self-fulfilling prophecy in, 123–24, 198
economic growth: inflation and, 319n10; supply-side economics and, 48. *See also* GDP growth in US
economic institutions, importance of narratives and, 3, 14
economic man, as rational optimizer, 120
economic models, contagion of, 24–28, 27f
economic narratives: analytical value of looking at, 238; anniversaries of past events and, 76; confluence of, 29–30; creative and

innovative, 75; defined, 3; distorting professional narratives, xiii; geographic pattern of spread, 296, 299; history of, going back to ancient Rome, 58–60; human significance of stories and, 79–80; immense complexity of landscape of, 266–67; international, 110; judging which are important, 89–91; key features of, 87; medical model of epidemics and, 21–23; names attached to, 94–95; narratives that become economic, 74; originating with one or a few people, 71–72; oversimplified variants of, 26; predictable workings of, 77; recurrence of, 107–8, 109–10, 238; self-censorship of, encouraging panic, 115; seven key propositions with respect to, 103. *See also* constellations of narratives; contagion of economic narratives; moral dimensions of economic narratives; mutation of economic narratives; narrative economics; narratives; viral narratives
economic policy. *See* policy
economics profession: behind other disciplines in attention to narratives, 12–13, 13f; events as natural experiments in, 72–73; potential of collaborative research for, 17, 302n1
economic stimulus: Keynes and Samuelson on effects of, 27–28; in Republican policy of 1920s, 189; *stimulate the economy* as phrase in late twentieth century, 50–51
economic strength, perception of, 272
education, narrative-centered learning in, 77–78
efficiency experts, 184
Eichengreen, Barry, 133, 172
Einstein, Albert, 192, 199
Eisenhower, Dwight, 261
electric dollars, 193
electronic brain, 195
Elliott, Catherine S., 281
elliptic curve digital signature algorithm, 5, 9

emotions: affect heuristic and, 67, 233; Bitcoin epidemic and, 5–6; in construction of narratives, 65; of financial panics, 115; flashbulb memory and, 80–81, 307n13; of gold standard debate, 160, 172; Harding's references to normalcy and, 244; historians' explanatory use of, 14; in housing boom of 1997–2006, 217; perceptions of people's reactions to story and, 64; profiteer narratives and, 247, 249; in quantitative study of narratives, 287; in response to narratives, xi, 35, 54; revealed in stories, 79; risk assessment and, 67; studied in economics without being partisan, 279; underconsumption narrative during Depression and, 188. *See also* anger about inflation; anger at businesspeople; anger at oil crisis of 1970s; fear

The Engineers and the Price System (Veblen), 193

entrepreneurship: cryptocurrencies and, 4, 92; labor-saving machinery narrative and, 209; Reagan policies and, 52

The Epic of America (Adams), 151

epidemic curve, 18–24, 19f, 22f, 289–93, 291f

epidemics of diseases: AIDS, 24; co-epidemics with narratives, 23; recurrence and mutation of, 108; repeats of variants of, 271; size of, 292–93. *See also* Ebola epidemics; influenza; Kermack-McKendrick SIR model

epidemics of economic narratives: on automation, 199–200; on bimetallism, 22–23, 22f; on Bitcoin, 22–23, 22f; co-epidemics of diseases with narratives, 23; co-epidemics of narratives, 294–95, 322n9; on cost-push inflation, 258, 259f; on electronic brain, 195; forecasting and, xi, 295, 322n9; of "going viral" and "trending now," x; on housing market, 227; on leading indicators, 125; medical model and, 21–23, 22f, 292; not heard by everyone in the population, 292; on profiteer, 241–42, 243f; random events affecting, 75; repeats of, with unpredictable timing, 271; self-fulfilling prophecies and, 74; sizes and time frames of, 88–89, 292–93; on technological unemployment, 183–85, 294, 295; with varying contagion rates and recovery rates, 295; volatility and, 5; on wage-price spiral, 258, 259f. *See also* compartmental models of epidemics; Kermack-McKendrick SIR model; viral narratives

epidemics of narratives: random events affecting, 40, 99–100; recognized since ancient times, 58–60. *See also* epidemics of economic narratives; viral narratives

epidemiology, insights from, xviii, 14, 17, 23–24, 277, 289

Escalas, Jennifer Edson, 77

"Every day in every way I get better and better," 121

The Evolution of Beauty (Prum), 65

excess profits, 242

excess profits tax, of US during World War I, 249, 265

exogenous shocks to economy, 73, 75–76

expectations, and representativeness heuristic, 66–67

extraordinary popular delusions, 59, 119

Facebook, meme quickly going viral on, 88

fact-checking websites, 85, 96

fair wage-effort hypothesis, 250

fair wage narratives, 249–50

fake news, 84–85, 273

fake wrestling matches, 84–85

Falk, Emily B., 54

false narratives, 95–97

family circle, literature read aloud in, 274

Famous First Bubbles (Garber), 5

famous people: patterns of mentions in books, 24. *See also* celebrities

Farmer, Roger E. A., 74

farmers: impact of gold standard on, 157–58, 161, 163; labor-saving machinery and, 176–77, 183, 185, 187, 209

farmland: earlier real estate talk centered on, 212; as speculative investment, 213, 214

Farnam, Henry W., 72–73

fear: of automation, 196; brain structures involved in, 56–58; changing economic behavior years after relevant narrative, 109; extended to unrelated events, 67; false narratives and, 95; in financial crises, 55–58; during Great Depression, 109, 127–28, 141; of human irrelevance, 208; identified as cause of Great Depression, 132; of machines replacing jobs, 175; "of fear itself," 128; Roosevelt's exhortations about, 128, 129; suicides after crash of 1929 and, 233; technocracy movement leading to, 194. See also panic

Federal Reserve: cause of Great Depression and, 132–33; Consumer Expenditure Survey of, 282; control of inflation and, 262; creation of, 111, 117; J. P. Morgan and, 111, 117–18; warning about speculation in 1929, 126

Federal Reserve Act of 1913, 117

feedback loops: 1930s-style models of, 287; between postponing consumption and job loss, 144–45; of prices in speculative bubbles, 216–17

Feelings in History (MacMullen), 14

Ferguson, Hill, 219

Festinger, Leon, 218

fiat money, 156

fiction, xii, 16. See also novels

films: less luxurious during the Depression, 142; predicting the success of, 41–42

finance, lagging in attention to narratives, 13f

financial advisers, automated, 275

financial crises, 55–56, 86. See also bank runs; world financial crisis of 2007–9

financial panic narrative, 114, 115, 116f; crowd psychology and, 119–20, 120f; frequency of appearance of five major occurrences, 118f; J. P. Morgan and, 117–18; nineteenth-century worldviews and, 116–17; rekindled in 2007 in United Kingdom, 119. See also panic

"fire in a crowded theater" narrative, 127, 129

fiscal policy, motivations of, 281

Fisher, Irving, 75–76, 128, 247, 266

Fisher, R. A., 65

Fisherian runaway, 65

flashbulb memory, 80–83, 307n13; of stock market crash of 1929, 233; of stock market crash of 1987, 233

flipping, 223–24

Florida land boom of 1920s, 214, 215, 220–21

flu epidemics. See influenza

fMRI (functional magnetic resonance imaging): of brain activation by analogy and metaphor, 17; of sharing content in form of stories, 54

focused interviews, as research tools, 281

focus groups, 282–84

folklore studies, 15, 16

forecasting. See economic forecasting

forgetting, in epidemic model, x, 25, 296. See also memory

forgetting rates: differences in, 89; effect of slight changes in, 40; lowered by identified personality, 100; lowered by symbols or rituals, 62; lowered by visual detail, 45, 46. See also recovery rates

The Forgotten Depression (Grant), 242, 251

formula stories, 16

Forster, E. M., 181

founding-father story, 15

The Fountainhead (Rand), 50

framing, 66

free markets: forgotten nineteenth-century advocate of, 110; George's Progress and Poverty on, 111; inflation and, 263; twentieth-century narratives about, xii, 50–51

Free Men and Free Markets (Theobald), 210

Free Silver movement. *See* Silverites

Friedman, Irving S., 262, 263

Friedman, Milton, 73, 132–33, 307n3

"From each according to his ability, to each according to his needs," 102

frugality narratives: American Dream narrative in contradiction to, 155; in Great Depression, 136–37, 142–43, 252; in Japan after 1990, 150

Galbraith, John Kenneth, 233

Gallup, George, 118–19

Gallup Data Collection, 284

gambling culture, and booming stock market, 29

Garber, Peter, 5

Garrett, Geoffrey, 299

GDP data, limited value of, 74–75

GDP growth in US: not successfully forecast, xiv, 301n5. *See also* economic growth

The General Theory of Employment, Interest, and Money (Keynes), 27

geographic pattern of spread, of economic narratives, 296, 299

George, Henry, 111, 178–79, 188, 209, 310n1

Germany: hyperinflation after World War I, 247, 266; reparations from World War I and, xvii–xviii

Glass, Carter, 191

Gödel, Escher, Bach (Hofstadter), 47

Goetzmann, William, 67

"going viral": appearing in newspapers around 2009, x; mathematical model of epidemic and, 293. *See also* viral narratives

gold: fears and rumors about, at start of World War I, 94; mystique about, 157; public perception of value in, 5; seen as safest investment, xii; spiritual significance of, 165; still held by central banks, 156–57

gold bugs, 163–64

Goldman, William, 41

gold standard: adoption in US, 166; defined, 156; eighteenth-century origins of, 166; end of, 156, 172–73; impact on farmers, 157–58, 161, 163; length of Great Depression and, 132; meaning "the best," 158. *See also* bimetallism

Gold Standard Act of 1900, 157, 312n10

gold standard narrative: morality and rectitude represented in, 172; somewhat active today, 156; symbolism in congressional debate and, 165–66; two separate epidemics of, 158–59, 159f, 166; *Wizard of Oz* and, 171–72, 313n29

Google Ngrams, x, xiii; imperfect for narrative research, 280–81

Google's "OK Google," 207

Grais, R. F., 294

grand narrative, 92

Grant, James, 242, 251

Grant, Ulysses S., 157

The Grapes of Wrath (Steinbeck), 131

The Great Crash, 1929 (Galbraith), 233

Great Depression of 1930s, 111–12; angry narratives in, 239; bimetallism epidemic during, 23; blamed on loss of confidence, 130; blamed on "reckless talk" by opinion leaders, 127; confidence narratives in, 114, 122; consumption demand reduced after, 307n3; crowd psychology and suggestibility in understanding of, 120; deportation of Mexican Americans during, 190; depression of 1920–21 and, 243, 251–53; difficulty of cutting wages during, 251–52; Dust Bowl and, 130–31; fair wage narrative during, 250; family morale during, 138–39; fear during, 109, 127–28, 141; flu epidemic of 1918 mirroring trajectory of, 108; frequency of appearance of the term, 133, 134f; frugality and compassion in, 135, 136–37, 140–43, 252; gold standard narrative during, 158–59; labor-saving machinery and, 174; lists of causes created at the time,

Great Depression of 1930s (continued)
129–30; modern theories about causes of,
132–33; modesty narrative during, 135,
136–37, 139, 142–45, 147–48, 150;
narratives after 2007–9 crisis and, 95;
narratives focused on scarcity during,
129; narratives illuminating causes of,
ix–x; not called "Great Depression" at
the time, 133–34; not forecast by
economists, xiv; ordinary people's
talking about, 90–91; photos providing
memory of, 131; prolonged by avoidance
of consumption, 139, 142, 144–46; as
record-holder of economic downturns,
112; revulsion against excesses of 1920s
during, 235–36; robot tax discussed
during, 209; seen as stampede or panic,
128; technocracy movement and, 193–94;
technological unemployment narrative
and, 183, 184; today's downturns seen
through narratives of, 134–35, 264;
underconsumption narrative during,
188–90; women's writing about concerns
during, 137–40, 145–46
The Great Illusion (Angell), 95
Great Recession of 1973–75, 112
Great Recession of 1980–82, 112
Great Recession of 2007–9, 112; bank
failures as key narratives in, 132; fear
about intelligent machines and, 273;
fueled by real estate narratives, 212;
predicted by few economists, xiv; rapid
drop in confidence during, 272
Great Society, 50
Greenspan, Alan, 227
Gresham's Law, and bimetallism, 169, 313n27

hacker ethic, 7
*The Hacker Ethic and the Spirit of the
Information Age* (Himanen), 7
Hackett, Catherine, 140, 253–54
Halley, Edmund, 124
"Happy Birthday to You" (song), 97–100

Harari, Yuval Noah, 208
Harding, Warren, 244–45
"hard times," 134
*Hard Times: An Oral History of the Great
Depression* (Terkel), 234
Harris, Sidney J., 263
Harvey, William Hope, 161, 162, 312n10
Hazlitt, Henry, 247
"Heads I win, tails you lose," 110
health interventions, narrative presentation
of, 78
Heathcote, Jonathan, 214
Heffetz, Ori, 144
Hepburn, Katharine, 201
Hero of Alexandria, 175
Hicks, John, 24, 26
Hill, Napoleon, 121–22
Himanen, Pekka, 7
historical databases, 279; of letters and
diaries, 285
historical scholarship: compared with
historical novel, 79; economics learning
from, 78; use of narrative by, 14, 37
Hitler, Adolf, 122, 142, 195
HIV (human immune deficiency virus), 24;
coinfective with tuberculosis, 294–95
Hoar, George Frisbie, 178
Hoffa, Jimmy, 260
Hofstadter, Douglas R., 47
Hofstadter, Richard, 36
Hollande, François, 151
Holmes, Oliver Wendell, Jr., 127
Holtby, Winifred, 140
homeownership: advantages over renting,
223, 317n18; advertising promotions for,
219–20; American Dream narrative and,
154–55; condominium conversion boom
and, 223–24; seen as investment by many
buyers, 226–27
home price indexes, 97, 215–16, 222
home price narratives, 215–17; declining by
2012, 227; fueling a speculative boom,
217–18, 222, 223–24

home prices: available on the Internet, 218; construction costs and, 215, 317n6; falling dramatically with financial crisis of 2007–9, 223; only going up, xii; price of land and, 215; ProQuest references to, 213–14, 216; rising again from 2012 to 2018, 223, 225; social comparison and, 218, 220; supply of housing and, 222; supply of land and, 221–22; surge leading up to financial crisis of 2007–9, 222–23. *See also* housing booms

Homer, 174, 314n1

honesty: economic narratives about, 101; phishing equilibrium and, 61

Hoover, Herbert, 90, 91, 138, 188–89, 191, 253

Hooverville, 131

hormonal response to narratives, 54–55

House Lust (McGinn), 217–18

housing booms: from 2012 to 2018 and continuing, 223; conspicuous consumption and, 225; feedback loop of prices in, 216–17; fueled by home price narratives, 217–18, 222, 223–24; as investment in land rather than structure, 221, 223; peak in 2005 predicted by few economists, xiv; record-setting boom of 1997–2006, 217; world financial crisis of 2007–9 and, 154, 155, 217, 222–23, 226, 227. *See also* home prices; real estate boom in 2000s

"housing bubble": Internet searches for, 226, 226f; looking beyond headlines and statistics, 238; stories found by ProQuest in 2005, 227. *See also* housing booms

housing market: narratives about, before 2007–9 financial crisis, 227; speculative bubbles in, 216–17; surveys of US homebuyers in, 285–86; today's status of, 226–27

Howard, Milford, Wriarson, 166

Hull, Clark, 195

human interest of economic narratives: added by celebrities, xii, 100–102, 153;

impact on events and, 77; many dimensions of, 79–80

human interest of stories, 32

human tragedy narratives in Great Depression, 137, 141

Hume, David, 58, 71

hyperinflation in Germany after World War I, 247, 266

hypnosis narrative, 122

ICOs (initial coin offerings), 76

identity economics, xxi

"I Have a Dream" speech (King), 153–54

Iliad (Homer), 174, 314n1

immunity to disease, 20, 289

Index of Consumer Sentiment, 119

Industrial Revolution: labor-saving machinery narrative and, 9; narratives about confidence and, 114; real estate narratives and, 212; as term introduced in nineteenth century, 175

inequality: artificial intelligence narrative and, 273; Bitcoin and fear of, 8–9; burgeoning public attention to, 210–11; decline in modesty narrative and, 150; George's *Progress and Poverty* on, 111, 178–79; labor-saving machinery and, 178–79, 180; opposition to gold standard and, 166; origins of the boycott and, 240

infectives in an epidemic, 23, 289; declining contagion rate and, 296

inflation: anger about, 239, 245, 247, 263–64, 265–66; central bank role in control of, 261, 262; cost-push inflation, 258–59, 259f, 260; demand-pull inflation, 258; economic growth and, 319n10; economists' views of, in 1997 study, 263, 264; highest in US from 1973 to 1981, 262; hyperinflation in Germany after World War I, 247, 266; as negative terminology, 172–73; public views of, in 1997 study, 263–64; runaway US inflation of 1970s, 256; sources of evil blamed for, 263, 266;

inflation (continued)
  stock market response to decline in, 29;
  unusually tame now, 266; wage-price
  spiral narrative and, 258–62; during wars,
  265–66; after World War I, 243–49, 250;
  after World War II, 255–56
Inflation: A World-Wide Disaster (Friedman), 262
inflation targeting, 261, 262
influencer marketing, 274–75
influenza: new forms and new epidemics of,
  271; pandemic of 1918, 108, 198, 252; SEIR
  model of epidemics of, 294
information cascades, 300
information technology: changing
  contagion rates and recovery rates,
  273–75; communication of stories
  through, xviii; history of inventions in,
  273; for research in narrative economics,
  279. *See also* Internet; search engines
initial coin offerings (ICOs), 76
initial public offerings (IPOs), flipping of,
  224
interest rates: central bank changes of, xvi;
  expectations of future rates, 55–56; of
  limited value in understanding economic
  events, 74–75; no proven record of
  forecasting of, 55; wage-price spiral
  narrative and, 260
international economic narratives, 110
International Monetary Fund, xiv
International Social Survey Program, 282
Internet: changes in contagion caused
  by, 273, 297; cooperation using new
  technology and, 7; fear of automation at
  beginning of, 205; home price narrative
  and, 218; narrative of computer power
  launched by, 206; phrase "going viral" in
  relation to, x; SIRS model for memes on,
  297–98; views or likes on, x. *See also*
  dot-com boom; search engines; social
  media
Internet trolls, 67

interviews as research tools, 281–82
inventions, obvious but not adopted,
  38–39
investment: fear-related brain circuitry and,
  57–58; Keynes on decisions involved in,
  xvi, 63–64; labor-saving machinery
  narrative and, 209; profitable for some
  during World War I, 94. *See also* stock
  market
investment managers, stories told
  by, 15
irrational exuberance: exogenous effect on
  economy, 76; Greenspan on 1996 stock
  market and, 227
Irrational Exuberance (Shiller), 29
Isaacson, Walter, 208
IS-LM model, 24–26, 27f

Jackendoff, Ray, 35
James, William, 121
Japan: "lost decades" of 1990s and beyond,
  95, 150
Jenkins, Gwilym, 295
Jevons, William Stanley, 73–74
jigsaw puzzle craze, 148–49
Jobs, Steve, 208–9
Johnson, Lyndon, 50, 202
Johnson, Mark, 17
Jones, John P., 165
Jung, Carl, 15

Kahneman, Daniel, 66
Kasparov, Garry, 36
Katona, George, 66, 119
Katz, Elihu, 297
kayfabe, 84
keep-up-with-the-Joneses narrative, 136
Kempton, Murray, 230–31
Kendall, David G., 296
Kendall, Patricia L., 281
Kennedy, John F., 236, 307n13
Kennedy, Joseph, 236–37
Kennedy, Robert F., 260

Kermack-McKendrick SIR model, 289–93, 291f; chaotic solutions of, 299–300; information cascades and, 300; investment decisions and, 299; still workable for idea epidemics, 298; variations on, 293–98. *See also* compartmental models of epidemics

Keynes, John Maynard: animal spirits and, 138; "beauty contest" metaphor of, 63–64; business confidence and, xvi; consequences of Versailles treaty and, xvii–xviii, 26; current consumption and current income according to, 307n3; gold standard narrative and, 172, 173; IS-LM model and, 25–26; on stimulus leading to economic boom, 27–28

Kim, Dasol, 67

King, Coretta Scott, 153

King, Martin Luther, Jr., 153–54

Kingsley, Grace, 142

Kiplinger, Willard Monroe, 130, 132

Klages, Mary, 16

Klein, Melanie, 15

Koopmans, Tjalling, xv

Kranton, Rachel, xxi

Kristol, Irving, xvi–xvii

Krock, Arthur, 90–91

Kulik, James, 307n13

Kydland, Finn E., 24

labor-saving machinery narrative, 174–76, 175f; counternarrative to, 178; depression of 1873–79 and, 174, 176–78; depression of 1893–97 and, 174, 179–81; early history of, 174–76; economic decisions affected by, 209; economic effects of narrative itself, 211; fear during Great Depression and, 109; increasingly vivid before 1930, 182–86; office workplace and, 186; opportunity during dot-com boom and, 109; robots and, 181–82; underconsumption or overproduction theory and, 187–89, 191–92; unemployment and, xiv,

9, 130, 177–81, 187–88, 191–92. *See also* technological unemployment narrative

labor unions: associated by public with organized crime, 260; automation and, 200, 202; boycotts used by, 241; trends in public support for, 258–59, 266, 320n2; wage cuts in depression of 1920–21 and, 249, 251; wage-price spiral and, 258–60, 261, 263, 264

Lacoste, Jean René, 62, 63

Laffer, Art, 42, 44–45

Laffer curve narrative, xviii, 24, 42–47, 48, 51, 52; exogenous effect on economy, 76; impact on output and prices, 48; in supply-side economics constellation, 47–48; two epidemics in appearance of, 42, 43f

laissez-faire narrative, in second half of twentieth century, 50

Lakoff, George, 17

land: federal regulation of interstate sales of, 317n15; home prices and, 215, 216; narrative about its scarcity and value, 212; not depreciating like the home, 215; as percentage of home's value, 214, 317n5; sold as investment in undeveloped property, 220–21

land bubbles, 213

land speculation, 213; Florida boom of 1920s, 214, 215, 220–21; marketing of undeveloped land before Great Depression and, 220

Lang, Fritz, 203

Lange, Dorothea, 131

Laughlin, J. Laurence, 312n10

The Law of Success in 16 Lessons (Hill), 121–22

Lazarsfeld, Paul F., 297

leading indicators: in economic forecasting, 125, 309n10; epidemic models instead of search for, 295; narratives causing changes in, 276; underlying human behavior and, xv learning, narrative-centered, 77–78

Le Bon, Gustave, 59, 119

leveraged buyouts, 47

Levi Strauss Company, 148

libertarianism, and hacker ethic, 7

Liebhold, Peter, 44

Lincoln, Abraham, 101

Lindgren, Astrid, 49

Linglong's Dingdong, 207

linguistics and narrative, 16–17, 94–95

Linux operating system, 7

listening as a research method, 281

literary studies and narrative, 15–16, 286

Livermore, Shaw, ix

Loftus, Elizabeth F., 78

logos on clothing and shoes, 62–63; on blue jeans, 148

Long, Elisa F., 295

Lopokova, Lydia, 26

Lorayne, Harry, 46–47

"lost decade" story, 95, 150

Love Is a Story (Sternberg), 79–80

Lovejoy, E. P., 14

Lubell, Samuel, 200

Lucas, George, 203

Luddite event in 1811, 174, 176

Luddite narrative, 9, 185; in 1930s, 186–87

Lujan, Sterlin, 6

Machill, Marcel, 77

machine learning, 207–8, 211

machines replacing jobs. *See* labor-saving machinery narrative

"The Machine Stops" (Forster), 181

Mackay, Charles, 59, 119

MacMullen, Ramsay, 14

Malabre, Alfred L., Jr., 202

Mallon, Mary, 20

Mann, Dorothea Lawrence, 60

Marden, Orison Swett, 122

marketers: contagion rate engineered by, 60; lowering the forgetting rate, 62;

profiting from narratives, xiii, 62; recurrence of narratives due to, 109–10

marketing: with accelerated analytics, 20; appeals to patriotism in, 155; background music and, 67; bizarre mental images in, 46; book jackets and, 60–61; contagion of economic narratives and, 60–63, 297; detested by many consumers, 62; focus group methods developed for, 283; logos and, 62–63, 148; self-referencing in, 77; social media used for, 274–75; of "the news," 61–62

Marx, Groucho, 133

Marx, Karl, 102

master narrative, 92

master plots in fiction, 16

maximize shareholder value, 47–48

May, John Allan, 38

McCall, Samuel W., 168

McCormick, Anne O'Hare, 140, 143

McGinn, Daniel, 217–18

McKinley, William, 163, 164, 171, 313n29

McQuiggan, Scott W., 77–78

Meany, George, 202

"Measurement without Theory" (Koopmans), xv

Meeker, Royal, 245

Mellon, Andrew, 44

Meloney, Marie, 220

memes, 60, 88

Memoirs of Extraordinary Popular Delusions (Mackay), 59, 119

memory: aided by rituals and symbols, 62; aided by visual stimuli, 45, 46–47; collective, 60; contagion of narratives and, 252; fear-related brain circuitry and, 57–58; flashbulb memory, 80–83, 233, 307n13; source monitoring in, 84, 307n21. *See also* forgetting, in epidemic model

Men and Machines (Chase), 185

mentors for young people, 274

Merrill, Charles, 167

Merton, Robert K., 73, 198, 281

metanarrative, 92

metaphors, 16, 17; of economy as sick or
healthy, 79

meteorology narratives, 123

Metropolis (film), 203

Mexican Americans, deported during Great
Depression, 190

Michel, Jean-Baptiste, 24

Milosz, Czeslaw, 57

Mitchell, Wesley C., 125, 309n10

Mitterrand, François, 42

"modern monetary theory," 42

Modern Times (film), 195

modesty narrative: absent from George and
Veblen works, 310n1; in Japanese "lost
decades," 150; present decline in, 272

modesty narrative of Great Depression:
bicycle craze and, 143; blue jeans and,
147–48; conspicuous consumption and,
135, 136–37, 139, 142–45; decline in, 150

Modigliani, Franco, 301n13

Mokyr, Joel, 71

Moley, Raymond, 114

Monetary History of the United States
(Friedman and Schwartz), 73, 132–33

monetary policy: causal impact on
aggregate economy, 73; studies of
narratives to infer motivations of, 281;
wage-price spiral narrative and, 261

monetary system: inflation and, 262; typical
American's confusion about, 170

monetary theory: invoked by bimetallism
and Bitcoin, 22; "modern monetary
theory" narrative, 42

money narratives, 173. *See also* Bitcoin
narrative; gold standard narrative

money supply: gold discoveries of 1897 to
1914, 73; Great Depression and, 132–33

moral dimensions of economic narratives,
80; abstract economic forces and, xvii;
American Dream narrative and, 155;
anger at business and, 239; annoyance

with boycotts and, 241; concerns about
labor unions and, 258; databases of
sermons relevant to, 284–85; frugality
during Great Depression and, 143;
opposing pairs of narrative constellations
and, 113; Roosevelt's Depression fireside
chat and, 129, 278; about stock market
crash of 1929, 235–36; wage-price spiral
narrative and, 261–62, 266

morality in historical narrative, 37

Morgan, J. P., 111, 115, 117–18

Morson, Gary Saul, 16

Mullen, Thomas, 128

Muller, Jerry Z., 75, 306n5

multiplier-accelerator model, 24–25, 27–28,
27f, 303n7

music: brain structure and, 53, 54; narrative
and, 35; songs that are one-hit wonders,
41–42

Music, Language and the Brain (Patel), 35

music market of sociology experiment,
39–40

mutation in evolutionary theory, 64

mutation of diseases, 108

mutation of economic narratives, 108–9; by
attaching new celebrity, 102, 108–9; on
cryptocurrencies, 76; to more contagious
forms, 31, 40; within narrative constellations, 86, 107; randomness in, 31, 40; of
recurrent narratives, 107, 109–10, 238;
self-fulfilling prophecies derived from,
74; of technological unemployment
narrative, 196, 199

mutation of narratives: "Happy Birthday to
You" and, 98–99; from hypnosis to
autosuggestion, 122

Nakamoto, Satoshi, 4, 7–8, 108–9, 162, 193,
302n3, 302n8

names attached to narratives, 94–95

narrative economics: concept of, xi, 3;
consilience and, 12; earlier use of the
phrase, xi. *See also* economic narratives

narrative economics research: artificial intelligence in, 276; databases to be used in, 279, 281–82, 284–85; data collection in, 276, 279–86; economic theory and, 277–79; exact methods with humanistic approach in, 271–72; future of, 275–77; quantitative methods in, 279; remaining nonpartisan in, 278–79; textual analysis in, 279, 287; tracking and quantifying narratives in, 286–87

narrative psychology, 15, 65–67, 78, 287

narratives: academic disciplines attending to, 12, 13f; becoming economic narratives, 74; central to thinking and motivation, 31–32; conspiracy theories in, 35–36; defined, xi; disrupted by brain injury, 65–66; distinguishing humans from animals, 34–35; effective wording and delivery of, 271; historical, 37; hormones of listener and, 54–55; as human constructs, 65; names attached to, 94–95; norms of politeness in transmission of, 35; originating with one or a few people, 71–72; as particular form of story, 36; as scripts or social norms, 37–38, 74, 77; social change and, 32–33; universality of, 33–35. See also constellations of narratives; contagion of narratives; economic narratives; mutation of narratives; stories; viral narratives

National Association of Realtors, 216, 219, 220

National Bureau of Economic Research (NBER): biggest economic events in US since 1854 defined by, 111–12; chronicle of business cycles, 110; working paper database, 279

National Industrial Recovery Act, 132, 189, 252

"near-rational," 300

network models, 296

neurolinguistics and narrative, 16–17; synonyms and, 94–95

neuroscience and narrative: hormones involved in, 54–55; research methods and, 287. See also brain

Newcomb, Anthony, 35

"New Deal," coined by Stuart Chase, 185

The New Financial Order (Shiller), 38

news media: creative during major stock market corrections, 75; economic narratives spread through, 3, 21; improving retention with narrative presentation, 77; international economic narratives and, 110; marketing-driven, 61–62; in modified SIR model, 297; reminding public on anniversaries of events, 76; searching for words and phrases in, x

Nixon, Richard, 173

normalcy, 244, 252

North, Douglass, 14

Northern Rock bank run in 2007, 119, 135

novels: classical symphony as, 35; understanding human experience and, 16. See also fiction

Noyes, Alexander Dana, 127, 164, 231

Nudge (Thaler and Sunstein), 278

nudge units, 277–78

NVIDIA Corporation, 20

O'Barr, William M., 15

Occupy Wall Street protest, 8, 225

office workplace: automation of, 204; labor-saving machinery narrative and, 186

Ohanian, Lee E., 132

oil embargo of 1973, 256

one-hit wonders, 41–42

Only Yesterday (Allen), ix–xi, 139

organ donation, narrative presentation of, 78

overlapping generations model, 24–25, 27f, 303n8

overproduction or underconsumption theory, 187–92

"Ownership Society" (Bush reelection slogan), 155
oxytocin, 54
Oz: The Great and Powerful (film), 172

Palme, Olof, 48–49
panic: at beginning of World War I, 93–94; creation of Federal Reserve and, 117; in financial crisis, 55–56, 86; following complacency, 55–56; Great Depression seen as, 128; inflation in 1970s and, 262; stock prices and, 228. *See also* bank runs; fear; financial panic narrative
Panic of 1907, 94, 111, 115, 117, 118f
Part of Our Time (Kempton), 230–31
Patel, Aniruddh, 35
Pathways Back to Prosperity (Baker), 210
patriotic appeal of a narrative, 101, 102–3
Paul, Ron, 156
Pavlov, Ivan P., 56
Pearl Harbor attack, memories of hearing about, 81–82
Penfield, Wilder, 53–54
perennial narratives, 107–8; nine major examples of, 113, 266–67 (*see also specific examples*); as works in progress, 276
permanent-income hypothesis, 307n3
"permanently high plateau," 75–76
phantasies of Melanie Klein, 15
The Philosophy of Honest Poverty, 150
phishing equilibrium, 61
phools, 61, 62
Piketty, Thomas, 150, 210–11
Piore, Michael, 281
Plath, Robert, 38, 39
Plato, 34
policy: formulating with knowledge of narratives, 3, 287. *See also* monetary policy
policymakers: creating and disseminating counternarratives, 278; narrative studies to infer motivations of, 281, 321n14
poliomyelitis enterovirus epidemic, 295–96

Pollack, Andrew, 204
Polletta, Francesca, 32
Pomperipossa in the World of Money (Lindgren), 49
Ponzi, Charles, 220–21
Ponzi scheme, 220
populism: inflation after World War I and, 245; opposition to gold standard and, 166
portfolio insurance, 93
post-traumatic stress disorder (PTSD), 57
"postwar," 242–43
Pound, John, 298
poverty: decreasing basic-needs charity in today's US, 272; Depression-era attitudes toward, 143; Dust Bowl and, 131; nineteenth-century moral views of, 117; technological advances creating, 178
poverty-chic culture, 143, 148, 149
power age, 183
predicting economic events. *See* economic forecasting
Prescott, Edward C., 24
price controls, in US after World War II, 255
price per acre, references to, 214
price setting: interviews of executives about, 281. *See also* wage-price spiral narrative
prison inmates, telling stories, 15
professional narratives, xiii
profiteer narrative, 241–43, 243f, 246–49; abrupt end of 1920–21 depression and, 250–51; falling consumer prices and, 243–44; inflation after World War I and, 245, 265. *See also* excess profits
profits, corporate: taxes on, 45, 48; viral narratives associated with, 47–48
Progress and Poverty (George), 111, 178–79, 188, 209, 310n1
property taxes, taxpayer revolt focused on, 50
Proposition 13, 50
Propp, Vladimir, 16
ProQuest News & Newspapers, x

Proudhon, Pierre-Joseph, 6
prudent person rule, 37
Prum, Richard O., 65
psychoanalysis and narrative, 15, 16, 280
Psychological Economics (Katona), 66
psychological impact of opinion leaders, 127
Psychologie des foules (*The Crowd*) (Le Bon), 59, 119
psychology and narrative, 15, 65–67, 78, 287
The Psychology of Suggestion (Sidis), 121
PTSD (post-traumatic stress disorder), 57
Public Opinion Research Archive, 284
purchasing power theory of wages, 188
push a button, 179, 200
Putin, Vladimir, 103

qualitative research, 281
quarantines, 19–20
quasi-controlled experiments, 73
questionnaire surveys, 285–86

Rand, Ayn, 50
random events with major effects, 40, 75, 99–100
randomness of which narratives go viral, 31, 40, 64–65, 286
random walk theory of speculative prices, xiii
rational expectations models, 277, 295, 301n13
Reagan, Ronald, xii, 42, 51–52, 153
Reagan administration, tax cuts by, 48, 51
real business cycle model, 24–25, 27f
real estate boom in 2000s: automation narratives and, 205; Trump University and, 226. *See also* housing booms
real estate narratives, 212. *See also* home price narratives
real estate speculation: in second half of twentieth century, 213. *See also* home price narratives
Rebel Without a Cause (film), 148

recessions: in 1949, 256, 264; in 1950s and 1960s, 199, 200–201, 264; in 1957–58, 201, 264; in 1973–75, 239, 256–57; in 1980 and 1981–82, 204; in 2001, ended after terrorist attack, 82–83, 307n17; biggest in US since 1973, 112; causes listed by economic historians, 112; consumer confidence narrative and, 115; economists' reluctance to mention narratives underlying, 276; narrative infecting fraction of population and, 29; as narratives in themselves, 112; not successfully forecast, xiv, 301n6; popular belief in periodic nature of, 124–25; popular stories affecting, xii; reasons for hesitating to spend during, 75; self-fulfilling prophecy in forecasts of, 123–24, 125
reciprocity, human patterns of, 36
recovery in medical model, 18, 20–21, 23, 289; economic analogy to, 21
recovery rates: differences in, 89; difficulty of predicting, 41; models from epidemiology and, 20, 21, 23–24, 290; new technology leading to changes in, 273, 275; varying through time, 295. *See also* forgetting rates
recurrence of narratives, 107–8, 109–10, 238
redistribution proposals, 209–10
regulation: supply-side economics and, 48; twentieth-century reaction against, xii, 48, 50, 51
religious studies, narrative approaches to, 15
repetition of economic fluctuations, 124–25
repetition of narratives: contagion and, 97–100; meteorology and, 123
representativeness heuristic, 66–67
Republic (Plato), 34
Reserve Prime Fund, 135
retirement: homeownership as saving for, 219; ordinary people in nineteenth century and, 116
Rhys-Williams, Juliet, 210

Richards, George, 265–66

Riefenstahl, Leni, 122

risk assessment, by primitive brain system, 67

risk taking: entrepreneurial narratives and, 52; excessive complacency about, 55–56

Ritter, Jay, 224

rituals, reminding people of the narrative, 62, 303n9

Roaring Twenties, ix, 133, 135, 235

Robbins, Lionel, 111–12

Robey, Ralph, 125

robo-advisers, 275

robots: artificial intelligence and, 196; broad use of the term, 192; as cause of Great Depression, 191; in Chaplin's *Modern Times*, 195; coinage of the term, 181–82, 186; enormous spike in mentions during early 1980s, 202–3; fear of, 186; Great Recession of 2007–9 and, 273; labor-saving machinery narrative and, 181–82; military uses planned for, 195; in movies, 203–4; product line failing in 1980s, 203; technological unemployment narrative and, 186. *See also* artificial intelligence narrative; automation narrative

robot tax, 209

Rockefeller, John D., 236

Rollaboard, 38, 39

Romer, Christina, 307n3

Roosevelt, Franklin: Buy Now Campaign of, 255; Depression fireside chat, 129, 278; "fear of fear itself" and, 128; National Industrial Recovery Act and, 189, 252; running against Hoover in 1932, 90, 91, 188–89

Roosevelt administration: codes of fair competition and, 132; confidence narratives and, 114

Roper, Elmo, 196–97

Ross, Andrew, 7

Roth, Benjamin, 141

RSA algorithm, 9–10

Rubik, Ernő, 47

Rubik's Cube, 47, 52

Rumsfeld, Donald, 44

R.U.R.: Rossum's Universal Robots (Čapek), 181–82, 196

Ryōkan, 150

Sadow, Bernard, 38

Saiz, Albert, 222

Salganik, Matthew J., 39, 300

salon, literature read aloud in, 274

Samuelson, Paul A., 24, 27–28, 303n8

Sandow, Eugen, 122

Sartre, Jean-Paul, 31

Saver, Jeffrey, 65–66

saving: in early twentieth century, 219; in eighteenth and nineteenth centuries, 116–17; homeownership and, 219–20

Schank, Roger C., 37

Schapiro, Morton, 16

schizophrenia, narrative in, 66

Schwartz, Anna J., 73, 132–33

Scott, Howard, 193, 194

scripts, 37–38; bank runs of 1893 and, 164–65; of Bush's narrative after terrorist attacks, 83; economic narratives involving, 74, 77

search engines, x; changes in contagion caused by, 273; improvements needed for narrative economics research, 280–81

searching digitized data: companies offering intelligent searches, 287; differing meanings of words and phrases in, 93; of public documents and the media, 287. *See also* databases for studying narratives; textual analysis

secular stagnation: fears of, after 2007–9 financial crisis, 95; narratives in thinking about, 71

SEIHFR model, 294

SEIR model, 294; chaotic variations of, 299, 323n21

self-censorship of narratives, 115

self-fulfilling prophecies in economics, 73–74, 123–24, 125; optimistic stories after 1948 and, 198; temporary hardships creating pessimism and, 209

self-made man narrative, xii

self-referencing in marketing, 77

semantic search, 287

September 11, 2001, terrorist attacks, 82–83, 284

sexual selection, 64–65

Sharpe, William, 275

Shell, Karl, 74

Shiller, Robert, xviii, 29, 38, 61, 64, 67, 216, 285, 298, 301n13

Sidis, Boris, 121

Silber, William, 94

Silverites, 158, 159, 160, 162–63, 164, 167; Wizard of Oz and, 171, 313n29

Simonides, 46

singularity, 199, 204–5, 207

Siri (Apple), 8, 206–7, 287

SIR model. See Kermack-McKendrick SIR model

SIRS model, 294, 322n4; for Internet memes, 297–98

sit-ins, 32–33

Six Cylinder Love (film), 144

size of an epidemic, 88–89, 292–93

slavery, and Civil War, 33

Slichter, Sumner H., 184–85

Sloss, Louis, 168–69

Smith, Adam, 44, 304n6

Smith, Al, 191

Snowden, Philip, 183–84

social change, and contagion of narratives, 32–33

social comparison: narratives about home prices and, 218, 220; narratives about stock market bubbles and, 228

social media: changes in contagion caused by, 273, 297; complicating geographic models of spread, 296; economic narratives spread through, xviii, 3, 21;

home price narrative and, 218; reconstructing arc of narratives from, xiii; recurrent narratives and, 109–10; research using data from, 287. See also Internet

social media marketing, 274–75

social norms, 37. See also scripts

social sciences: controlled experiments in, 78; study of popular narratives in, 15

sociology: economics learning from, 78; narratives central to social change and, 32–33; storytelling and, 15

Socrates, 34

Something to Look Forward To (Rhys-Williams), 210

source monitoring, 84, 307n21

S&P/CoreLogic/Case-Shiller home price index, 216, 222

speculative bubbles: feedback loop of prices in, 216–17; information cascades and, 300; resembling sexual selection outcomes in animals, 65; valuation of Bitcoin seen as, 4, 5, 7

speculative investments: flipping and, 223–24; real estate as simplest of, 221; in undeveloped land, 220–21

speculative markets: before crash of 1929, ix, 125–26, 231; Keynes's explanation of, 63–64

spending: boycott narrative and, 240, 254; hesitation during a recession, 75; postponed after World War I, 245–46, 249; postponed after World War II, 256; postponed during 1957–58 recession, 264; postponed during Great Depression, 129, 253–55; postponed in response to rising prices, 239; reduced by fear of automation, 201; reduced in 1973–75 recession, 256–57; revived after depression of 1920–21, 251; Roosevelt's Depression fireside chat and, 278; women making most decisions in 1920s and 1930s, 254. See also boycott narrative;

consumer confidence narrative; consumption

Sproul, Allan, 262

Star Wars trilogy (Lucas), 203

Steinbeck, John, 131

Sternberg, Robert, 79–80

Steve Jobs (Isaacson), 208

Stewart, William Morris, 166

stimulus. *See* economic stimulus

stock market: automated advisers for, 275; biggest expansion in US history, 1974–2000, 206; conversations and news media during corrections, 75; Keynes's "beauty contest" metaphor and, 63; prices as indicator of public confidence, 129, 228; questionnaire surveys of investors, 285; speculative bubbles in, 216–17; survey of investors' decision-making, 298–99; World War I and, 93–94, 283; World War II and, 94, 283, 308n6

stock market boom in 1920s: baffling to economists, 230; crowd psychology and, 119; Groucho Marx's take on, 133; ticker projector and, 228–29

stock market boom in 1990s, 109, 206

stock market bubbles, 228; popping in 2000, 29, 83

stock market crash narrative, 228–29, 232–33, 232f; exaggerated assessments of risk and, 67; in Great Depression, 252; in Great Recession of 2007–9, 272; idea of divine punishment and, 236; lingering today, 238

stock market crash of 1929: American Dream narrative and, 231; battle between Wall Street and the Fed prior to, 126; blamed on surplus of goods produced by technology, 186, 192; *boom and crash* going viral after, 229; consumption demand falling immediately after, 307n3; disillusionment with optimistic predictions and, 126–28; economists'

puzzlement over, 229–30; evidence of danger prior to, 231–32; Fisher's "permanently high plateau" phrase and, 75–76; high price-earnings ratio prior to, 231–32; moral narratives about, 235–36; narrative of human folly associated with, 228; narratives in 1920s and, ix–x, 72; overproduction or underconsumption theory and, 188; references to 1920–21 depression during, 252–53; rising unemployment prior to, 185–86; shoeshine boy narrative and, 236–37; "stock market crash" reminding us of, 17; suicide narratives associated with, 233–35

stock market crash of 1987: discussion of portfolio insurance and, 93; learned about by word of mouth, 89; narrative compared to 1929, 235; narrative of, 232f, 233; news media reminding public about, 76

stock price indexes: declining from 1929 to 1932, 230; public attention to, beginning in 1920s and 1930s, 97; public fascination with, 229

stories: basic structures of, 15–16; brain structure and, 54; emotion revealed in, 79; narrative as particular form of, 36; preference to share information in form of, 54; revealing personal values, 15; spread if we think others will spread them further, 63, 64; thinking in analogies and, 17. *See also* narratives

Stowe, Harriet Beecher, 33

structuralist literary theory, 16

Success Fundamentals (Marden), 122

suggestibility, 119–22, 120f; of less consumption during the Depression, 142

suicides after crash of 1929, 233–35

suitcases with wheels, 38–39

Sullivan, Mark, 172

sumptuary laws, 136

sunspots, 73–74

Sunstein, Cass, 277–78

super-spreaders, 20, 294

supply-side economics narratives, 48–52

surplus of goods produced by technology, 186, 192, 210

survey research, 285–86

susceptibles in epidemic, 20, 23, 289–90, 291f, 292, 294

Swing Riots in 1830, 174, 176

symbols, reminding people of the narrative, 62

synonyms, different connotations of, 94–95

talk shows, economic narratives spread through, 21

Talleyrand, 172

tax cuts: Laffer curve and, 42, 48, 51; of Reagan administration, 48, 51; supply-side economics and, 48–52

taxes: on corporate profits, 45, 48; Henry George's single tax on land, 209; narratives of people paying more than 100%, 49; Rand's *Atlas Shrugged* and, 50; reducing incentive to earn and create jobs, 42, 44; on Social Security benefits combined with Medicare surtax, 305n20

taxpayer revolt around 1978, 50

tax rates, of limited value in understanding economic events, 74–75

Taylor, Zachary, 110

teach-in, 33

technocracy, 192–94

technological unemployment narrative, 174, 175f, 183–86; automation with broader scope than, 200; concentration of business and, 190; during depressions, 176; economic effects of narrative itself, 211; epidemic models for, 294, 295; in Great Depression, 252; mutating after World War II, 196, 199; not strong in 1920s, 186–87; in run-up to World War II,

194–95; saturating the population in 1930s, 194; underconsumption and, 189. *See also* automation narrative; labor-saving machinery narrative

"technology taking over our lives" narrative, 8–9

Temin, Peter, 133, 172

Terkel, Studs, 234

The Terminator (film), 203

textual analysis, 279, 287. *See also* databases for studying narratives; searching digitized data

Thaler, Richard, 277–78

Thatcher, Margaret, 42, 51

Theobald, Robert, 210

theory of mind, 63–64

The Theory of the Leisure Class (Veblen), 310n1

"They say that . . . ," 92

Think and Grow Rich (Hill), 122

Think Big and Kick Ass in Business and Life (Trump with Zanker), 150

Thompson, Anne Kinsella, 226, 285

ticker projector, 228–29

time and motion studies, 184

Tmall Genie (Alibaba), 8, 207

Tobias, Ronald B., 16

Tracy, Spencer, 201

traffic light, replacing policemen, 182–83

Trans-Lux Movie Ticker, 228–29

"trending now," x

trickle-down economics, 44

Triumph of the Will (film), 122

Trohan, Walter, 51

Trulia, 218

Trump, Donald J.: *bigly* and *yuge* coined by, 244; downplaying modesty and compassion, 150; gold standard and, 156, 173; modeling ostentatious living, 272; narrative of, xii, 225–26

Trump administration, less generosity toward the poor during, 272

Trump supporters, resembling Silverites, 162–63
Trump University, 226
trust, in business dealings, 101
trusts, public anger about, 181
tulip mania in 1630s, 4, 5
Tversky, Amos, 66
Twain, Mark, 124
Twitter: meme quickly going viral on, 88; retweeting of mostly false stories on, 96–97
Typhoid Mary, 20
tyranny of metrics, 75, 306n5

Uchitelle, Louis, 150
Uncharted: Big Data as a Lens on Human Culture (Aiden and Michel), 24
Uncle Tom's Cabin (Stowe), 33
underconsumption theory, 187–92
Understanding the Process of Economic Change (North), 14
unemployment: artificial intelligence narrative and, 273; automation and, 199–200, 204; constant reminders of possibility of, 89; crime and, 141, 142; in depression during 1890s, 111; employee morale and, 147; gold standard and, 172; in Great Depression of 1930s, xiv, 111, 132, 141, 142, 143, 146–47, 172, 187, 189–91, 193; Kiplinger's 1930 list of causes of, 130, 132; labor-saving machinery narrative and, xiv, 9, 130, 177–81, 187–88, 191–92; narratives focused on massive occurrence of, 129–31; Nazi Party's rise in Germany and, 195; robotics and, 209; technology raising specter of, 8–9, 130; underconsumption theory and, 187–91. *See also* labor-saving machinery narrative; technological unemployment narrative
unemployment rate, first measurements by US government, 131, 184, 185
unfair behavior, human eagerness to punish, 36

universal basic income, 209–10
universals: anthropologists' study of, 33–35; social comparison as, 218

Valenti, Jack, 41
Van Evera, Stephen, 95
Vartanian, Oshin, 17
Veblen, Thorstein, 154, 193, 310n1
Versailles treaty, Keynes on consequences of, xvii–xviii, 26
viral diseases. *See* Ebola epidemics; influenza; Kermack-McKendrick SIR model
viral narratives: affecting economic activities without regard to truth, 95–96; American Dream as, 151–54, 152f; appearance of term "going viral," x; about bimetallism, 170, 172; about boycotts, 241; causal elements of, 72; choice of celebrities and, 100; confluence of, 29; creators of, 60; experimental evidence relevant to, 39–40; of "fire in a crowded theater," 127; about gold standard, 168, 172; about hypnosis, 122; about labor-saving machines, 195; mathematical model of epidemic and, 293; needing personality and story, xii; news publishers' financial success and, 61; about office automation, 204; randomness of which stories become, 31, 40, 64–65, 286; Roosevelt's quote about fear, 128; sit-ins and, 32–33; about stock market boom and crash, 229; about technological unemployment, 185; about wage-price spiral, 259–60
visual images: changed in mutated narrative, 108; memory aided by, 45, 46–47; power of Laffer curve narrative and, 45, 48
vivid mental images, jury members' response to, 78
volatility, and epidemic quality of economic narratives, 5
Vosoughi, Soroush, 96–97

wage cuts: anger at business over, 239; criticized during Great Depression, 251–52; National Industrial Recovery Act and, 252

wage lag hypothesis, 264

wage-price spiral narrative, 258–62, 259f, 263, 264, 266

wages: interviews of managers on decisions about, 281; of limited value in understanding economic events, 74–75; National Recovery Administration and, 189; purchasing power theory of, 188. *See also* labor unions

Wagner, Robert, 184

Walker, Edmond, 250

Wall Street Journal "Mansion" section, 224–25

Wanniski, Jude, 44–45

war metaphors, 17

Warner/Chappell Music, 98

wars: inflation during, 265–66. *See also* Civil War, US; World War I; World War II

war to end all wars, 242

Washington, George, 100–101, 102, 117, 177

Washington Mutual (WaMu) bank run, 135

Watson, IBM computer on *Jeopardy*, 207

The Way the World Works (Wanniski), 44

"We are the 99%" protests of 2011, 8, 225

weather forecasting, 123–25

Weems, Mason Locke, 100

Weiman, Rita, 139

Welch, Ivo, 300

welfare mother, narrative on, 49–50

When Washington Shut Down Wall Street (Silber), 94

Whewell, William, 12

White, Hayden, 37

Whitman, Walt, 165

Wicked (Broadway musical), 172

Wicked (Maguire), 172

Wikipedia, 7

Wikiquotes, 102

wikis, 7

Williams, James D., 147

Wilson, E. O., 12

Windmill, Alexander, 59

Wizard of Oz (film), 171–72

Wolman, Leo, 241

The Wonderful Wizard of Oz (Baum), 171–72, 313n29

Woolf, Virginia, 26

word of mouth: cultural change completed by, 297; cultural changes in use of, 274; investment decisions and, 298–99; in learning about stock market crash of 1987, 89; popular stories spread through, x, 3

word-of-mouth marketing, 15, 297

world financial crisis of 2007–9: advertisements for homeownership around time of, 220; automation narratives and, 205; housing bubble that collapsed during, 154, 155, 217, 222–23, 226, 227; interpreted as harbinger of "lost decade," 95; predicted by few economists, xiv; risk taking by banks ten years later, 55–56; seen through Great Depression narrative, 134–35; stock market expansion following, 206; thousands of boycotts during, 257

World War I: "Cult of the Offensive" false narrative and, 95; depression following, 197; excess profits tax imposed by US during, 249, 265; Harding's appeal for normalcy and, 244–45; Hitler's appeal in aftermath of, 122; inflation during, 243–49; monetary policy and, 73; profiteer narrative and, 241–43; stock exchanges closed at beginning of, 93–94

World War II: Keynes on Versailles treaty and, xvii–xviii, 26; meaning of "postwar" and, 242; modesty narrative during, 137; monetary policy and, 73; optimistic narratives after, 198; Pearl Harbor attack and, 81–82; positive market reaction to beginning of, 94, 308n6; technological unemployment narrative and, 194–95, 196; "victory vacations" shortly after, 198; worldwide depression preceding, 112

wrestling matches, fake, 84–85

Xi Jinping, 151

Yandex's Alice, 207
Yellen, Janet L., 250, 300
Young, Kay, 65–66
Young, Warren, 25
"Your World in 90 Seconds," 103

Zak, Paul J., 54
Zhao, Laijun, 297
Zillow, 218